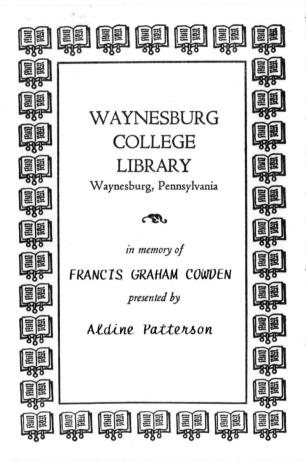

This book presents a detailed survey and analysis of the surviving corpus of biblical drama from all parts of medieval Europe. Over five hundred plays from the tenth to the sixteenth centuries are examined from the point of view of the communities who performed them and the stories they dramatised in a mixture of sermons and suffering, comedy, pathos and the realities of everyday, mainly urban, life. Remarkable in their variety and quality, fascinating in their evolution and development, these plays offer unique insights into the medieval interpretation of sacred texts.

The volume is arranged in such a way as to present a detailed overview of major aspects of medieval biblical theatre, including the theatrical community of audience and players; the major plays and cycles; and the legacy of medieval drama in the modern world. Specially prepared maps illustrate the number and distribution of towns involved in dramatic activities, and an Appendix provides information on the liturgical context of the plays, including the Church calendar, processions, and the Mass, the Office and the Creed.

The biblical drama of medieval Europe will be a valuable resource for scholars and students of medieval theatre and for enthusiasts of early drama.

The biblical drama of medieval Europe

The biblical drama of medieval Europe

LYNETTE R. MUIR
formerly Reader in French, University of Leeds

CAMBRIDGE
UNIVERSITY PRESS

Published by the Press Syndicate of the University of Cambridge
The Pitt Building, Trumpington Street, Cambridge CB2 1RP
40 West 20th Street, New York, NY 10011-4211, USA
10 Stamford Road, Oakleigh, Melbourne 3166, Australia

First published 1995
Reprinted 1996

Printed in Great Britain by Woolnough Bookbinders Ltd, Irthlingborough, Northants

A catalogue record for this book is available from the British Library

Library of Congress cataloguing in publication data

Muir, Lynette R.
The biblical drama of medieval Europe / Lynette R. Muir.
p.   cm.
Includes bibliographical references (p.   ) and index.
ISBN 0 521 41291 9 (hardback)
1. Religious drama – History and criticism.
2. Drama, Medieval – History and criticism.   I. Title.
PN1880.M85   1995
809.2′516 – dc 20   94-15701   CIP

ISBN 0 521 412919 hardback

CE

Contents

x   Contents

Illustrations

Maps

Preface

The aim of the present study is to make available to the increasing number of scholars working in the field of medieval drama, and to the even larger number of people who attend performances of such plays, a detailed survey and analysis of the surviving corpus of biblical drama from all parts of medieval Christian Europe. The number of plays is very considerable, their variety and quality remarkable and the history of their development and evolution fascinating.

Inevitably in a work conceived on a European scale, the need for translation discourages discussion of the stylistic and linguistic qualities of the plays. Nor, though the book is essentially comparatist in its approach, can it avoid some national divisions, for they are an essential part of the evolution of the genre. Very little secondary literature has been cited since the overall purpose is to encourage and facilitate detailed and comparative critical investigation of the plays, not to provide it.

The origin of the book goes back to the early 1970s when interested members of the Leeds Centre for Medieval Studies met on Wednesdays for a working lunch and hammered out the principles of a catalogue and episode-guide to the medieval religious plays. The catalogue was eventually abandoned (partly because of the work being done by Lancashire, in England, and Lippman, Bergmann and Neumann in Germany) but some of the material gathered was published in *The staging of religious drama in Europe in the later Middle Ages*, edited by Peter Meredith and John Tailby, in 1983.

In 1974, the Leeds Centre organised the first international colloquium on the medieval theatre, which led (during the second colloquium in Alençon in 1977) to the formation of the Société internationale pour l'étude du théâtre médiéval (SITM). Meanwhile in 1975 the Leeds Centenary Cycle – the first modern production of the York cycle on pageant waggons – initiated a series of such productions in both Europe and North America.

Having been working for a number of years on the comparative treatment of subject-matter in Old Testament plays from different language areas, I was encouraged by the success of *Staging* and the stimulus of the cycle productions and SITM meetings to attempt a general history and analysis of biblical plays from the whole of Europe based partly on the original subject-index prepared for the now defunct catalogue. The present volume is the outcome.

The material is presented in two parts: in the first the theatre is considered from the point of view of the organisers and performers – the theatrical community. The question of who performed plays, when and why, is examined, with a brief outline of how and where the plays were performed.

In part two, the subject-matter and sources of the theatrical text are analysed following the biblical narrative from Genesis to the Book of Revelation and including as far as possible all known examples of the Old Testament themes and a selection of the more interesting and unusual variants of the prolific Christmas and Easter plays.

As the purpose of this book is to provide a comprehensive picture of European medieval biblical drama, I have tried to include references to all texts composed before 1500 (with the exception of some unpublished material). Between 1500 and 1550 the only texts omitted are those which have no medieval links at all – mainly humanist and polemical plays – whereas after 1550, plays are only included if they relate to the medieval traditions, for example the Dutch rhetoricians' plays and the Stonyhurst pageants. In doubtful cases, the text is always included. The arabic numbers following play titles refer to the pages of the edition given in the bibliographical index of plays at the end of the book.

The changes that take place in the drama during the sixteenth and early seventeenth centuries are discussed in the conclusion, which also studies the survival and revival of the medieval dramatic traditions. An appendix describes the liturgical context in which the plays were created and performed.

The maps indicate the principal known (or surmised) locations of plays and performances. Since political boundaries changed constantly in the six hundred years covered by the survey, rivers have been preferred as a guide to the position of less well-known towns. The place names on the maps are the medieval ones and modern changes are indicated in the index. English forms are used throughout where applicable.

The illustrations, taken from some of the many productions which have delighted audiences on both sides of the Atlantic in the last twenty years, are chosen less for their intrinsic quality than for their exemplary value in the recreation of medieval staging techniques and practices.

All drama is a communal effort and this book is indebted to an enormous number of people: to include their names in the acknowledgements is but feeble return for all they have done for me. But my greatest debt is to the original stalwart 'Wednesday-lunchers' and it gives me great pleasure to dedicate this book to those three wise men of Leeds, Peter Meredith, Richard Rastall and John Tailby, in gratitude for their advice, help and friendship over the last twenty years.

Acknowledgements

This book would not have been possible without the help and advice of many friends and specialists. General assistance and information on plays in different language groups was given by Leeds colleagues, including Richard Andrews, Peter Meredith, Jane Oakshott, Richard Rastall, Anne Rees, Penny Robinson, and Irmgart and John Tailby. In addition, Alan Knight and Graham Runnalls have provided me with advance copies of French plays not yet published as well as answering many questions. Elsa Strietman and Wim Hüsken have kept me straight on the Dutch material, and the Eastern European texts have been identified and translated for me by Sonja Dekanić-Janoski (Serbo-Croat) and Irena Janicke-Śviderske (Polish). I have also had advance information or texts from Cyrilla Barr, Joyce Hill, Wim Hüsken, Alexandra Johnston, Hans-Jürgen Linke and Gerard Nijsten. Other contributions are acknowledged in the footnotes, and the bibliographies list the work of numerous scholars, masked but not concealed by the acronyms of *REED* and *RORD*, EDAM, SITM and *MeTh*.

Illustrations and permission to reproduce them have been provided by Alistair Doxat-Pratt, Helen Taylor, Eleonora Udalska and Black and White Pictures (Chester). The photos were prepared for publication by Fred Johnson of Chester and the Domino Agency, York.

I have also had much help in the preparation of the text. Peter Meredith, Richard Rastall, Elsa Strietman and Elizabeth Williams read parts of the typescript and made many useful suggestions. Barbara Douglas devoted a great deal of time and care to preparing the maps. Jenifer Fairpo spent many hours putting the bibliographies in order and Gavin Fairpo enabled me to use a computer. The editors for the Cambridge University Press, especially Victoria Cooper and Janet Banks, have been endlessly helpful and patient.

Without all this assistance there would be many more errors of omission and commission in this book. For those that remain the fault and the responsibility are mine.

> *Ce que avons de faultes commis*
> *Et que en noz fais avons obmis..*
> *Prions vostre benivolence*
> *Que le nous voeulliés pardonner,*
> *Suppleer et nous excuser,*
> *Car le Mistere est tres pesant.*

Abbreviations

Bergmann: Bergmann, K. *Katalog der deutschsprachigen geistlichen Spiele und Marienklagen des Mittelalters*. Veroffentlichungen der Kommission für deutschen Literatur des Mittelalters der Bayerischen Akademie der Wissenschaften, 1. Munich and Zurich, 1986.

Evans: Blakemore-Evans, M. *The passion play of Lucerne: an historical and critical introduction*. New York and London, 1943.

CFMA: Classiques français du moyen âge.

D'Ancona, *Origini*: D'Ancona, A. *Origini del teatro italiano*. 2 vols. Rome, 1966 (repr. 1981).

De Bartholomaeis, *Origini*: De Bartholomaeis, V. *Origini della poesia drammatica italiana*. 2nd ed. Turin, 1952.

Donovan: Donovan, R. B. *The liturgical drama in medieval Spain*. Toronto, 1958.

EDAM: Early Drama, Art and Music.

EETS: Early English Text Society.

Hummelen: Hummelen, W. M. M. *Repertorium van het rederijkersdrama, 1500 – c.1620*. Assen, 1968. (Addenda to the *Repertorium* in *Dutch Crossing*, 1984, *22*: 105–28).

Lancashire: Lancashire, I. *Dramatic texts and records of Britain: a chronological topography*. Toronto, 1984.

Malone: Malone Collections, Malone Society, London.

MeTh: Medieval English Theatre.

Mill: Mill, A. J. *Medieval plays in Scotland*. Edinburgh and London, 1927. [repr. New York, 1969].

Mons: *Le mystère de la passion . . . joué à Mons, 1501*. (Ed. G. Cohen. Paris, 1925.)

Neumann: Neumann, B. *Geistliches Schauspiel im Zeugnis der Zeit. Zur Aufführung mitteralterlicher Dramen im deutschen Sprachgebiet*. 2 vols. Münchener Texte und Untersuchungen zur deutschen Literatur des Mittelalters, 84, 85. Munich and Zurich, 1987.

Newbigin: Newbigin, N., ed. *Nuovo corpus di sacre rappresentazioni fiorentini del Quattrocento*. Bologna, 1983.

Petit de Julleville: Petit de Julleville, L. *Histoire du théâtre en France. Les Mystères II*. 1880. [repr. Geneva, 1969].

PMLA: Publications of the Modern Language Association of America.

REED: Records of Early English Drama.

RORD: Research Opportunities in Renaissance Drama.

Rouanet: Rouanet, L., ed. *Coleccion de Autos, Farsas, y Coloquios del siglo XVI*. 4 vols. Barcelona and Madrid, 1901.

Roy, *Mystère*: Roy, E. *Le Mystère de la passion en France du XIVe au XVIe siècle*. Paris, 1905.

SATF: Société des anciens textes français.

Shergold: Shergold, N. D. *A history of the Spanish stage from medieval times until the end of the seventeenth century*. Oxford and London, 1967.

SITM: Société international pour l'étude du théâtre médiéval.

Staging: The staging of religious drama in Europe in the later Middle Ages: texts and documents in English translation ... [etc.]. Eds. Peter Meredith and John Tailby. EDAM monograph series, 4. Kalamazoo, 1983.

Toledo: Torroja Menéndez, C., and Rivas Palá, M. *Teatro en Toledo*. Madrid, 1977.

Woolf: Woolf, R. *The English mystery plays*. Berkeley and Los Angeles, 1972.

Young: Young, K. *The drama of the medieval church*. 2 vols. Oxford and London, 1933.

ZDA: Zeitschrift für deutsches Altertum und deutsches Literatur.

ZDPh: Zeitschrift für deutsche Philologie.

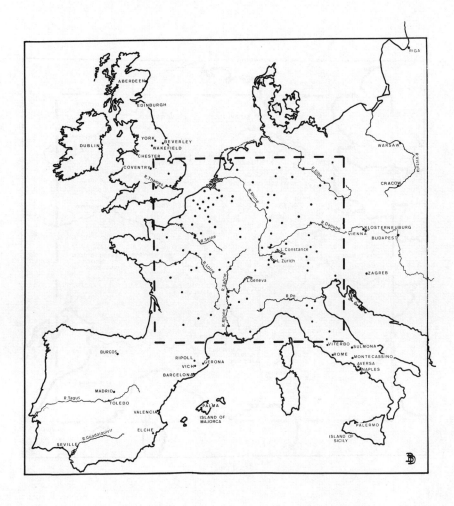

Map 1 Medieval Europe showing locations of principal play-texts and records cited in this study. (For names of towns in central area see maps 2 and 3.)

Map 2   Enlargement of central area showing locations of liturgical and feast-day plays
as defined in chapter 1.

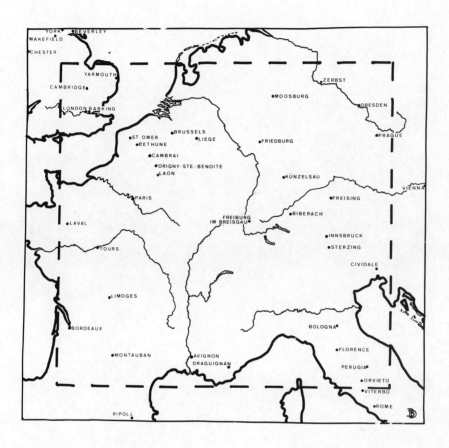

Map 3   Enlargement of central area showing locations of civic and community plays
as defined in chapter 2.

Introduction: Christian Europe and the Play of God

Passion plays and Corpus Christi cycles, like Arthurian romances and Gothic cathedrals, are among the outstanding cultural monuments of medieval Europe. However, theatre is an essentially evanescent art form: texts and records can provide at best a skeleton of the drama which, for a brief moment, combined the verbal, musical and visual arts with the beliefs and faith of Christendom. The medieval bones of this body are plentiful and widely dispersed: play-texts and records of performances; accounts, costume lists, contracts and minutes of town meetings; contemporary reports and eye-witness descriptions. All these survive in their hundreds, for biblical drama flourished in Western Catholic Europe for more than five hundred years and its roots go back to the very beginnings of Christianity.

Like Judaism, Christianity had at its core a regular ceremonial re-enactment of the saving activity of God. Under the Old Covenant, Moses instructed the children of Israel in the annual commemoration of the Passover: 'You shall observe the rite as an ordinance for you and your sons for ever' (Exodus 12: 24). Christ took this Law and reinterpreted it in the form of the New Covenant, bidding his disciples: 'Do this in remembrance of me.' From the earliest centuries the Christian Church obeyed his commandment through the celebration of the sacrament of the Mass.

The other principal sacrament of the early Church was Baptism, for which a long preparation was required. Before being made a member of the Church each candidate had to affirm his belief in the basic tenets of the Christian faith as expressed in the Apostles' Creed. Whereas the Mass commemorated the sacrifice of God in the Passion, the Creed recorded the threefold action of God in Christ as Creator, Redeemer and Judge. In the West, its recitation was (and has remained) an integral part of the daily round of prayer and praise.[1]

The description of the worship in Jerusalem in the fourth century left

by the noble Roman lady, Egeria,[2] shows that already by that date a
third element of worship had been added to the liturgy and the Mass:
on major feasts the Church also encouraged ceremonial re-enactments
of the events of the Life of Christ. Her description of the Palm Sunday
procession makes it clear that this is not a dramatic, representational
approach to the Triumphal Entry into Jerusalem but an act of worship,
no different in kind from the numerous processions, often with a
wooden figure of Christ on a donkey, still found in parts of Europe
today.[3] The veneration of the True Cross[4] on the site of Golgotha itself
was likewise an act of worship that could not become drama, whereas
the ceremonial interment on Good Friday, a thousand miles away and
several centuries later, of a cross bearing the image of the crucified
Christ, could.

Soon after Egeria's visit, the Church (like the Roman Empire itself)
divided into two parts with a Byzantine Emperor and a Greek-speaking
Church in the East; a Roman Emperor and a Latin Church in the
West.[5] Biblical plays did not develop from the liturgy of the Eastern
Church, which had its own 'incarnation' of the Word of God in the
icons, a custom defended by John of Damascus during the eighth-
century iconoclastic controversy: 'Of old, God the incorporeal and
uncircumscribed was never depicted. Now, however, when God is seen
clothed in flesh and conversing with men, I make an image of the God
of matter who became matter for my sake.'[6] Such a theology could not
lead to representational drama, though it has been claimed that a
group of Greek homilies, preserved in manuscripts of the ninth to
eleventh centuries but dating back to the period before the eighth-
century iconoclastic controversy, contain the relics of dramatic scenes
and dialogues which together make up a considerable body of what
might be considered Greek sermon-drama. The central figures of these
scenes are the Virgin Mary, John the Baptist and Christ, and the
material covers three main areas: the Annunciation, including Joseph's
doubt about Mary; the Baptism and Temptation of Christ; the death of
John the Baptist and his arrival in Limbo with the patriarchs, followed
by the Harrowing of Hell.[7] These sermon-plays, if one may use the
term, are essentially dogmatic and theological in their emphasis; there
is no certainty that they were ever in fact performed and they certainly
did not influence the few genuine biblical plays written in Greek, such
as the *Paschon Christos* and Cyprus *Passion*.[8]

Medieval biblical drama as we know it, therefore, developed
exclusively in the Western Church. Its Bible was the Vulgate,

St Jerome's new, fourth-century, version of the Bible in Latin which replaced the *Vetus Latina* (Old Latin) translation which had become corrupt in the process of manuscript transmission, while its version of the Old Testament had been translated not from the Hebrew but from the Greek Septuagint version.[9] Jerome, who was a considerable scholar and translator, revised the text of the New Testament from the Greek and produced a new version of most of the Old Testament from the Hebrew original.[10]

The catalyst that was to enable the translation of the Bible into the biblical play, and was to have far-reaching consequences for both the Church and ultimately the drama, came in the following century when St Benedict wrote his *Regula* (*Rule*). Designed for the monastic order he founded in Montecassino, for the next thousand years this Rule governed the life of scores of religious communities all over Europe. At its heart was the *Opus Dei* (Work of God): a series of short services sung or recited every three hours during the day (hence the familiar name, Hours). This Daily Office which, combined with the celebration of Mass, formed the basic obligation of all Benedictine religious,[11] included lections (or readings) from the Bible which were gradually arranged in a sequence or cursus for the whole of the Church year.[12]

The monastic liturgical calendar based on the life of Christ laid down the structure of the feasts and fast-days of the whole Christian Church. Beginning in Advent with the prophecies of the coming of Christ and the reminder of the Second Coming on the Day of Judgement, it proceeds through the life of Christ from Nativity to Ascension, including the major feasts of Christmas, Epiphany and, above all, Easter. The Coming of the Holy Spirit at Pentecost leads into the last part of the year, celebrating the work and witness of the Church. Like the Creed, the liturgy as a whole emphasised the triple activity of God as Creator, Redeemer and Judge through the tradition of reading the Old Testament in its relationship to the New, starting from the references to the Old Testament in the gospels (especially Matthew) and the epistles (particularly Hebrews). The prophets, especially Isaiah, form part of the lectionary (the book of readings) during Advent, and the story of the Fall of Man was read during the period before Easter, beginning on Septuagesima Sunday and continuing through Lent with the patriarchs and the story of Moses. Throughout the year the biblical lections are supplemented by readings from the sermons and commentaries of the patristic writers, especially

Augustine, but including John Chrysostom, Gregory, Ambrose and (later) Bede.

The Office was essentially an act of worship, so the readings from the Bible made up only part of the liturgy, which included sung acts of praise, intercession and repentance. Both here and in the Mass many of the texts and musical settings were arranged for antiphonal performance, with a soloist and choir or two half-choirs singing alternately. There was also ritual and processional movement. In structure and presentation, the Office and, especially, the Mass were performances. But they were not drama, for they did not have the essential audience without which there is no theatre.[13] Nevertheless it was from this liturgy of the Benedictine communities (for drama is essentially a community activity) that there developed by the end of the ninth century the first examples of Latin drama of the type usually described as liturgical (see p. 14).

Liturgical drama remained important and widespread throughout the medieval period, but in the twelfth and thirteenth centuries a series of social and religious developments encouraged the birth of what was to become the vernacular lay-drama of the later Middle Ages. The liturgical and patristic forms which dominated the first church plays were challenged by the great cultural and spiritual renaissance of the twelfth century with its stress on the primacy of the individual.[14] Theologically, the Church, which had been focussed on crusades against the threat to Christianity from pagan and heretical groups, began to pay more attention to the spiritual needs of its own flock at home. Regular confession, repentance and penance were increasingly stressed, first by writers and teachers like St Bernard and St Anselm, and then by the newly formed orders of friars, the Franciscans and the Dominicans, whose mission took them out of the enclosed monastic circle to preach to the laity in the towns and villages of Europe.[15] An additional stimulus to this new lay popular piety was given by the preaching of Joachim of Flora, who early in the thirteenth century pronounced the imminent arrival of the Day of Judgement.[16]

As a genre which combined art, literature and popular piety, the biblical drama could not fail to be influenced by this revival of religious enthusiasm and the movement towards greater stress on the individual, on emotions and personal relationships – a movement which was reflected in the shift from Romanesque to Gothic in art and architecture, from epic to romance in literature, from the divine *Christus victor* reigning from the Tree of Life to the agonised suffering of the human Jesus on the cross of shame in works of theology and devotion. These changes encouraged also a growing emphasis on the earthly life of Jesus, with its natural concomitant of a growth in the role of the Virgin and a generally greater interest in the lives and feelings of the individual characters.

Two thirteenth-century Latin works exploited this new approach so successfully that they dominated popular devotion and religious drama for centuries. The *Legenda Aurea* (*Golden Legend*) by the Italian Dominican, Jacobus de Voragine, is a commentary on a sequence of readings (legends) for the different feast-days of the Church year. The *Meditationes vitae Christi* (*Meditations on the Life of Christ*) attributed in the Middle Ages to the Franciscan, St Bonaventure, were written as a devotional guide to the life of Christ.[17] A number of other Latin texts were also influential, including the *Postilles* (commentaries on the Bible) of Nicholas of Lyra,[18] and Vincent of Beauvais's *Speculum historiale* (*Mirror of History*). Vernacular narratives of biblical events, especially the Passion, became increasingly common and, enriched with stories and legends from apocryphal sources, provided many material details for the translation of gospel narratives to the popular stage.[19]

A new community now became associated with the biblical plays: the laity, whose involvement in drama first burgeoned in the thirteenth century. In different parts of Catholic Europe neighbourhood groups, trade guilds, literary societies and pious confraternities, began to create a lay religious theatre that was to spread throughout Europe; but it was above all the inhabitants of the centres of commerce whose growing civic self-awareness encouraged them to celebrate with processions, and eventually plays, their new pride and status.[20] They had watched (and built stands for) the jousts and *pas d'armes* which were the preferred amusement of the fighting aristocracy, but though the tales of chivalry and courtly love which inspired the entertainments and maskings in court and castle remained popular reading, they were apparently considered inappropriate to the public spectacles of a merchant class and had only a limited appeal to the growing urban communities.[21]

Instead, inspired by the plays they saw and heard in church on the feast days of obligation, and especially by the new feast of Corpus Christi with its obligatory civic procession, the merchants and trade guilds began to present biblical and hagiographic plays, whose setting in the urban and pastoral life of the Holy Land made them peculiarly suitable material for the towns which still retained close links with their surrounding countryside: seed-time and harvest were still significant in the life of the most urbanised merchant or mastercraftsman. The courts of Arthur and Charlemagne which, in an age of warfare and disorder, could provide little comfort for the inhabitants of a besieged city in a wasted countryside, were replaced by the Court of Heaven with its more powerful and, hopefully, more merciful rule. If the Kingdom of Heaven seemed a long way from the daily horrors of fourteenth-century Europe, at least the new Jerusalem was awaiting the faithful hereafter.

In parts of Europe, especially northern France and the Netherlands, this period of expansion in urban and civic drama suffered a set-back during the wars, plagues and famine of the fourteenth and early fifteenth centuries. But in the century that followed the end of the Hundred Years' War in 1450, it was in the credal cycles, especially those associated with the feast of Corpus Christi, and in the big cyclic passion plays where Church and laity combined in an act of theatre which was also an act of worship, that the genius of the medieval biblical drama found its ultimate flowering.

'The emphasis of Jesus' teaching is upon God, rather than upon man – upon what *God* has done, is doing, and shall do for His people.'[22] Medieval biblical plays were essentially theocentric, pre-senting the two Testaments as the total work of God: Creator, Redeemer and Judge. The chronicler who recorded the performance in Latin in Cividale in 1298 of a sequence of scenes from Passion to Judgement, gave it the name *Ludus Christi* (Play of Christ).[23] Six years later, when the same clerics performed a full credal cycle from Creation to Judgement, they might have called that *Ludus Dei* (Play of God) for this was the title used two hundred years later in the prologue to the Mons *Passion* – a cycle from Creation to Pentecost – whose author declares they intend to present the acts of Christ:

> en la forme tres belle
> Que le Jeu de Dieu on appelle.

(In the very beautiful form which is called the Play of God.)[24]

The Play of God is peculiar to Western Christendom, and especially to those parts of Constantine's Christian empire that had been occupied and civilised by his Imperial pagan predecessors. France and Germany, Italy, England and the Low Countries were the heartlands of the biblical plays, a remarkable number of which were performed in or on the ruins of Roman cities from the Coliseum to York Minster, beneath whose crypt lie the Roman barracks where Constantine himself was proclaimed Emperor.

From the dramatic point of view, the historical geography of Europe was primarily one of frontiers – linguistic and religious rather than political. Plays were particularly common along the border areas between France and the Holy Roman Empire which dominated the areas east of the Rhine. By the end of the fifteenth century, the map shows concentrations of drama records in the trading centres of the Netherlands, Dutch-speaking Antwerp and Brussels, francophone Mons, Lille and Valenciennes. Like shrines on the Road to St James of Compostella, play-performing towns are spread along the route which led between the Rhone and the Rhine through Lorraine and Burgundy towards the south, where the towns of Savoy and Dauphiné on the west and the silver-rich Tyrol towns on the east kept the passes into Italy along which travelled an endless river of traders, travellers and troops.

On the south-western edge of Catholic Europe, Catalonia, though it had lost its Mediterranean trading pre-eminence and its political independence to the united crowns of Aragon and Castile, kept its traditional plays and processions, especially in Elche, Barcelona and Valencia. The absence of liturgical and early vernacular drama in the rest of Spain and in Portugal is a consequence of the Moorish occupation and the late restoration of Christianity. By the end of the fifteenth century there was a flourishing tradition of Corpus Christi drama and court theatre throughout the Peninsula.[25]

In contrast to the liturgical drama of the Western Catholic tradition, the Byzantine sermon plays never inspired vernacular civic drama, which is unknown in the towns of Eastern, Orthodox Europe till after the end of the medieval period. This was partly because many of the towns themselves were stunted in their development by the Turkish invasions of the fourteenth century. The clearest example here is the dual tradition in the two Balkan states of Serbia and Croatia. The latter had been part of the Roman *imperium*, was Catholic and remained virtually free of Turks. It also had strong trade links with Venice; examples of both Latin liturgical and vernacular civic plays survive there. Serbia was Orthodox and overrun and had neither.[26]

Native biblical drama generally developed late in the vernaculars of the Catholic countries of Eastern Europe – Poland, Bohemia, Hungary – which were for a long time dominated culturally and politically by the mainly German-speaking Holy Roman Empire. Bohemia was the first to produce native drama, and a number of Czech plays survive from the fourteenth century, but the Protestant Hussite movement (which was opposed to drama) gave a new direction to the expression of nascent nationalism.[27] Hungary's earliest vernacular drama from the fifteenth century includes some Christian and biblical elements but retained also much of its unique pagan folklore.[28] Russian drama did not develop till the end of the seventeenth century[29] and Slavonic Catholicism found its chief exponent in the late medieval period in Poland. Many medieval Latin texts survive but the earliest extant text in Polish is from 1580 though it may have an older source. The *History of the glorious Resurrection*, as its title implies, is an Easter play and includes also the Harrowing of Hell; there are directions for staging it between Easter and Ascension (with the permission of the ecclesiastical authorities) either in church or in the graveyard. The thirty-five characters may be played by only twenty-one actors, and a number of mansions are required, especially a substantial Hell with a solid door, fire and a horrible smell.[30]

The importance of not only the Roman liturgy but also the Roman *civis* and the political ethos of the old Roman empire in the development of religious drama, shows up also in the Celtic countries of the far west of Europe. In Ireland, the most politically and culturally isolated of the group, never influenced by Roman occupation or the Roman Church, only Dublin (founded by the Vikings and already an English outpost in the twelfth century) and the Anglo-Norman settlement of Kilkenny have records of liturgical and civic drama. Vernacular biblical drama is also unknown in the other Celtic territories; no biblical plays are recorded from Wales or Brittany till the very end of the medieval period, when they evidently came under the influence of their more powerful neighbours. Cornwall, smallest and least independent politically of them all, had a trilogy of plays, somewhat on the French model, the *Ordinalia*, known to have been composed and performed *c.* 1376.[31] Scotland has no Gaelic drama from the Celtic Highlands but a flourishing tradition in the Scottish dialect of English survives from the Lowlands and the towns of the East coast.[32]

There is a similar absence of biblical drama in the Scandinavian countries, partly due to the late date of their conversion to Christianity. Perhaps also the strong tribal and family traditions of the Northmen were less suited to community drama than to poetry and saga. The court and aristocracy were well versed in the popular epics and romances of the day, and the Church, at least in Sweden,[33] has some dramatic forms of its own, but once again the Roman 'civilisation' in its most literal sense of the *civis* or town is absent.

From whatever part of Europe they came, the medieval writers did not limit themselves to simple transfers of biblical stories, characters and dialogue to the stage. Their approach was essentially theocentric but for them the Word of God was the incarnate Christ, the Logos, not simply the Holy Scriptures in which his acts were recorded. In the preface to his *Monologium* or meditation on the being of God, St Anselm explains the method he has been following: 'that nothing in Scripture should be urged on the authority of Scripture itself, but that whatever the conclusion of independent investigation should declare to be true, should ... be briefly enforced by the cogency of reason, and plainly expounded in the light of truth'.[34] The biblical drama of medieval Europe was not a meditation on the *being* of God but a representation *par personnages* (as the French dramatists put it), of the *doing* of God. The authors freely adapted and altered the Scriptures, adding characters and emotions, commentaries and debates to create plays which, lacking the brevity advocated by Anselm, have yet often the 'cogency of reason', while the modern parallels adduced and the use of contemporary settings gave a unique opportunity for independent examination within the framework of the Christian Church.

Such freedom of thought and personal interpretation could not survive the religious upheavals of the sixteenth century. In the age of reform and counter reform, the medieval emphasis on God incarnate in contemporary society was replaced on the one hand by the Inquisition-enforced authority of the Church and on the other by the equally strict control of the ministers of the Word of God and a fundamentalist approach to the Bible.[35] The results, reflected in the differences between the medieval and the later biblical plays discussed in the conclusion, pose the question: could the Play of God exist outside medieval Europe?

PART ONE

The theatrical community

We do not ask that a play communicate for ever; we do ask that a play communicate in its own time, through its own medium, for its own community.

(J. L. Styan, *Drama, stage and audience*)

CHAPTER I

Liturgical and feast-day drama

FROM LITURGY TO DRAMA

As indicated in the previous chapter, the first biblical plays developed within the liturgical office of the monasteries founded by St Benedict, first of all in Italy but soon spreading throughout Catholic Europe. The Benedictine Office was sung not spoken and a variety of chants were used in the different parts of Europe, for there was considerable flexibility even within the Benedictine order. This was inevitable at a period when communication was difficult, and the influence of local cultures helped to encourage variations within local liturgies.

A dominant variant was the so-called Gallican liturgy in the Western Frankish empire (France), noted for its predilection for variety and ornamentation in the Daily Office.[1] In the ninth century the Emperor Charlemagne tried to reform the Church in Gaul and insisted on the reintroduction of the Roman rite as revised by Pope Gregory the Great in the previous century. Part of Gregory's reform involved a simplification of the music which in many religious houses had become extremely elaborate. But although the music returned to the simpler mode laid down by Gregory and Charlemagne, it was the turn of the texts to be embroidered. Additional sections of narrative or dialogue were introduced into the liturgy of the major feasts, especially at Easter.[2] The most influential and crucial development for the history of the drama was the dialogue sung at the beginning of Easter Day Mass, and known from its opening words as the '*Quem queritis?*' (Whom do you seek?) trope.

In the oldest surviving manuscript (*c.* 933 AD), the trope appears in the following form: before the introit (the opening chant of the Mass) part of the choir (representing the angels at the tomb) sings the phrase, '*Quem queritis in sepulchro, O Christicole?*' (Whom do you seek in the tomb, O Christians?). The other half of the choir (for the Marys and all Christians) responds: '*Jesum Nazarenum, O celicole*' (Jesus of Nazareth, O heavenly ones). Then the whole choir sings the joyful tidings of the Resurrection in the introit to the Mass: '*Resurrexi et adhuc tecum sum, alleluia*' (I rose up and am with you still, alleluia).[3] The peculiar interest of this dialogue lies in its source. It does not derive from one of the gospel accounts of the Resurrection itself but from John's narrative of the arrest of Jesus, sung as part of the Passion on Good Friday. Jesus twice asks the soldiers, '*Quem queritis?*' to which they reply, '*Jesum Nazarenum*' (John 18: 5–7).

The later history of this brief exchange and its appearance in a variety of dramatic contexts will be considered below. It is sufficient here to point out that, as the introduction to the greatest feast of the Church's year, the *Quem queritis?* dialogue had no opportunity of realising its dramatic potential. One more step was needed. The dialogue was moved from the rigidly ordered liturgy of the Mass to the more flexible Office of Mattins and a play was born.

We have no way of knowing the exact time and place of this nativity but by the late tenth century the *Quem queritis?* is evidently quite widely used in the Benedictine houses of north-western Europe. The earliest manuscript to contain it is the *Regularis concordia* (*Agreement of the Rule*) compiled in England *c.* 970 on the instruction of King Edgar as part of the restoration of Benedictine monasticism after the Viking invasions.[4] The *Concordia*, as the introduction tells us, was designed to ensure uniformity of practice in the observance of the Benedictine *Rule* by the different houses in England and their conformity to the best continental practice, represented apparently by the abbey of St Benoît-sur-Loire at Fleury, in France, and St Peter's abbey, Ghent.[5]

A substantial part of the *Concordia* deals with the liturgy of Holy Week in accordance with general practice among continental Benedictine houses. Three ceremonies are mentioned which seem relevant to the development of the drama. In writing of the night Office on Maundy Thursday, the compiler (probably St Ethelwold of Winchester) adds:

We have also heard that in churches of certain religious men a practice has grown up whereby compunction of soul is aroused by the outward representation of that which is spiritual. [This practice involves a particular addition to the regular Office sung by the choir.] Therefore it seemed good to us to insert these things so that if there be any to whose devotion they are pleasing they may find therein the means of instructing those who are ignorant of this matter; no one however shall be forced to carry out this practice against his will.   (*Concordia* 36).

This concept of the 'optional extra', to be used if it is found to be helpful, is repeated for an item on Nones on Maundy Thursday (39) and, with a significant comment, on Good Friday when it is suggested that 'if anyone should care or think fit to follow in a becoming manner certain religious men in a practice worthy to be imitated for the strengthening of the faith of unlearned common persons and neophytes we have decreed ...' Then follows the well-known ceremonial of the Burying of the Cross in a 'sepulchre' (here a curtained-off part of the altar) 'in imitation as it were of the burial of the body of our Lord Jesus Christ' (44).

With so much stress on conformity on the one hand, and the possibility of using certain additional items for the instruction of the faithful and the increase of devotion on the other, it comes as something of a surprise when the play based on the *Quem queritis?* trope and normally referred to as the *Visitatio sepulchri* (Visit to the Sepulchre) is introduced with no hint of choice or reference to devotion. It is not an optional extra. The *Concordia* emphasises that the canonical Hours of Easter Day are to be celebrated as set down by the blessed Gregory in his *Antiphonar*: this refers to the Roman or secular office as distinct from the monastic.[6] It is apparently as part of the normal Office, then, that

while the third lesson is being read, four of the brethren shall vest ... One of them, wearing an alb and carrying a palm goes to the place of the sepulchre [the altar, as on Good Friday] while during the third respond [following the lesson] three others vested in copes and holding thuribles in their hands shall advance as though searching for something. Now these things are done in imitation of the angel seated at the tomb and of the women coming with perfumes to anoint the body of Jesus.

After the singing of the *Quem queritis?* trope right through in dialogue form, the three Marys turn to the choir and sing: '*Alleluia, resurrexit dominus*' (alleluia, the Lord is risen). Then the angel summons the Marys to the sepulchre, which is empty, the cross buried on Good Friday having been removed from the sepulchre and put back in its usual place early in the morning by the sacristans. The shroud is lifted out, held up to show it is empty and then laid on the altar while the antiphon is sung. Then the prior 'rejoicing in the triumph of our king in that he had conquered death and was risen, shall give out the hymn *Te Deum laudamus* and thereupon all the bells shall peal' (49–50).

The reference to the prior's 'rejoicing' explains the whole difference

between the semi-dramatic ceremonies of the earlier part of the week
and this actual play. The former were to be used, at will, for increase of
devotion or the instruction of the ignorant. The latter is prescribed,
without choice, as part of the rejoicing for the Resurrection. Like the
bells and the *Te Deum* it is an integral part of the celebration of Easter
Day.

LATIN PLAYS FOR EASTER AND CHRISTMAS

The play described above is the oldest of an enormous group of
medieval *Visitatio* plays from all parts of Europe (more than a thousand
manuscripts survive) but it is not the only type of play to develop from
the *Quem queritis?* trope which by the end of the tenth century had also
been introduced (with different music) as part of the introit of the other
great feast of rejoicing, the Nativity. In an eleventh-century manuscript
from St Martial de Limoges in Provence, part of the choir sing: '*Quem
queritis in praesepe, pastores, dicite?*' (Whom do you seek in the manger,
shepherds, say?), to which the rest reply: '*Salvatorem, Christum Dominum,
infantem pannis involutus secundum sermonem angelicum*' (The saviour Christ
the Lord, a child wrapped in swaddling bands as the angels said). The
dialogue continues for several more lines before they all sing the
anthem: *Puer natus est* (a boy is born).[7]

This scene is already more developed than the Easter trope had
been, with an elaboration of the gospel narrative. The final shift from
antiphonal singing by an anonymous choir to a brief but genuinely
dramatic dialogue was achieved when the interlocutors became
specifically shepherds and either '*mulieres*' (women) or, in the Christmas
play from Freising, '*obstetrices*' (midwives).[8]

Only comparatively few examples of this *Officium pastorum* (Office of
the Shepherds) have survived, the more important dramatic development of the Christmas season being associated with the Feast of the
Epiphany on 6 January, which commemorated the manifestation of
Christ to the Gentiles in the persons of the wise men or magi (Matthew
2: 1–15). By the fourth century the unnumbered magi had become
three in number, and kings; the reference in Psalm 71: 10 'the kings of
Tharsis and the islands shall offer presents, the kings of the Arabians
and of Saba shall bring gifts' presented many opportunities for
liturgical and dramatic embellishment. Though never as popular as the
Visitatio play, the *Officium stellae* (Office of the Star) flourished in the
eleventh and twelfth centuries.[9]

A notable example from Freising in the late eleventh century includes scenes of the magi meeting the shepherds, as well as the biblical dialogue with Herod (considerably expanded) together with a visit and gift-giving at the stable.[10] Despite its rather scrappy dialogue and abrupt changes of scene this is by far the most elaborate play surviving from the eleventh century; above all it introduces us to the main dramatic problem of the Christmas liturgy: the fact that it covers twelve days. The meeting of the magi with the shepherds links 6 January with 25 December; while a hint of the Slaughter of the Innocents at the end of the play introduces the feast celebrated on 28 December.[11]

In this play, then, we see the shape of things to come and can understand some of the pressures which were soon to drive many plays out of the liturgical cursus altogether. Many churches chose to celebrate feasts like the Ascension or Pentecost with symbolic ceremonial rather than dramatic action[12] and this more formal presentation is already evident in the last dramatic development associated with the Christmas season to appear in the eleventh century, the *Ordo prophetarum* (Procession of Prophets).[13]

The earliest example of an extra-biblical addition to the Easter *Visitatio* play appears in the early twelfth century when the *Mercator* (merchant, sometimes also called the *Unguentarius*), who sells the Marys their spices before they go to the sepulchre, makes his debut in a text from the Catalan abbey of Ripoll. He was to play a major role in later Easter plays, both Latin and vernacular.[14]

This introduction of additional characters and scenes in both the Easter and Christmas plays was only one of the new developments in the biblical drama. By the end of the eleventh century the first play had been composed that was partly in vernacular and partly in Latin and, more significantly, had no specific performance slot within the liturgy. The *Sponsus* represents the earliest example of what will henceforth be referred to as extra-liturgical drama.[15] These texts, which will be discussed in the next chapter, may retain their Latin liturgical form and even be designed for a church performance at the end of Mattins or Vespers but they have no fixed and regular place in the annual round of worship. Innovations of language and form, especially the introduction of vernacular, are also found, however, in the plays produced within the liturgical framework in the following centuries. The new extra-liturgical drama developed in parallel with the old; it never replaced it.

FESTIVAL DRAMA OF THE LATER MIDDLE AGES

There were several developments in the liturgical plays between the twelfth and sixteenth centuries. Easter and Christmas Latin plays continued to be performed in many parts of Europe in more or less elaborate forms but new feasts attracted plays in the same sung Latin tradition and the first passion plays developed.

The Latin Easter play reached its height in the thirteenth century.[16] Two notable examples from this period are from Origny-Ste-Benoîte and Barking Abbeys, both of them communities of women. The former play, unusually, has all its rubrics in French as well as some of its text; it includes beside the basic *Quem queritis?* dialogue, the visit of Peter and John to the tomb (John 20: 2–8) and the scene between Christ and Mary Magdalene usually known as the '*Noli me tangere*' (Touch me not): John 20: 11–18). The version of the *Visitatio* play from Barking Abbey includes a detailed rubric:

since the congregation of the people in these times seemed to freeze in devotion, and human torpor greatly increasing, the worthy lady, Lady Katharine of Sutton [the Abbess] then being responsible for their pastoral care, desiring to get rid of the said torpor completely and the more to excite the devotion of the faithful to such a renowned celebration ...

instituted the performance of the *Visitatio* play.[17] This performance, then, is a celebration like the first English version in the *Regularis concordia* but it is also considered as an aid to devotion.

A similar purpose may have inspired the introduction of scenes for Pilate and the soldiers guarding the tomb and being bribed by the priests in the early thirteenth-century *Ordo paschalis* (Order of Easter) from Klosterneuberg, for this play had at least in part a lay audience, as can be seen from the reference at the end – *Et populus universus iam certificatus de Domino, cantor sic inponit: 'Christ der ist erstanden'* (and then the whole population having been assured of God, the cantor intones [the hymn]: 'Christ is risen').[18]

Sung Latin plays connected with other feasts of Our Lord are also found in the latter centuries of our period but only in small numbers. The most common is the play based on the meeting between Christ and the disciples on the road to Emmaus (Luke 24: 13–33), usually called the *Peregrinus* (Pilgrim) play and often performed on Easter Monday. Latin plays of the Ascension are rare. The most notable, that from Moosberg, includes details of costumes for the disciples and Mary and is indisputably dramatic rather than ceremonial though it does use a statue for the ascending Christ.

Plays composed for feasts of Our Lady become increasingly common and are found in many countries in both Latin and vernacular. The play of the Presentation of Mary in the Temple performed at Avignon in the late fourteenth century was written by Philippe de Mézières who also composed the Office for the feast. This elaborate and spectacular Latin play was produced in Avignon between 1372 and 1385.[19]

The Annunciation, always a major feast of the Church, developed a splendid semi-dramatic presentation of the gospel of the day known as the *Missa aurea* (Golden Mass) and performed in many churches including St Paul's cathedral, London and the collegiate church of St-Omer in northern France.[20] But the most popular feast of Our Lady by the end of the Middle Ages was the Assumption (15 August). Numerous annual performances of plays on the subject are recorded, especially in Spain; most of them were vernacular though a Latin version survives from Vich (Catalonia) and contains an interesting variant of the ubiquitous *Quem queritis?* trope.[21] The annual Assumption play still to be seen at Elche in south-east Spain has an unbroken performance tradition of five hundred years.

Not all these later liturgical plays were celebratory, however. Just as the *Visitatio* play at Barking had been performed to increase devotion in the torpid faithful, so the devotion of the faithful to the mournful events of Good Friday received a dramatic impetus in the thirteenth century with the introduction of the *Planctus Marie* (Lament of the Virgin Mary). Often found, like the Sibyl's prophecy, as simply a set-piece, the *planctus* may be considered dramatic when, as at Cividale in the fourteenth century, it is provided with rubrics for gesture and separate roles for the Marys and John as well as the Virgin. Here the liturgical performance occasion is clearly indicated by the title: *Hic incipit planctus Marie et aliorum in die Parasceven* (Here begins the lament of Mary and others on Good Friday).[22]

A different kind of liturgical, or liturgically associated, passion drama developed from the thirteenth century onwards as part of the Lenten preaching of the friars, especially the Franciscans. St Francis himself, with his sermon preached over the relic of the Crib preserved in S Maria Maggiore in Rome, had set an example of the use of such devotional aids. With the increased emphasis on the popular piety of the laity and the importance of repentance and penance at Easter it is not surprising that the preaching orders should play a considerable role in the development of lay liturgical drama. The *planctus* performed in 1476 in the German monastery at Jasenitz is specifically described as a lament designed to inspire those who repeat it and those who hear it to tears and compassion '*sicut facit sermo*' (as a sermon would do) on Good Friday (Neumann 817). The performance includes a symbolic adoration of the cross during which St John holds a sword to the Virgin's heart. In Laval, in 1507, a Franciscan made use of costumed local people in tableaux to illustrate his Lenten sermons.

Italy was more ambitious: in Perugia in 1448 a friar preached the Passion out of doors in the square. Then a group of laymen presented the Way of the Cross with the Virgin Mary 'weeping and speaking sorrowfully as was done in the similar play of the Passion'. At the appointed place the cross was laid down and a crucifix set up. The Virgin and some others repeated part of the *planctus*, then followed the Deposition including the *pietà* (the lament of Mary with the body of Christ in her arms) and the Entombment. 'Throughout the people continued to weep loudly.'[23]

Lay vernacular commemorations of Good Friday are also found without a sermon. The sixteenth-century English Bodley plays of the Burial and the Resurrection were intended to be performed, probably by a convent, on Good Friday and Easter Day and the Breton *Passion* is introduced by the 'Witness' with the reminder: 'Today the Son of God the Father died of his own free will for the sin of Adam.' As in the Bodley manuscript, this play ends with the Entombment and a separate Resurrection play for Easter Day follows.[24]

The Catalan *Passion* from Cervera was performed in Holy Week from Palm Sunday to Holy Saturday from the fifteenth right through to the eighteenth century and a group of Easter plays that were at first performed strictly on their correct liturgical occasions have survived from the Tyrol. From about 1430 onwards regular performances on Maundy Thursday, Good Friday and Easter Day were presented in the towns along the route through the Brenner pass, from Hall (near Innsbruck) to Bozen (nowadays Italian Bolzano).[25] The plays continued to be performed until about 1530 though there is evidence that there was no longer a definite liturgical link between their subject matter and the day of the performance. The complex seven-day performance that took place in Bozen between Palm Sunday and Ascension day in 1514 (the longest recorded from a German-speaking country) will be considered in the next chapter.

An important distinction between the Latin and the vernacular plays associated with liturgical performance is that the former derived their material from the texts originally composed for the monastic Office while the latter, being intended primarily for laymen, were as likely to use material found in the Propers (the prescribed lections of the Mass of the particular day being commemorated: see Appendix). Nowhere does this discrepancy reveal itself more clearly than in the Italian *laude*.

In the second half of the thirteenth century the flagellant movement in many parts of Europe brought together bands of young men inspired, by the preaching of Joachim of Flora and fears of the approaching end of the world, to do penance for the sins of Christendom.[26] In Italy the *disciplinati* (as they were called) alternated sung *laude* or praises with periods of self-flagellation. Starting in Perugia the movement spread rapidly through Umbria and subsequently to other parts of Italy. Many of these *laude* based on the gospel readings at Mass on the different Sundays and feasts of the church year were simple lyrics, but others soon developed into genuine sung vernacular plays.

The earliest extant manuscript collection of these *laude*, the Perugia *laudario*, includes a Judgement play to be performed in Advent and a Passion sequence for Holy Week. Other later collections have plays of the Creation as well as a variety of incidents from the gospels.[27] The survival of lists of costumes and properties from several of these confraternities makes it certain that the texts were actually presented dramatically rather than being mere sung dialogues, like the Latin tropes.[28] By the fifteenth century many of the original, simple plays had become more extensive and elaborate extra-liturgical *rappresentazione* (performances); others remained within the routine of the church year.[29]

Several different groups of *disciplinati* in Rome joined together to create the company of the *Gonfalonieri di Santa Lucia* (Bannerbearers of St Lucy) which staged a passion play on Good Friday morning in the Coliseum annually from *c.* 1460–1540. The text of this play – the most substantial extant liturgical Italian *Passion* – has survived as well as the list of costumes and properties. Pilgrims celebrating Holy Week in Rome attended the play as part of the Good Friday observances, as we learn from the eye-witness account by the German, Arnold von Harff, who saw it in 1498.[30] Although the *laude* provided plays for a much wider range of liturgical occasions than any other type of drama, and created a sequence for the church year that parallels the liturgical ritual itself, they were never, of course, performed in cycles. That peculiarly medieval dramatic form developed only after the proclamation, almost contemporary with the early *laude*, of a new feast which was to have an influence on drama throughout medieval Europe: the feast of Corpus Christi.

PLAYS FOR CORPUS CHRISTI AND CORPUS CHRISTI PLAYS

The feast of Corpus Christi, which was to play such a significant role in the development of vernacular biblical drama, was first celebrated in the diocese of Liège (then an independent archbishopric within the Holy Roman Empire) in 1246 by Bishop Robert, inspired by the visions of blessed Juliana of Cornillon. The original intention behind the celebration was twofold: to encourage greater veneration of the Eucharist with more frequent communion by both clergy and laity, and to emphasise the true importance of the Sacrament whose institution on Maundy Thursday was overshadowed in the Holy Week liturgy by St John's emphasis on the Washing of Feet and the beginning of the Passion.[31]

Pope Urban IV, who formally established the feast in 1264 by the bull: *Transiturus de hoc mundo* (Preparing to leave this world), had been archdeacon in Liège at the time of Bishop Robert and was also encouraged by the Dominican, Hugo von den Chor, papal legate to that region of the Empire. The feast was celebrated in a number of churches in France and Germany in the last years of the thirteenth century but the death of Pope Urban the year after the bull was promulgated, delayed universal acceptance of Corpus Christi until Clement V and the Council of Vienne took up the matter in 1311/12 and strongly recommended the new feast. Even then, it was only in 1317 that Clement's decree was officially promulgated by John XXII and that the Thursday after the Octave of Pentecost (which might fall between 21 May and 24 June) was fixed on for the celebration of the feast of Corpus Christi.

From its inception, this was a feast for the laity[32] and since vernacular liturgical drama was already so well established in Italy as a result of the *disciplinati* movement, it is not surprising that what is probably the oldest surviving Corpus Christi play-text is to be found in the *laudario* from Orvieto.

According to this version, the feast was instituted as a result of the celebrated Miracle of the Bleeding Corporal of Orvieto. (The corporal is the white linen cloth laid on the altar underneath the communion vessels. It represents the shroud in which Christ was wrapped.) The miracle, as presented in the play, is recorded on marble tablets in the Chapel of the Corporal in Orvieto cathedral which dates from *c.* 1360. A German priest who has doubts of the Real Presence of Christ in the Eucharist is sent by his confessor on pilgrimage to Rome and on his way home he stops in the little town of Bolseno near Orvieto and goes to celebrate Mass in the church of St Christina. Two bystanders see him fall, rush forward and see the miracle: blood is dripping from the consecrated wafer on to the corporal. The pope is summoned, declares: 'We have here a great miracle of the *"Corpo di Cristo"* ', and summons Thomas Aquinas to compose the Propers for a new feast.[33]

Although modern scholarship has cast doubt on the validity of the miracle and its influence on the founding of the feast, its association with Corpus Christi was certainly accepted in medieval Italy. Pope Pius II writing in his memoirs in the 1460s described a visit to Orvieto cathedral and the miracle of the Corporal and adds: 'This miracle was authenticated by Urban IV and therefore was instituted the feast of the most Holy Body of Christ which is celebrated yearly with the profoundest solemnity and devotion by the nations of the entire Christian world.'[34]

No other dramatic *lauda* for Corpus Christi is extant but plays associated with the feast are recorded from every part of Catholic Europe during the second half of the Middle Ages. Three types of drama can be distinguished: a simple play on any subject and possibly staged by a Corpus Christi guild; a processional play with floats and tableaux, walking figures and some dramatic presentations, staged by the religious guilds, the church or the city; and the processional cycle plays, often called Corpus Christi plays, presenting a series of scenes from the Old and New Testaments and usually staged by the craft guilds. These will be considered in turn.

The place of the feast at the culmination of the Church's year, after the commemoration of the Resurrection, Ascension and coming of the Holy Spirit at Pentecost, meant that the whole triple structure of the Creation, Redemption and Judgement of Man, set forth in the Apostles' Creed, was suitable material for dramatic presentation on that one day. All surviving texts and records of independent Creed plays are associated with this feast: the fourteenth-century Innsbruck *Fronleichnamsspiel*, the oldest extant German Corpus Christi play, is a mixture of Creed and Prophet play with tributes to the Sacrament by characters from the Old and New Testaments and a final speech by an unidentified 'pope'.[35]

References to plays for Corpus Christi are recorded from a number of towns in the British Isles, which had a strong dramatic tradition connected with the feast,[36] but the most unlikely subject recorded for a Corpus Christi play must be that performed in Perugia in 1450, when, after the morning procession and dinner, they presented Theseus Slaying the Minotaur. One explanation might be the similarity of this classical theme to the story of St George and the Dragon which was a popular part of the Corpus Christi processions described below.[37]

It was above all the public procession of the Sacrament on Corpus Christi day, established in 1320 by the Synod of Sens, which stimulated dramatic activity. The decrees of Urban and Clement had stressed particularly the importance of repentance and communion but the procession of the Sacrament, already recorded in Germany before 1317, soon replaced the original emphasis on lay communion. Though relics and other venerable objects were often processed, the Sacrament was rarely taken outside the church (except for the Last Rites) and public processions of which it was the focal point were virtually unknown before the end of the thirteenth century. The Corpus Christi procession had, therefore, to be more worthy of its festive occasion than the most venerable patronal and Rogationtide procession[38] so it is not surprising that accounts of decorated streets and the ordered marching of local groups, guilds, confraternities and dignitaries, with banners and candles, recur constantly in the records. The Real Presence of God himself in the Sacrament must ensure an outstanding attention by the whole community to this very special liturgical celebration.

Predictably, figures and ornaments were soon added to the stations where the procession halted. The adornment of these altars of repose, on which the Sacrament rested for a brief time, encouraged the presentation of the tableaux which were so popular and regular a part of civic life on special occasions in the later Middle Ages. Each guild or parish or group of supporters vied with the others to produce the most impressive display.[39] As early as 1328 the tailors of Lincoln were fined for failing to take their part in it; Vich and Valencia in Catalonia both had processions with floats and tableaux by the middle of the fourteenth century and in Bohemia, in 1371, the Archbishop banned 'ludos theatrales' (dramatic plays) from the Corpus Christi processions.[40] However, the great age of the Corpus Christi procession and its associated drama is the fifteenth century.[41]

The towns least likely to be moved to this form of celebration were naturally those which already had an annual or regular procession with representations: the feast of St John the Baptist, in Florence, Bordeaux and Dresden; Candlemas at Aberdeen (where, however, the old-established procession with plays seems to have been taken over by the Corpus Christi celebration after 1530). The feast of St Anne had a procession at Lincoln, and a number of towns in France and the Netherlands celebrated feasts of Our Lady with dramatic processions. In Bozen, in the Tyrol, Corpus Christi was known popularly as 'Antlass' (entlassen = 'freeing') from its association with the flagellant processions on Maundy Thursday when the penitents were 'freed' from their sins before Easter (see Appendix note 9). The Bozen Umgang described in the archives included scenes from the Old and New Testaments.[42]

Given the importance of the new feast and the popularity of plays as a part of the celebration of other liturgical feasts such as Easter or the Assumption, the final step towards a genuine vernacular liturgical drama for Corpus Christi was easily taken. Towns that presented actual plays as part of the Corpus Christi procession did so in a variety of ways. Bologna had a procession with a mixture of real drama (on waggons), tableaux and figures. The subjects represented included the Creation; scenes from the life of Christ; and a long tail of walking groups of saints and biblical characters. Turin also included plays with the procession; in 1510 the Nativity and Ascension are mentioned.[43]

The Catalan processions were organised jointly by town and church groups like the processions in Italy, but with the difference that in Spain the church often took the financial responsibility for the feast while the actual performances were put on by lay guilds. The Toledo cathedral accounts for Corpus Christi in 1493 indicate the presence of genuine plays, for they include payments to performers (as well as costumes and properties) for the Temptation, Woman in Adultery, the Harrowing of Hell (with rockets), Resurrection and Assumption. Between the last two scenes came the play of the 'Man who exploded'.[44] A few examples of these 'mixed' processions, with tableaux, plays and walking figures, are recorded from France and the Netherlands and many more from the British Isles.[45]

The last group to be considered are what I have called the processional cycle plays. Evidence of series of short plays covering the whole span of the liturgical year from Creation to Doomsday is to be found in several continental countries, especially Germany, but the best known are the English Corpus Christi plays, though not all of these were in fact performed on that feast.

It is a peculiarity of these cycles that with rare exceptions[46] the full-span play, the whole sequence of the Acts of God including the Judgement, is not staged by religious confraternities, civic or church authorities but only by groups of craft guilds. Though such craft-guild cycles are occasionally found in Spain and France[47] the most important examples of the genre come from Germany and England.

Only one German cycle text is extant that dramatises the full sequence and was performed annually: that of Künzelsau. The plays in this cycle are short and some include only one character; each episode is introduced by the *rector ludi* (play director) who explains its significance. It is probable that these plays were performed at each of the three stations at which the procession paused. The cycle is 4,300 lines long (approximately four to five hours' playing time) and at the end of the manuscript, which bears the date 1479, there is an additional series of more elaborate plays for Christmas and Easter which were apparently added to the procession at a later date. Between the Pentecost and Judgement plays there is a Creed play with the twelve apostles.[48] Descriptions of other Corpus Christi plays associated with processions in different ways are extant, but whatever the variety of length and performance arrangement in these German cycles (many of which come from the Imperial 'free towns' of the southern area of the Empire on the Swiss border)[49] they all have in common a sequence from Creation to Doomsday performed by craft guilds like the plays performed in England, where the Corpus Christi cycle reached its apogee.

Examples of lost processional plays performed by craft guilds are recorded by Lancashire and others. The four surviving complete cycles are all on this pattern; yet by the end of the fifteenth century, only York and Coventry had a Corpus Christi play cycle that continued to be performed annually on its liturgical day. Chester was performed at Whitsun and later at Midsummer and there are also records from the town of a play by the cathedral clergy performed on the feast itself. The N. town play, as its name suggests, has no fixed location or occasion for performance and the links between the Towneley cycle and the records of a Wakefield Corpus Christi play, though strong, are not conclusive.

A solitary continental parallel comes from the town of Eger (Cheb) in Bohemia on the frontier of the German-speaking Empire. Here there are records of a Corpus Christi processional play and, in a separate manuscript, the text of a three-day cycle which covers the sequence from Creation to the Resurrection and Christ's appearance to Doubting Thomas. The disciples recite the articles of the Creed during the Last Supper, and the Resurrection scenes follow closely the liturgical pattern of the extended *Visitatio* plays.

It sems likely therefore that these plays, which are so similar to the guild Corpus Christi cycles – with their structure based on the Creed, their use of occasional Expositors, the strong liturgical overtones in the choice and treatment of the subjects, and the annual performance – once belonged to the feast-day drama that developed within the Church's celebration of Corpus Christi. It may be that Eger, like Chester and N. town, outgrew its original context as centuries before the Easter plays from Fleury and Benediktbeuern had done. Certainly in England, with the exception of the York cycle, which remained in uneasy double harness until its originating procession was abolished in 1567, the cycles ceased to be plays for the feast of Corpus Christi and became simply a particular form of civic drama described by the sixteenth-century scribe, at the beginning of the eclectic N. town manuscript, as 'The Plaie called Corpus Christi'.[50]

CHAPTER 2

Civic and community drama

EXTRA-LITURGICAL CHURCH PLAYS

The development of drama took a new turn in the twelfth century with the evolution of plays that were not specifically linked by subject-matter or performance occasion with the feasts of the liturgical year. Certain of the plays for the Christmas season had already shown signs of bursting out of their liturgical bonds (see p. 17). The process is accelerated in the twelfth century with the introduction into biblical plays of an increasing amount of vernacular speech, so that we are faced with a considerable number of unattached plays composed for an occasion we cannot pinpoint and a purpose we cannot divine: floating masterpieces in a world of ordered formulae. The question then has to be asked: who wrote, performed and watched this drama? Many of the early extra-liturgical plays are traditional in form, and present sung Latin dramatisations of biblical incidents from both Old and New Testaments outside of the usual range of Christmas and Easter plays. It is reasonably certain that they were still linked with the church, for drama must have a community to flourish in and the church (including the church schools) is the only place at this date where Latin playwrights could be expected to be found. But as not all the texts are preserved in liturgical books other information must be sought in the play-texts themselves.

The twelfth-century *Isaac* play from Austria, which is simply a loose sheet of paper pasted into a book of sermons, has elaborate staging and music for part of the text which suggests a church performance without indicating the occasion. The same is true of the *Joseph* play found in the same Laon Troper as the *Ordo stellae* and *Ordo prophetarum*.[1] However, the inclusion in the Fleury play-book (so-called from its modern location, since the abbey of Fleury has no record of liturgical drama)[2] of several miracles of St Nicholas, the patron of scholars and the only

28

non-biblical saint to feature in Latin plays,[3] may suggest a scholarly source for these extra-liturgical plays. Hilarius, the earliest named author of biblical plays, has been described as one of the *vagantes* or wandering scholars. His *Daniel* play requires church facilities for performance but has no occasion for which it is particularly suitable, though the author suggests ending with the *Te Deum* if the play is performed at Mattins or the *Magnificat* if at Vespers.[4] These and other Latin plays could all have featured as part of a church's celebrations outside of the normal liturgical sequence performed for (partially at least) lay audiences by groups of clerks, students or scholars such as those whose plays are recorded from Deventer (see p. 56).

Prophet plays have more obvious liturgical association than these other Old Testament texts since prophecies of the Redemption were an important part of the readings in Advent. It is interesting therefore that the earliest *Ordo prophetarum*, from St Martial de Limoges in Provence, is in an eleventh-century manuscript collection which also includes another play linked with the Advent theme of judgement and preparedness. The *Sponsus* (bridegroom) based on the parable of the Ten Virgins (Matthew 25: 13)[5] is the earliest surviving play we have which includes a substantial amount of vernacular sung dialogue: one third Provençal to two thirds Latin. This is a church play, then, but with concessions to the presence of an illiterate (i.e. non-Latin-speaking) congregation.

Even the fully vernacular texts can be divided (as established in the previous chapter) between those plays such as the Castilian *Auto de los reyes magos (Play of the Kings)* which were performed on their appropriate liturgical occasion – here the feast of the Epiphany – and others like the Anglo-Norman *Adam* whose three episodes, the Fall of Man, Cain and Abel, and a prophet play, cannot be liturgically located.

Moreover, with the introduction of vernacular into the plays, a clerical performance now becomes open to question. So long as the Virgins are lamenting or rejoicing in musical forms, the change from Latin to Provençal is only significant on an emotional level. With the introduction of spoken rather than sung dialogue the real difference becomes apparent. The next wave of vernacular/bilingual plays used more or less normal speech with character variation and development expressed through words rather than sounds. In the Anglo-Norman *Adam*, moreover, the characters think and speak theologically.

Information about the patrons and performers of these extra-liturgical vernacular plays can sometimes be deduced by an examination of the history of the manuscripts. The *Reyes magos* is incomplete, and none of the small number of stage-directions can help decide by and for whom it was performed. *Adam*, however, is a very different matter. Though it is now generally accepted that the play was originally composed in the mid-twelfth century in Anglo-Norman, few scholars have considered the significance of the fact that the surviving manuscript was copied in the thirteenth century not in England but in Southern France, on paper from Moorish Spain (it is the oldest paper manuscript in French) by a Provençal-speaking scribe with indifferent knowledge of Latin. It is also known that the manuscript belonged to an aristocratic family during the sixteenth to seventeenth centuries and passed from them (via the celebrated Benedictine house at Marmoutier) to Tours only in the late eighteenth century.[6]

Whether written for church performance or an aristocratic audience, plays of the Old Testament or lives of saints were important novelties in the early development of the extra-liturgical drama, just because they were not easily linked to liturgical occasions. They were an extra, outside of the seasonal calendar. But they were not an alternative to the ceremonies of the liturgy. This position was held by the two major groups of non-liturgical vernacular plays which were to develop in the next three centuries: plays for the Christmas season including the whole Nativity sequence from Annunciation to Innocents and, above all, the play which dominates the civic drama of Europe and, in its cyclic form, absorbed the whole history of God's relationship with man: the passion play.

PASSION PLAY AND PASSION CYCLE

The term Passion has two meanings in liturgical usage. Passiontide is the period of two weeks from the fifth Sunday in Lent (Passion Sunday) to the Saturday of Holy Week (see Appendix). During this period the crucifixes in the church are all veiled and special readings begin to commemorate the events leading up to the Death and Resurrection of Christ.[7] These include the raising of Lazarus, which St John explains precipitated the Jews' determination to have Christ put to death, and the meal at the house of Simon when Mary Magdalene anoints Christ's feet (John 12) or head (Matthew 26: 6–13; Mark 14: 3–9) as preparation for his death.

In Holy Week itself, the 'Passions' according to the four evangelists, that is to say the whole account of the Arrest, Trials, Crucifixion,

Death and Burial of Christ, were read in turn, except on Maundy Thursday when the gospel for the day was taken from John's account of the Last Supper. On Good Friday the gospel of the day is the Passion according to John. In the liturgy, however, in contrast to the non-liturgical narrative or dramatic passion texts, the gospels are never harmonised: each Passion is read independently.[8] Liturgically, then, the term 'Passion' can refer either to the immediate events surrounding the Crucifixion or to the whole sequence of events recounted during Passiontide; passion plays may follow either usage.

Liturgical drama included the *planctus* on Good Friday and the semi-dramatic singing of the Passion, but the principal Latin drama of the Easter season remained the Resurrection play,[9] with only a few liturgical plays, all of them vernacular, staging the Crucifixion and Death of Christ on Good Friday. However, in the twelfth century three extra-liturgical texts, two Greek, one Latin, dramatise not only the Crucifixion but also some of the surrounding events. The Greek *Paschon Christos*, which centres on the Virgin Mary and includes her lamentations before and during the Crucifixion (in which Christ has a small speaking role) is preserved in a twelfth-century manuscript, but was said to be the work of the sixth-century Gregory of Nazianzus, which would make it the oldest biblical play extant.[10] The other Greek play, the Cyprus *Passion*, was composed in the late twelfth or early thirteenth century by an Orthodox monk at a time when the Venetian Latin Christians had taken over the island of Cyprus. The manuscript gives only an outline (or Scenario, as the editor calls it) with stage directions and *incipits* for many of the speeches, which follow the Bible closely. There is an interesting introductory speech on the proper way to stage the play.[11] It seems probable that both these texts were performed in churches by clerical actors and probably for a primarily clerical audience.

Though these Greek plays are interesting and curious, they are isolated examples of the genre – unlike the important twelfth-century Latin Montecassino *Passion*, which is incomplete at the beginning and end but seems to have covered the events from the Betrayal to the Resurrection. The end of the text is only known from a fourteenth-century actor's role for a Fourth Soldier, from Sulmona.[12]

The Montecassino play was probably performed in the monastery church. A church location is also likely for the two versions of the *Ludus de passione* from the group of plays in the thirteenth-century Benedikt-beuern *Carmina burana* manuscript which also includes a prophet play explicitly set in church. Recent scholarship suggests that the manuscript may originate in the Tyrol.[13] The *Ludus breviter de passione* stages only the Last Supper, Arrest and Crucifixion but the second, longer text (given the name *Ludus de passione* by Young) begins with a lengthy staging direction as Pilate, Herod and the high priest, each with followers, takes his place '*in locum suum*' to the singing of the reponsory, '*Ingressus Pilati*' (Pilate having entered). The play includes scenes from the Ministry, Entry into Jerusalem and other events of Holy Week including the Crucifixion and Death of Christ. Who performed these German passion plays? The presence in the Benediktbeuern manuscript of the *Carmina burana* (a group of student songs) and the example of the plays of Hilarius (including *Daniel*) suggests that the clerical performers might have been *vagantes*, wandering scholars. This could also explain the partial introduction of vernacular in the worldly scenes with Mary Magdalene.

There are also records of plays for which no texts have survived such as those performed for the instruction of the pagans in Riga (Latvia) in 1204; or the Fall and prophet play in Regensburg in 1194. The latter seems to have been aimed at an already Christian audience judging by the reference to the pope and the emperor. Since the scenes were '*celebratus*', a clerical performance seems probable.[14] It was certainly the clergy of Cividale which performed plays in the diocese of Friuli in 1298 and 1304. These two cycles – for such they must be considered – were performed on Whitsunday and the following days in the presence of the local nobility and clergy.[15]

The fourteenth century saw a marked decrease in Latin extra-liturgical plays and a corresponding increase in the vernacular and bilingual drama. But whereas Easter plays, such as the Muri *Osterspiel* or the fragmentary *Trois Maries* from Reims may have been performed in religious houses (the use of vernacular is not uncommon in liturgical works from houses of nuns),[16] the extra-liturgical vernacular passion plays, with multiple staging and large casts, were probably performed by townsmen rather than clerics. The number of performances recorded for the fourteenth and early fifteenth centuries is limited, partly because of the disasters of war, famine and plague which ravaged the countries of Western Europe at this time, but during the fifteenth and early sixteenth centuries this trickle swelled to a flood and by the end of the Middle Ages there are biblical plays extant from the Celtic lands of the west to the newly emergent nations on the eastern fringes of the Empire.[17] But it is in France and Germany that the majority of texts and records can be found.

In France, texts like the fourteenth-century Palatinus *Passion* contain very little Latin and are already moving along a very different path from the liturgical plays with no indication of church involvement.[18] Who performed these French plays and when? In 1333 in Toulon, a group of about a hundred townsfolk presented an elaborate play of the early life of Mary and the Birth of Christ. The significance of the record is that all the participants are named, and all belong to the leading families of the city. This is the earliest record of what was to become a common practice of French drama: a group of eminent townsfolk deciding to perform a play and asking for (and usually receiving) assistance from the town council.[19] In Mons, for example, in 1455, a number of people petitioned the council for permission to put on a play and asked them to appoint a group of leading councillors (*echevins*) to organise the performance.[20] In other parts of France groups like the *Confrérie du Saint-Sacrament* in Amiens oversaw the town's plays. Best known of all was the *Confrérie de la Passion* in Paris.

Paris stands out on the continent for its unique organisation of religious drama in the later medieval period. There are references from the end of the fourteenth century to performances of passion plays in Paris and the surrounding area; in 1401 the king, Charles VI, granted letters patent to a *Confrérie de la Passion* formed of a group of townsfolk, who had been doing an annual passion play before the king 'which they have not been able properly to continue because we were not then able to be present'. The Brotherhood had apparently asked the king's leave to play publicly which 'would be to the profit of the Brotherhood' and this is granted 'so that everyone as an act of devotion may and should join them and be of their company'. By this unique charter, the *Confrérie* had the monopoly on all public dramatic performances in the capital, a right they were to retain for nearly three centuries till the *Confrérie* was finally abolished by Louis XIV in 1676.[21]

Unfortunately we have almost no direct evidence of the activities of the *Confrérie* during the early part of its existence. How many members there were in the group and how they were chosen we do not know; certainly the later plays used huge casts. The plays in the St Genevieve manuscript, which include a biblical sequence from Creation to Acts as well as a series of plays on the life of St Genevieve (the patron saint of the city) herself, may well have formed the repertory of the company, but we cannot be sure. There are references in printed play-texts to Paris performances of the *Passion* in 1473, 1490, 1498 and 1507, and to the *Sacrifice of Abraham* (1539). The *Abraham* is part of the huge *Viel*

Testament (Old Testament) cycle of plays which was performed as a whole in 1542, the last known production before the *Parlement* (the supreme legal authority in Paris) banned the *Confrérie* from putting on plays on religious subjects.[22]

Outside of Paris the drama, especially passion plays, flourished after the end of the Hundred Years War and the civil war between the Armagnacs and the Burgundians. More than a hundred performances of the Passion are attested from all over the country between about 1440 and 1550. The most influential extant text is the *Passion* composed around 1440 by Arnoul Gréban, a canon of Notre Dame cathedral in Paris (and, later, at Le Mans). It survives in a number of manuscripts and printed editions and, with revisions and additions, it was still being used a hundred years later.[23]

One of the distinctive features of the French passion plays is their comprehensive range: Gréban's play opens with a Prologue of the Fall; then a brief prophet scene in Limbo introduces the Nativity sequence, followed by the Ministry, Passion and Resurrection. Some performance texts include an Old Testament sequence and end with Pentecost and the Assumption. Separate passion plays independent of the Gréban tradition (which dominated northern France) survive from Semur in Burgundy and the Auvergne.

The German plays are numerous, with a wide range of recorded performances, but they are shorter and less comprehensive than the French. Though there is none of the complex tradition created in France by the use of printed editions of the basic texts, there are examples in Germany of groups of related plays from towns in the same area. The best known group are from the west central area of Germany, centred on Frankfurt. The first civic German passion play is preserved in the bilingual fourteenth-century Frankfurt *Dirigierrolle* (Director's copy) from which evolved the fully vernacular Frankfurt *Passion* of the fifteenth century, with related texts from Alsfeld, Heidelberg, Marburg and Friedberg. The German passion plays often remained close to their liturgical roots, perhaps because so many German towns also had Corpus Christi plays,[24] and part of the *Dirigierrolle* in which each speech is sung in Latin then spoken in German is closely related to the Latin Benediktbeuern play. Other major passion texts are those from Redentin and St Gallen. North Germany has only a few examples of biblical drama, the most important being Immessen's *Sündenfall*, while the only *Passion* in Low German/Dutch is from Maastricht.[25]

Some of the imperial free towns and the early members of the Swiss confederation had a rich dramatic tradition. These include Fribourg, Neuchâtel and, especially, Lucerne, from which detailed records have survived together with variant versions of the passion play which was performed from the late fifteenth through to the early seventeenth century at intervals of about twenty years.[26] Zurich, which became Protestant, nevertheless had a notable playwright in Adam Rueff who wrote a *Fall* play and a *Passion* which were performed early in the sixteenth century.[27]

A particularly interesting group of plays have been preserved from the Tyrol.[28] The plays from Bozen were collected by the Latin schoolmaster, Benedikt Debs, who, in a major passion play performed in 1495, reintroduced the bilingual tradition found in the early German plays. After Debs's death in 1515 his manuscripts (a total of fifteen vernacular plays) were taken over by Vigil Raber who continued to write and produce plays in the area which included the towns of Brixen, Bozen, Hall and Sterzing. Raber's own work included *Passion* and Old Testament plays and two incomplete dramatisations of John's gospel – a return to the liturgical concept of separate gospel traditions not commonly found in medieval drama.[29]

Passion plays are comparatively rare in Italy, which has a great variety of traditions because of its fragmentary political state at this period. The confraternity that staged a passion play in the Coliseum in Rome has been mentioned in the previous chapter; a second, unpublished passion text survives in a manuscript from Rome.[30] There are also passion texts among the very large number of plays composed and printed in Florence but no performance details are available. None of these texts is cyclic except the most notable passion play from Italy, that written for and staged by the small Piedmont town of Revello in 1492. This three-day *Passion* on the French model, beginning with prophets and covering the Nativity, Ministry, Passion and Resurrection, was an explicitly civic production.[31]

Vernacular drama also flourished in the south of France and on both sides of the Pyrenees. The fourteenth-century Provençal *Passion* has vernacular text and stage directions throughout.[32] In Spain, the drama was mainly associated with the feast of Corpus Christi, but two *Passions* feature in the sixteenth-century collection from Madrid (which contains over a hundred, mainly biblical, religious plays) and there is an *Auto de la Passion* from Toledo written by a cathedral canon, Alfonso del Campo, who was also responsible for the Corpus Christi procession.[33]

This suggests a situation similar to that of Freiburg im Breisgau, where the *Passion* was performed in an interval of the Corpus Christi procession.[34] Such an arrangement may perhaps also underlie the only real passion play extant from England, that from the N. town manuscript which appears (though this is still a matter for debate) to contain a conflation of a Corpus Christi processional cycle with fixed-location plays on the early life of Mary and two versions of the *Passion*.[35]

Not all the great civic plays were *Passions*. There are also separate nativity plays and plays based on selected biblical episodes from the Old and New Testament. In addition, a number of cycles or groups of plays, like the Corpus Christi plays discussed in the previous chapter, were composed for and performed (sometimes annually) on specific but civic occasions.

CIVIC DRAMA: OCCASIONAL PLAYS

Civic drama was used in several countries to celebrate a local patronal or other religious festival. These plays are rarely found in the same towns as Corpus Christi drama: it seems that citizens who already had a special festival, even if it had no dramatic element, did not choose to add drama to the obligatory procession of the guilds and townsfolk on the new feast of Corpus Christi. There is an indication of this attitude in the journal entry of the Bourgeois de Paris which describes a week of processions instituted in 1419 in support of the King's struggle against the Burgundians. Detailed accounts are given of the processions on each day of the week except for Thursday which has the terse entry: 'The Thursday was the day of the Holy Sacrament; the traditional procession took place.' This lack of enthusiasm is compensated for by the description of the crowds who on Friday accompanied the miraculous Host in the 'most beautiful procession ever seen'. This latter procession included a tableau of the burning in 1290 of a Jew who had desecrated the Host.[36]

Many towns had non-biblical patron saints and there are numerous saints' plays extant written for these towns. Civically honoured biblical patrons, however, are limited to two: Our Lady and John the Baptist. One of the most important Marian cycles comes from Brussels, which from at least 1448 until 1556 had an annual feast of Our Lady organised by the town guild of archers (*boogschutters*) consisting of a procession (*ommegang*), together with a play on one of the seven *Bliscapen* (Joys) of

Mary. One *Bliscap* was performed each year in a seven-year cycle, but only the first and seventh play have survived. Tableaux on carts of the Seven Joys of Mary also formed part of the Procession of Our Lady from Leuven where they followed a series of walking episodes (each sponsored by a separate guild) of famous women from the Old Testament including Sarah, Rebecca, Ruth and Jael who carried a hammer and was followed by Sisera with the nail in his head. This combination of tableaux on floats and episodes acted out by walking figures on the street is also found in the Procession of the Holy Blood from Bruges which has a continuous performance tradition from the fourteenth century to the present day (see fig. 1).[37]

Also performed to celebrate a feast of Our Lady are the processional plays in the recently discovered Lille manuscript. A number of individual plays on biblical, hagiographic or historical subjects were prepared by the different neighbourhood groups into which the town was divided.[38] The procession was founded in 1270 under the sponsorship of the collegiate church of St Peter but the plays were not added till the fourteenth century. The procession took place two weeks after Pentecost and only three days after the later-established Corpus Christi procession which it overshadowed. The plays were usually organised by a Canon of St Peter's who each year was elected Bishop of Fools, and from 1431 prizes were awarded for the best plays entered. When the Duke of Burgundy attended the plays in 1448, particularly sumptuous prizes encouraged the town to put forth its best efforts.

The Lille *Evesque des fous* was a cleric but the Abbot of Bonaccort who presided over the '*haliblude*' (holy blood) play in Aberdeen in 1440 and 1445 was elected from among the towns' leading citizens. In 1442 there was also a reminder to the craft guilds of Aberdeen of their obligations for the annual procession and plays at Candlemas including biblical and hagiographic episodes 'in the honour of God and the blessed Virgin Mary'. This suggests two different dramatic efforts in the one town.[39]

John the Baptist, who was often associated with the cloth trade because of his iconographic appearance holding a lamb (derived from his words: 'Behold, the Lamb of God', John 1: 36), was patron of Florence, and from at least the fifteenth century the city celebrated the nativity of her patron saint (24 June) with a procession and sequence of plays from the Old and New Testaments. Several play-texts have survived, together with eye-witness accounts of the presentation. It is a distinctive feature of this cycle that from 1428 onwards it did not include the Passion, which was considered inappropriate for a festive occasion.[40] Bordeaux also held its annual procession and plays on John the Baptist's day; as did Dresden.[41] There are no surviving texts from Dresden but the expense accounts for the annual processional performance indicates a range of episodes including the Fall, Annunciation (and possibly the Nativity), as well as the Baptism and the Decollation of John the Baptist. The sequence also includes the Passion and ends with the Resurrection. It seems appropriate to mention here that in the late fifteenth century the Chester cycle play was moved from Corpus Christi day to the Midsummer festival (24 June, i.e. the feast of John the Baptist) which was traditionally celebrated with a mayoral procession in the town. The Midsummer show in London sometimes involved tableaux if not actual plays.[42]

A different kind of civic occasional drama is that recorded from towns which performed a play once (or regularly) as a thank-offering for being spared in plague or other disaster. In 1565 the town of St Jean-de-Maurienne in Savoy swore an oath in the town council that if they were spared in the plague that threatened them they would perform the Passion of Christ. The plague passed them by. A few years later a council member with an inconvenient memory brought the matter up again and pointed out they must either do it or be forsworn. The play was performed in 1573.[43]

GUILD AND COMMUNITY DRAMA

Not all urban dramatic occasions were on a large scale. There are many instances of small numbers of people from a parish, neighbourhood or guild getting together to stage plays.[44] Not all of these plays were biblical – indeed for many we have no record of the subject – but there are enough known cases to justify including them here.

During the thirteenth century, a number of craft guilds and associated religious confraternities were formed in towns in the German-speaking Empire, England and Scotland. In Italy the unique development of the flagellant drama has already been mentioned (see p. 21). Many French towns had literary guilds or *puys*, often with a religious element built into them, which might bring together the professional minstrels or *jongleurs* and the local bourgeois.[45]

In towns of the French-speaking Netherlands which did not have *puys* or chambers of rhetoric, neighbourhood groups of actors were already flourishing in the fourteenth century. In 1397 it was forbidden to perform on '*cars*' (waggons) or any other kind of staging in the streets and squares of Lille: fines of '*20s*' would be levied against those who infringed the edict and on the owner of the cart (or the horses and harness), used for such plays.[46] Since the edict was repeated at intervals over the next century it was evidently not taken too seriously, and by 1415 groups of players from Lille are taking part in the inter-city play contests which were a feature of dramatic life in the Netherlands for several centuries. Unfortunately we are not usually told the subject of the plays performed by these players. Nor do we know details of the plays presented by the neighbourhood group – led by Jean Wastelet, a barber's apprentice – in nearby St-Omer, which also took part in a number of play contests.[47] However, the three 'figures' Wastelet presented for the procession on the feast of St Omer, patron of the town, were probably biblical. A neighbourhood group from Haut-Pont in St-Omer acted plays for Corpus Christi from 1413 onwards and in 1456 they were given £6 to prepare and refurbish the Tree of Jesse and other props and costumes for the forthcoming feast.[48]

Another sort of community drama is that recorded from villages and small towns in England, especially the south-east. In East Anglia, several villages would combine, take up a collection and import a 'Property player' to organise and stage a series of local performances. In other places such as Reading, the locals would go out in groups 'gathering' to raise money for a play in aid of church funds; their texts include at least one biblical play of Adam and Eve.[49] The only extant reference from France on this scale is the story of the three inhabitants of the village of Athis-sur-Orge near Paris who bound themelves together by contract to stage a group of three plays, including one on the Selling of Joseph.[50] We do not know where these plays were performed but as one of the group was the local innkeeper, a playing-space in the yard is a possibility. Local plays were also occasionally performed indoors. At the end of the Schwabian Christmas play, for example, the angel explains the Holy Family must flee and asks the audience for contributions of food, or 'if anyone has no cakes and doughnuts money will be welcome'. Then Joseph tells the audience that they are setting off – not for Egypt, but to the house of N-. where they will find a warm room.[51]

Many towns in both French and Dutch Netherlands had chambers of rhetoric which performed plays both publicly and for their own members. Among the surviving texts are a considerable number of biblical plays.[52] Some of the rhetoricians' drama was performed indoors in what were called dinner-plays; the name can also serve for the plays performed at the annual dinner of a guild or religious confraternity. The Cangé manuscript of plays based on miracles of the Virgin which were performed annually for the Paris Goldsmiths' guild includes a *Nativity* in three scenes.

Perhaps the ultimate in dinner-plays was that given at the Council of Constance in 1417. The English bishops (including London and Salisbury, with 'other honest citizens of their group') entertained the other bishops at the council to dinner and performed a nativity play between the two courses of eight dishes each. The play, which may have been a mime, was presented very lavishly with a moving star and fine clothes for the magi. The eye-witness account concludes with the judgement that the play was performed with great skill and humility (*mit grosser Gezierd und Grosser Demuht*). It was repeated the following Sunday before the emperor.[53] There are also many examples of small groups performing for royal entries or other aristocratic occasions.

PRINCES AT PLAYS AND PLAYS FOR PRINCES

Princes (to use a general word for all royal and aristocratic persons) were involved in the mainly civic biblical drama in two ways: as visiting dignitaries or as patrons. Many examples are recorded of towns celebrating royal entries and other civic, princely occasions with plays or tableaux, sometimes with miming or spoken, rhymed commentaries. Quite a number of these presentations include episodes from the Bible, even part or all of a Corpus Christi cycle; but whereas the usual medieval biblical play is theocentric, the tableaux for a royal entry are centred on the prince rather than God: the prince is both spectator and actor. The choice of theme reflects this change of focus though a distinction may be made between some of the early presentations which included the Passion, and the later more allegorical and secularised events. The former are focussed on the town itself; the latter on the town's honouring of the prince.[54]

In Paris in 1313, two craft guilds – the *corroyeurs* (leather-workers) and the *tisserands* (weavers) – presented a long series of tableaux from Adam and Eve to the Judgement (including the Passion), in the streets through which Philip the Fair of France escorted the visiting Edward II of England and his French wife, Isabelle. A century later, in 1420, when the French and English kings again entered Paris together, this time after the Treaty of Troyes, the Bourgeois de Paris describes the '*moult piteux mystere'* (most pitiful mystery) of the Passion presented on a series of scaffolds stretching a hundred yards down the street; and claims that no-one saw them '*a cui le cueur ne apiteast*', (whose heart was not moved to pity, Petit de Julleville 189). In these two instances the emphasis is still on the play, still on God. In contrast, when Charles VII returned to Paris in 1438 (after the Treaty of Arras which, more or less, ended the civil war) he was greeted with as great a festival '*comme on povoit faire a Dieu*' (as could be made for God) (Petit de Julleville 192). The king is now the focus of the event.

In the fifteenth and sixteenth centuries, the choice of tableaux which adorned royal occasions in the capitals of Western Europe often reflected the person being honoured. When the Duke of Bedford (regent for Henry VI) returned to London from Paris in 1427, he was greeted with a whole series of Old Testament heroic, warrior figures including Judas Maccabaeus. Henry's queen, Margaret of Anjou, was honoured in 1445 with Noah's Ark (symbol of the saving of the chosen people) and the prophets Elijah and Enoch in Paradise where they waited their time to confront and defeat Antichrist.[55]

Not all triumphs (as they had become) took place in the capitals. David and Goliath greeted Louis XI in Orleans in 1461, perhaps as a tribute to the young king's successful handling of his powerful vassal, the Duke of Burgundy (Petit de Julleville 196). In the Burgundian Netherlands, successive Dukes were shown scenes of Christ and the apostles, Solomon, Job or David; but the most frequent subject was Gideon, for the hero of the book of Judges was the patron of the Order of the Golden Fleece founded by Philip the Good in 1429. Occasionally the incidents chosen for these special occasions were less flattering. In 1469 the burghers of Arras greeted Charles the Rash with a number of tableaux including one of Rehoboam who was noted in the books of Kings as a particularly cruel and oppressive ruler who came to a divinely appointed bad end. Perhaps this was intended as a hint?[56] When Mary Queen of Scots entered Edinburgh in 1561, one tableau represented Abiron and Dathan who were swallowed up by the earth for idolatry (Numbers 16: 27–33). This was apparently a deliberate attack on popery. The Queen was not amused.[57]

The costumes, and sometimes the whole production, from a civic play might be utilised for the royal visit: the *Confrérie de la Passion* regularly contributed a biblical scene (usually the Passion) outside their theatre at the *Hospice de la Trinité*.[58] Coventry's reception for Edward IV (1461) included the Smiths' pageant.[59] In Mons in 1455, the process was reversed: a group of townsfolk preparing to do a Passion play asked for and received the costumes used in the visit of the Duke of Burgundy earlier in the year.[60] An unusual variation occurred in Aragon in 1413 when the new king, Fernando, asked to borrow the angels' 'heads [haloes?], wings and robes' from the Corpus Christi procession in Valencia to adorn his coronation celebrations in nearby Saragossa. After consideration the town council agreed on condition that financial sureties were given by leading citizens. The surviving account of the coronation festivities includes several references to angels on floats singing and playing musical instruments.[61]

There are many records of princes attending public performances of biblical plays with consequential benefits to the townsfolk. In Calw in 1502 a *Ludus Paschalis* was presented on the Sunday after Corpus Christi by the town clerk for the delectation of the visiting Papal Legate, the Margräfin of Brandenburg, and other notables. The Legate proclaimed an indulgence of 240 years for all those who attended – which may explain the estimate of ten thousand spectators given by the chronicle. When an Easter play was staged again in 1507, the noble lady Heroide of Brandenburg gave *multas preciosas vestes* (many rich garments) for the play.[62] In 1437 in Metz (an independent bishopric within imperial territory with a strong tradition of civic drama) the prince-bishop Conrad of Boppard arranged for performances of the *Passion* and the *Vengeance of Jesus Christ* to which he invited a large number of German notables (Petit de Julleville 12). René d'Anjou, King of Sicily, was a fervent patron of the drama and sponsored performances in Angers of the *Passion, Resurrection* and the *Marriage at Cana*.[63] The Duke de Longueville, overlord of Châteaudun on the Loire, was the moving spirit behind the town's passion play of 1510, being involved in the organisation to an unprecedented degree.[64]

Plays for princes – biblical plays at court – go back to the earliest days of Latin drama. What is probably the oldest extant non-liturgical Latin biblical play, the *Cena Cypriani* (Cyprian's banquet) was first composed in Italy in the fourth century and revised in the ninth first by Rabanus Maurus and then by John the Deacon, among whose works we find the text of this most original biblical play. A rich man prepares a great banquet (cf. Luke 14: 16–25) and invites numerous guests, all of them biblical characters. They are given appropriate places to sit – Eve under a fig-tree, Samson on a broken pillar, Cain on a plough – and suitable wedding-garments to wear (cf. Matthew 22: 11–13): for Abel a lambskin, for Jacob a hairy goatskin, and for Adam, of course, a fig-leaf. This deliberately humorous linking of appropriate items with suitable people is the whole theme of this quite long play and would be of interest only to persons very familiar with the Bible. Such an audience would not be difficult to find in the tenth century, and John the Deacon suggests it might have been intended for a performance at either the papal or the imperial court. The simplicity of the action and the generally humorous approach would certainly be more suitable for a court entertainment than as an aid to devotion.[65]

A court audience would also have been appropriate for the Tegernsee *Antichrist,* one of the most elaborate of the Latin extra-liturgical plays. It includes seven kings, both Christian and heathen, among those who follow Antichrist or attempt to foil him, and stresses the role of the German Holy Roman Emperor. The play dates from the twelfth century and is usually linked to the reign of Frederick Barbarossa. It is noteworthy, therefore, that in 1153 Frederick encouraged the people of Hagenau (Alsace) to perform *comedias, dramata et processiones* (Neumann 385) for the increase of religion and devotion to the mystery of Our Lord's Passion, in the church recently constructed to hold relics of the Crown of Thorns, the Spear, and a Nail from the Crucifixion.[66]

The most frequent subjects of court drama were the Nativity and the Passion. In Spain the Catholic Monarchs and the nobility were strong supporters of religious drama and texts of nativity plays were specially commissioned for the court entertainments at Christmas.[67] At Amboise in 1496 a magnificent nativity play was presented before Charles VIII and his queen, Anne of Brittany, in the castle grounds *'davant le roy et par son commandement'* (before the king and at his command).[68]

In 1227, a passion play performed by clerics in the castle of Eisenach was financed and attended by Ludwig IV of Thuringia before he set out on crusade. In several towns in Italy, the ruling house commissioned religious plays, notably the d'Este family in Ferrara who had passion plays performed on Good Friday in 1481, 1489 and 1490.[69]

Long after the medieval civic plays had been discontinued, biblical drama, reformed and renewed, was still sometimes performed for princes and it is ironical that the Sun King himself, Louis XIV of France, having finally disbanded the *Confrérie de la Passion* in 1676, found himself a few years later, in 1689, taking great delight in an amateur performance of a biblical play by a most professional playwright: Racine's *Esther* acted by the young ladies of St Cyr.

PLAYS FOR THE PERFORMING COMMUNITY

Where did these many different groups of players find their texts? It is clear that liturgical manuscripts were copied widely and transmitted through movement within the religious communities, while from the twelfth century onwards many vernacular plays were specially written for the town or community concerned. The plays created for Corpus Christi or other civic occasional processions are normally anonymous, though groups of plays may be linked on stylistic grounds with a single author such as the Wakefield Master.

The identities of a number of German and French playwrights, however, are known. They are usually not professional poets but educated men. Among the French dramatists, Gréban was a cathedral canon, Michel a doctor (and royal physician) and Floichot (of Semur) was a lawyer. Renwart Cysat was town clerk of Lucerne and Vigil Raber, of Tyrol, was a painter who revised the work of Benedikt Debs, a schoolmaster. In the Dutch Netherlands, where the majority of the plays were sponsored, written and performed by the chambers of rhetoric in the different towns, many of the plays are by known authors, some of them professional. A large proportion of the texts listed in Hummelen's *Repertorium* of plays are by known authors.

In Spain and Italy, where the majority of the extant texts are single-episode plays performed as part of Corpus Christi processions, however, many are known to have been commissioned from professional writers and survive mainly in printed texts. In Florence, too, professional poets involved in drama include Feo Belcari and Castellano Castellani in the fifteenth century, and the sixteenth-century Giammaria Cecchi, author of *Farse spirituali* (religious comedies).[70] In the Spanish Peninsula, authors known to have written Christmas plays include Gil Vicente, who wrote in both Castilian and Portuguese, and Juan de Encina.[71]

By the end of the sixteenth century therefore, civic, community and even church plays with local or unknown authors had largely given way to the professional theatre. But in Elche, Bruges, Oberammergau and a host of unsung towns and villages, despite Reformation, Renaissance and Revolution, amateurs of the European biblical drama still maintained the tradition of the Play of God.

CHAPTER 3

Performance and the community

RECORDS OF PERFORMANCE

Information about the performance of biblical plays comes from two principal sources: the texts themselves which often include stage directions and instructions for the decor, and the records of churches, towns and community groups. Other sources include letters, contemporary or eyewitness descriptions, and decrees, both civic and canonical.[1]

As the two previous chapters have indicated, these records offer a picture of flourishing and varied dramatic activity in towns and villages all over Europe. Religious subjects make up the greater part of the surviving repertory and dominate the records. They were performed in churches and palaces, streets, squares and graveyards. They might be staged in a single (often indoor) location; in a processional or stational mode; or on a multiple, fixed-location set. The organisation of these different types of play varied from country to country and from group to group, but in all cases a high proportion of the information comes from the financial records of town or court, confraternity, guild or church. For although most medieval drama was technically amateur, costumes, properties and often, though not always, scaffolds (the commonest medieval term for a raised stage) had to be provided for even the simplest plays.[2]

Since it is impossible to consider this huge subject in detail, this chapter will be concerned mainly with three aspects related to the performing community: the interrelationship of audience and actors in the different kinds of staging; the financial organisation of the plays; and the place of women in the theatrical community.[3]

PLAYS IN CHURCH

Growing out of the celebrations of the liturgical seasons, church theatre began as closed-community drama: a few of the choir monks as actors

presented a scene for the rest – the audience – and then the whole
community was reunited in its liturgical act of worship. At this stage
the distinction between performers and audience is a very fine one. In
some of the semi-dramatic liturgical observances it is even finer.
Nevertheless, the distinction is there and becomes more marked in the
course of the early centuries. The Mass was never intrinsically a play
because there was no division of actors and audience – the whole
worshipping group was one: 'For we, being many, are one bread, one
body, all that partake of one bread' (I Corinthians 10: 17). The essence
of the Mass is the unity of the Church. It is not surprising, therefore,
that the liturgical drama removed itself from the Mass at an early
stage, particularly when the lay congregation became involved in
cathedral and parish churches.[4]

Even when they had grown from a single incident to a sequence of
episodes, as in the more elaborate Christmas and Easter scenes or the
extra-liturgical plays from Fleury or Benediktbeuern, plays performed
in churches generally retained certain basic characteristics throughout
the medieval period. One or more fixed locations were used within the
building; if the actors moved between them, they did so in processional
or formal order. The audience presumably accompanied them.[5] Since
there were no seats in a medieval church except in the quire and
sanctuary, we can talk therefore of a mobile, standing audience
watching a play at one or more stations.

In some countries churches were also used for vernacular plays. In
Italy, the flagellant groups performed regularly in the church of their
patron; and the *Presentation of the Virgin in the Temple* staged by Philippe
de Mézières in the church in Avignon is a large-scale processional and
stational play with a carefully stage-managed production for which we
have a gratifyingly detailed account.[6] Many of the early extra-liturgical
texts – the Fleury Old Testament plays, the plays from Benediktbeuern, or the Montecassino *Passion* – imply a fixed-location form of
staging of the style usually known as 'mansion and *platea*' in which a
number of scaffolds or other *loci* (places) are set round or in a general
playing area (*platea*). This format also predominates in the earliest
vernacular and bilingual plays: the Muri Easter play, the Provençal
Sponsus and the *Seinte Resurreccion*, whose prologue describes a series of
locations but not the site in which they are established. All these may
have been, and quite probably were, performed in church.[7]

That vernacular plays using this mode were staged in church is
confirmed by the Catalan *Consuetas* performed on a series of platforms

in the cathedral in Majorca in the fifteenth century.[8] The fact that the plays, though vernacular, were sung, may suggest either a clerical group of performers (including the boys of the choir) or something similar to the Italian *disciplinati* groups. Later vernacular plays known to have been performed in churches include many Assumption plays, especially those from Spain that utilised the *aracoeli*, a device that descended from the roof of the church bringing Christ to earth and then took the Virgin to Heaven.[9] There are also sketch-plans for a passion play in a church in Bozen (Tyrol) and for one from Villingen.[10]

The relationship of audience and stage is less clear for the big productions in Florentine churches of the Ascension and Annunciation plays described by the Russian patriarch, Abramio, and presented during the ecumenical council of 1439.[11] The *Ascension* was performed every year by the *Compagnia di S Agnese* in the church of S Maria Carmine but when (as in 1439) there were distinguished foreign guests in the city, the town contributed to the costs of the performance.[12] The action took place on the high stone 'bridge' (similar to a rood-screen but without the figures) in the centre of the church. There were several separate locations, including the mountain and the city (Jerusalem). Christ's ascension was effected by means of seven ropes some of which guided the clouds and angels who were involved in the very elaborate scene.[13] We have no indication of seating but even if it were standing facing the central playing place, this audience, at least, was probably not mobile.

Even in churches, there were cases of uncontrolled audience reaction especially during the Christmas season. The Herod plays in Freising or Vich became an excuse for spectator participation that was more wild than worshipping.[14] Nevertheless, misbehaviour by the laity at church plays was, perhaps, not as common as the complaints might suggest; often the actors appear to have been the ones to blame. In Amiens, in 1496, the chapter allowed the *vicaires* (minor clergy) to perform the *Life of Joseph* in the quire on condition that neither they nor the choirboys ran about the town by day or night or committed the *customary* excesses.[15] It is notable that no cases of trouble are reported from the records of convent drama.[16]

PLAYS IN THE STREET

An urban variant of the ecclesiastical stational drama is found in the processional or waggon play.

In Corpus Christi processions, royal entries or other festive occasions, the pageants or walking groups might perform at a prearranged station or move from one location to another. Where the plays were very brief (or merely tableaux, perhaps with a commentator) the action might take place during the movement of the waggon. In every case the mass of the spectators were on foot and potentially moving along the line of the route, as in the Digby *Conversion of Paul* where *Poeta* (poet, i.e. the commentator) tells the audience: '*Ffynally of this stacon thus we make a conclusyon, besechyng thys audyens to folow and succede ... this generall processyon.*'[17]

In Germany, Italy and Spain, Corpus Christi plays were often performed before, during or after the obligatory procession of the Sacrament. In Spain, where in the later period the plays were performed on two adjacent waggons, there might be a series of performances at fixed points before the local dignitaries or, in Madrid, the king himself. Some of the German towns performed their plays at one of the stations on the route, usually in a market place or other convenient location, where the Sacrament was placed on an altar of repose which became the focus of the plays. In Innsbruck, for example, the kings made their offering to the Sacrament, rather than to the Virgin.[18] Here, as for all the processional cycles, the audiences were big and close to the waggon but the presence of the Sacrament was a great inhibitor of bad behaviour. The difference is noticeable in those plays which, like the Florence and Dresden St John's day plays or some English cycles, were separated from the religious procession.[19] It is perhaps significant that the English cycles are the only processional plays to introduce comedy into the actual biblical scenes. Cain's mock tithing or Mrs Noah's recalcitrance, though theologically defensible, could have been considered inappropriate in the presence of the Sacrament.

In all street plays, since most of the performers were local citizens and the audience only a few feet away from the stage, there was a problem of creating the proper atmosphere (see fig. 2). The necessary distance for the most sacred characters had to be created by visual distinctions. Heaven is imitated with magnificence of hangings, costumes and machinery. The English plays sometimes mention a gilded mask for God or haloes for Christ, the Virgin and the apostles as part of the scenes on earth.[20] At the other end of the cosmic scale were the devils, whose proximity to the audience and grotesquely masked appearance could raise an agreable frisson of fear.[21]

Problems with street audiences at these annual processional plays certainly existed but are rarely recorded in detail. Lille is unique in its attitude to actor–audience relations. The plays of the *Procession de Lille* were not staged by craft guilds or religious confraternities but by neighbourhood-groups based on a local district or '*place*'. It can be inferred from the scanty records that the Church arranged this to discourage the groups from less peaceful activities of a secular nature, which led to riots and fights between rival gangs. With all the potential trouble-makers on the waggons there was some hope of a peaceful procession.[22]

THEATRES AND PLAYING-PLACES

Instead of the church or street, a play might be performed in an outdoor, fixed location of considerable size: a town square, a quarry, an old amphitheatre or a filled-in moat on the edge of the town. Churchyards and the cloisters or courtyards of religious houses were also used as playing-places.[23]

One problem with a very large set is the distance of the audience from the action. If it is in the round as in the Cornish *Ordinalia*, for example, they may be beside one scene and a long way across the whole round to the next (see figs. 3 & 4).[24] On the other hand, at Mons and Valenciennes the play seems to have been performed on a wide stage with a row of mansions running from Hell on the stage left to Heaven on the stage right. The cheapest audience places were in the standing area, behind which were tiered seats. The spectators in the back rows of these spectator scaffolds, or the family boxes behind the seats, would have been at a considerable distance from everything. Châteaudun and Lucerne had an audience in two rows of seats or boxes stretching along parallel to each other facing the central playing area with Heaven at one end and Hell at the other. Lucerne did not charge admission so we have no evidence for which end was favoured, but at Châteaudun the boxes opposite Hell cost more than those next to it.[25]

Apart from Lucerne, only a few records from Germany refer to the actual stages. In Frankfurt, where there was a fairly regular passion play, the '*machinen*' (stage) was set up and taken down by the carpenters, but we have no indication of size. In Dortmund in 1513 a play of Antichrist was performed on the feast of St Dorothy (5 February) on six *burgen* (mansions) set up round the square, two of them near the *Rathaus*

(town hall). *Burgen* were also used for a play on the Markplatz in
Stolberg in 1457. In 1488 the town council of Strasburg issued an edict
forbidding anyone, man or woman, young or old, to climb on the stage
where the passion play was performed, under pain of a fine of 10s.
Moreover, spectators were not allowed to stand on carts, ladders or
benches among the audience but must set up these viewing points
behind or to one side so that they did not impede the view of those on
the ground. It was also forbidden to erect audience stands (*gerüste*) or to
take money for them; the penalty was 30s.[26]

From Lucerne we have a great deal of information, especially for the
sixteenth-century performances, including plans for each of the two
days of the play. The stage in the Weinmarkt made use of existing
buildings (especially the *Haus zur Sonne*) as well as purpose-built
structures. The sixteenth-century director of the play, Renwart Cysat,
the town clerk, seems to have favoured an all-seated audience with
processional entry into the *platea* of the performers at the beginning of
the day's session.[27]

The decor of fixed-location plays can be classified under two main
headings: sequential or simultaneous. A century ago, Gaston Paris, in
his edition of Gréban's *Passion*, explained: '*Au lieu d'être successive, si l'on
peut parler ainsi, la mise-en-scène est simultanée*' (instead of being sequential,
if one may so express it, the action is simultaneous). He claimed that
this was the principal element in the success of the *mystères*. France
presented the longest plays in Europe though the amount performed
on any one day was gradually reduced over the years. Michel's 1486
Passion has 30,000 lines divided into four days; the Valenciennes play of
1547 has 35,000 lines in twenty-five days. Amiens and many plays had a
dinner break for actors and audience, whereas in Lucerne, the play
continued all day with the actors eating lunch inside the mansions out
of sight: for example, the director decided John the Baptist could eat
concealed in his prison. The play lasted two days of about six thousand
lines each.[28]

A number of devices were used to hold the attention of the
'groundlings' during these complex and often very lengthy plays. The
Trial in Heaven in Gréban's play as performed at Mons is more than a
thousand lines long – it is immediately followed by a long but very
much more lively devil scene (*diablerie*). Indeed the devils in French
simultaneous staging have almost the same role as clowns in a circus,
with the difference that in some texts the *diablerie* is actually part of the
action, or a parody of the preceding scene. Fiendish noises are equally

utilised in appropriate contexts, often accompanying the exit of a soul to Hell.[29]

Another common technique is the use of instrumental or vocal interludes: music played a considerable role in many plays and directions for a *sillete* (musical item) in Heaven while characters are moving across the stage, are common.[30]

Most of the fixed-location plays were either one-off or occasional performances. There is however, one medieval example of a civic and amateur company performing regularly in a fixed, indoor location: the *Confrérie de la Passion* in Paris.[31]

Considering the numbers involved in fixed-location plays and the length of these performances, the audience seem to have been reasonably well behaved; strong measures were rarely required, at least while the play was actually in progress. The principal problem for the actors was (then as now) getting the audience to be quiet 'and let those listen who want to'.[32] Some playwrights took special precautions: on the second day of his *Passion*, Jean Michel recommends that if there is too much noise the *Prologue* should be delayed and the daughter of the Canaanite woman be sent on 'raving like one possessed' until suitable quiet should be achieved.[33] At the first performance of Michel's *Passion*, in 1486, the Angers city council seems to have been expecting trouble. It arranged for a group of important citizens, including the chief of police and a senior member of the university, to impose quiet on the audience under threat of fines or prison. It was also proposed that in order to start well, they might consider it expedient to have Mass said on the stage '*sur ung autel honnestement droissé*' (on a decently-prepared altar).[34] In Autun when the play of St Lazarus was performed, the record claims that the whole audience was 'silent'. This is probably as much of an exaggeration as the figure of eighty thousand given for the said audience.[35]

The crowds of outsiders pouring into the towns for the big occasional plays might cause problems, as is clear from the precautions noted by the councils of Mons or Angers, Lucerne, Revello or Frankfurt. In most towns they doubled the guards at the town gates and set up additional watchmen. Sometimes these were to guard the playing-area and the stage as at Mons or Romans. They probably also helped prevent thieves taking advantage of the crowds. Inns and hostelries had to notify the authorities of the names of their temporary residents, and dogs were locked up. Mons also erected a chain across the entrance to the market place to keep out carts and pack animals. Within the *parc* (auditorium) admission was refused to the old and infirm, the pregnant and children under ten.[36] In Grenoble in 1535, the bishop asked leave of the town authorities to cross the ramparts, from his palace to the convent of the Cordonniers where the play was taking place, rather than have to push his way through the streets. It was allowed but, specifically, only for the duration of the play.[37]

Despite these precautions, trouble both during and after a performance was not of course unknown. There were disasters on stage though rarely among the audience. Actors might be burned by fireworks, have heart attacks during the crucifixion or nearly be strangled when hanging; there are at least two stories of fatalities with gunpowder, but they were during rehearsals.[38] The common problem with audiences was brawls. An entertaining variant on the more bloody encounters is that recorded from Dijon in 1511: a group of young people in the audience, including a 'girl of marriageable age', criticised the performance of one of the actors. His wife, who was sitting nearby, objected and struck the girl, who retaliated. Both were arrested and charged with a breach of the peace. Unfortunately the end of the story is not known.[39]

PAYING FOR THE PLAYS

Religious drama was essentially an amateur affair. With few exceptions actors were not paid, though even for church plays they might receive a gift of wine. In Germany, when the guilds performed Corpus Christi plays the town often gave them a small reward or *Trinkgeld* (money for drink).[40]

In all forms of presentation, the great majority of the audience – all of them in a church play – enjoyed the spectacle for free; in outdoor plays, both processional and fixed-location, a few spectators might pay for a seat or standing room, while local dignitaries and distinguished visitors would have a seat provided for them at the town's expense.[41] Sometimes these distinguished spectators repaid their entertainment by contributions to expenses, relief from taxes, or other assistance given to towns or groups performing plays.[42]

In England, the processional plays were usually performed and paid for by the trade guilds, who were obliged to 'bring forth their pageant' in decent order and at regular intervals. That this financial burden was resented on occasion is attested by the records.[43] There is little extant evidence for the finances of the processional and Corpus Christi plays from France and Italy. In Spain, even where the guilds performed the Corpus Christi plays the financial arrangements were usually in the hands of the city, as in Valencia, or of the church, as the records of Toledo Cathedral make quite clear.[44]

Civic authorities would often give post-performance contributions to the expenses of a group if they felt it had brought honour to the town.[45] It is generally true, however, that in civic plays the town, either directly or through the guilds and confraternities, paid for the play – 'to the glory of God and the honour of the town'.

In France alone there are clear indications from the beginning of the fifteenth century that plays were seen as a way of attracting money as well as glory. When the king gave the *Confrérie de la Passion* its charter, this was explicitly to ensure its recouping the money already spent on its performances: 'for which performance and play the said Brotherhood has laid out and spent much of its goods ... if they played publicly to the community it would be to the *profit* of this Brotherhood. We who desire the welfare *profit* and advantage of the said Brotherhood and the rights and *revenues* thereof to be increased ...' (my italics).[46]

In France, then, financial benefit, not the mere recovery of outlay, was to be expected in putting on a play, whether the subject were religious or secular. Unfortunately we have no details of the finances of the *Confrérie* till the very end of its active life in the sixteenth century. At this time it was attracting very large audiences who paid to attend performances of the *Viel Testament* (1539) and the *Actes des Apostres* (1541). The success of the performances is clear from the restrictions imposed on them by the *Parlement* in 1542: they might only act the *Viel Testament* on certain feast days (not the major ones); they could charge only 2s per session or 30 *ecus* for a box for the whole season. Moreover they had to pay £1,000 to the fund for the poor to compensate for the drop in collections at church. They accepted all these limitations and went ahead with the production nevertheless. We do not know the length of the performance but it must have been at least thirty days to make the undertaking viable.[47]

The *Confrérie* was not the only French group to charge admission – it seems to have been widespread by the end of the fifteenth century for the big civic productions, and records of such charges come from many towns, especially in the north and from the provinces of Dauphiné and Savoy.[48] There are a number of records of church and civic authorities combining to finance plays: in Romans in 1509, the town and the local chapter shared the costs (and the takings) fifty-fifty. In Amiens in 1500 when the town approached the cathedral chapter to join in such a venture, the chapter was not interested and the town decided to go it alone. A rare example of a university contributing to a civic play comes from Angers. When the Passion was played there in 1486 the town voted extra money to help pay for the very complex *feintes* (special effects), and the Angevin '*Nation*' (student group) at the university contributed ten pounds because the play was being presented by Angevins.[49] These occasional productions were on a very substantial scale, attracting audiences of thousands in specially constructed 'theatres' and involving elaborate machinery and effects. It is not surprising therefore that even with large audiences and the admission charges they paid, the plays rarely made a profit: unlike the *Confrérie* they had to build their theatre, and the construction of the scaffolds and the enclosing of the *parc* (auditorium) was the most expensive part of the production. Various difficulties might also hamper these theatrical entrepreneurs: bad weather (Metz, Seurre); political troubles (Seurre, Bourges); or over-hastily prepared and faulty special effects (Poitiers). Châteaudun appears to have been the only town to have taken the precaution of having an understudy for Jesus: 'And because it was feared that illness or some other mishap might befall the *escuier* Larrivé who played God' (139), Fleurentin Boucher was rehearsed in the role and was promised £7 if mishap befell Larrivé so that he had to play.[50]

Despite all precautions most performances lost money, but the towns were content to recoup a proportion of their outlay and set off the rest against the real and 'invisible' benefits to the community. For against the occasional mishaps could be set the overall effectiveness of the great plays which were talked of for years and, in a few cases, even passed into popular proverbs.[51]

WOMEN IN THE THEATRICAL COMMUNITY

From the earliest centuries women were involved in religious drama. The first recorded author is Hrotsvitha of Gandersheim; other notable women in the early days include Hildegard of Bingen, composer of the *Ordo Virtutum*.[52] From the twelfth century onwards there are a number of liturgical plays listed from religious houses occupied and run by women in England, France and Germany. The rubrics of the plays from the convents of Origny-Ste-Benoîte and Troyes in the thirteenth century are in French, not Latin.[53] There are at least two examples of a woman singing the prophecy of the Sibyl in the Christmas Office in Majorca, presumably in a convent.[54] A bilingual play of the Ten Virgins from the convent of Eisenach is linked with the Office of Profession of a Nun.[55]

In the Latin play of the *Presentation of the Virgin Mary in the Temple* by Philippe de Mézières, the role of the young Mary was to be taken by a three- or four-year-old girl, and her accompanying virgins were also played by girls.[56] This is the earliest example of a woman playing the Virgin. The only person to have achieved even greater dramatic heights in church drama must be the nun from Origny who, in the thirteenth century, took part in a semi-dramatic ceremony as '*celle qui fait Dieu*' (she who plays God: Young, I 689). These were all plays performed in church. The fifteenth-century vernacular Christmas plays written and performed by the convent of the White Ladies of Huy, near Liège, were probably performed in the community room. The plays include an extra number of female roles: St Anne and the Virgin's sisters (Mary Cleophas and Mary Salome) visit the new born Christ child on two occasions before the Flight into Egypt.[57] We can be sure that the plays had a well-behaved audience since they would be under the authority of the convent's superior; and that the same order prevailed even when outsiders attended is born out by a remark from a sixteenth-century convent play in Florence performed in the '*sala*' (hall). In the epilogue one of the actresses declares: 'We young girls (*noi giovanetti*) thank you for being a favourable and quiet audience.'[58]

Women's part in the theatrical community stretched far beyond the convent walls. Royal and noble ladies were well-known patrons of the drama in every country[59] and Queen Marguerite de Navarre was also a notable author.[60] In the production of St Barbe before the Duke of Burgundy at Nancy, in 1506, a woman performed the principal role.[61] More complex and interesting, however, is the involvement of women as performers in the vernacular civic and community plays. There is a clear distinction to be made between plays presented by guilds and confraternities on the one hand and plays put on by the civic community on the other.

There is little evidence for women taking part in Corpus Christi plays, whether these were put on by trade guilds or religious confraternities. In England girls took part in the Digby *Candlemes* 'as many as a man wylle' (III, and see pp. 108–9) The 'wives of Chester', who are listed among the guilds in the records from 1499–50 and 1539–40 as putting on the Assumption of Mary play, may or may not have actually taken part in the scene. In view of the fact that there is only one woman's role in the play, their actual participation seems unlikely, although the Chester plays by these dates had long since broken away from their Corpus Christi roots.[62]

However, women appeared in non-liturgical urban plays from quite an early date. Records from the Imperial town of Deventer in the Lower Rhineland show regular payments from 1327 to the *virginibus civitatis* (after 1366 when the records are kept in the vernacular they are referrred to as *joncfrouwen*) for their play. Unfortunately we have no indication of the nature of this play or who the young ladies were. All the plays recorded are in the Christmas season and often mentioned in conjunction with performances by the *scolaribus* (scholars). In Basle in 1519, one Anna Bechimerin played Mary in an Epiphany play organised by the schoolmaster on the Sunday after Epiphany – a very cold day (*die frigidissima*).[63] The earliest real 'breakthrough' by a woman was, perhaps significantly, in a play commissioned and paid for by a noble lady, Catherine de Baudoiche, in Metz in 1468. A young girl played St Catherine of Siena with a resounding success which led to her own marriage.[64]

In the sixteenth century women played an increasing number of roles in civic vernacular passion and saints' plays. In the French-speaking Netherlands, especially Mons (1501) and Valenciennes (1547), girls (not married women) played a variety of roles including the young Virgin Mary (up to the Nativity), the daughters of Jerusalem and Herod's step-daughter.[65] In the south-eastern provinces of Savoy and Dauphin, older women appeared on stage including a married woman playing the torturer's tart in the saints' play from Romans in 1509. In this production women played all the female roles except the devil, Proserpina. The following year, men and women also acted together in the *Passion* at Châteaudun on the Loire (115) including some whole families (97). The married woman who played Mary Magdalene was given special coaching by one of the directors (162).[66]

The seven-day passion play in Bozen in the Tyrol in 1514 (the biggest recorded from Germany, with a cast of nearly two hundred) included women playing all the female roles, except the female damned souls and the Virgin. A woman was at first put down in the list to play Mary but her name was then crossed out and replaced by a man. The reason is not known.[67] So it was a French woman, Françoise Buatier of Grenoble, who in 1536 was the first recorded adult woman to play the Virgin in a civic passion play.[68]

However, the Tyrol does have a notable first in this field: in 1578, Barbara Fröchlin of Sterzing was paid 3 florins for having produced a play in the *Rathstuben* (Mayor's Parlour). The subject, though not known was probably religious since it was performed on 6 April which was Low Sunday. It seems appropriate that the first known woman-director should have been a schoolmistress (*Schuelmaisterin*).[69]

1. Tableau on moving waggon: the trial before Pilate (Holy Blood Procession, Bruges, 1992).

2. Stage in square. Moses and Pharaoh (Alençon, 1977)

3. Stage amongst the audience: David and Bathsheba (Cornwall 1969).

4. Playing in the round: the Entry into Jerusalem (Cornwall, 1969).

PART TWO

The theatrical text

The need for some means of presenting before the mind the God to whom our worship is offered is imperative ... Some portrayal of God we must have; and it is of supreme importance that the portrayal be right.

(W. Temple, *Personal religion and the life of fellowship*)

CHAPTER 4

Creation and Fall

> In the beginning was the Word and the Word was with God ...
> all things were made by him.
>
> (John 1: 1, 3)

In the following analysis I have tried to mention at least in passing all the medieval plays on Old Testament subjects that have been published or listed in bibliographies. The inevitable omissions are unintentional. The texts and details mentioned specifically are of two main kinds: those that are common to a number of plays from different language groups and those peculiar to one play for which a source may or may not be available. Extra material is given from the less easily accessible texts – the two unpublished Valenciennes plays in French, for example, or the Dutch rhetoricians' plays. The existence of the widely available, detailed analysis of the English cycles by Rosemary Woolf has allowed me to treat these well-known plays less fully.[1]

Some plays in both Latin and vernacular contain only material from the Old Testament, usually a single episode or related group.[2] More commonly a sequence of Old Testament episodes or at least a scene of the Fall of Man is found at the beginning of cyclic Corpus Christi or passion plays, for, as Gréban puts it in the prologue to his Passion, '*La creacion du monde est la chose sur quoy depend tout ce qui vient apres*' (the creation of the world is the event on which depends all that happened after: 13).

In Corpus Christi cycles which follow the credal triple structure of Creation, Redemption and Judgement, the choice of Old Testament episodes may be based on Augustine's doctrine of the Seven Ages of the World described in the *City of God*. The first four Ages are those of Adam, Noah, Abraham and Moses. Most authors then make the fifth age that of prophecy, the sixth age is of Christ and the seventh age is that of the Spirit and the Last Judgement.[3] Sometimes the Old

Testament episodes are selected instead on an explicitly typological basis but only the Heidelberg *Passion* includes a series of Old Testament prefigurations intercalated into a New Testament play.[4]

GOD THE CREATOR

> Christ is the image of the invisible God, the first-born of every creature. Whether thrones or dominations or principalities or powers: all things were created by him and in him.
>
> (Colossians 1: 15–16)

A number of Old Testament plays begin with a speech of God the Creator[5] who sometimes refers to himself as Alpha et Omega and in all the plays speaks as God in Trinity.[6] Having created Heaven and earth, God then creates light. At this point about half the plays introduce the episode of the fall of the angels and the war in Heaven. Originally composed under the influence of Egyptian angelology and written down in the Jewish apocrypha of the first century AD,[7] the story became important in Christian tradition for two reasons: it explained the origins of the tempter who was to challenge Christ in the gospels; and, especially, it motivated the enmity between the fallen angels and Man which led to the Temptation and Fall of Man, the need for Redemption and the Incarnation.

The tradition is principally based on two passages from the prophets. Isaiah describes the fall of Lucifer (the daystar) as a parable of the downfall of Babylon:

> How art thou fallen from Heaven, O Lucifer, who didst rise in the morning? How art thou fallen to the earth, that didst wound the nations? And thou saidst in thy heart: 'I will ascend into Heaven, I will exalt my throne above the stars of God, I will sit in the mountain of the covenant, in the sides of the north. I will ascend above the height of the clouds, I will be like the most high'.
>
> (Isaiah 14: 12–14)

In Ezekiel, the King of Tyre is described in similar terms as a falling angel:

> Thus saith the Lord God: 'Thou wast the seal of resemblance full of wisdom and perfect in beauty ... Thou a cherub ... wast perfect in thy ways from the day of thy creation, until iniquity was found in thee ... and thou hast sinned and I cast thee out from the mountain of God and destroyed thee. O covering cherub ... thou art brought to nothing and thou shalt never be any more.'
>
> (Ezekiel 28: 12–19)

In the New Testament this condemnation was applied to Satan in Christ's words, 'I saw Satan fall as lightning from Heaven' (Luke 10: 18) and was developed in the account in Revelation of the war in Heaven: 'And there was a great battle in Heaven, Michael and his angels fought with the dragon and the dragon fought and his angels' (Revelation 12: 7). Subsequently the dragon is equated with the serpent of the Temptation, the devil and Satan 'who seduceth the whole world' (Revelation 12: 9).[8]

The earliest reference to a play of the fall of the angels is in a cycle from Regensburg in 1194 which included an *Ordo creacionis angelorum et ruina Luciferi et suorum* (Of the creation of the angels and the fall of Lucifer and his followers).[9] Like the Fall of Man, the story of the fall of the angels is divided into three episodes: creation, rebellion and expulsion.

The creation of the angels is usually on the first day, immediately after light;[10] often God names all nine orders of angels, though in Chester 3 this is done by Lucifer.[11] All the texts include a scene of the angelic host praising God, sometimes based on the *Te Deum*, especially the verse 'To thee Cherubim and Seraphim continually do cry.'[12] In Towneley 3 the angels praise God for making Lucifer so beautiful; all the texts include a description of his pre-eminence in beauty (cf. Ezekiel 18: 12) and his brightness (Isaiah 14: 12) – the name Lucifer means light-bearer and in Künzelsau 4 Lucifer says he is holding the sun, while in *Viel Testament*, I 47 he is to have a blazing sun behind him.[13]

When God exits, Lucifer rebels. Boasting of his power and beauty, he attracts a number of followers[14] and, declaring his intention of claiming his rightful place, he sits on God's throne.[15] At this point Semur 6 has a unique scene in which *Orgueil* (Pride) arrives on horseback, accompanied by *Dame Oysseuse* (Lady Idleness) and a train of followers, to attend the coronation of Lucifer.[16] This is the only text that makes dramatically explicit that the sin of Lucifer was pride.

God returns and the expulsion follows. In a few plays God personally drives out Lucifer, who falls and is transformed into a devil. In the other texts God gives the task to Michael: 'Michael and his angels fought with the dragon' (Revelation 12: 7).[17] Many plays then include a scene of angry lamentations by the devils; Lucifer swears to be avenged on man, whom he blames for taking his place.[18] The plays then continue with the story of the creation of the world and especially of man.

ADAM AND EVE

For as in Adam all die so in Christ shall all be made alive.

(I Corinthians 15: 22)

There are a number of references to the Fall in the New Testament and the liturgy of the medieval Church, following the patristic exegetes, made good use of the parallel between the first Adam and the second: Christ. The Creation and Fall of Man was performed at Regensburg in 1194 and the Creation of the First Parents formed part of the cycle of plays presented at Cividale in 1304; both were probably in Latin but there is no actual Latin text extant of a Fall play although it was a favourite topic with the authors of the vernacular plays.[19]

A few dramatists are content to translate the story straight from Genesis and make the Redemption an act of simple grace,[20] but most take the opportunity to include at least some mention of the theological implications of the Fall and look forward to the atonement. Two main doctrines of the atonement were current in the Middle Ages. The older or classic one which goes back to Irenaeus sees the Redemption as a conflict between God and the devil who had seized man away from his rightful lord. As part of this doctrine God pays a ransom of himself to the devil. The outstanding example of this doctrine is the Anglo-Norman *Adam*, but a number of other plays also reflect it.[21] The later doctrine laid down in the twelfth century by Anselm in his *Cur Deus Homo* (*Why God [became] Man*) stresses that it is God's justice to whom man owes a debt which, however, he is powerless to pay. The Redemption then becomes an act of God's mercy. This doctrine is adumbrated in the Fall plays of the big French passion cycles (and several other texts)[22] and clearly set out in the scenes of preparation for the Incarnation, especially the Trial in Heaven.

There are two accounts of the creation of man in Genesis. The first simply states 'and God created man to his own image, to the image of God he created him, male and female he created them' (1: 27). The man and woman are then instructed to multiply and are given dominion over the created world. A more detailed creation story with the difference between man and woman, the entry into Paradise, the Temptation, Fall and Expulsion is recounted in Genesis 2: 7 to 3: 24. It is the latter account which forms the basis of the stage texts and provides a quite astonishing range of iconographical variations. Almost all the plays stress that Adam was created with free will.

The creation of man involved two elements. The first was physical: the making of the body from the dust of the earth; and the second spiritual: God breathed on this dust so that man 'became a living soul' (2: 7). The creation of Adam (and subsequently Eve) from the dust of the earth may be staged with the help of a cover or hiding place from which God can raise them up.[23] Only three plays, two of them late, dramatise the scene where Adam gives names to the animals (2: 19–20).[24]

Since Eve was always played by a youth, the nakedness of the newly created pair was simulated by leather suits. Alternatively, as in Anglo-Norman *Adam*, they wear fine garments (*sollempnes vestes*) symbolic of their glorious state.[25]

Some plays eschew the creation scene altogether and open with the already created couple being instructed by God in their relationship to each other and to him. The Anglo-Norman *Adam* opens with God joining Adam and Eve in marriage and instructing them to love and honour each other: '*Tel soit la loi de mariage*' (let such be the law of marriage 21).[26] Elsewhere God simply places the couple in Paradise and pronounces the ban on eating the fruit of the tree.[27]

The temptation of Eve, central to all Fall plays, is preceded in two texts by a temptation of Adam. In Anglo-Norman *Adam*, the tempter is not disguised as a serpent and is recognised by Adam, who rejects him in words that echo the temptation of Christ: 'Get hence from here – you are Satan, you give ill counsel' (33; cf. Matthew 3: 10). Bologna also describes the tempter as the *Demonio* (though Eve speaks of the 'serpent' when excusing herself to God).[28]

The relationship between the devil and the serpent in the temptation of Eve presented problems for the producer. The tempter may be Lucifer or Satan or even simply the serpent.[29] A number of plays portray the serpent with a female face.[30] Some of the plays which retain a devil or a non-female serpent make the tempter approach Eve with flattery of her beauty and femininity: words which would be inappropriate in the mouth of a serpent with a maiden's face.[31] The temptation is sometimes to pride and the desire to be equal to God; at others it is to gluttony: 'the woman saw that the tree was good to eat' (Genesis 3: 6).[32]

Having succumbed to the serpent's temptation, Eve proceeds to tempt Adam. Many texts show Adam succumbing to appeals to his love for Eve rather than to a desire to eat the apple for its own sake.[33] After the Fall, the plays which showed the couple in robes mention a change to garments of leaves.[34]

Most plays follow the biblical words for the dialogue between God and the fallen protoplasts and the cursing of the serpent – which in the *Sündenfall* avoids God by leaving before he arrives.[35] The expulsion is variously carried out by God himself (as in Genesis); the cherub or seraph with the fiery sword; St Michael, as in the fall of Lucifer; Michael and Gabriel together, or even Uriel.

Although Anglo-Norman *Adam* has Adam using a rake and Eve a hoe, most plays follow the biblical account that on earth Adam will dig and Eve spin: in Cornish *Creation* 83 Michael tells them they will find the necessary tools on earth; in *Ordinalia* 29 Adam has to beg God to grant them the power to till the earth, which at first resists him. God ultimately grants them sufficient land to feed themselves and their children.[36]

Many Adam and Eve plays end here even when there is a scene to come for Cain and Abel. Anglo-Norman *Adam* 53 has them taken off to Hell by devils and other plays end with lamentations and hopelessness.

The texts which stage the later life and death of Adam and Eve will be considered after the Cain and Abel scene.

CAIN AND ABEL

By faith Abel offered to God a sacrifice exceeding that of Cain, by which he obtained a testimony that he was just.

(Hebrews 11: 4)

The story of the first murder probably owes its importance in the plays to its liturgical position as the twelfth responsory among the readings for Septuagesima. 'And the Lord said to Cain: "Where is thy brother Abel?" and he answered, "I know not. Am I my brother's keeper?" And he said to him "What hast thou done? the voice of thy brother's blood crieth to me from the earth"' (Genesis 4: 9–11). In the gospels Christ threatens the scribes and pharisees with God's judgement for the death of the innocent 'from the blood of Abel the just' (Matthew 23: 35; Luke 11: 51) and in exegesis, art and drama this became a type of the death of the innocent Christ (cf. Pilate's: 'I am innocent of the blood of this just man' and the Jews' reply: 'His blood be upon us and upon our children'; Matthew 27: 24–5). In his first epistle, John warns that Christians must not be like Cain 'who was of the wicked one and killed his brother. And wherefore did he kill him? because his own works were wicked and his brother's just' (I John 3: 12).[37]

The Cain and Abel plays also use scenes from contemporary life which echo in medieval terms the biblical context.[38] In Anglo-Norman *Adam* 57, Abel tries to persuade Cain to tithe his corn and Cain tells his brother to stop preaching; the Breton and Cornish *Creations* stress his grumbling and his wickedness in giving God poor offerings (in the latter they include cowpats: 93). The English plays (especially Towneley) make him a really comic character.

Stage directions sometimes require the sacrifices to be presented with symbolic effects: the fire on Abel's altar burns brightly and the smoke goes straight up. Cain's sacrifice merely smoulders with choking, earthbound smoke.[39]

The weapon with which Cain kills his brother is usually unspecified: in Jewish tradition it was a stone. A few texts mention a jawbone – obviously derived from the story of Sampson (Judges 15: 15).[40] After the murder, Cain sometimes hides Abel's body (Valenciennes 20-day, f.11r, Cornish *Creation*, 97) or it is buried by Adam and Eve (Gréban 25),[41] before God confronts Cain with the biblical question: 'Where is your brother?' and receives the well-known reply 'Am I my brother's keeper?' The Mark of Cain (Genesis 4: 15) is often mentioned but only two plays specify what it is: in the Cornish *Creation* he is marked with an Omega on the forehead (99) and in *Viel Testament*, I 109 he is seized with an unceasing and uncontrollable trembling.[42]

The legend of the killing of Cain by Lamech is related in only a few plays; there are brief scenes in N. town and Eger and in two plays the role of the blind huntsman who kills Cain accidentally is extended to make him a wicked man and the first bigamist.[43]

SETH AND THE OIL OF MERCY: THE DEATH OF ADAM

For as in Adam all die, so in Christ shall all be made alive.
(I Corinthians 15: 22)

Eleven plays dramatise the death of Adam and all link it with the legend of Seth and the Oil of Mercy.[44] The story derives originally from the *Gospel of Nicodemus* where Seth narrates it to the prophets in Limbo before the Harrowing of Hell; it was taken over almost verbatim by *Legenda* and became part of what is known as the Holy Rood legend: the story of the wood from which the Cross was made.[45]

According to *Legenda*, when Adam is dying he sends Seth to Paradise to ask for the Oil of Mercy which God had promised him at the expulsion.[46] Seth asks how he shall find the way to Paradise and is told to follow the path where the grass is burnt – that was the way Adam and Eve came after the Expulsion.[47] Seth sets out and comes to the gates of Paradise where he is stopped by the angel with the fiery sword. He is shown the tree from which will come the Oil of Mercy but not for 5,500 years.

Other plays, based freely on the vernacular Rood legends, describe how the cherubim with the fiery sword allows Seth to look inside Paradise and describe what he sees. In *Ordinalia* 59 and *Sündenfall* 136 he sees a dead tree with a serpent in it whose roots go down to Hell and in its top is a swaddled child. In Cornish *Creation* he sees two trees. One is dead and has a serpent in it: this is the Tree of the Fall. The other is the Tree of Life: its roots go down into Hell where Cain is imprisoned; in its topmost boughs are the Virgin with a child. Seth is told this child will be the Oil of Mercy (147). In all three plays the angel gives him three seeds from which three small trees will grow up which eventually will become one tree whose fruit will produce the promised Oil of Mercy for Adam.[48]

Several plays include the scene of the burial of Adam, by his sons and grandsons (*Viel Testament*, I, 162; Valenciennes 20-day, f.16r); Seth and Eve (Mons 17); or Eve alone (*Sündenfall* 141).[49]

Some plays proceed straight from the death of Adam to the prophet play and most of the plays that include the story of Seth also stage the Trial in Heaven between Justice and Mercy. None of the processional or sequential plays includes the death of Adam which emphasises their dependence on the liturgical lections for their choice of episodes. These plays either end their Old Testament scenes with the expulsion or move on through Cain and Abel to the story of Noah (as did the lectionary).[50]

Plays with more extended dramatisations of the Old Testament may include, between the death of Adam and the Flood, scenes designed to explain God's decision to bring about the death of all mankind.[51] The choice of incidents was perhaps influenced by the description in the gospels of the coming of the Son of Man at an unexpected time: 'For as in the days before the flood, they were eating and drinking, marrying and giving in marriage, even till that day in which Noah entered into the ark' (Matthew 24: 38–9; cf. Luke 17: 26–7).

From early days exegetes taught that the decision of the Sons of God to marry the Daughters of Men, for which God shortened man's life to 120 years (Genesis 6: 2–3), referred to the descendants respectively of the righteous Seth and the cursed Cain.[52] In *Viel Testament* their relationships and the series of orgies and dissipations which they indulge in are interlaced with the arguments of Justice and Mercy in Heaven (the former demanding the death of all men for the sins of bigamy, homosexuality and lust) and with the beginning of the Noah play (I 192). Similar scenes occur in Valenciennes 20-day, f.17r, which shows three Sons of God and three Daughters of Men courting each other in a formal pattern almost like a dance.[53] Indeed they do dance later before indulging in a banquet which is only ended by the Flood. 'And they knew not till the flood came and took them all away' (Matthew 24: 39). In Mons 19, Human Lineage and the Seven Deadly Sins feast and dance together, accompanied by devils.[54]

THE STORY OF NOAH

By faith Noah framed the ark for the saving of his house.

(Hebrews 11: 7)

A considerable number of Corpus Christi and other processions included a tableau of Noah's Ark for its symbolic association with the Church; also, the ark was an easily distinguished structure to put on a float.[55] The story of Noah formed the lections and responsories for Sexagesima Sunday and was often dramatised in cycle-plays whether they were linked with Corpus Christi or not.[56]

The plays fall into two distinct groups, depending on the presentation of the character of Noah's wife. The majority portray Noah and his family as righteous in their obedience to God, an obedience which is seen as directly opposed to the disobedience of Adam.[57]

A small, mainly English, group follows an Eastern legend which makes Mrs Noah succumb to a temptation of the devil (as Eve had done before her) and seek to prevent Noah's salvation. The closest to the original story is the Newcastle *Noah* play (all that survives of a Corpus Christi cycle there) which includes the scene of the devil tempting Mrs Noah and urging her to give Noah a drink so that he will then tell her what he is doing.[58]

Other English plays omit the explicit temptation by the devil but use the legend to justify an anti-feminist portrayal of Mrs Noah as disobedient and bad-tempered.[59] The Ark was seen by the patristic exegetes as the Church in which the faithful were saved from the destruction which overwhelmed the world: therefore, once Mrs Noah has been (forcibly if necessary) made to enter the Ark/Church her unrighteous behaviour ceases and she becomes one of the righteous.

The presentation of the Noah story depended on the staging form being used. A literal flood and live animals were not feasible on a pageant waggon and painted creatures were used (see fig. 5), though live birds are sometimes mentioned for the raven and dove sent out from the ark, with an artificial dove for the return.[60]

After the flood is over most of the plays portray the sacrifice of thanksgiving and God's sending of the rainbow.[61] Some plays simply conclude with the rejoicing but *Sündenfall* adds the death and burial of Noah (150). Only *Viel Testament* and Semur go on to stage the scene of the drunkenness of Noah (Genesis 9: 20–26). The former (I 246) as usual follows the biblical story closely, including the quarrel between the sons over Ham's mocking of his father's nakedness, and Noah's cursing of his son: 'Cursed be Ham (Chanaam) a servant of servants shall he be unto his brethren' (Genesis 9: 25).[62]

In the Semur play there is more emphasis on the cultivation of the vines – not surprising in a Burgundian text (30).[63] When Noah curses Ham, he is immediately transformed into a *rusticus* (peasant). His wife and children also change both their clothes and their names, becoming *uxor rusticus* and *filius/filia rusticus*. The *Rusticus* and his wife then become recurrent figures in the rest of the play in scenes from both the Old and the New Testament.

Some plays now continue with the prophets, but many Corpus Christi cycles and cyclic Passions and some individual plays present other episodes from the Old Testament.

CHAPTER 5

The Covenant and the Kingdom

ABRAHAM AND THE PATRIARCHS

Christ Jesus was a minister of the circumcision ... to confirm the promises made unto the fathers.

(Romans 15: 8)

Although the story of Abraham occupies fifteen chapters of Genesis (11–25) and formed the lections for Mattins of Quinquagesima Sunday, the only episode to be dramatised regularly is the sacrifice of Isaac. However, a handful of plays treat other episodes in the story and the *Viel Testament* play of Abraham (which follows immediately after the scene of the fall of Babel) is 5,000 lines long and covers most of the Genesis account.[1]

Abraham's defeat of the kings who attack Sodom and imprison Lot leads on to the meeting with Melchisedech, king of Salem, who 'bringing forth bread and wine, for he was the priest of the most high God, blessed him' (Genesis 14: 18–19). For the Church this brief incident was a figure of the Eucharist: Melchisedech's gift typifies the priest's offering of the sacrifice of Christ in the bread and wine. The incident forms the basis of one of the responsories in the Corpus Christi liturgy, so it is not surprising that the texts which present it come mostly from Corpus Christi plays.[2]

The stories of Lot and of God's Covenant with Abraham, leading up to the birth of Ishmael, are dramatised occasionally.[3] Then follows the visit of the three angels who foretell the birth of Isaac (Genesis 18: 1–16); Lille includes the typological detail that one of the three angels whom Abraham entertains is in fact Christ himself: 'He saw three and worshipped one' (cf. responsory to the fifth lesson on Quinquagesima Sunday).[4]

Abraham's sacrifice of Isaac, read during Quinquagesima, was a popular subject for plays since the story combined typological

75

significance with a moving human dilemma.[5] The German versions merely tell the biblical story very briefly and without humanising additions. The Northampton play includes a role for Sarah and is the most emotional of the English texts, all of which stress the dramatic pathos of the relationship between father and son. There is some attempt at pathos in Semur (which is incomplete) and in *Viel Testament*; in Aversa, Abraham has difficulty in raising the knife to slay his son (255). The Castilian *Abraham's Sacrifice* opens with preparations for a feast to celebrate Isaac's weaning, which stresses the horror of Abraham's dilemma, while the emphasis on the newly weaned child recalls the stories of Samuel or the Virgin Mary's being taken to the Temple.

In many plays Isaac bears the wood for the sacrifice – a figure of Jesus carrying the cross: 'And he took the wood for the holocaust and laid it upon Isaac his son' (Genesis 22: 6).[6] Some of the plays draw another typological parallel: Abraham's willingness to obey God's command and slay his only son, was seen as a figure of God the Father offering his own Son for the redemption of the world.[7]

After the sacrifice of Isaac, *Viel Testament* continues its relentless dramatisation of Genesis with the death of Sarah and the marriage of Isaac and Rebecca. This last theme was also dramatised in Lille and twice in Castilian.[8] Then follows the birth of Esau and Jacob. A twelfth-century Latin play from Austria stages the scene of Jacob stealing Esau's birthright by deceiving his father, Isaac (Genesis 27; cf. responsories 5–12 for the Second Sunday in Lent). The incomplete text is interspersed with a chorus commenting on the typology of the play: Jacob, the younger, taking precedence over Esau, the firstborn, is a figure of the Church replacing the Synagogue. The dialogue is formal but the staging is described with great detail.[9]

A few plays treat of Jacob's later life, including his wrestling with God and the rape of Dinah.[10] A scene in Egypt telling of the imprisonment of Pharaoh's servants brings *Viel Testament* to the last chapters of Genesis and the story of Jacob's sons, Joseph and his brothers (Genesis 37: 39–50).

Joseph, like Jacob, was seen by the Church as a forerunner of Christianity, sufficiently significant to be mentioned in the lections for the Third Sunday in Lent and treated in detail in the twelve responsories for that day. In Heidelberg 127, Joseph's being sold into slavery by his brothers is the figure for Judas' selling of Christ.[11]

The twelfth-century Latin *Joseph* fragment from Laon is a straight-

forward dramatisation of the Bible story which breaks off before
Benjamin goes to Egypt (Genesis 43), while the *Viel Testament Moralité* of
the Selling of Joseph covers the whole story down to the death of
Joseph.[12] There is an unusual Castilian Corpus Christi play of the
Marriage of Joseph based on the reference to Joseph's marriage to
Aseneth (Spanish: Senec), daughter of Putiphare the high priest
(Genesis 41: 45).[13] Putiphare tells his daughter Joseph is coming to visit
them and he hopes Joseph will marry her. She is shocked at the idea of
marrying a wretched foreigner.[14] When Putiphare offers Joseph his
daughter's hand, however, Joseph explains that his race is not allowed
to marry heathens or idol-worshippers. He leaves, promising to return
in a week. Up in her room, Aseneth throws down her idols. An angel
appears and in an Annunciation-like scene tells her she is an honoured
virgin, an 'immaculate rose'. He has brought her the 'bread of
incorruption' and she shall drink the holy chalice; he will anoint her
with holy oil and chrism. After a lengthy speech of instruction in the
Sacraments, the angel leaves her.[15] Joseph returns and Pharaoh
himself comes to honour their marriage which is celebrated with great
rejoicing and music. This *auto* emphasises the role of Joseph as a type of
Christ with Aseneth seen as the *Sponsa* (Bride of Christ) and also the
Virgin Mary.[16]

MOSES AND THE TEN COMMANDMENTS

> And Moses indeed was faithful in all his house as a servant for a
> testimony of those things which were to be said.
>
> (Hebrews 3: 5)

Moses figures in four books of the Old Testament – Exodus, Leviticus,
Numbers and Deuteronomy – and also in the New Testament as the
symbol of the Law at the Transfiguration in the synoptic gospels. In the
liturgy he is the subject of the lections for the Fourth Sunday in Lent
and the week following it. Although not himself a figure, his actions
were often taken as types of future events: these will be indicated in
their place in the analysis.

As with the patriarchs, *Viel Testament* presents a comprehensive
dramatisation of the life and works of Moses. Elsewhere, only certain
elements are found. The birth of Moses and his upbringing by
Pharaoh's daughter is narrated in Eger 31 and Florence *Moses*, which
includes the scene of Moses refusing to suckle from a pagan nurse so

that a Hebrew woman has to be sent for – his own mother (172). Both *Viel Testament* and Florence 177 include the incident of the child's being lifted up by Pharaoh, who sets his crown on Moses' head only to have it thrown to the floor by the child who, in *Viel Testament*, is old enough to speak (I 251). Pharaoh sees this as an omen and wants him put to death, but it is suggested that it was only a childish trick and they prove this by giving Moses a pan of hot coals mixed with jewels to play with. When he tries to eat the hot coal and burns his mouth it is taken as a sign that he is only a child.[17]

As a grown man, Moses fights with Egyptians who are ill-treating the Jews and is forced to flee from Egypt. He marries Zipporah, daughter of Jethro, a priest of Madian.[18] In the Castilian *Marriage of Moses*, he helps Jethro's daughters to water their sheep (Exodus 2: 21). They take him home to Jethro who in true Castilian style asks him his birth and lineage (II 328). This enables Moses to tell the story of being left in the bulrushes and his adoption by Pharaoh's daughter. Delighted, Jethro plans an immediate marriage and 'since the musicians are already here' they end with a round dance and song.

The next episode in Moses' life is one of the most important typologically – his vision of the burning bush (Exodus 3: 2) which was seen as a type of the Virgin Birth because it burned but was not consumed. In the plays the scene usually includes God's instructions to Moses to go to Pharaoh and demand that he free the Israelites.[19] The plagues are briefly mentioned in *Ordinalia*, then follows the Exodus with Gabriel opening the sea. *Ordinalia* then includes a unique scene of Moses finding the rods which have grown up from the seeds planted in Adam's mouth (see p. 209); he cuts the rods and takes them with him, saying they are a symbol of the Trinity. Any sick person who kisses them is healed (131).[20]

The miracle of the water from the rock is in several plays, and even more stage the miracle of the manna in the wilderness which, like the offering of Melchisedech, was a well-known iconographical type of the Eucharist.[21]

The giving of the Law and the story of the golden calf (Exodus 32: 4) are common episodes in the drama.[22] Semur includes an interesting stage direction: God is to enter a *domus ignea* ('house of fire' made with the help of burning spirit) to represent the fire on Mount Sinai (39). Künzelsau 27; Eger 33; Lucerne 164; and *Viel Testament*, I 360, include scenes of dancing round the calf; the Lucerne sequence is particularly extensive and vivid.

A few plays feature other incidents from the Moses story, including the flowering of Aaron's rod (Numbers 17: 8; cf. the Marriage of Joseph and Mary). In Heidelberg 232 the episode of the brazen serpent (Numbers 21: 6–9) is a figure of the Crucifixion: cf. 'And as Moses lifted up the serpent in the desert, so must the Son of Man be lifted up' (John 3: 14).[23] Joshua bearing the bunch of grapes back from the promised land (Numbers 13: 24, cf. *Viel Testament*, I 392), is also a type of the Crucifixion.[24]

THE KINGDOM OF ISRAEL

Lord, wilt thou at this time restore again the kingdom to Israel?
(Acts 1: 6)

The history of the Kingdom of Israel, which falls between the end of the Pentateuch and the prophetic books, is the least dramatised part of the Old Testament in the Middle Ages, perhaps because God rarely intervenes directly. As the story of Samuel puts it: 'and the word of the Lord was precious in those days, there was no manifest vision' (I Kings 3: 1).[25]

'The time would fail me to tell of Gideon, Barac, Samson, Jephthah, David, Samuel and the prophets' (Hebrews 11: 32). All these characters appear in at least one play and several also in non-dramatic processions. The scenes dramatised with any frequency show God's intervention through human agency: the stories of David and Goliath, Esther and Judith belong in many ways to the tradition of the saints' plays which flourished side by side with the biblical cycles. A certain number of these plays have also a specific typological or figurative value and are used as such. Indeed this whole period in Jewish history is treated by the dramatists mainly as a prefiguration of the development of the Early Church after Pentecost, when the new Kingdom replaced the old.[26]

The first four characters listed by the author of the letter to the Hebrews figure in the book of Judges, parts of which were read liturgically during July and August. The story of Sampson and Delilah (Judges 16) appears in Heidelberg 155 as the type of the betrayal and binding of Christ. Gideon's miracle of the fleece covered with dew on dry ground was a type of the Virgin Birth (Judges 6: 37–8; cf. Ps. 71: 6). As patron saint of the order of the Golden Fleece, he often appears in processions in the Burgundian Netherlands.[27] Barac was the victorious

Israelite general from whose chariots Sisera fled and was slain by Jael
(Judges 4: 16–22). Jephthah's rash vow (Judges 11: 30–4), which
became a popular theme in post-medieval biblical drama, appears in
the sixteenth-century Castilian *Jephthah's Sacrifice*.[28]

The books of Kings were read during the first six Sundays after
Trinity. There are few plays of Samuel or of Saul[29] but two scenes
from the story of David occur with some regularity: his fight with
Goliath and the marriage with Bathsheba, mother of Solomon. David
slays Goliath in *Viel Testament*, IV 130, plays from Aversa and Sterzing
and one of the pageants in the Norwich Corpus Christi cycle. In
Heidelberg 111, the scene prefigures the crowd's rejoicing at Christ's
Entry into Jerusalem.[30] The story of David and Bathsheba (Lille; *Viel
Testament*, IV 130; *Ordinalia* 159 and a Ghent procession) tells how David
fell in love with her when he saw her bathing. To conceal their liaison,
David deliberately sent her husband, Uriah, to his death in battle
(II Kings 11: 1–17).

David also appears in *Ordinalia* in another episode from the Legend
of the Cross: inspired by a dream from God, David finds the rods
planted by Moses and carries them to Jerusalem in honour. Overnight
it is discovered that the three have grown up into a a single tree. A ring
of silver is set round it to mark the growth (147).

Solomon also appears most commonly in two scenes: the judgement
between the two mothers and the meeting with the Queen of Sheba.
Both of them manifest his wisdom; the book of Wisdom was read in the
liturgy on three Sundays in August. In *Sündenfall*, the Judgement of
Solomon (III Kings 3: 16–27) is included in the big prophet scene (165,
and see p. 88) as is his meeting with the Queen of Sheba which was
treated more fully in *Viel Testament*.[31]

The *Ordinalia* completes the story of the Holy Cross with a scene
from the building of the Temple in Solomon's reign: the great triple
tree planted by David is cut down to form the king beam of the
Temple but proves to be unusable as its length constantly changes, so
the tree is set aside in the Temple where St Maximilla is inspired by it:
when her clothes catch fire she prays aloud to the Trinity and is healed.
(In some versions she calls on the Name of Jesus.) She is stoned to
death for blasphemy (201).

Material dramatised from the later books of Kings include several
episodes featuring the prophets Elijah and Elisha. Elijah's ascension in
the fiery chariot (Lille) was a common iconographical type of the
Ascension of Christ. In Heidelberg the ascension of Elijah is part of the

scene of Elisha being mocked by the children – a type of the mocking of Christ (210). Elijah also appears in the New Testament at the Transfiguration, as a representative of the prophets (Luke 9: 30), and with Enoch in the Antichrist plays. Elijah healing the son of the widow of Samaria appears in Dutch and is a figure of the raising of Lazarus in Heidelberg 98. Elisha heals Naaman of leprosy (Lille, Dutch (2), Castilian).

Stories from other Old Testament books were included among the lections prescribed for the Sundays after Trinity. Some represent incidents manifesting the faith of the eponymous heroes or heroines. The acts of Esther and Judith show the intervention of God in the affairs of his people the Jews.[32] The feast of Ahasuerus is the type of the Last Supper in Heidelberg 142 – a unique usage. The story of Tobias from the book of Tobit was seen as a justification of old Tobit's faith and the healing of his blindness prefigures the miracles of the New Testament.[33] The Book of Job formed the lections in the Office for the Dead and his patience (suffering) as a type of the passion (suffering) of Christ is staged in Heidelberg 182.[34] There are Haarlem and Lille plays from the history of the Maccabees.

Before considering the prophets as forerunners of the Redemption – their main role in the medieval plays – it will be convenient to mention here the few independent episodes from the prophetic books of Jonah and Daniel. Jonah's rescue from the whale's belly is a common iconographic figure of the Resurrection, but in Heidelberg 253 the swallowing of Jonah prefigures the burial of Christ. The Haarlem *Jonah* begins after this scene and dramatises the repentance of Nineveh and the scene with the ivy (AV has 'gourd') by which God rebukes Jonah for his condemnation of the people of Nineveh (Jonah 3–4).[35]

There are several incidents dramatised from the book of Daniel: two Latin twelfth-century plays (one by Hilarius, the other from Beauvais) include the episodes of the writing on the wall (also found in Dutch) and Daniel's being imprisoned by King Darius in the lions' den for the first time (Daniel 5: 14). Aversa *Daniel* 108 dramatises in detail the cause of Daniel's second incarceration with the lions: his destruction of Bel and the Dragon (Daniel 14). The Latin plays, as well as the vernacular ones, include the incident of Habakkuk bringing Daniel food with the help of an angel (Daniel 14: 32–38) although this incident strictly belongs to the second, not the first lion scene.[36] Aversa makes Habakkuk a comic peasant complaining about his uncomfortable shoes (125). There is a Castilian *auto* of Nebuchadnezzar's dream of the statue which is broken (Daniel 12) and in *Viel Testament*, IV 173, Daniel's interpretation of the dream, with the episodes of Bel and the dragon and the consequent, second imprisonment among the lions, are interlaced with the story of Susannah (Daniel 13). This chaste wife was falsely accused by her unsuccessful seducers but her innocence is proved by the young Daniel. The incident was dramatised in many countries and in Heidelberg 80 is a figure of the Woman taken in Adultery.[37]

The other plays based on the prophetic books will be considered in the next chapter.

CHAPTER 6

Prophets and precursors of Redemption

And beginning at Moses and all the prophets, he expounded to
them in all the scriptures the things that were concerning him.

(Luke 24: 27)

PROPHETS AND PROPHET PLAYS

There are frequent references in the New Testament to the fulfilling of
prophecies. The liturgy, too, includes many texts from the prophetic
books as lections in the Office, or adapted as the theme for an
antiphon, responsory or other musical form, especially during Advent
and the Christmas season.

It is not surprising, therefore, that a large number of the plays on the
life of Christ, especially those which stage the Nativity, include a
preliminary scene or scenes of such prophetic utterances which may
include any or all of the sixteen biblical prophets, especially the four
major ones: Isaiah, Jeremiah, Ezekiel and Daniel. Of the twelve minor
prophets, Habakkuk is most commonly cited, though all appear in at
least a few plays. In a large number of texts other biblical, historical or
allegorical characters, especially Moses and David, figure among the
speakers.

These prophetic scenes may be divided into two groups: in the first,
a single prophet or a series of prophets come on stage and speak (or
sing) the prophetic text; in the second, a group of prophets may be
brought on stage together (usually in Limbo) and their prophecies are
part of a dialogue. The plays are too numerous to treat inclusively, but
examples of each type will be considered in turn.

The earliest form of prophet play, the Latin *Ordo prophetarum*
(Procession of prophets) derives from a *Sermon against Jews, Pagans and
Arians* attributed in the Middle Ages to St Augustine and read as one of
the lections during the days immediately before Christmas.[1]

The speaker calls upon a series of prophets (including David and Moses) to bear witness to Christ: '*Dic et tu*' (And you say). In addition to the Jewish prophets, the *Sermon* includes three Gentiles: Virgil, Nebuchadnezzar and the Erythraean Sibyl, each of whom was widely regarded as a prophet of Christ. Virgil's claim rests on the so-called 'Messianic Eclogue';[2] Nebuchadnezzar is included because when he cast the three holy children into the fiery furnace, he declared that he saw four men in the furnace 'and the form of the fourth is like the Son of God' (Daniel 3: 92; cf. the Castilian *auto* of *Nabucdonosor quando se hizo adorar*). The Sibyl's prophecy of the Fifteen Signs of Judgement was quoted and commented on by St Augustine in the *City of God*.[3] A separate semi-dramatic rendering of the Sibylline prophecy is found in many liturgical books from Spain, especially Catalonia, from the eleventh century.[4]

The dramatic possibilities of the Pseudo-Augustinian *Sermon* are obvious. Two surviving texts, one from Salerno and one from Valencia, present a partially dramatised form of the *Sermon* with speakers' names in the margin of the text. The Valencia version also includes one vernacular stage direction: the Sibyl is to be 'already prepared and seated on her throne dressed as a woman'.[5] Although these versions are closest to the original *Sermon* in form they are from late manuscripts and cannot therefore be used to chart the development of the *Sermon* into something more like a play. The earliest genuinely dramatic adaptation of the *Sermon*, the *Ordo prophetarum* from St Martial de Limoges, occurs in a twelfth-century manuscript. Processions of prophets are also extant from Laon in the thirteenth century and Rouen in the fourteenth. These three texts vary considerably in detail but include substantially the same prophetic texts (though Rouen has more) and are clearly based on the *Sermon*.

The Procession of Prophets which forms the third part of the twelfth-century Anglo-Norman *Adam* includes a range of figures and quotations differing considerably from the *Sermon* and the Latin texts. Abraham and Solomon are added, Virgil and the Sibyl omitted and Isaiah's prophecy is turned into a dialogue with a Jew.[6] The genuinely dramatic nature of these processions is clear from the descriptions of costumes and movements in the Rouen, Laon and *Adam* versions.

Anglo-Norman *Adam* is the first play to include the pagan Balaam as a prophet (68; cf. Numbers 22: he is not in the *Sermon* or Limoges). He is described as *equens* (riding) but there is no attempt to present the dialogue betweeen him and the ass, whereas in Laon and Rouen, when

Balaam strikes the ass, a boy hidden underneath speaks for the animal (II 150, 159; in the Rouen text, Balaam also has spurs and uses them). The scene with the angel and the ass becomes the central feature in two later Balaam plays, but whereas Chester (in the pageant of *Moses and the Law*: 83) treats the matter with considerable humour, it is presented in *Viel Testament*, III 407 with the customary, invariable gravity.

A considerable number of vernacular cycle and passion plays include a version of the Procession of Prophets commonly but not exclusively before the Nativity.[7] Sometimes the prophecies are spoken by a Doctor as in York 110, or listed by God himself as at the beginning of the Towneley *Annunciation* (86). A *Demonstrazione* of the Annunciation was performed at the wedding of Duke Ercole's son, Alfonso d'Este to Lucrezia Borgia at Ferrara in 1503. Isabella, his sister, describes in detail the performance which was staged by a '*spiritello*' (religious) who began by narrating the prophecies of the Nativity. As each prophet's name was mentioned he entered and spoke his prophecy in the vernacular. The Annunciation scene followed.[8]

The prophet play which opens the thirteenth-century Latin play from Benediktbeuern is exceptional in many ways. It is based on the *Sermon* and includes Augustine to summon the prophets, but it also has a group of Jews, led by *Archisynagogus*, who attack the prophets and deny their words. The scene includes an almost pantomime type of comedy with the Jews reiterating: '*Res neganda!*' (Untrue!) and the prophets: '*Res miranda!*' (A marvel!) several times (*Hoc fiat pluries*).[9]

The N. town prophet play is in the form of the *Radix Jesse* (Jesse Tree). Thirteen prophets alternate with thirteen kings with prophecies foretelling the reign of Christ (65).[10] Another unusual sequence is found in the Innsbruck Corpus Christi play where the prophecies alternate with the apostles reciting the articles of the Creed (148).[11]

Nebuchadnezzar does not appear in any of the vernacular prophet plays after Anglo-Norman *Adam* but a tableau of the three youths in the fiery furnace, with music and splendid special effects, was included in the Modena Corpus Christi procession in 1556, while a French traveller who attended a Byzantine rite in Constantinople in the fifteenth century said it included '*un mistere de trois enfants que Nabuchodonosor fist mettre en la fournaise*' (a mystery play of three children whom Nebuchadnezzar had put in the furnace).[12]

Many plays also omit the Sibyl, though she is included by Semur (44) and appears in Limbo in the Sicilian *Resurrection* discussed below. In a number of the later Italian and some Spanish versions, however, the sibyls multiply and become an alternate series of prophets.[13] *Viel Testament*, VI 215 has a procession exclusively made up of sibyls but in this text it forms part of the episode of Octavian and the Sibyl.[14]

In contrast to the formal, ordered processions so far considered, there also developed a number of scenes which, ignoring time and space, present a dialogue between two or more prophetic characters. St Genevieve *Resurrection* prologue ends with the expulsion, but in *Nativity*, after the Fall, Amos and Elijah discuss their prophecies before the scene of Seth and the Oil of Mercy (107); a similar scene between two unnamed prophets occurs at the beginning of each of the two surviving Coventry pageants (1; 33).

The majority of these prophet dialogues, however, are set in the one location where a group of prophets might legitimately be found – Limbo.[15] Here, surrounded by the lamentations of the protoplasts and patriarchs, the prophets await the fulfilment of their own words. In Gréban the scene is simple: Adam and Eve lament and are consoled by David, Isaiah, Ezekiel and Jeremiah (34). In St Genevieve *Nativity*, there is a second prophet scene after the death of Adam: in Limbo he and his wife are consoled by Isaiah and Daniel; the devils overhearing are troubled and fear their power will be overthrown (112). In Rouen after lengthy lamentations there is a cosy domestic scene between Adam, Eve, Abraham and Jacob. Eve is shown as meek and submissive: each speaker asks in turn '*Vous plait-il, Eve?*' (Do you agree?) to which she replies '*Chacun sache que ouy*'(Be sure I do). Eli, father of Joseph, then arrives in Limbo and announces the accomplishment of the prophecies and the imminent birth of the Messiah (64).

An original touch, derived from the liturgy for Advent (and commented on in detail in the *Legenda* introduction to the Season), is the use by the prophets in Valenciennes 20-day, f.c4v and Grandi's Sicilian *Resurrection* 26 of texts from the great 'O' antiphons sung at vespers in Advent (see Appendix). In Grandi's play, these antiphons are sung just before the Harrowing of Hell but their use and the inclusion in the scene of the Sibyl, the Magi and the Innocents suggests rather a prophet play associated with Christmas.[16]

Valenciennes 20-day is one of a group of plays from different traditions which all have a common (and so far inexplicable) structure and details. N. town, *Bliscap*, *Sündenfall*, Rouen and Valenciennes 20-day and 25-day do not limit their scenes to Limbo but use a variety of messengers to bridge the space between Limbo and Heaven for the celebrated scene of the debate between the Four Daughters of God, or Trial in Heaven.[17]

THE FOUR DAUGHTERS OF GOD

These allegorical ladies, who feature in a very large number of medieval texts both narrative and dramatic, first appear in a sermon on the Annunciation by St Bernard based on the reference in Psalm 84: 11: 'Mercy and Truth have met each other: Justice and Peace have kissed.' Where Bernard showed how the Incarnation reconciled Justice and Peace, St Anselm (and many of the authors who adopted Bernard's allegory) looked rather at the problem of reconciling God's Justice and his Mercy (or compassion):

For though it is hard to understand how thy compassion is not inconsistent with thy justice, yet we must believe that it does not oppose justice at all, because it flows from goodness, which is no goodness without justice; nay, that it is in true harmony with justice ... truly thou art compassionate even because thou art supremely just. (*Proslogium* ch. 9)

The theme is presented in the biblical plays in two different forms. The Arras *Passion* and Gréban stage a formal trial with the principal antagonists, Justice and Mercy, supported respectively by Truth and Peace. God the Father appears as judge but takes no part in the discussion till the four Virtues, aided by Wisdom, have settled that the only way to reconcile Justice and Mercy and save man is for God the Son to be made man and suffer death (see fig. 6). The debate in Gréban is about 1,200 lines long with much theological and scholastic detail, so it is interesting to find that the version in the acting text from Mons is almost verbatim: evidently French audiences enjoyed the dialectic (40).[18]

A markedly different treatment of the Four Daughters, used in a large number of plays,[19] is found at the beginning of *Meditationes*: the angels are the first to ask God to have pity on Man; then follows the debate 'according to the ... sermon of the Blessed Bernard on the Annunciation' (6). After listening to the four Virtues, the King (i.e. God) then writes his judgement: 'Let death become good and each will have what she desires. Let someone be found who is not guilty but willing to die for man and he can be redeemed.' Truth searches on earth and Mercy in Heaven but nowhere can they find one who is innocent and willing to die. God then announces he will save the man he has created.

In three texts, N. town *Mary* 67; *Bliscap* 104; and the Castilian *Divine Justice and Adam*, there is a debate of the whole Trinity at this point, ranging from a brief but effective three quatrains in N. town *Mary* to more than two hundred lines in the Castilian text during which the Trinity settle a number of important matters such as the Seven Deadly Sins, the nature of sin itself, the impassibility of God, and so forth.[20]

As already mentioned, some of the plays link the debate in Heaven with the prophets. Valenciennes 25-day, f.25v and *Bliscap* 93 introduce the character of Prayer (*Oraison; Innich Gebet*) who moves from Limbo to Heaven. Valenciennes 20-day, f.30r presents a series of prophets themselves trying to approach the throne of grace, and only succeeding after many efforts. The same principle is followed in the most comprehensive and original of all these plays, the *Sündenfall*, in which Solomon invites all the prophets and all the sibyls to dinner (165). While they are at table their royal host adjudicates the case of the two mothers and the dead child and also entertains the Queen of Sheba. Then the tables are removed (stage direction) and a massive prophetic teach-in follows. The prophets quote themselves and each other, and Adam joins in from below with the '*De Profundis*' (Out of the depths have I cried unto thee, O Lord: Psalm 129). Meanwhile the Four Daughters are arguing in Heaven with the Father and the Son. At intervals one of the prophets goes up to Heaven to plead with God: Isaiah first, then Jeremiah, then David. At last David goes a second time and, helped by Michael, obtains audience with God and is told the result of the debate.[21] The play ends with the Conception of Mary and the promise of Redemption.

The Trial/Debate of the Four Daughters ends the Old Testament sections of the plays. The cycles go on to either the Annunciation to Joachim and Anne or the Annunciation to Mary and the beginning of the promised act of Redemption. The Bologna Corpus Christi play sums up this moment of change most effectively. After a Procession of Prophets and a Trial scene, there is a pageant of Aaron praying and censing the Ark of the Old Covenant. Then appears the Old Testament riding on a horned ass and escorted by the Jews. She is preceded by two angels with bats' wings bearing a torn veil on poles. The Old Testament recalls the Fall of Man, and laments that she was deceived by the serpent and rejected from Paradise for her disobedience (III 223). The circle is complete: she is followed by the pageant of the Annunciation.

THE EARLY LIFE OF THE VIRGIN MARY

The early part of the gospel story is preserved only in Matthew and Luke but, as with the Old Testament, there are many apocryphal additions and a small number of plays intercalate between the end of the Old Testament and the beginning of the gospel accounts of the Incarnation of Christ one or more scenes of the early life of the Virgin Mary. The material is drawn from the apocryphal *Protevangelium* from which two successive texts developed: the *Gospel of Pseudo-Matthew* (attributed to St Jerome but probably not composed before the eighth century; versions are extant in many languages) and a revised Latin version of it known as the *Gospel of the Nativity of the Virgin Mary*.

Material from all three texts was used by later medieval writers especially in *Legenda* and *Meditationes*, but details and proper names make it clear that the playwrights move freely about among the available source texts.[22] Their choice of incidents may also have been dictated by liturgical usage, for new feasts of the Virgin were established in the latter part of the Middle Ages. Plays that include this Marian material are extant from all the major language groups except Spanish.[23] It is curious that Spain, which has the greatest number of extant Assumption plays, has nothing on the early life of the Virgin.

For purposes of comparison the material may be grouped under three headings: Conception and Birth; Mary in the Temple; Marriage to Joseph. Unless otherwise stated the story is given according to *Pseudo-Matthew*.

The story of Joachim and Anne, parents of the Virgin, owes much to the biblical account of the birth of Samuel (I Kings 2: his mother's name, Hannah, is the Hebrew form of Anne). Joachim, of the royal house of David, marries Anne, daughter of Ysachar of the priestly house of Levi (Valenciennes 25-day, f. 6v; *Mystère*, f. 8v). After twenty childless years, they vow to give any child God may send them to the Temple (Orvieto A, I 349; N. town *Mary* 32), and divide their goods into three parts, keeping only one for themselves and giving one to the poor and one to the Temple (cf. Tobit 1: 4; N. town *Mary*; *Sündenfall*; Valenciennes 25-day; *Mystère*). Nevertheless, when Joachim goes to offer in the Temple on the Feast of Dedication he is rejected by the high priest because he is childless (Orvieto A; Valenciennes 20-day, f. 45r).[24]

Joachim leaves home and goes to the fields with his flocks. He and Anne separately lament their barrenness (most texts). In the *Protevange-*

lium, Anne compares herself unfavourably with the sparrows who have young; this is echoed in Valenciennes 20-day, f. 49v and Orvieto B, I 360. God sends an angel to announce the forthcoming birth of a daughter, Mary.[25] The angel reminds Anne of the barren women of the Bible who have borne notable sons including Samuel, Joseph, Sampson and Isaac (Orvieto A; N. town *Mary*; Valenciennes 20-day. In *Mystère*, f. 18r; the angel tells this to Joachim). The couple are bidden to meet again at the Golden Gate and embrace. In art this frequently represented scene is sometimes entitled the Immaculate Conception: Augustine had taught that Original Sin was transmitted by the father during the sexual act, and there was considerable theological debate over the claim (first put forward by Duns Scotus in the eleventh century) that Mary was conceived without Original Sin.[26]

Although several plays include the meeting at the Golden Gate, and Orvieto A includes in its title that the conception of Mary took place at 'the meeting with Joachim at the Golden Gate in Jerusalem' (I 348), most of the play texts suggest a normal conception. In Valenciennes 20-day, Satan tells Lucifer he tried to sully the conception but was foiled by the powerful protection surrounding Mary (f. 55r). Valenciennes 25-day, uniquely, presents the act of conception in a curtained bed on the stage, surrounded by angels who keep away the devils who are trying to inflame Joachim's concupiscence (f. 15r).

Before Mary goes to the Temple, in several plays there is a stage direction for the disappearance of the infant Mary and the appearance of a three-year-old one (Mons 48 specifies seven years old). Some also include a dialogue in which Mary assures her parents she is willing to go into the Temple. (In Aquila this scene opens the *lauda* described as being for the Marriage and Feast of the Virgin: 56.) In Valenciennes 25-day, f. 18v, Anne insists on waiting till the child is weaned before she will go up to the feast (cf. Hannah and Samuel, I Kings 2).

The most important visual, and therefore dramatic, moment in this episode is when the child Mary climbs the fifteen steps to the Temple unaided. It is the centrepiece of the only Latin play in the group, that for the feast of the Presentation of Mary in the Temple composed in the late fourteenth century by Philippe de Mézières who had been instrumental in reintroducing the feast into the Western Church from Cyprus.[27] In N. town *Mary* 43, Mary recites the *incipits* of the fifteen gradual psalms as she climbs up; in Aquila 57, Joachim explains and lists the psalms; in Valenciennes 25-day, f. 22v she prays as angels escort her, unseen by the onlookers; in Valenciennes 20-day, f. 59v she mentions the psalms but then quotes fifteen gifts of the spirit. *Mystère*, f.24r includes the scene but without details.

While Mary is in the Temple, several plays follow *Meditationes* 12 which tells how she was fed by angels and gave her own food to the poor (Valenciennes 20-day, f. 61v; Valenciennes 25-day, f. 24r; and *Mystère*, f. 26r; in N. town *Mary* 49 the angels bring her manna in a golden cup; Aquila says she was comforted by angels but there is no reference to food). The *Protevangelium* stresses her skill in spinning which leads to her being given the finest thread, the purple and scarlet, to work after she has left the Temple. Several French plays transfer this element to her life in the Temple: in *Mystère*, f. 25v she is described as weaving on a small loom; in Valenciennes 20-day she sews with silk and in Rouen she weaves 'an excellent purple'(237).[28]

The Orvieto *lauda* of the Marriage of Mary is described as being based on the *Gospel of Nicodemus* from which comes a reference to the marriage of Mary and Joseph during the trial of Christ before Pilate when the Jews claim Jesus was a child of fornication not of marriage.[29] The other plays follow the usual sources and there is general agreement about the first part of the story. When Mary reaches the age of fourteen (*Protevangelium*; St Gallen, I 152; *Mystère*, f. 27r says she was thirteen)[30] she is told she must leave the Temple and marry as is the custom for temple virgins. She declines, very politely and humbly, and explains she has vowed her virginity to God.

The high priest confers with his fellows on how to solve the dilemma. In St Gallen the discussion is between Cleophas, second husband of Anne, and Joseph, his brother.[31] (In some plays this is the opportunity for a description of Mary's holy way of life in the Temple.) The priests pray for guidance and God sends an angel (usually Gabriel) with instructions to summon the men of the tribe of David to bring their rods and lay them on the altar (cf. Numbers 17: 7–9), and God will make known who is to be the husband and guardian of Mary.[32] In Aquila, twelve men come, one from each tribe. Joseph complains of his age and infirmity which make him unsuitable for the role of husband to Mary. *Protevangelium* adds that she is young enough to be his grandchild.

References to Joseph's previous marriage are only found in *Protevangelium* and *Pseudo-Matthew*. From *Nativity of Mary* onwards there is no mention of it, indeed, in *Mystère*, Aquila, Valenciennes 20-day and Valenciennes 25-day Joseph explains his reluctance on the grounds that he has vowed to live in virginity.[33] The author of the

Limburg *Echtverbintenis* (Betrothal) criticises those who talk of Joseph as aged and comical, saying it is inappropriate for one who was chosen to be the husband of the Virgin; the author adds categorically that Joseph was only forty years old.[34]

Two variants of the miracle of the rod are given in the sources: in *Protevangelium, Pseudo-Matthew* and *Nativity of Mary* a dove emerges from the rod but there is no mention of its flowering. In *Legenda* (followed by Rouen, I 273; Valenciennes 25-day, f. 37v; Aquila 64; Valenciennes 20-day, f. 66v) the rod flowers and a dove comes and perches on it. N. town *Mary* 59; Eger 49; Mons 54; and *Bliscap* 136 have only a flowering rod and no dove.

In *Pseudo-Matthew*, a priest called Abiathar has already offered gifts to the high priest if Mary will marry his son. This episode may have inspired a scene in Valenciennes 20-day, where one of the young men, Agabus, is so besotted with Mary's beauty that he conjures up the devil and offers to sell his soul to Satan in exchange for making him the chosen husband (f. 64r). After the miraculous flowering of Joseph's rod, Agabus repents and becomes a Carmelite. This order had a special devotion to Our Lady and St Anne and was very active in the Netherlands from the late fifteenth century onwards.[35]

After the marriage, Joseph sends Mary home to Nazareth while he goes to Bethlehem to finish the house he was building (*Protevangelium; Bliscap* 137; Eger 49; Mons 55). Rouen and Valenciennes 20-day add the detail that she is accompanied by some of the temple virgins. In N. town *Mary* 63, Joseph leaves her in the Temple then returns to escort her to Nazareth.[36] In later episodes Mary's mother and family are shown to be living in Nazareth.[37] In addition to the plays, these Marian incidents also featured in a number of processions.[38]

THE PRECURSOR: JOHN THE BAPTIST

> There was a man sent from God, whose name was John. This
> man came for a witness ...
>
> (John 1: 6–7)

Although John the Baptist was seen from earliest times as the Precursor or messenger of Christ, most plays pass directly from the prophets or the early Marian material to the Annunciation and Visitation and omit the story of John's birth recorded in Luke's gospel.[39] One probable reason is that John the Baptist's nativity was celebrated at Midsummer and not at Christmas so there is no mention of it in the biblical readings of prophetic texts for the period of Advent leading up to Christmas which include also a commemoration of the feast of the Annunciation (25 March).[40]

The annunciation to Zacharias of the birth of a son to his elderly, barren wife, Elizabeth (Luke 1: 5–25) is staged as a brief, separate incident in Künzelsau 48; Lucerne is somewhat longer with Gabriel's speech to Zacharias including a reference to John's being filled with the Holy Spirit while in the womb (I 192). Neither text stages the birth and naming of John. A Spanish auto of the *Conception of John the Baptist* (written in 1528 for performance on St John's Day) omits the Annunciation, adds the motif of the Virgin Mary's being present at John's birth (*Legenda*) and includes a humorous episode of the maid making milk-toast. Other plays of the birth of John will be considered after the Annunciation.[41]

THE ANNUNCIATION

Scenes and semi-dramatic liturgical ceremonies of the Annunciation were common in Latin and vernacular throughout Catholic Europe over the whole medieval period. Normally followed by the Visitation, it is the subject of many separate plays and is included in almost every Corpus Christi and passion cycle: the following examples are only representative.[42]

Many of the plays begin with a scene for prophets or the Trial in Heaven, or with God sending the angel Gabriel on his errand. In the Dutch *Eerste Bliscap*, whose title refers to the Annunciation (the First Joy of Mary), there is only a brief, mainly biblical, scene between Mary and Gabriel – less than a hundred lines out of a play of more than two thousand which includes the Fall, prophets and early life of Mary. In Maastricht which also begins with the Fall, the Annunciation (310) is followed by a speech in which *Ecclesia* tells Mary of her eventual Assumption and Coronation in Heaven: this was the Seventh Joy (*Sevenste Bliscap*; see Assumption plays, p. 146). Is there a hint here of an earlier Dutch Joys of Mary sequence? The Haarlem play of the Annunciation, on the other hand, is mainly a morality.[43]

In Rouen, God prepares Gabriel for Mary's vow to preserve her virginity and tells him to reassure her it will not be lost (I 299). In Valenciennes 20-day, God has quite a long discussion with Gabriel, who wants to understand exactly what is happening; eventually the archangel apologises for talking too much and sets off (f. 71r). His descent here, and in many accounts, is accompanied by celestial rejoicing and music. In Semur 54 Gabriel sings the *'Veni Creator Spiritus'* (Come creator Spirit) as he approaches. There are also a number of accounts of machinery being used for the descent, the most elaborate being that staged in Florence and described by the Patriarch Abramio in 1439: 'a fire comes down from God ... towards the middle of the scaffold ... rising up again in flames'. More flames pour forth, lighting all the lamps in the church and only subsiding after Gabriel has returned to Heaven. There was also a spectacular arrangement with lights in Ferrara on the occasion of the marriage of Duke Alfonso to Lucrezia Borgia (1503).[44]

The Virgin may be presented either reading or praying to God that she may meet and serve the Virgin who, according to Isaiah, is to bear the Messiah (Bologna, III 224; Belcari, I 188; Rouen, I 300).[45] Some texts follow the biblical account of the Annunciation very closely. Belcari gives the whole dialogue in Latin (I 179), though a variant manuscript of his play has it in vernacular. Eger 50 and Hesse, III 905 use alternating sung Latin and spoken vernacular speeches. Elsewhere there are simple verbal additions, including Gabriel telling Mary she will bear the Second Person of the Trinity (Coventry 3) and the Augustinian image of the sun passing through glass as a metaphor of the Virgin birth (St Genevieve *Nativity* 132). In Valenciennes 20-day, after Gabriel's departure, Mary describes herself as the earth opening to the heavenly dew to germinate and nourish the Saviour (f. 72v). The same image is used by the prologue to the York *Annunciation* 111.[46]

A number of plays introduce more substantial variants. Mary's fear on seeing the angel is often mentioned because of the biblical 'Fear not, Mary' (Luke 1: 30); however, in Rouen, Gabriel says she is not afraid of him, since she is accustomed to speaking with angels in the temple; her astonishment is at the tenor of his message (I 302). A very *un*fearful Mary in St Genevieve *Nativity* (greeted by Gabriel with the Ave/Eva pun also found in N. town *Mary* 73), declares that it is just as likely that 'this rod will blossom in the pot' as that a Virgin will bear a child (132). When it immediately flowers she declares her acceptance of God's will.[47] The Semur Mary is neither sceptical nor afraid, but asks to be shown by *'raison clere'* (clear reason) how this can be. Gabriel (rather tartly) tells her to read Isaiah on the subject (55). In N. town *Mary* (one of the richest Annunciation plays), Gabriel explains to Mary at length the importance of her consent to the Incarnation and enlarges on the tension of the whole of creation waiting to hear her acceptance of God's plan (74). This play also has an unusual stage effect for the Incarnation: the persons of the Trinity descend with '*bemes thre*' to Mary, '*and so entre all three to here bosom*' (75). It is generally accepted that this implies some representation of beams of light.

The visually striking performance seen in Florence by the Orthodox Patriarch Abramio also contained some unusual dialogue. When the angel appears, says Abramio, Mary rebukes the 'young man' for daring to come into her house with his foolish speech and adds 'Go away, young man, lest Joseph should see you and cut off your head with an axe' (trans. *Staging* 245). There is no such speech in any Western European text of the Annunciation, but it does have a possible parallel in one of the Greek dramatic sermons: Mary begs the angel to 'go away from my city and go away from my country and leave my dwelling place in haste'; when Joseph finds Mary pregnant he orders her to 'expose the plotter against my house, bring into public view the one who has disordered it that I may take off his head with my craftsman's knife because he has dishonoured my grey hairs'. Since the Florence play was almost certainly in Italian (which the Russian Abramio may not have understood well) it seems possible that he is here putting into the mouth of the speaker a text with which he himself was familiar.[48]

Often the moment of Incarnation is symbolised by a dove sent down from Heaven. Several such mechanisms are recorded from liturgical Annunciation ceremonies and a dove is also mentioned in several plays.[49] In Lucerne there was a special mechanic, the *Stern und Heiliggeist Leiter* (Star and Holy Spirit handler) in charge of the dove, symbolic of the Holy Ghost, and the star. At the direction: *Winck dem heilig geist* (signal the Holy Ghost), he sent the dove on wires from the upper floor of the *Haus zur Sonne* down the length of the square (I 196).

A most unusual Annunciation play from Bozen opens with a liturgical rubric: '*In festo Annunciationis* ... there shall be a procession of the angel, the Saviour and Mary to the prescribed place' (I 337). A number of Jews enter singing '*cados*' (is this meant to be the Jewish '*Kadish*'?) led by *Archisynagogus* and '*Talmueth*' (obviously the Talmud). They are joined by prophets and all discuss the matter. The young and argumentative Pinkchenpanckh and his fellows heckle Isaiah when he speaks of the Virgin who shall conceive. Ezekiel joins the group and finally Isaiah describes the salamander as a bird who can pass through fire unhurt (presumably he means the phoenix?) and compares it to the

Virgin, with a passing reference to Moses and the burning bush. After this notable display of mixed metaphors, the play ends abruptly. A boy sings the Gospel for the day and the congregation are dismissed with prayers and warnings.

THE VISITATION AND THE BIRTH OF JOHN THE BAPTIST

> And thou, child, shalt be called the prophet of the Highest.
>
> (Luke 1: 76)

In the cyclic plays the Annunciation is normally followed by the Visitation.[50] Most texts follow the Lucan account quite faithfully and feature the *Magnificat*.[51] Valenciennes 20-day, f. 73v has Zacharias greet Mary by signs and Elizabeth explains he is dumb until his son is born. A few plays follow *Legenda* and show Mary remaining with her cousin until the actual birth. In Eger, Elizabeth and John reverence Mary but in Mons and Valenciennes 25-day, Mary, acting as midwife, presents the child to Elizabeth.

The fifteenth-century *Natività di Giovanni Baptista* composed in Rome for the confraternities of *disciplinati* united under the title of the Banner-bearers of St Lucy (*Gonfalonieri di S Lucia*), is notable for its unusual structure: Luke the Evangelist is the narrator/commentator and his speeches are interspersed with dialogue scenes of the events he has just described. Though there is no indication of actual breaks in the action, the effect is similar to a series of episodes in a Corpus Christi play such as Künzelsau, each introduced by the *rector processionis*. After the annunciation to Zacharias, Luke is described as addressing the apostles: '*Dice Luca all'Apostoli*'. At the Annunciation, Mary is actually asked by Luke to tell him what happened and agrees; the dialogue with Gabriel then follows. The play is completed by a brief scene of the Visitation, the birth of John, and Zacharias pronouncing a vernacular version of the *Benedictus* (also found in Valenciennes 25-day, f. 42v; and Mons 58, where Mary is present at the circumcision and naming of John). She and her accompanying maidens then leave for home and the epilogue to Valenciennes 25-day announces the events to be staged the following day. These include Joseph's Doubt about Mary (cf. Matthew 1: 18–25), which in many plays immediately follows Mary's return from the Visitation or even precedes it. In the Perugia *laudario*, however, it is the subject of a separate *lauda* for Christmas Eve.

N. town *Mary* ends with Mary's departure from Elizabeth's house but the main N. town play has a unique episode of the Trial of Joseph and Mary as described in *Protevangelium* and *Pseudo-Matthew*. Accused of breaking the terms of the betrothal because Mary is pregnant, they are tested according to the procedure laid down in the Law (Numbers 5: 12–31) and triumphantly cleared (139). In this text Joseph is sympathetically portrayed but the English plays generally present Joseph as the typical comic, cuckolded and complaining elderly husband – a tradition also followed to a lesser extent in French. In Rouen, Joseph complains on his way home to Nazareth because of his age: he nowadays only wants a comfortable bed and a well-filled plate but he has to look after Mary and go on working. But when he sees Mary is pregnant his concern is to save her from the penalty for adultery: burning or stoning. A similar attitude is found in Arras and Valenciennes 25-day.[52] In St Genevieve, Joseph expresses his doubt directly to Mary and tells her he is going away and she will be burned: '*se poise moy, ne vous puis aidier*' (I am sorry I cannot help you: 137). In Revello, Joseph's doubt of Mary is aroused by Satan even before the Annunciation, after which Joseph immediately accuses Mary of being pregnant (32). God sends Michael to dispatch Satan and reassure Joseph. Most other texts follow Luke closely and are brief and dignified. In Lucerne the angel reassures Joseph before he has even seen that Mary is pregnant. The sole Spanish reference to Joseph's Doubt is a brief speech in the *Representacion del Nacimiento (Representation of the Nativity)* by Gomez Manrique.[53] A number of Greek homilies include a dialogue between Joseph and Mary with the angry Joseph threatening the humble but steadfast Mary.[54]

This is the end of the season of Advent. Christmas follows.

CHAPTER 7

The Birth and childhood of Jesus

> And the Word was made flesh and dwelt among us, (and we saw
> his glory, the glory as it were of the only begotten of the Father),
> full of grace and truth.
>
> (John 1: 14)

THE JOURNEY TO BETHLEHEM AND THE NATIVITY

Since there are a very large number of plays linked with the Christmas season it is only possible to mention some of the most original and interesting examples of each episode.

Many processional plays, including Bologna and the Florence procession of 1439, present only a tableau of the Mother and Child. Others (including Liège and Künzelsau) merely stage the adoration of the newly-born infant by various groups: angels, shepherds and kings. (Although the cyclic plays often continue to refer to the protagonist as 'God' or 'Saviour' even during the scenes of the Incarnation, other plays (and this analysis) follow the gospels in referring to him as 'Jesus' until the Ascension.) The bare bones of Luke 2 are sometimes fleshed out, however, with a variety of details and traditions, most of which are to be found in *Legenda*.

Some plays begin with the sending out of the 'decree from Caesar Augustus that all the world should be taxed'.[1] The most elaborate scene is that in the second day of the Rouen *Incarnation et Nativité*, where the Romans are the first to pay their tax. Cirinus, the governor of Syria (Luke 2: 2) learns of Caesar's order and tells his secretary to prepare plenty of paper. The latter assures him he has got a pile of it and plenty of pens also (I 38). A group of Jews and a group of Gentiles discuss the summons and set off to pay their tax.

In *Legenda* and some plays this scene is interwoven with the episode of Octavian and the Sibyl: the Roman Senate wishes to pay to Caesar the honours due to a God because he has established universal peace. (Sometimes there is reference to the building of the Temple of Peace containing the statue of Romulus which will never fall.) Octavian insists on first consulting the Tiburtine Sibyl to know if there will ever be born a greater man than he. The Emperor and the Sibyl are together on the day of the Nativity when she (or they) sees a vision in the sun of a Virgin holding a child (cf. Valenciennes 20-day, f. 86r). A voice is heard saying that this woman is the *Aracoeli* (Altar of Heaven). The Sibyl explains that this child will be greater than the Emperor.[2]

Versions of this legend were widespread in the Middle Ages and the plays show considerable variety of detail. In the Florentine *Festa di Ottaviano* (one of the plays composed for the St John's day procession), the temple falls, revealing the actual Nativity scene (75). In Revello 44 the Emperor is reassured by Gabriel that the vision was true: he kneels, holding a thurible, and adores the new-born child. Valenciennes 20-day, f. 80r stages the fall of the temple and the destruction of the statue of Romulus.

In St Genevieve *Nativity* 119, the Emperor is troubled by a message which appears on the base of the statue of Jupiter, *'Dum virgo mater pariet, Ista ymago corruet'* (when the Virgin bears a child this statue will crumble). His wise man tells him of the prophecies, including that of the Sibyl (who does not however appear). Chester narrates the miracles and tells of the founding of the commemorative church of Santa Maria in Aracoeli (124). In most of the plays (*Viel Testament*, VI 180; Florence *Octavian;* Rouen; Valenciennes 20-day and 25-day; Lille; Revello) the Emperor accepts gladly the Sibyl's revelations.[3] Towneley, exceptionally, makes the Emperor a Herod-like tyrant who intends to arrange Christ's death as soon as possible (83), while the Catalan *Fet de la Sibilla* introduces not the Tiburtine Sibyl but the Erythraean one who tells the wicked Emperor of the second coming of Christ, not the first, and threatens him with the Fifteen Signs of Judgement. His only defence is to banish the Sibyl from his lands.[4]

A comparatively small proportion of plays actually stage the journey to Bethlehem. Joseph and Mary set off on their journey, with Mary either walking, or riding on the ass. Several plays follow Nicholas of Lyra in having Joseph taking the ox to sell to pay their expenses and the tax.[5] In other plays the animals are already in the stable. Rouen, II 82; and Chester 113 include the *Legenda* story of the two groups of people Joseph and Mary meet, one laughing and the other crying. Mary wonders at this and an angel (Uriel: Rouen, II 96) explains that the joyful ones are Gentiles who rejoice because they know that soon they will receive the blessing of Abraham (Genesis 12: 3, cf. Galations 3: 14); the sad are Jews who know that the end of their election is near.[6] The quest for accommodation is treated by several plays including Eger, Troyes and Rouen. In Coventry 10, Joseph leaves Mary outside Bethlehem while he goes to look for shelter and returns to find the Child has been born. In Mons there is a direction for Eliezer (who accompanies them) to go from lodging to lodging: 's'en doit despechier' (without speaking or dawdling: 63). The Hesse Christmas play individualises the interlocutors: one, Czulrich, rejects Joseph's plea because he can see they will need a cradle and his house is too small; also they will stay too long and he likes to have his house to himself (III 908). In Marguerite de Navarre's Comédie de la Nativité 5, three landlords reject them, each (as Joseph points out) because of a different sin: one will only take the rich (avarice); the second will take only the important (pride); the third wants only good company (volupté: pleasure).[7]

In Rouen, Joseph repairs the shed with bundles of broom which Mary hands him (Meditationes 26 suggests he would have used his carpenter's skills to repair their poor dwelling) then comments on the lack of a fine palace with crenellated towers and painted rooms with paved floors, hung with tapestries and matting to keep out the cold. Where are the fine beds with fur coverings? he asks. 'The Creator of the Heavens will be poorly lodged.' To all these regrets, Mary simply answers, 'It is God's will it should be so' (II 139).

Once they are settled in the stable, Joseph goes away to find fire, food and other necessaries. First he insists on giving Mary the cushion off the ass's back to sit on (Meditationes 35; and Rouen, II 216). In Gréban 72 he returns with clothes and milk; Lucerne actually has him cooking the milk for the Child (I 202). In Valenciennes 20-day, f. 78v he makes fire by striking two cailloux (pebbles) together but it does not last long, so when the Child is born Mary takes off her veil and wraps him in it lest he suffer from the cold (f. 79v). She remains unveiled (cf. Meditationes 27). In the Perugia Nativity, the shepherds give Mary their cloaks to wrap the Child in, while St Genevieve 141 includes the legend of Joseph asking a marischal (blacksmith) for fire and being refused unless he can take it in his giron (lap). The marischal throws the fire at Joseph but sees he is not burned by it, repents and is converted.[8]

In nearly all the plays Mary is alone for the actual birth except for angels.[9] As the Child is born a bright light appears: a standard theme from the Protevangelium onwards and based on Isaiah, 9: 2: 'The people who sat in darkness have seen a great light.' The birth takes place at midnight on a Sunday (*Meditationes* 26; Künzelsau 56; Schwabian *Christmas*). In the fifteenth-century Sarum Missal during the first Mass of Christmas two clerics sing an elaborated version of Isaiah's prophecy of the birth of Christ which includes the line, 'And at midnight great light shone upon the shepherds.'[10]

Mons, following Nicholas of Lyra, explains that Mary did not need help at the birth, which was painless (69). In *Legenda*, however, Joseph calls two midwives because it was a custom of the country. In Arras 22, Mary asks Joseph to find her some women for the same reason.[11] One of the midwives, Salome, refuses to believe Mary is still a virgin and determines to test it. In Chester 118 when she tries to touch Mary *in sexu secreto* her hand withers (cf. N. town 160, Revello 40) but when she asks the Child's forgiveness, she is healed. In Arras 24 and Rouen, II 279, she touches the Child to see if he is really God: one hand withers. After Mary's intercession and her repentance she touches him again and is healed.

A variant on the scene occurs in St Genevieve, where Joseph and Mary are guided to shelter by Honestasse who apologises for the poor shed and promises to find them something better later. Joseph asks her to help Mary but she says she has no hands, only stumps. When she touches the Child she is healed.[12]

The birth is followed by the adoration of the Child, first by Mary and then by the angels, either in Heaven or at the stable, accompanied by bright lights and music. At this point Valenciennes 25-day, f. 46r had a special effect of flying angels (*voleries*) which was much admired.[13]

In addition to the adoration of Mary, Joseph and the heavenly Host, there are scenes of adoration by the daughters of Sion (St Gallen); virgins (Hesse); St Anne with the Virgin's sisters, Mary Salome and Mary Cleophas (Liège).[14] Rouen has a direction that if available there should be *corps fains* (models) of the ox and the ass kneeling before the Child and warming him with their breath (II 375).

The Hesse Christmas play is particularly original and includes several well-known Christmas Latin hymns. When the Child is born (III 909), Joseph brings a cradle and Mary asks him to help rock it. Then Joseph with a servant dances round the cradle singing '*In dulce jubilo*'. The angels sing '*Sunt impleta*', followed by the Christ Child singing '*Virgo deum genuit*'. Mary then sings a lullaby, calling on all the elements and the heavenly bodies, sun, moon and stars to rejoice with her. A group of virgins greet the Child with singing in Latin and in

German, and the concert ends with the Child dancing with Joseph and
the servant as they sing '*Trinitatis speculum*', followed by a short dialogue
between Mary and the Child who asks her, 'Must I suffer great pain
from the Jews?' She lulls him to sleep with comforting words and songs
in Latin and German from the angels.[15]

There is an interesting mingling of pagan and Christian themes in
the *regös* play from Bucsu in Western Hungary performed during the
mid-winter solstice celebrations. In the fourth of the play's seven
scenes, three birds appear and, led by moonlight, fly to Jerusalem and
greet the Saviour there. The birds are identified as St Peter (like an
eagle); St Michael (an owl); and God the Father (a peacock). There are
probably associations here with the old, pagan totem-animals.[16]

THE SHEPHERDS

The structure of the biblical shepherd scene makes it particularly easy
to dramatise: setting, dialogue and action are all set out in the few
verses of Luke (2: 8–20). It is scarcely surprising, therefore, that a huge
number of shepherd plays are extant in both Latin and vernacular
from all over Europe.[17]

Even where the scene is part of a longer Christmas sequence, many
texts are content to add only a few details to the basic Latin *Officium
pastorem*.[18] The shepherds are given names and some identifying
characteristics – old, young, boastful, wise. Sometimes (on analogy
with the traditional development of the magi) the shepherds are three
in number, but this is by no means universal: from two to five
shepherds (or even more, including wives and servants) are found. The
scene of the angelic annunciation is often enhanced not only by music
but also by a bright light, either staged or described verbally. In
Gréban 72, Gabriel is instructed to go towards the shepherds with a
lighted torch (*atout torche alumee*), while in Arras 25 the dazzled shepherds
repeatedly ask 'Where did they get all those candles?'[19] This may be
followed by a discussion, humorous or serious, as to the exact nature
and meaning of the angels' words. In Benediktbeuern, II 187, *Diabolus*
joins the discussion at this point and tempts the shepherds to reject the
angel's announcement.

The shepherds then make their way to Bethlehem where the
adoration, usually conventional in form, is enriched with examples of
rhetorical praise of the Child. Some plays give the Virgin a speaking
part of some length; Joseph occasionally speaks (Florence *Christmas*, I

197; Hesse, III 916); elsewhere he is merely a spectator, probably dressed as Benediktbeuern requires '*in habitu honestu cum barba prolixa*' (in decent clothes with a full beard: II 180; in Chester 147 the shepherds comment on Joseph's bushy beard).

Generally the shepherds give gifts to the Child. This custom probably derived from the gifts of the magi; indeed some of the early Fathers criticised the shepherds for going to the manger empty-handed.[20] The nature of the offerings may have been influenced by the liturgical tradition of the *munera populi* (peoples' gifts).[21] Many of the gifts would be quite suitable: food (milk, cream, cheese, fruit, bread, wine); or clothes (gloves, mittens, hoods, cloaks, bags and pouches). Other gifts are typical of the pastoral life, including animals (usually dogs, occasionally a lamb) and musical instruments such as shepherds' pipes or flutes. The gifts all emphasise the *humanity* of Jesus though some can be considered symbolic and some are deliberately humorous.[22]

The distinctive feature even of the plays which follow the Bible closely, is the atmosphere of reality. Not only is the Old Testament rich in pastoral scenes (which also feature in the plays of the Conception of Mary), but the New Testament, in addition to the Nativity, also uses the familiar figure of Christ as the Good Shepherd. Moreover, even for an urban population in the late fifteenth century, many of whom were involved in the cloth trade, shepherds and sheep were a familiar and normal part of life.[23]

It is this sense of familiarity which dictates the development in a certain number of plays of extended preliminary scenes in which the 'shepherds abiding in the fields' become local men and, occasionally, women: in Semur and the *Comédie* the shepherds' wives play a major role in the pre-adoration scenes. Many plays show them eating and drinking; wrestling or playing 'odds and evens' with chestnuts.[24] A few texts have the shepherds talking over the biblical prophecies (N. town) or being instructed by one of their number in matters theological, a variant particularly common in Spain where the Christmas plays were generally shepherd-centred.[25] In Towneley 101 the talk is of the hard times they live in, while in the printed short Parisian *Nativité* of 1500, the shepherds praise their idyllic way of life.[26] Unique in its kind is the sheep-stealing episode in Towneley *Second Shepherds*.

The stress on contemporary affairs is used rather differently by the Rouen author whose long series of shepherd scenes (more than 2,500 lines) includes a sequence of prophecies with commentaries, a lesson in musical theory and a discussion on great shepherds of the past, including Abel, Moses, Jacob and David.

Music, especially singing, plays an important role in many parts of the episode. Often the shepherds echo (or try to) the angels' song. In Revello they do a set dance; elsewhere they sing on their way to the manger. The return may be accompanied by both singing and dancing (Revello 42; Siena, II 209; Mons 74). Many Spanish plays include dancing and there is one complete dance play of the Nativity by Suárez de Robles.[27]

THE CIRCUMCISION AND NAMING OF JESUS

A few plays insert, between the shepherds and the kings, a scene of the Circumcision. An Arras stage-direction describes the scene as being done according to the Law (31). Joseph and his kin, with the midwives, take the Child to the Temple where the priest circumcises and names him.[28] In Lucerne this was apparently a striking visual effect with the priest holding a bag full of blood in his hand (207). In the Castilian *Circumcision* the actual operation takes place off stage at the end of a play in which the priest and Temple officials discuss the new-born Child and a shepherd enters the Temple looking for a meal, recognises the Holy Family when they arrive and tells of his visit to the stable. This is the only play in which Mary goes to the Temple. In *Meditationes* 44 and several French plays (Valenciennes 20-day, f. 90r; Mons 77; *Mystère*, f. 62v) the operation is performed by Joseph, at home.[29]

THE VISIT OF THE MAGI

For many centuries, Epiphany (6 January) was a more important feast than Christmas because it was the manifestation (Greek: *epiphaneia*) of Christ to the world. The simple story of the unnamed and unnumbered magi in Matthew's gospel was expanded and elaborated from an early date. The story is developed at length in *Legenda* from which many later texts took their material.

In contrast to the episode of the shepherds with its limited development in the liturgical drama and major elaborations in the pastoral idylls or rustic realism of later vernacular plays, the story of the magi changes only in details from the earliest Epiphany ceremonies in the ninth/tenth centuries to the elaborate spectacular presentations in procession and play five hundred years later.[30] Three main scenes make up the play of the kings: their meeting together and journey led by the star; the confrontation with Herod; and the offering at the stable.[31]

The early texts still call them magi as do some later Italian plays (Perugia, I 75; Florence *Christmas*, I 199).[32] In almost every other case they have become the three kings: usually called Melchior, Caspar (Jaspar) and Balthasaar. Their kingly status and countries of origin are derived in the first instance from Psalm 71: 10: 'The kings of Tharsis and the islands shall offer presents: the kings of the Arabians and of Saba shall bring gifts.' This verse is quoted in the eleventh-century play from Freising and other Latin texts, though they are still called magi not kings (II 96). In *Legenda*, Melchior is the eldest and gives gold as a symbol of kingship; Caspar the youngest gives incense for the Godhead; Balthasaar gives myrrh for mortality. The symbolism of the gifts is also found in the Latin plays (cf. Freising and Sicily, II 62).[33] The twelfth-century *Auto de los reyes magos* uniquely has the kings prepared to offer the Child a choice of the three gifts as a test of his nature. Since the text is incomplete we cannot be sure how it was developed though it is generally assumed that he would have accepted all three, thus revealing himself as king, man and God.

A few plays dramatise the first meeting of the kings and their explanations to each other of the star they saw and the gifts they are carrying (Valencia 114; Lucerne, I 209; Valenciennes 20-day, f. 91r). In Revello, they are told what gifts to take by an angel (42). At the beginning of St Genevieve each king explains to the audience that he has been at war with other kings for a long time but will not let that stop him following the star. As soon as they meet they hasten to ask each other's pardon and all go on together. In Eger 63, each king tells of a miracle which accompanied his vision of the star. Melchior had a new-born son who foretold the birth of the Child from a pure Virgin, who will live to be thirty-three years old and suffer death for all mankind: 'as surely as I shall die on my thirty-third day so will this happen'. The star appeared containing the Virgin and Child and Melchior's son died. Balthasaar has a cedar tree taller than his palace. It blossomed with a miraculous sweet-smelling flower from which came a small bird 'like a robin' which sang with a human voice and told of the Child born of the maiden. From the top of a high mountain Balthasaar saw God's face in a star which had just appeared. Caspar's miracle also involved a bird. He had an ostrich which laid two eggs: out of the first came a '*leb*' (lion) and from the second a lamb. In the star he saw a vision of the Child with a cross on its head in the maiden's arms.[34] There is an echo here of the description of the star in *Legenda* as being in the form of a Child with a cross on its head (cf. Valenciennes 20-day, f. 86v). In Revello at the adoration of the kings in the stable, the Child is also described as having a cross on his head (49).

The kings often journey on horseback, especially in processions and processional plays (Eger 71; Erlau, III 942; Valenciennes 20-day, f. 88r; Chester 161). At Lucerne the horses wore artificial heads to make them look like an elephant, a dromedary and a camel (Evans 201). In Valencia 122 a sage quotes Isaiah that they will travel '*ab dromedaris, gamells*' (with dromedaries, camels). For dromedaries see also Chester and Valenciennes 20-day.[35]

In a few plays, mainly liturgical, the kings meet the shepherds on their way home. In Benediktbeuern, II 188 and Freising, II 96, it is the magi who ask the question from the *Officium pastorum*: '*Pastores, dicite quidnam vidistis?*' (Say, shepherds, what did you see?) and receive the standard response. St Gallen has quite a long meeting, in which the shepherds give directions for finding the Child (I 169). In Erlau the shepherds make their way to Jerusalem and visit Herod's court where Herod himself begins the responsory, '*Quem vidistis?*' The shepherds sing the rest. Before they leave, the shepherds tell Herod of the angels' song and their visit to Bethlehem (III 941).[36]

The scene between Herod and the kings is substantially the same in most of the plays, the variations coming from the choice of advisors (Annas and Caiphas are often included; in Lucerne, one of the king's attendants is Longinus) and the degree of Herod's anger at the news. In the Florence *Christmas* play the advisors quote many prophecies including Isaiah and the sibyls, giving Herod a life-history of the Messiah (I 200).[37] In Florence *Magi* 195, they bring a whole case of books to court. In the *Joyeulx mystère* by Jean Abondance 103, Herod tells the advisors that the kings have said they are going to worship the true king in Bethlehem. The sages agree that Bethlehem is mentioned by the prophets.[38] In Liège, Herod asks the clerks where '*Jhesuchrist*' will be born, before the kings have arrived. He then tells his '*peuple*' the news and they swear they will have no king but Herod himself (11).[39]

Herod's rage is described in the gospel but only at the end of the episode, when the magi fail to return (Matthew 2: 16). It featured in the plays from the eleventh century onwards,[40] but the extent of his wrath in the scene with the kings varies considerably. In some of the fixed-place cycle plays, there is only a general irritability at this stage and a sense of his cunning in getting the kings to bring him news of the Child's whereabouts. The full rage only bursts forth after the discovery that the kings have tricked him and gone home another way. In plays which are immediately followed by the Slaughter of the Innocents, however, Herod may show great wrath earlier – even, in the Latin Bilsen play, going so far as to imprison the kings (II 77). Although his outbursts of anger are common, his claim to be a god and the Lucifer-like boasting of his beauty and greatness are peculiarly English. They are probably based on the account in Acts of Herod Antipas, who was acclaimed by the people as a God 'and forthwith an angel of the Lord struck him because he had not given the honour to God and, being eaten up by worms, he gave up the ghost' (Acts 12: 23).[41]

The kings' journey from Jerusalem to Bethlehem led by the star is sometimes expanded with meetings with the *Rusticus* (Semur) or the *Vilain* (Abondance). In Arras 43; Gréban 93; and Valenciennes 25-day, f. 59v, they pause near the town and send a servant to the inn to make arrangements for a night's lodging.[42]

The adoration scenes vary little except in length and the range of high-flown language which accompanies the offering of the gifts. Sometimes they all offer all three gifts, greeting the Child as '*Vray Dieu, vray homme et roy parfaict*' (True God, true man and perfect king).[43] Perugia, I 82 (following St Bernard as quoted in the *Legenda* and emphasised by Nicholas of Lyra) adds a second significance to the gifts: gold is to balance the poverty of the stable; incense to purify the place; myrrh to strengthen the Child's body. Only Valenciennes 20-day, f. 96r and the Valencia *Herod* 125 follow *Meditationes* 51 in having Mary subsequently send Joseph to give the gifts to the poor.

In several French plays and Revello 50 the kings then go to the inn where they are served a meal before they go to bed: a realistic interpolation to allow the angel to speak to them 'in a dream'. In Arras (the most extended scene) the whole bill for the kings and their servants is two besants (48). In Troyes, which follows Gréban closely here, they stay at the sign of the Swan (a local inn: 312).[44] In Erlau each king sings a different Latin responsory as he approaches Jesus; after the adoration all sing a responsory together as they withdraw, but they are interrupted by the appearance of a man (*vir*, not an angel) who warns them that Herod has already sent out his soldiers to kill the children. The kings finally exit singing an antiphon (III 946).[45]

There are a few references to them going home by the sea-route. Revello has a long scene of bargaining with the shipmaster and then a stage battle between their '*nave*' (roundship) and two '*galioti*' (galleys) which attack them. The *nave* sails on with the boatman still singing gaily, leaving the galleys on the stage '*rotte*' (broken: 52).[46]

THE PRESENTATION OF CHRIST IN THE TEMPLE

The arrangement of the Presentation and Flight into Egypt episodes, one recorded by Luke and one by Matthew, presented the medieval playwrights with a problem: the Slaughter of the Innocents, which precipitated the Flight into Egypt, was commemorated on 28 December but obviously did not take place until after the visit of the magi. The Presentation of Christ in the Temple was often called the Purification of Mary, since it commemorated also her ritual cleansing after childbirth according to Jewish law. It was celebrated on 2 February (forty days after the Nativity as in the Law of Moses) but must predate the Flight into Egypt. Evidently therefore it was impossible to follow both the liturgical order and the logical one. The processional cycle plays with their normally chronological sequence of episodes had the worst problem, and often preferred to complete the Matthean story of the kings' visit and its consequences before returning to the Lucan narrative.[47] In contrast, some of the interlaced French and German texts actually have the news of Simeon's glorification of Christ in the Temple brought to Herod by a messenger and this new information, coupled with the kings' failure to return, finally motivates the Slaughter.[48]

The two main strands in a Presentation/Purification play are the fulfilment of God's promise to Simeon that he shall see the Messiah, and the offering of the first-born child according to the Law of Moses. Additions to the gospel account of the event are often quite small, such as Simeon lamenting his increasing age and infirmity.[49] The liturgically important *Nunc dimittis* (Lord now lettest thou thy servant depart: see Appendix) is normally included but it may be sung or spoken, in Latin, vernacular or a mixture; in Arras 52 and Valenciennes 25-day, f. 60r, Mary tells Simeon the song is 'melodious and well-founded on reason'.

A few plays introduce more original additions to the gospel. In N. town 186 and Arras 53 (followed by *Mystère*, f. 70v, Valenciennes 20-day, Valenciennes 25-day) Mary redeems her first-born by a money payment according to the Law: 'Every first-born of men thou shalt redeem with a price' (Exodus 13: 13). Digby *Candlemes* includes a chorus of temple virgins who dance at the beginning and end and join Anna in worshipping the child; after Simeon has pronounced the *Nunc dimittis* in English, these virgins '*as many as a man wylle*', holding candles, are assembled by Anna for a procession of worship of the Child. They sing *Nunc dimittis* in Latin, while Simeon explains the symbolism of the candle whose wax, wick and flame signify respectively Christ's humanity, soul and Godhead (112).[50] Simeon's words are an echo of the prophecy: 'Behold, I have given thee to be the light of the Gentiles, that thou mayest be my salvation even to the farthest part of the earth' (Isaiah 49: 6). In a recently discovered French *Purification* from Paris, Simeon interprets the three parts of the candle as signifying the Father, Son and Holy Spirit. This unique play includes the characters of Anastaise and St Anne, mother of the Virgin, and has no known analogues.[51]

The most original Purification play is from Florence. It begins with a series of prophets (Jacob, Daniel, Malachi) appearing to Simeon to tell him of the imminent arrival of the Messiah. Then the shepherds decide to return to the stable taking bigger and better gifts, including doves and a sackful of food, to the new-born Saviour. Joseph welcomes their gifts and says the doves will be used for the offering at the Purification. He and the shepherds share the wine, then Joseph prepares to set off to Jerusalem. The shepherds offer their company across the dangerous desert area. When Joseph declines they take umbrage and have to be reassured that God, who knows all hearts, will have appreciated their offering. The rest of the play is conventional: Mary resists the priest's suggestion that she should dedicate the child to the Temple where he would be well cared for, and redeems him with five silver *denarii* (I 220). At the end Joseph invites Simeon and Anna to join in a song of rejoicing and they sing a *lauda* together.

THE SLAUGHTER OF THE INNOCENTS

Whether Herod is made angry by the kings' visit alone, by their failure to return or by the news of Jesus' Presentation in the Temple,[52] the actual scenes of the killing of the innocents are substantially the same in all texts: an opportunity for some exciting violence and the pathos of the lamenting mothers. The soldiers, like the tormentors at the crucifixion later, are often given names which hint at their violent and pagan lifestyle.[53] The women may also be named but here the emphasis is on Jewish-sounding names and in several texts one or more of the mothers is called Rachel from Matthew's quotation of Jeremiah's prophecy: 'A voice in Rama was heard, lamentation and great mourning; Rachel bewailing her children and would not be comforted because they are not' (Matthew 2: 1).[54] Chester and several French plays include the motif (found in *Legenda*) of Herod's own son being killed, despite his nurse's protests.[55] Valenciennes 20-day, f. 108v includes the story of the imprisonment and death of Herod's eldest son, Antipater, as recounted in *Legenda*.

Sometimes the scene just ends with Herod rewarding his soldiers (Semur 95; Eger 90) but several plays end with the death of Herod. The most vivid death scene is in N. town 195 where Death appears in person during Herod's feast of rejoicing and kills Herod and two of his soldiers.[56]

THE FLIGHT INTO EGYPT

At some point in most of these plays, Joseph is warned by an angel to take Mary and the child to Egypt.[57] A few texts add extra details and miracles connected with the Flight. Several plays give the story from *Legenda* of the miracle of the sower who sees the Holy Family pass while he is sowing his grain. The wheat miraculously sprouts and grows tall at once. When the soldiers arrive soon afterwards he tells them he has seen no one since he sowed his corn.[58] Other miracles (derived ultimately from *Pseudo-Matthew*) are the spring which gushes out in the desert when they stop and are thirsty, and the tree which bows down to the Child in homage.[59] In Revello 57 two robbers, Dismas and Gestas, plan to attack the travellers but when Dismas sees the Child he declares he is so beautiful he must be the Son of God and forces his fellow-robber to leave them alone. This preparation for the penitence of Dismas in the crucifixion scene is recorded in the *Gospel of Nicodemus*.

The most popular legend, found in both *Legenda* and *Meditationes* 68, describes how the idols fall when the child enters Egypt. This is based on the prophecy 'and the idols of Egypt shall be moved at his presence' (Isaiah 19: 1).[60]

Revello gives details of their life in Egypt, with Mary earning money to buy food by sewing and spinning. A benevolent lady gives her bread, wine and salt meat. Then angels are sent by God: Uriel bears 'white bread in a cloth at his neck and a silver goblet of wine in his hand; the other has some food in a covered dish'. Before taking the offered food, Mary washes her hands (59). The eucharistic parallel in the scene is obvious.

In the Burgos *Flight into Egypt* 21, robbers steal the clothes of the Child while Joseph is sleeping but repent, return them and are pardoned by the Virgin, while in the Castilian *Flight* Joseph and Mary meet an old man who escorts them to a village. They are turned away from the inn but befriended by gipsies who foretell the events of Christ's life and death (II 382). After Herod's death the Holy Family leave them and return home.[61]

During the return from Egypt, Valenciennes 20-day, f. 113v, and the Italian *S. Giovanni nel deserto* (following *Meditationes* 82) describe a meeting between the child Jesus and his cousin John the Baptist in the desert: they foretell the Baptism. This is loosely based on Luke's reference to John: 'and the child grew and was strengthened in spirit and was in the deserts until the day of his manifestation to Israel' (1: 80).[62]

JESUS AND THE DOCTORS IN THE TEMPLE

This is the last story of Jesus' childhood in the New Testament though a number of legends grew up and were recorded in the apocryphal gospels. The incident formed the gospel reading for the First Sunday after Epiphany.

The two elements in this scene are the discussion with the doctors and the anxious search for the child by Joseph and Mary. The latter varies only in length and number of people taking part; the former is less fixed. The most common themes discussed are the fulfilment of prophecies showing that the Christ has been born or the Ten Commandments.[63] The Spanish *Farsa de los doctores* includes one of the shepherds who went to the manger. He bears witness of what has happened but they do not believe him until Jesus expounds the events for them. They break into a paean of praise of Jesus, and when Mary arrives and reproaches her son, they ask her to leave him in the Temple. She refuses and after the Holy Family have departed the doctors realise it is the Lord himself whom they have seen. In the Florence *Disputa al Tempio*, the doctors speak of the promised coming of the Messiah to free man from sin; Jesus shows that he is already come as prophesied, and the delighted rabbis honour the child and join in a *lauda* in his praise. When Mary comes to find him, Rabbi Samuel tells her that her son is so well instructed in the faith that he will win any joust ('*sare' vincitor d'ogni gran giostra*': I 240).

The fourteenth-century Cangé *Nativity* omits the Slaughter and

Flight and moves from the Purification to the scene with the doctors in the Temple. Jesus borrows a book of the prophecies from the *libraire* (librarian) promising to return it in good condition (I 231). He then reads Isaiah (35: 5, cit. Matthew 11: 5) and claims 'This day is the prophecy fulfilled.'[64] They challenge his knowledge and he replies 'I will tell you if you tell me if John's baptism was of God' (cf. Matthew 21: 23). The discussion continues on this level as if both Jesus and John were already adults. The subjects include the much-married woman, the greatest commandment and whether the Messiah will be the Son of David (Matthew 22). The masters are furious but decide to console themselves with a good dinner (I 242). Jesus returns home with Joseph and Mary. 'And he went down with them and came to Nazareth and was subject to them. And his mother kept all these words in her heart' (Luke 2: 51).

From this point onwards all four gospels present the adult life of Jesus beginning with the Baptism and Ministry. So do the plays.

CHAPTER 8

The public life of Jesus

And Jesus went about all Galilee ... preaching the gospel of the
kingdom: and healing all manner of sickness.

(Matthew 4: 23)

The story of the Redemption as told in the four gospels comprises two
main parts: the three years of Jesus' ministry of teaching and healing;
and the events of Holy Week culminating in the Crucifixion and
Resurrection. Plays on the latter section are extremely numerous and
there are also a considerable number of texts which include some
episodes from the Ministry. Unlike the infancy stories treated in the
previous chapter, the main incidents of the Ministry and Passion are
told by all four evangelists though in a different sequence and with
variations of detail and emphasis; even the three synoptic gospels,
Matthew, Mark and Luke, show considerable individuality, and John's
gospel is very largely original.[1]

To cover the very large range of dramatic accounts in detail is
beyond the scope of the present study, and only the more significant
episodes and some of their variants can be considered.[2]

THE WITNESS AND DEATH OF JOHN THE BAPTIST

For I say to you: amongst those that are born of women, there is
not a greater prophet than John the Baptist.

(Luke 7: 28)

All four gospels begin the adult life of Jesus with some account of the
witness of the Precursor, John the Baptist.[3] Some plays begin with a
scene of Jesus taking leave of Mary (and sometimes Joseph) as he
prepares for his Ministry.[4] In others the sequence begins with John
being summoned from the desert: in Revello 62, Uriel appears to

113

John in the desert and tells him he is to baptise everyone so that they may be saved. He will also baptise God, whom he will recognise by the dove that hovers over him. John gives thanks to God.[5] In N. town John preaches repentance to the audience; in the Florence *Decollation*, his sermon is constructed on a series of stanzas, each beginning 'Prepare ye the way of the Lord' and echoing various prophets including David, Solomon, Isaiah and Jonah (118). In other plays there are various groups of characters who ask questions and/or receive baptism.[6]

Although several plays imply the use of some kind of representation of water, either to bathe in (immersion) or to pour over the candidate's head (affusion), only Lucerne has records of how it was done: Cysat, the director, rejected his first idea of using the fountain or a well, because the Jordan was neither. Instead he arranged for a stream to be diverted across part of the Weinmarkt at the appropriate moment so that the Baptism could take place, with topological propriety, in running water.[7]

In John's gospel (which does not mention the actual Baptism of Christ) the Baptist points to Jesus and hails him as the Lamb of God: '*Ecce Agnus Dei*'. Many plays introduce this incident either before or after the Baptism, and a few specifically mention John's pointing finger.[8]

The plays, like the gospels, include some discussion between John the Baptist and Jesus (as the former urges his unworthiness to baptise the Messiah), and during the Baptism the synoptic gospels all mention the appearance of the Holy Spirit in the form of a dove and a voice from Heaven saying 'This is my beloved Son.' Not surprisingly, therefore, these elements also appear in most of the plays.[9] A few plays have special directions for God: St Gallen *Passion* 103 has a third, hidden voice which speaks for God (in addition to the two angels) and Michel 26 suggest three voices of different pitches, low, medium and high, speaking together.[10] In the gospels, the Baptism is followed by the Temptation, but some plays continue with the story of the imprisonment and death of John the Baptist.[11]

The marriage betwen Herod the Tetrarch and his brother Philip's wife, Herodias, is staged exceptionally in Abruzzi *Decollation* 45, where the devils tempt Herodias and she leaves Philip for Herod who then banishes Philip, while Valenciennes 25-day f. 8or has a lengthy scene of Herod visiting his brother; he woos and wins Herodias, who returns to Jerusalem with him.[12] Many plays stage a scene of John upbraiding

Herod: in Revello 64, John preaches on the sin of *luxuria* (lust) in the royal presence; in the Castilian *Decollation* John enters the palace and addresses the Tetrarch as 'insatiable beast, generation of serpents' (II, 50); in Lucerne 254, John preaches at Herod and Herodias in their palace. After John's arrest and imprisonment his disciples bring him the news that Jesus is the fulfilment of prophecy.[13]

Theatrically, the most popular scene is, of course, the feast at which Herodias's daughter dances and receives John's head on a platter as a promised reward.[14] Most of the plays follow the gospel and imply that Herod was genuinely reluctant to have John executed. In Auvergne the devils deliberately lead him on to make the promise in order to bring about John's death (92).[15]

The execution may take place on stage. In a performance at Casteldurante (near Urbino) in 1488, a false head was used to make the decollation convincing.[16] In Lucerne 343 John puts his head through his prison window (cf. *Meditationes* 183) and it is cut off. In Abruzzi the gaoler tells John, 'You see what comes of telling the truth!' (48). When she sees the head, Herodias rejoices and sticks a knife into it as a sign of vengeance.[17] After John's death an angel takes his soul to Limbo in a cloth (Revello 85). In Auvergne 112 the angels come and escort the soul to Limbo and drive away the devils who try to seize it. Later John's disciples ask Herod for the body and bury it.[18]

THE TEMPTATION OF CHRIST

Found only in the synoptic gospels but typologically important because it echoes and reverses the Temptation of Adam and Eve, this story occurs in almost all the cycles and cyclic plays as well as a few separate ones.[19] Some plays begin with a council of the devils, who boast of their skill as tempters.[20] The tempter of Jesus is normally Satan, though Lucerne, I 261 has Lucifer.[21] Many plays follow *Meditationes* 122 in emphasising that the triple Temptation is to gluttony, vainglory and avarice: the three sins of Adam. The devil explains he needs to know whether Jesus is God or Man but at the end he is still bewildered. Several authors stress Jesus' humility in allowing the devil to touch him, even carry him on his shoulders to the top of the pinnacle or the mountain. In Arras 81, Jesus says the 'three who are one' (the Trinity) will allow Satan to do this.[22] In several plays Satan disguises himself: as a hypocrite, and then theologian (Revello 70), hermit, doctor and king in turn (Michel 35).[23]

In all the plays, after the devil has departed one or more angels come to minister to Jesus. In Revello 71 they bring him food and wine and clothes; in Michel 39 and Auvergne *Baptism* 124 the food is eucharistic in form: wine in a chalice and 'bread from Heaven' (Ps.77: 24; cit. John 6: 31). Auvergne *Baptism* 124 and both Abruzzi versions (119, 128) follow *Meditationes* in having the angels also bring food prepared by the Virgin (125).

THE MINISTRY OF JESUS

The Corpus Christi cycles and the separate individual plays in Italian, Spanish and Dutch include few of the incidents recounted in the gospels between the Temptation and the beginning of the events of Holy Week. In contrast, two Sterzing plays dramatise the whole of John's gospel up to the Betrayal, and several German and French cyclic Passions (together with Revello) treat the material at some length. This very considerable body of material will be considered under two headings: the miracles and signs including the Transfiguration, and the story of Mary Magdalene, Martha, and their brother, Lazarus. Two additional sections will look at the dramatised parables and the plays on the Judgement of Jesus Christ.

Signs and miracles; the Transfiguration

The first miracle recorded in the Ministry is the turning of water into wine at the marriage at Cana in Galilee: 'This beginning of miracle did Jesus in Cana of Galilee and manifested his glory' (John 2: 11). The incident sometimes precedes the calling of the apostles and in St Gallen 101 it precedes the Baptism. From Jerome onwards there had been a tradition that the bridegroom was John Zebedee, the evangelist; in Lucerne, where the episode was added in 1597, the invitation to the marriage is given personally to the Virgin by her sister, Mary Salome, whose husband, Zebedee, organises the feast.[24] Gréban does not mention the bridegroom but in the other French plays he is always John.[25] In Michel 66 the Virgin Mary is invited to attend the marriage of 'her nephew John' with her son and his disciples. At the end of the meal Jesus urges John to live in chastity with his wife. Both John and his bride agree (72; cf. 'If any man come to me and hate not his ... wife ... he cannot be my disciple' Luke 14: 26).[26]

Whereas John's gospel stresses the manifestation of Christ's divinity through his miracles, or 'signs', for the synoptics this divinity was revealed above all in the Transfiguration (which John omits).[27] Many cycles, on the other hand, omitted the Marriage at Cana and John's other 'signs', but included the Transfiguration.[28] The staging of this scene varies considerably. The English waggon-plays rely on the words of the apostles to indicate the sudden brightness and whiteness of Jesus' appearance; Revello 87 directs that sunlight or (if it be cloudy) candlelight should be reflected on to Christ from a silver basin. Michel specifies a golden sun behind Christ, who has secretly changed his purple robe for a white one and gilded his face and hands (125). Mons spent a large sum of money on a special robe of white silk material for Christ and had a concealed lift for him to use so that he could leave his disciples on the stage, change his clothes and reappear in the white robe on top of the mountain (177). Moses is usually portrayed carrying the Tables of the Law while Elijah is sometimes described as wearing a Carmelite habit or head-dress, because he was the traditional founder of the Carmelite Order who took their name from Mount Carmel in the Holy Land.[29]

A few examples of what may be called miracles of dominion over nature are included in the plays: many staged the withering of the fig-tree that had been cursed (Matthew 21: 19) and Mons 170 had a special effect for the storm on the Sea of Galilee (Matthew 8: 24–7) but the majority of the miracles presented in the plays are miracles of healing.[30]

The French and German plays show great variety in their choice and ordering of these episodes.[31] Scenes of the casting out of devils were obviously good theatre and brought Jesus into dramatic confrontation with the Jews because it raised the whole question of power and authority.[32] Healing the sick generally did not, unless done on the sabbath or coupled with the forgiveness of sins, as in the frequently dramatised healing of the man born blind (John 9: 1–41). As so often in John's gospel, the emphasis is on the consequences of the event: in this instance the man and his parents are thrown out of the synagogue for claiming Jesus is a prophet.[33]

It was the miracle of the Raising of Lazarus which finally brought to a head the clash between Jesus and the Jews. 'From that day therefore they devised to put him to death'(John 11: 53). In the liturgy, the miracle is read on the Friday before Passion Sunday.[34] In the plays it often forms part of a larger group of episodes featuring Mary Magdalene and Martha.

The story of Mary Magdalene, Martha and Lazarus.

From an early date, references in the gospels to a woman who was a repentant sinner and anointed Jesus' head during a meal (Luke 7: 36–50) and to Mary of Magdala from whom Jesus cast out seven devils (Luke 8: 2), were linked with Mary of Bethany, sister of Martha and Lazarus (John 11: 2), who anointed Jesus' feet (John 12: 2).[35] In the conflated version found in the narrative and dramatic accounts, four scenes can be distinguished: the worldliness of Mary Magdalene; her conversion and repentance; the meal at Bethany and the raising of Lazarus from the dead. Since they are based on incidents in different gospels, these scenes may be presented in various sequences, but the following analysis uses the order given above.

A scene of the worldliness of Mary Magdalene[36] occurs in many cyclic passions and a number of separate plays, the earliest known being the Benediktbeuern *Passion*, I 520 where Mary sings, dances, and buys unguents from the merchant to redden her cheeks so that she will attract the young men; while she sleeps an angel appears and warns her of the danger of such a life. The two scenes are repeated three times, with Mary's lover appearing in the second. Eventually the angel's third warning moves her to repentance and the lover goes away, together with the devil who is first mentioned here.[37] At the other end of the dramatic spectrum is the scene of the worldliness of Magdalene in Michel's *Passion* 125 (followed by Mons and Valenciennes 25-day) which is very long and includes details of Mary's clothes, hairstyle and toilet in a discussion with her attendant, Pasiphae, before her meeting with her lover and their song. When she goes to meet her lover, Pasiphae sprinkles rose water on the ground around her; later Mary will pour rose water on the head of Jesus. Many of the plays show Magdalene singing and dancing with her suitors but Arras, most originally, portrays her as a young woman desperate for a lover but not finding one despite all her efforts (117).[38]

Several plays include scenes of Martha and/or Lazarus trying to turn Mary from her sinful life. This is particularly elaborated in the Florence *Conversion*, where Martha first of all consults the Virgin Mary and begs her to intercede with her son on Magdalene's behalf, then pleads repeatedly with her sister despite the latter's often insulting replies. Eventually Martha persuades Mary to come and listen to the new prophet, Jesus, who has healed her.[39] At the end of a very long sermon on the parables of the talents and the prodigal son, Magdalene is weeping and penitent.[40]

In many texts Magdalene comes to the house of a certain Simon who has invited Jesus to a meal[41] and, falling at Jesus' feet, she washes them with her tears and dries them with her hair.[42] In most versions she then anoints Jesus' feet but in a few she anoints his head.[43] Some plays include the scene where she purchases ointment from the apothecary.[44] Simon murmurs to himself because Jesus allows a sinner to touch him and Jesus responds with the parable of the two debtors (Luke 7: 40–8).[45] In some plays the scene is played after the Entry into Jerusalem, and Judas criticises Mary for wasting the ointment that might have been sold and the money given to the poor (cf. John 12).[46]

The episode of the meal in Bethany (John 12: 2; Luke 10: 38–42) sometimes begins with Lazarus inviting Jesus to dinner (Florence *Conversion* 286). In Revello 100, having heard from Mary of her repentance and forgiveness, Lazarus writes a letter addressed to: 'Jesus Christ, sent from God as the prophets foretold, who is the Son of the eternal God'. A servant carries it across the stage to Jesus. John is asked to read the letter, in which Magdalene, Martha and Lazarus ask Jesus to come to lunch or dinner (*o a disnare o a cena*) because of the great love he has showed to Magdalene. Jesus asks the messenger to wait and instructs John to write and say he hopes to come to '*disnare*' the following day with his followers (*mya brigata*). The messenger takes the answer John has written from 'Jesus Christ, born in Nazareth, without spot or sin, of the pure Virgin Mary as it was written in the prophecy' back across to the Bethany 'mansion' where Lazarus reads it aloud to the two sisters.[47]

In most plays the scene in Bethany follows the gospel account fairly closely, with Martha fussing about the serving while Mary sits at Christ's feet listening to him. In the Castilian *Martha's Hospitality*, Jesus praises Martha for her charitable acts but confirms that Mary has the 'better part'. This incident led to Mary and Martha being seen as symbols respectively of the contemplative and the active life.[48] In plays where the scene follows the Raising of Lazarus the meal is sometimes the occasion for Lazarus to describe what he saw in Hell during the four days he was dead.[49]

Plays that do not include the story of Mary Magdalene nevertheless usually stage the miracle of the Raising of Lazarus (there are versions in Latin as well as many in all the vernaculars including Dutch),[50] perhaps because of its importance in the development of the trouble between Jesus and the Jews. It is characteristic of the French plays to name both the followers and the opponents of Jesus among the Jews: Auvergne, for example speaks of the meeting of groups of '*mali judei et boni*' (bad Jews and good: 180; cf. Troyes 410: '*Y doivent estre tous les Juifz bons et mauvais*' (All the Jews, good and bad, should be there)). The German plays, on the other hand, follow the Johannine tradition and speak of the group opposed to Jesus simply as 'the Jews' or the synagogue. John's gospel has been called (by a Jewish writer) 'the gospel of Christian love and Jew-hatred' (quoted in Kirk, *Vision of God*, 82). It is also worth remembering when discussing the question of anti-Semitism in the German plays that in the fifteenth century when most of the plays were written, England and France had already expelled the Jews and Spain was preparing the Inquisition, whereas in Germany and parts of Italy, Jews were a part of the everyday life of the towns. In Freiburg im Breisgau in 1338, where the Jews had been placed under the personal protection of the Count, it was stated that 'no one should make a play about them in Freiburg that might cause them trouble or shame' (Neumann 337). In Frankfurt, however, in 1469, when a play of Antichrist and the Last Judgement was to be performed, the council decreed that 'the Jews must remain at home during the play' (Neumann 312), presumably to prevent possible disorder.[51]

Scenes of Lazarus's illness, death and burial sometimes precede the Raising. In Florence *Conversion* 292, two doctors attend him and Martha provides a white cloth for a shroud, while in Eger (where the news is brought to Jesus while he is still at table with Simon the Leper) four *tumulans* (entombers) carry Lazarus to the monument (114).[52] Some plays characterise the mourners: Gréban includes Simon the Leper who, in Michel 186, invites Jairus to join them. Arras 106 includes a number of women who help nurse Lazarus and then mourn him.

The moment of the actual Raising of Lazarus is still, in most versions, more or less biblical: Jesus comes to Bethany, has a conversation with Martha about the Resurrection, consoles Mary, weeps over Lazarus[53] and then at the climax of the scene orders the stone to be taken away. In a few plays of the Michel group, the Jews emphasise Martha's warning about the smell: 'Lord, by this time he stinketh'(John 11: 39), and conspicuously hold their noses as they remove the stone (Michel 190). The biblical command 'Lazarus, *veni foras!*' (Lazarus, come forth!), retained in most texts, is sometimes given in both Latin and vernacular (cf. Sterzing *Palm Sunday* plays 50, 139).

Fleury (perhaps to avoid any risk of humour in the movement of a
bound man) simply has Lazarus sit up and sing a thanksgiving to
God (II 208).[54] Towneley 390 and Rouergue 85 introduce here the
description of the Pains of Hell. A few plays end with a warning of the
consequences of the miracle: the stage is set for the final confrontation
between Jesus and the Jews. Before analysing the plays of Holy Week,
however, there are two other groups of texts to consider: plays which
dramatise the parables, and those which treat of the Judgement of Jesus
Christ.

PLAYS OF THE PARABLES

And he spoke to them many things in parables.

(Matthew 13: 3)

Dramatisations of the parables are basically morality plays, and only
one actually appears in the biblical sequence. The story of the Ten
Virgins (Matthew 25: 1–13), already in the gospel linked with the
warning of the Judgement, appears in that position in several plays.[55]

Parables may be dramatically treated in several ways: as a
straightforward staging of the biblical story with little addition to the
text; as a retelling of the parable in contemporary, medieval, terms; or
as a formally allegorised text. Examples of each of these methods will
be found in the following brief study.

The story of the Prodigal Son (Luke 15: 11–32), is by far the most
commonly dramatised parable, with examples in many languages both
during and since the Middle Ages.[56] The fifteenth-century Catalan
Consueta del Fill Prodich is a morality play. The father (who gives his
departing son as much advice as Polonius does Laertes) clearly
represents God, and the prodigal is tempted away to a riotous life
offstage by Vanity, while the elder son promises his father to serve him
faithfully. The most unexpected detail in this version is the explicit
identification of the *caballer* (gentleman) who leads the prodigal astray
as the devil, who rejoices in having trapped one who, he believes,
cannot escape because he will not beg for mercy. At the end the elder
son finally accepts his father's invitation to join in the feasting because
he 'is always obedient to your will' (288). In contrast to this moralised
approach, in the earliest and most original play, *Courtois d'Arras*, the
story is transferred not merely to the Middle Ages but to the town and
area of Arras, and the main part of the play is set in a tavern.[57]

Courtois, a would-be gentleman, having left home because he was tired of the humdrum life – symbolised by a diet of bread and pease (*pain et pois* 2) – enters on a realistically presented rake's progress. Two prostitutes and the innkeeper help him spend his money then rob him of his good clothes. Destitute, he tries to earn his living by looking after the pigs but the inedible bread given him by his new master and the dry husks trodden underfoot by the swine remind him of the bread and pease he rejected at home. He repents sincerely and prays for help; then, his pride humbled, makes his way back to his father who welcomes him home and forgives him. This central part of the play is flanked by short scenes between the father and the unsympathetically portrayed elder brother. The triple pattern of worldliness, repentance and reconciliation (typical of the Mary Magdalene plays and many saints' lives) is symbolised by Courtois' three coats: the fine one stolen from him in the tavern, the rags he wears as a swineherd and the best robe given him by his father on his return home.[58]

A contrast between riches and poverty is the basis of the other popular parable play: the story of the rich man and the beggar, often called Dives and Lazarus (Luke 16: 19–31).[59] The emphasis in most versions is not on the riches of Dives but on his lack of charity (the parable occurs shortly after Jesus' warning that 'you cannot serve God and Mammon'). In Haarlem he is the *Rijcken Wrecke* and in Toledo 46 the *Rico Avarieto* (Greedy rich man). The French *Maulvais riche* (the wicked rich man) is so irritated by the clicking of the leper's rattle when the poor man comes each day to beg for food, that he orders the dogs to be set on him. In a scene reminiscent of the story of Daniel and the lions, the leper prays for help and the dogs lie down and lick his sores (cf. Luke 16: 21). Particularly realistic in its treatment of the episode is the play from Sterzing[60] where the playwright introduces a *Precursor* to moralise on the scenes, which are presented in universally recognisable settings without local special references. The brief account in the gospel is much enlarged (the play is nearly a thousand lines long) by the introduction of attendants on the rich man who help him to take his pleasure – the minstrel joins him in a drinking bout, for example – and make only feeble efforts to help the dying man at the door. Lazarus dies and angels take him to Abraham's bosom while the devils lament the loss of a soul. Then it is Dives's turn. He dies surrounded by wife, doctor and servants but none can help him, and even before her husband's decease the upper servants are urging the wife to collect as much of Dives's goods as she can before the five brothers come. The scene between Abraham and Dives is very close to the gospel and there is no suggestion of Hell effects: the devils do not even appear. Then the play has a long coda in which the brothers fight over their inheritance and finish by killing each other, while four peasants philosophise on the vanity of riches before going home to their meal of curds (*sauer milch*). The *Precursor* drives the moral home for the audience.

Parable plays were especially popular in the Netherlands and most of these dramatisations are heavily allegorised.[61] The expositor of the Lille *L'honme quy descendit de Jerusalem en Jherico* (the man who went down from Jerusalem to Jericho), the text of the Dutch *Geslacht des Menschen* (Mankind) and Vicente's Portuguese *Geraçâm humana* (Mankind) all present the story of the Good Samaritan (Luke 10: 30–7) as an allegory of the Fall and Redemption. Mankind leaving Jerusalem and journeying down to Jericho '*nous magnifeste Adam*' (represents Adam) in Lille. (Vicente starts with the glory of Adam in Paradise and keeps the name throughout). In the Dutch play, the thieves that bring him into danger on the road and leave him for dead are the devil and his followers; the priest and the Levite (representing the Law and the Prophets) pass him by on the other side without helping him, then comes Christ, the Good Samaritan and brings Mankind to the Inn of God's Grace where the innkeeper will care for him with the help of the Samaritan's two pennies: '*teen es mijn vleijs en tander mijn bloet*' (one is my flesh and the other my blood). The play ends with Mankind's expression of thanksgiving.[62]

THE JUDGEMENT OF JESUS CHRIST

'In this we have known the love of God because he hath laid down his life for us.'

(I John 3: 16)

Legal debates and court scenes are very popular in the biblical and morality plays, culminating in the Last Judgement.[63] In addition to the gospel Trials of Jesus (see below), five plays from different language areas present an earlier judgement play: the Judgement of Jesus Christ. Although the theme was a favourite one with the preachers all these plays derive ultimately from a fifteenth-century sermon: the *Passio secundum legem debet mori* (according to the Law he ought to die – John 19: 7) which was widely disseminated in Latin and vernacular in both manuscripts and printed editions.[64] The Rouergue *Jutgamen de Jesus* is part of a fifteenth-century sequence of plays. The *moralité, Secundum legem* by Jean Abondance, the Sterzing *Ain recht das Christ stirbt* and the Aversa play *La licentia di Cristo a matre* are all from the sixteenth century. In the Revello *Passion* the Jewish leaders demand Christ's death before Pilate, using the same arguments as in these Judgement plays.

The theme of the plays is theological: was the death of Christ necessary to salvation? The subject is treated at length by Aquinas who concludes that, although God could have saved Man by a simple act of his will, the death of Christ was necessary for three reasons: it fulfilled the prophecies; it reconciled the Justice and Mercy of God, and it showed God's love for man.[65]

The action is substantially the same in all the plays. Human Nature appeals to the Judge to be freed from Hell as God had promised; to achieve this Christ must die.[66] Christ is summoned before the court, and appears accompanied by his mother. Throughout the plays Christ never joins in the debate or questions the sentence; it is always the Virgin who tries to save her Son from death.[67]

The first judgement is that of the Law of Nature. Charity pleads for Man to be saved and calls on Adam and the patriarchs, who point out that they are the figures of how Christ must die: Adam died through the wood of a tree, so the death of Christ must also be through the wood of a tree; Noah was shamed by his son when he was drunk, so Christ must die naked;[68] Abraham sacrificed his son who bore the wood on his shoulders, so Christ must bear the cross. Jacob's ladder is the figure of the mount of Calvary and the cross up which Christ must go to his death (cf. crucifixion *in sublimo* p. 135). Innocence protests that Christ is guiltless so should not die.[69] The verdict is against him but the Virgin pleads for the right to appeal and it is allowed.

The court then moves to the Law of Scripture.[70] The prophets (David, Solomon, Isaiah, Jeremiah) say Christ must die to fulfil God's word spoken through their prophecies.[71] The Judge agrees. The Virgin again appeals against the verdict and the third court is summoned: the Law of Grace. The Judges are the four evangelists.[72] The council for Man, here, is Necessity: Christ must die to show God's grace; the evangelists prove this from their gospels. The sentence is read out condemning Christ to die and he accepts it. The Virgin faints but is comforted by Christ with the promise of future joy. In the sermon and Abondance's *Moralité* the Passion follows.[73] In the *Licentia*, after the verdict, Death appears and announces that Christ's end is near. The Virgin flees in terror. Christ rebukes Death for frightening his mother, sends John to console her and, when she returns, asks 'licence' of her to die. She reluctantly gives him her blessing. The Jews lead him off and she gives way to her grief.[74]

The theme of these Judgement plays is echoed in some of the Corpus Christi cycles and cyclic passions with a scene in which the Virgin pleads with Jesus not to allow himself to be put to death (see p. 127). Only during the Agony in the Garden, does Jesus himself express reluctance to face the suffering necessary to save Man, and he always accepts that God's will should be done. In N. town *Passion* 81, for example, he prays:

> *O, Father, Father, for my sake*
> *this great passion thou take from me,*
> *which be ordained that I shall take*
> *if Man's soul saved may be.*
> *And if it behove, Father, for me*
> *to save Man's soul that should be lost [spylle],*
> *I am ready in each degre*
> *the will of thee for to fulfil.*
>
> (My modernised spelling)

CHAPTER 9

The Passion and Resurrection

We bring before your eyes, as best we can, corporeally, played out by men, this mirror of devotion so that you may look in it and humbly reflect on it.

(Gréban, 267)

The events of Holy Week culminating in the Resurrection on Easter Day were dramatised innumerable times in the Middle Ages. Although I have tried to mention all the recorded or published vernacular texts, references to particular motifs are not comprehensive unless specifically stated. A number of the more unusual details and variants are also described.

THE ENTRY INTO JERUSALEM

On Palm Sunday, the gospel account of Jesus' triumphal entry into Jerusalem was read at the beginning of Mass before the procession during which the Palm Sunday anthems took up and amplified the gospel accounts.[1] A number of plays include a scene of the disciples being sent to fetch the ass.[2] There is often a keeper of some kind (Luke 19: 34 refers to the owners) who only allows them to take the ass when he knows 'the Lord hath need of him'. In *Ordinalia*, I 239 the keeper hands the ass over willingly when he knows who it is for, and wishes it were worth 'a thousand pounds in good red gold to Jesus'; whereas in Arras 123 he begins by calling them thieves and says they should have come by night to steal it. Semur 154 goes further by introducing the recurrent figures of the *Rusticus* and his wife as keepers. He insults the apostles and argues with them, even when he knows who wants the ass.

In most of the plays the most important variation between the texts is in the forms of greeting sung or spoken as Jesus arrives in Jerusalem. Many different Latin or vernacular songs are mentioned and most plays include the strewing of the ground with flowers or branches. Revello III has an angelic choir as well as one of boys (*putti*) who, accompanied by pipers, sing the '*Gloria in Excelsis*' and the biblical anthem: 'Hosanna! Blessed is he who comes in the Name of the Lord' (John 12:13).[3] The Gréban/Michel group of plays include a welcoming party organised by one of the Jews and mention the homely detail of a small boy, Benjamin, wearing his best coat for the occasion (Michel 217). York, in contrast, presents a group of burgesses clad only in their shirts who cast down their cloaks for Christ to walk on as he dismounts, and welcome him with a series of stanzas beginning 'Hail!' and including many images from the Palm Sunday anthems (218).[4] In the Perugia *lauda* for Palm Sunday (I 197), the crowd greets Christ with the words '*Gesu Cristo viva, viva*' before continuing with the traditional hymn '*Gloria, laus et honor*' (All glory laud and honour: sung also in N. town *Passion* 62).[5]

The other scenes at the beginning of Holy Week vary considerably from play to play; only the Cleansing of the Temple and the Betrayal will be treated here.[6] In a few plays Jesus immediately goes to the Temple for the scene of the Cleansing (Matthew 21: 12–17).[7] Before he drives out the sellers with a whip there is sometimes a brief dialogue between the different traders. In the Castilian *Entry* 269 the traders indulge in praise of their wares; in Lucerne, II 39 they boast of the quality of their doves; *Ordinalia*, I 247 includes a cloth-seller among the merchants. Semur 157 introduces the wife of the *Rusticus* who asks the fruit-seller for a '*poire d'angoisse*' (an old form of pear-shaped gag) for her husband, who himself argues with the other vendors over his increasingly obscene demands.[8]

THE BETRAYAL

According to the synoptic gospels, during the early part of Holy Week Jesus and his disciples left Jerusalem each evening for Bethany (Matthew 21: 17). In the medieval elaborations of the story they stay in the house of Mary, Martha and Lazarus where the Virgin Mary is also staying. Many plays include a farewell scene between Jesus and his friends and especially his mother before the Passion.[9] In Brixen, the Virgin reminds Jesus that an angel had promised her she should not suffer pain; he agrees that 'we, the Trinity' had said this but that this was in the time of joy and bliss. Now is the hour of pain and anguish which he must suffer to redeem mankind (Tyrol 359). Some French plays include here the Virgin's plea to her son to grant her one of four requests: that he should save humanity without dying for them; that his death, if essential, should not be agonising; that she should die before he does; or that if she must see him suffer, it should be without feeling or pain. Jesus explains why he cannot grant any one of these requests.[10]

Several plays include at this point the scene of Magdalene's anointing Christ with the precious ointment and Judas' anger at what he sees as the waste of money.[11] Often it is straight from this scene that he goes to the Jews to betray Christ, demanding money because he feels he has been cheated out of his share of the three hundred pence that the precious ointment would have fetched. John's gospel explicitly states that Judas was a thief and kept the purse and helped himself from it (12: 6). From this there developed in exegesis the idea that the thirty pieces of silver (Matthew 26: 16) was a 'tithe' to which Judas felt he was entitled.[12]

A number of plays include a reference to the story of the doomed birth of Judas, found in *Legenda*, in which he suffers the fate of Oedipus: exposed by his real parents because of the oracles, he is rescued and brought up by the queen of Iscarioth. Later he enters Pilate's service, in the course of which he kills his real father and marries his mother. Only Michel 58 (followed by Mons 142, and Valenciennes 25-day, f. 76v) includes a dramatisation of all these events but many texts refer to it in some way, often in the form of a soliloquy by Judas at the time of the Betrayal, the Arrest or just before his own death.[13]

Judas' selling of Christ is sometimes deferred until after the Last Supper and conflated with the preparations for the Arrest, alternatively the events may be interlaced. N. town *Passion* 234 (revised text), Palatinus 99 and Autun 73 associate Mary's repentance and anointing of Jesus' feet with the Last Supper scene, linking it in this way with Maundy Thursday – the day on which the Holy Oils used in anointing the sick were blessed for the coming year, and also, perhaps more significantly, the day when sinners who had been doing penance during Lent were readmitted to the congregation in preparation for their Easter communion.[14]

THE LAST SUPPER

In many plays the Last Supper takes place in the house of Simon (variously described as *Hospes*, Leper, Pharisee, or 'of Bethanie'). In Revello 122, Simon is helped by his wife and the servant, with whom he argues that the food is cold. In Troyes 643, Judas insists on helping serve because he loves to wait on his master; in Autun 71 and Palatinus 95 Judas is told to sit by his master 'as usual'.

The two principal elements in the gospel accounts of the Last Supper are the Institution of the Eucharist (Matthew, Mark and Luke) and the Washing of Feet (John). Most plays include both (though there are a few exceptions) and since there is no liturgical basis on which to determine the order of the two incidents they can occur either way round. Towneley and Cyprus follow John and omit the Institution. Abruzzi *Minor Passion* and Künzelsau omit the whole episode.

The Institution of the Eucharist generally follows the biblical accounts[15] though in many plays there are details which echo the celebration of Mass: the bread which Jesus breaks is referred to as a host or 'oble' and the distribution as a 'communion'.[16] In Michel, where Judas serves the lamb (257), the gospel meal is followed by a formally prepared and staged Communion of the Apostles with a special seating plan and the liturgical manual acts (266).

John's gospel provided the lection for the Maundy Thursday Mass, which included the ceremonial washing of the feet of twelve men by the presiding priest, bishop (or even pope).[17] Most plays follow the Johannine narrative closely though one version of Lucerne provides Jesus with an assistant to carry the basin (II 64: this suggests liturgical influence).[18]

After the washing there is usually the warning that one of the disciples will betray Jesus, and the giving of the sop to Judas, after which he leaves the room. In Michel 270, when Judas eats the sop there is a storm in Hell and Satan comes, takes hold of Judas and produces an artificial little devil from Judas' shoulders (cf. John 13: 27; the devil also appears in Breton *Passion* 61). In Donaueschingen 141, Judas lets a black bird fly out of a bag by his feet before he goes out. In several plays the disciples comment on his departure, and in Revello 126 Judas explicitly tells them he is going to buy something (cf. John 13: 29).

A number of plays pick up Jesus' reference to the need to have a sword and the reply 'Here are two' (Luke 22: 35–8). Arras actually interrupts the scene by cutting to the shop of the armourer, who has a long speech listing the weapons he has for sale before Peter and James the Less enter and bargain for two swords. They cost eight *sous*. As they have no money Peter leaves his cloak in pledge (131). They return to the Upper Room and explain 'Lord behold here are two swords.'[19]

The rest of the episode – including parts of the Johannine discourses and the warning to Peter that he will deny Jesus – may be interlaced with the Betrayal and preparations for the Arrest. Semur 165 and Alsfeld 685 stage the Passover meal being prepared and eaten by the Sanhedrin. In Revello 127 the episode includes a visit by the Virgin Mary and her dialogue with Jesus on the necessity for his death.

THE AGONY IN THE GARDEN AND THE ARREST OF JESUS

This episode occurs in all four gospels, with varying details. Most plays include the reference to the angel coming to comfort Jesus and to the Bloody Sweat that fell from his face (Luke 22: 43–4).[20] Probably because it is the most emotional and personal moment for Jesus in the Passion sequence, Anton Lang of Oberammergau described the scene in the Garden as 'the hardest in the Passion Play'.[21]

The Provençal *Director's Notebook* 26 suggests two alternative ways of producing the Bloody Sweat: either Jesus can have a sponge of blood under his wig and press it at the right moment, or there can be someone hidden under the place where he is praying to paint the sweat on his face. Revello 129 and Lucerne 85 specify someone hiding while in Donaueschingen 149 Jesus is instructed to prostrate himself for the duration of a *Pater Noster* ('a good *Pater Noster* long') before showing the Bloody Sweat, which may suggest some device like the sponge full of blood.[22]

Many texts, following Luke 22: 43 have a reference to the angel who appears to Jesus. Often the angel carries a chalice: a visualisation of the prayer 'My Father, if it be possible let this chalice pass from me.' In the *Gospel of Nicodemus* the angel is named as Michael and reminds Jesus of the necessity for his sacrifice.[23] Heidelberg, however, specifies that there shall not be a 'strengthening' angel: *non angelum confortantem* (167).

During the scenes in the Garden (also referred to as the Mount of Olives) preparations may be going on elsewhere for the Arrest. In *Ordinalia*, I 307, the soldiers are led by Prince Annas. In Lucerne 87 and Donaueschingen 150, Caiaphas borrows soldiers from Pilate while in Valenciennes 20-day one of the tyrants promises to collect a million cut-throats, brigands, ruffians and so on from local lodging houses. His Rabelaisian list is followed by a longer one of the armour and weapons they will have, ranging from *belle artillerie* to swords, crossbows and clubs (f. 269r). This text and a number of others include, among the guards or the tormentors of Jesus, names taken from the *Gospel of Nicodemus*. In Michel 278, lanterns are borrowed from an old hag,

Hedroit, who delightedly leads the group to the Garden; later Hedroit is the porteress involved in Peter's denial and also forges the nails for the crucifixion. In the Savoie *Passion* she keeps a drinking-house (Chocheyras *Savoie* 175).[24] In Heidelberg, the betrayal and binding of Jesus is prefigured by Samson and Delilah (155).

In some plays Judas expands the biblical 'Hail, master!' with false expressions of friendship (York 240, Semur 178, *Ordinalia*, I 309). In Hall after the arrest a Jew tells Annas that Judas was clever to deceive Jesus by the kiss: 'he's a good fellow' (*guet gsell*: Tyrol 311). Several plays follow *Legenda* and include Judas' suggestion that he will kiss Christ so they shall not mistake him for his kinsman, James the Less.[25] When Judas and his followers arrive, Jesus sometimes greets them with the biblical Latin text '*Quem queritis?*', to which the reply is *Jesum Nazarenum* (John 18: 4; this is of course the origin of the '*Quem queritis?*' trope: see p. 13). Elsewhere the question is asked and answered in vernacular. Many plays include variations of the incident of the soldiers falling to the ground when Jesus speaks. In Semur 177 they declare they were blinded by a great light – an obvious borrowing from the Conversion of St Paul (Acts 9: 3).[26]

Almost all plays include the healing of Malchus's ear (John 18: 10–11 is the only version which gives the name). In Eger 164, Malchus declares, 'Jesus is a magician but I've got my ear back'; in Künzelsau 133 Jesus tells him: 'Stop yelling, I'll heal it'; whereas in Castellani's *Passion*, Jesus promises Malchus he will heal his ear miraculously: 'I intend to show how humane I am towards these hostile and cruel people' (I 312).[27]

The scene normally ends with Jesus, bound, being led off to Annas and Caiaphas, often being beaten and ill-treated by the soldiers on the way. In Alsfeld 693 the soldiers dance along, singing that they have caught Jesus '*der Trogener*' (the traitor). They also sing in Revello and try to make Jesus join in (132). Peter and John follow at a distance. A few plays include the incident of the young man who flees naked leaving his linen cloth in the hands of his pursuers (Mark 14: 51–2).[28]

THE REMORSE AND DEATH OF JUDAS

In the gospel account Judas' remorse and attempt to return the thirty pieces of silver follows the trials before Annas and Caiaphas, when Jesus is being taken to Pilate. Many plays set it earlier, perhaps for theatrical convenience while the Sanhedrin are still on the stage.

Montecassino *Passion* 70 specifies that Judas throws the money onto a table but usually it is the floor. In Künzelsau 138, the Jews tell him that if he chooses to throw the money down they will be quite happy to pick it up. The section of the Cervera *Passion* for Good Friday morning opens with Judas approaching, shouting. At first the Jews think it is soldiers, then someone suggests it is Jesus' mother; finally Judas himself appears. Many plays include a reference to the later use of the money (Matthew 27: 6–7). In *Ordinalia*, I 347, Caiaphas's crozier-bearer sells the Sanhedrin a field as a burial place – not for strangers (Matthew 27: 7) but for Christians, so that their stink will not pollute Jewish ground or kill Jews.

In York 283, Judas' remorse at first seems genuine, and he tries to persuade the Jews to free Jesus and take him as a slave instead. In Künzelsau 137, Misericord comes to him but he rejects her; in Arras he begs the Jews '*humblement*' to free Jesus in exchange for the money. Only when his attempts fail does his despair burst forth (151). He constantly shows himself guilty of the sin of pride, by claiming that his deed is too appalling for God's mercy. In Semur he addresses Jesus and is answered by the Virgin (who is present at the Trials). She urges him to repent, but he declares his heart is of marble and tells her to leave him, for her pale face hurts him. He calls on devils to counsel him, and *Mors Inferni* and the Herald of Hell (*Clamator Inferni*) oblige with a recommendation to hang himself (188).[29]

Judas' suicide is mentioned only in Matthew (27: 7) where he hangs himself, and in Peter's speech to the apostles where the detail is added that 'he burst asunder in the midst and his bowels gushed out' (Acts 1: 18). Most plays show the hanging, and several include the idea (found in *Legenda*) that Judas' evil soul cannot pass the lips with which he kissed Jesus so the devils must rip him open to take it: in Frankfurt 472 they use a dummy body and in Mons Judas has a bag of pig's entrails under his robe (306 n.3).[30]

THE TRIALS OF JESUS

In the gospels, from the moment of the Arrest the role of Jesus becomes verbally extremely limited.[31] Most plays retain the biblical dialogue and, in the early trial scenes, expansions (if any) are limited to the physical brutalities of the guards and the venom of the Jews, especially Annas and Caiaphas. A vivid passage in *Meditationes* describes this succession of beating, noise, torment, mocking and abuse as a 'continuous battle' with Jesus in 'great pain, injury, scorn, and torment' (318). In Towneley the two Trial plays are called after the two main scenes of violence, the Buffeting (*Coliphizacio*) and the Scourging (*Flagellacio*).[32]

Interlaced with the violence is the sequence of Peter's denial. A few plays give to the maids or soldiers who challenge him names and individuality and in the Coliseum *Passion* Peter is addressed as Old Man and insists he is merely a travelling Jewish pilgrim (29). In Alsfeld, the cock had a speaking part and walked in the procession (858). His words cleverly echo the sound of a cock crowing: '*Gucze gu gu gu ga!/ Peter lug lug lug nu da!*' (The first line is meaningless but the second says: 'Peter lies lies lies now then!' 697). In Sterzing in 1496 the actor playing the serving maid doubled as the cock ('*et gallus*': Neumann 651). After his denials Peter laments; in Semur he goes into a ditch (*fovea*) to do so. The second part of his long speech parallels antithetically the despair of Judas' speeches: having confessed his sin, Peter declares his need for his master's forgiveness and his certainty that God will pardon him (185).[33]

Apart from the Scourging and the Crown of Thorns, in most plays there is less general emphasis on violence in the scenes before Pilate than in the earlier ones before the Sanhedrin. The *Gospel of Nicodemus* stresses even more than the other gospels Pilate's opposition to the violence of the Jews and his belief in Jesus' innocence. Several plays include a 'pomping' (boasting) speech for Pilate, but, although he is weak and vacillating Pilate is not actively wicked: the only really evil Pilate is in Towneley (Woolf 248). Sometimes Pilate's attitude is influenced by the respectful action of the servant who (inspired, he explains, by the Entry into Jerusalem) lays down his cloak for Jesus to walk on and/or by the miracle of the standards which bow to Jesus when he enters the hall, despite all the efforts of the standard bearers.[34] Several plays follow the *Gospel of Nicodemus* with a Jew speaking on Jesus' behalf and recalling his deeds of healing.[35]

The order of events varies but all sources and most plays agree in having Pilate repeatedly try to avoid sentencing Jesus to death, firstly (recorded only in Luke 23: 8–12) by sending him to Herod, where Jesus remains silent despite all Herod's questions. In N. town *Passion* Herod has him whipped, then Satan enters the playing area in the '*most orryble wyse*' and has a long speech while the soldiers put Jesus' clothes back on him and '*overest a whyte clothe*' (108). Then the devil is sent to Pilate's wife. In *Ordinalia* the learned doctors argue before Herod about Jesus' claim to be both Man and God. One says this is impossible because two different things cannot be combined. The other retaliates with the example of the mermaid which is half woman and half fish (I 361). The white robe (Luke 23: 11) in which Herod (encouraged by his queen in Revello 151) dresses Jesus before sending him back is usually described as a fool's garment: in Breton *Passion*, Herod's fool laments the loss of his robe which has been put on Jesus (104).[36]

Many plays include at some point in the story Pilate's wife's dream (Matthew 27: 19; further elaborated in the *Gospel of Nicodemus*) and most follow Comestor and Nicholas of Lyra in showing the dream as being inspired by the devil.[37] Usually the news of the dream is brought to Pilate by a messenger, but sometimes she goes to him in person – like 'a mad woman' (N. town *Passion* 110); accompanied by her son and daughter who both plead for Jesus (St Genevieve 178).

Pilate next tries to have Jesus released as the Passover prisoner but is defeated by the demand for Barabbas, who in a few plays has a small speaking role before running off free. Pilate finally says he will have Jesus flogged then let him go. This scene is included in all texts, usually combined with the Crown of Thorns. It may be followed by the '*Ecce Homo*' (Behold the Man) when Jesus is put into the purple robe and shown to the people as their king (cf. John 19: 15–16). Ultimately, however, as *Legenda* puts it, Pilate betrays Jesus out of fear and washes his hands of the blood 'of this innocent man' because he is afraid of Caesar. The scene occurs in all the plays; in Palatinus, Pilate's son, Joel, holds the basin (147).[38] In Matthew (27: 30–31), *Gospel of Nicodemus* and many plays the Flagellation and Crown of Thorns follow the Washing of Hands (Matthew 27: 30–1) and the condemnation of Jesus by Pilate.[39] '*Her was more rancore shewed than equitee*' (Bodley *Burial* 145).

Ordinalia introduces here another part of the legend of the Rood: the tormentors use for the cross the beam thrown into the brook Cedron after it had been cast out of the Temple in Solomon's day (I 425). In Arras 180 one of the Jews narrates the legend and suggests the beam be now used for the cross.[40]

Some plays also stage the legend of the smith who refused to forge the nails, claiming he had hurt his hands. When his wife said he was lying a miracle occurred and his hands were covered in sores. The wife herself then forged the nails with the help of one of the tormentors. In Semur 204 they sing a song together while forging. Michel omits the legend of the smith and the forging is done by Hedroit with one of the tormentors (383).[41]

THE CRUCIFIXION

The four gospel accounts of the Crucifixion were conflated in the plays, often following the order of the liturgical devotion of the Stations of the Cross popularised in the late Middle Ages by the Franciscans. The first Station was the condemnation by Pilate, the last the entombment. In the following analysis the Stations will be indicated in Roman numerals.[42]

The cross is loaded onto Jesus by the tormentors (II) and the procession sets off for Calvary.[43] The first fall (III) is often followed by the meeting with his Mother (IV); both offer opportunities for violence and abuse by the soldiers and lamentations by the Virgin. In Abruzzi she embraces Jesus and is forced away by the soldiers. Jesus then declares he is so weakened by sorrow for his mother that he cannot lift the cross.[44] Most plays follow the three synoptic gospels in presenting a reluctant Simon of Cyrene (Simon Leper: Arras 186, *Ordinalia*, I 431) being made to carry the cross (V). Usually he is bullied and threatened into helping but in Auvergne 193 he agrees because it will cost him money otherwise. By far the most developed and original Station is the legend of Veronica, the woman who wiped Jesus' face with a cloth on which the face became imprinted (VI). The story occurs in Latin versions of the *Gospel of Nicodemus* and was widespread in the later Middle Ages.[45] The second fall (VII) is followed by the other biblical Station (VIII), the meeting with the Daughters of Jerusalem (Luke 23: 28–31).[46] Few plays have the third fall (IX).

In *Nicodemus* it is said that after Jesus has been stripped (X) they girded him with a cloth, but in *Meditationes* and some plays the Virgin uses her veil to cover his nakedness (Alsfeld 786; Eger 235; Michel 398).[47] Many texts limit the speech of Jesus during the Crucifixion to the traditional Seven Words of the gospels but in some Jesus prays before he is crucified.[48]

The representations of the nailing to the cross (XI) depend on which method is being used (see figure 7). *Meditationes* talks of Christ climbing on to a cross that is already set up: crucifixion *'in sublimo'* (*Paschon* 181; Donaueschingen 207; and probably St Genevieve 196 – the text is not clear). *Meditationes* also mentions that the nailing may have been done on the ground before the cross is raised: *'in humilo'*. This is the usual practice in the plays which also generally follow the tradition that the holes were bored in the wrong place so that the tormentors stretch Jesus to fit: 'strung as tight as a bow' (Michel 400).[49]

In some plays Pilate writes the label for the cross in the palace, in others he is brought parchment and ink at Calvary (Semur 214); in Michel (and Valenciennes 20-day) he is advised to write in every language so that all the spectators will know who is being executed (401). In Towneley 274, one of the tormentors explains the label to the others.[50]

None of the gospels and only a few of the plays (Rueff is one) include all the Seven Words from the Cross and the Roman numerals used here merely indicate the traditional liturgical order. Plays may include the Latin text as well as a vernacular paraphrase and there is scope for dramatic development in the dialogue with the Penitent Thief (II. Luke 23: 39–43) or the Virgin and St John (III. John 19: 25–7). The scene with the thieves is extended with complaints and cursing by Dismas and expressions of repentance from Gestas. In Breton, Jesus tells Gestas he will be saved by 'my merits'(141).[51] The roles of John and of the Virgin are also enlarged. Although she and the other women are rudely treated by the soldiers (literally kicked aside in Lucerne 182) they remain near the Cross, their lamentations alternating with the Words of Jesus and the jeering of the Jews (see fig. 7).[52]

In Alsfeld 772, while the soldiers divide the clothes, Jesus sings the Latin prophecy '*Diviserunt*' (They divided [my garments among them]: Psalm 21, cit. Matthew 27: 35).[53] In several plays the soldiers, instead of casting lots, play dice for them.[54]

Many plays refer to 'the darkness that fell over the land from the sixth hour to the ninth hour' (Matthew 27: 45). The effect may be presented visually (Revello 171; in Lucerne it was effected by belching dark smoke from the Mount of Olives; see Evans 200) but in Alsfeld 795 the Moon and Stars have speeches of lamentation. Gréban 347 and Lucerne, III 78 introduce St Denis (Dionysius) commenting on the eclipse.[55] The marvels which accompany Jesus' death at the ninth hour are variously staged. The rending of the veil in the Temple (mentioned by all three synoptics) was sometimes portrayed in the Good Friday Liturgy by the rending of a cloth by deacons during the singing of the Passion. In Semur, the veil and the '*ydole*' in the Temple fall and the priest, Damp Godibert, declares he has heard a voice saying that this and the darkening of the sun is the work of the crucified enchanter (218). Lucerne had a bright golden sun hanging in Heaven which at this point was reversed to appear blood-coloured (see Evans 149). In Auvergne, God in Heaven declares he will frighten the Jews by making the earth tremble and he sends Michael to destroy part of the Temple (224). Other plays also include the earthquake, opening graves and

appearance of the Risen Dead in the streets (Matthew 27: 51–3).[56]
Lucerne 208 directs the dying Jesus to let his head drop to the right; in
Semur 218 Jesus' death is indicated by the release of a white dove.

After Jesus' death many plays include the centurion's claim: 'Indeed
this was the son of God' (Matthew 27: 54).[57] Occasionally he is
identified with the soldier who pierced Jesus' side (John 19: 34). The
latter is more commonly St Longinus (feast day 15 March) whose story,
as told in *Legenda* and many plays, makes him a blind soldier, often
accompanied by a servant or boy. In the twelfth-century *Seinte
Resurreccion* 13, after Joseph has asked Pilate for Jesus' body, Pilate sends
soldiers to see if Jesus is truly dead, and they offer the blind beggar,
Longinus, twelve pence to thrust the lance into the body.[58] In Eger
259; Alsfeld 796; Frankfurt 525; Benediktbeuern 298; and Coliseum 59,
Longinus kills Jesus to shorten his agony. More commonly he is an
enemy of Jesus or ignorant of the identity of the man he is striking till
the blood from Jesus' side falls on his hand and, when he touches it to
his face, his sight is restored. He repents and laments what he has
done.[59] Meanwhile, the thieves have died as a result of having their
legs broken. Several plays show their souls being taken respectively to
Heaven by an angel and to Hell by a devil (Alsfeld 805; Lucerne 210; in
Michel 424 the souls speak as they are led away). In Welsh, before
Longinus enters, Pilate's knights remove the thieves' bodies for speedy
burial because they smell badly (191). Elsewhere they are often left on
stage till after the Deposition.

DEPOSITION AND ENTOMBMENT

In some plays the Harrowing of Hell precedes the Deposition, but most
plays follow the Creed and put the Entombment first. The episode
usually begins with Joseph of Arimathea going to Pilate to ask for Jesus'
body. In York, Pilate gives Joseph the body 'our sabbath to save' (331).
In Sterzing (1486) 119, Joseph and Nicodemus tell Pilate they want to
remove the body before the Passover festival lest the Jews use the
holiday to continue their jeering at Jesus.[60] In several French plays
Joseph buys a shroud, and in one play Nicodemus also buys the
ointments (John 16: 39–40).[61] In the *Dirigierrolle* 363 Joseph and
Nicodemus wear albs and stoles for the Deposition. Often ladders
are used to enable them to remove the nails and lower the body to
the ground, where Mary receives it and holds it on her lap while
she laments (Frankfurt *Passion* 532, Bodley 160). In Revello 175 and

St Genevieve *Resurrection* 346 she accuses the prophets of falsehood and Jacob appears to explain that their prophecies are being fulfilled. The burial of Jesus is prefigured in Heidelberg 253 by the story of Jonah. The body is buried (York 332) or put in a sepulchre (*Ordinalia*, I 475). In Sterzing 123 it is carried out to the sacristy. In Frankfurt, angels with candles precede and follow as the body is carried to the tomb (532).

Although the setting of the watch on the tomb actually takes place the following day (Matthew 27: 52–6) many plays include the incident immediately after the Entombment, while others leave it till the Resurrection episode. In the *Seinte Resurrexion* 37, the soldiers are made to swear on a copy of the Law of Moses that they will guard the entombed body against all comers.[62] A few plays here introduce from *Nicodemus* the story of the imprisoning of Joseph by the Jews because he had befriended Jesus.[63]

Several plays include the Debate between *Ecclesia* and *Synagogua* at various points in the story: after Pilate has washed his hands (Alsfeld 731); beside the cross (St Genevieve *Passion* 213; Berlin *Redemption*, see Bergmann 67; Donaueschingen 223 where they are called Christiana and Judea); after the Ascension (*Dirigierrolle* 372); at the beginning of the Gothaer *Destruction of Jerusalem*; near the end of the procession but before the Last Judgement (Künzelsau 169).[64]

THE HARROWING OF HELL

From the fourth century, Christ's descent into Hell was included in the Apostles' Creed. It also formed part of the Athanasian Creed, but never the Nicene (see Appendix). Though the incident is not part of the canonical gospels, there are statements in the New Testament which can be taken as referring to the redemption of the justified dead: 'In the spirit ... he preached to those spirits that were in prison' (I Peter 3: 18–19). Supported by many of the Church Fathers, including Augustine, it became a generally accepted tradition. Aquinas speaks of it at length, and in the Middle Ages it formed a regular part of the Easter Celebrations with a place in the liturgical ritual.[65]

The principal source for the episode is the second part of the *Gospel of Nicodemus, Discensus Christi ad Inferos* (Christ's descent into Hell, usually rendered as the Harrowing of Hell.[66]

Before the arrival of Christ, there are often scenes of the souls in Limbo rejoicing at the prospect of deliverance while the devils prepare to defend their citadel.[67] In the *Discensus* the extensive scene of the patriarchs and prophets includes Seth's story of the Oil of Mercy and the promise of eventual redemption.[68] Christ approaches, often accompanied by angels, wearing a crown and carrying a banner with a cross on it. In *Ordinalia*, I 463 the devils describe the dying Christ as a banner hanging on a cross-shaped standard: they prepare to defend Hell.[69] In the *Discensus*, *Legenda* and many plays Christ summons Hell to surrender with the cry: '*Atollite portas*' (Lift up your gates [O ye princes and be ye lifted up O eternal gates and the King of Glory shall enter in] Psalm 23:7).[70] In Towneley he tells the devil, in the words of Moses to Pharaoh, to 'let my people pass' (299). Christ is joyfully received by the righteous but criticised by the devils for stealing those whom they had justly imprisoned. In Toledo where the scene was staged twelve times, the patriarchs are seated at a banquet (55). Sometimes the debate between Christ and the devils is considerably extended.[71] Lucifer and the other devils are left lamenting (and sometimes bound) as Christ leads the redeemed souls out of Hell.[72] A few plays include the scene of their arrival in Earthly Paradise (usually escorted by Michael) where they meet Elijah and Enoch, who have not yet died and will return to earth to fight against Antichrist. The Penitent Thief appears carrying his Cross and narrates how he was saved by the dying Jesus (Sterzing 151; Revello 180; *Ordinalia*, II 17; Arras 244). The scene with the Thief precedes the Harrowing in Provençal 68 and also in Semur where Jesus is enthroned in Paradise amid the souls who are crowned with flowers by the angels (247).[73]

THE RESURRECTION AND VISIT TO THE SEPULCHRE

Although there are many vernacular and many hundred Latin plays of the Resurrection, the actual Rising of Christ only occurs in vernacular plays.[74] In several German plays Christ is summoned to rise by an angel with the words from the introit for Sexagesima Sunday '*Exurge! quare obdormis, domine?*' (Rise up, why are you sleeping, lord?: Psalm 44: 23). He steps from the tomb, singing the antiphon for Maundy Thursday, '*Ego dormivi*' (I laid me down and slept [and rose up again]: Psalm 3: 6).[75]

In *Dirigierrolle* 364, after the Harrowing, Christ returns to the tomb, there is an earthquake and he is 'seen to have risen' while in Semur the *Anima* re-enters the tomb *subtiliter* (247) with a throng of angels; after a hymn he rises again and exits. Mons (using Gréban's text) directs Jesus to step out of the tomb right foot first, accompanied by smoke of

incense and lights (412). The English cycles show Christ stepping from
the tomb (after the Harrowing of Hell plays) and addressing the
audience with a lyrical complaint.[76] In Welsh, after the Harrowing, the
Spirit of Christ says 'Now I go to my body and I command it to appear
bodily to my beloved Virgin mother' (225). The appearance to the
Virgin here and elsewhere precedes the Visit to the Sepulchre by the
other Marys.[77]

The *Visitatio sepulchri* or visit of the women to the tomb on Easter
Day is (with the possible exception of the Greek *Paschon Christos*) the
oldest extant scene in the biblical drama.[78] An important addition to
the episode was the buying of ointments from a merchant or spice
seller (*Mercator, Unguentarius*; cf. Ripoll; Donaueschingen; Eger; *Dirigierrolle*; Delft; Origny; Tours; Gréban; Rouergue). Some French scenes
include a long '*dit*' in which the merchant boasts of his wares (Arras
247; Semur 231; Palatinus 231). In the Bohemian *Mastickár* the servant
Ruben boasts of his master's skill which is famous in 'Austria, Hungary,
Bavaria, Poland and Russia' (335). Ruben also appears in the Polish
Glorious Resurrection and German plays from Melk and Innsbruck, in
comic, sometimes obscene, episodes with the merchant, his wife, son,
and apprentice (often called Pusterpalk or Lasterbalk).[79]

The story of the guards from the sepulchre may be interlaced with
these early Resurrection scenes. Most plays show them as boastful and
easily frightened. In German the angels sometimes strike them down
with a flaming sword; elsewhere they sleep, or are stunned by the
earthquake. Some texts considerably extend also the scene with the
Jewish authorities and the argument over how much the guards should
be paid to hold their tongues (cf. Matthew 28: 11–5). In Gréban they
demand 10,000 besants because they are selling something very rare
and precious: Truth.[80]

The Resurrection appearances vary from one gospel to another in
order and persons; in addition, St Paul mentions appearances to Peter
and James as well as to groups of apostles (I Corinthians 15: 5, 7); he
does not mention the visit to the Tomb or the Marys.[81] In the core of
the Resurrection plays, the Visit to the Sepulchre, the *Quem queritis?*
dialogue with the angel is often included even if only in vernacular. In
the *Ordinalia*, II 63 there is apparently a deliberate alteration in the
sequence. The Marys lament at length, then the angel says: 'I know
whom ye seek; Jesus is not here.' Many German texts also include sung
Latin liturgical pieces such as the '*Quis revolvet?*' (Who will roll aside?)
and '*Victimae Paschali*' (The Paschal victim) with spoken vernacular

glosses. Semur 256 develops the liturgical scene of displaying the empty
shroud: Magdalene calls on the spectators to observe the marks of the
1,500 wounds of Christ on the blood-stained cloth.[82]

The great majority of plays also include the meeting between Mary
Magdalene and Jesus *in specie ortulani* (in the form of a gardener; John
20: 11–18).[83] Some texts include Jesus' meeting with the other Marys
(Matthew 28: 9; Admont 88; St Genevieve *Resurrection* 377; Arras 255;
Cyprus 209) but most continue with the visit of Peter and John to the
tomb and Jesus' appearance to the group of apostles. Bodley *Resurrection*
interpolates a whole section of the Latin text (190) then continues in
vernacular. The play ends with Peter and John visiting the tomb and
announcing the Resurrection.

The episode often known as the *Peregrinus*, from the title by which
Jesus is addressed in the gospel (and the consequent custom of dressing
him as a pilgrim in art and drama) describes Christ's meeting with two
disciples on the way to the village of Emmaus. They discuss the events
of the last few days, then, at supper, Jesus manifests himself to them by
breaking bread (Luke 24: 13–35). In addition to the Emmaus scenes in
the cycle plays, Latin and vernacular versions were sometimes
performed separately on Easter Monday when the incident formed the
lection of the day.[84] The Bozen *Emmaus* plays include two versions of
the scene: one, like the Latin and English texts, is a straightforward
rendering of the biblical account, but the other includes the innkeeper
and much crude comedy as the disciples, after Jesus has disappeared,
eat and drink heartily before returning to Jerusalem (300). There is a
comic scene also in Rouergue *Resurrection* where the innkeeper, finding
Jesus gone, accuses the disciples of having murdered him (120). Other
French plays limit the humour to the non-biblical innkeeper and his
family. In Arras 266 he stands at the inn door extolling his wine, food
and beds. In Breton *Passion* 201, the innkeeper accuses his serving-maid
of stealing eggs and milk to make skin cream. Arras, Gréban and N.
town also extend the dialogue between Jesus and the disciples about
the prophecies of his Resurrection.

The other Resurrection appearance commonly dramatised is the
story of Doubting Thomas (John 20: 19–31). Many texts stress the
disciples' rejection of the evidence of the women because women are
unreliable. Although the gospel specifies that the appearance to
Thomas was on the Sunday following the Resurrection, Bozen 159;
and Sterzing (1486) 164 include it in the Easter Day plays. Thomas
comes to the tomb where Magdalene tells him she has seen the risen

Christ. He expresses his disbelief but Jesus himself appears and
Thomas is convinced and repents. In N. town 379 he refuses to believe
either Magdalene or the disciples returning from Emmaus. The
Cornish Thomas is particularly obstinate, despite the efforts of the
apostles, Magdalene and the disciples from Emmaus to convince him
(73).

Probably because of the staging problems involved, the scene of the
miraculous draught of fishes and the charge to Peter: 'Feed my sheep'
(John 21: 1–20) is dramatised only in Lucerne (1616); Lille; plays of the
Arras/Gréban group; and the Angers *Resurrection* 727.[85]

THE ASCENSION AND ENTRY INTO HEAVEN

Although the best-known scene of the Ascension is that in the first
chapter of Acts, there are scenes of farewell and mentions of ascension
at the end of the synoptic gospels as well. These include the so-called
Commissioning of the Apostles, when Jesus tells them to go out into all
the world and preach (Luke 16: 15–18) and baptise in the name of the
Father and the Son and the Holy Ghost (Matthew 28: 18–20).
Extended versions of this scene are found in the Gréban and Angers
plays and in brief references in St Gallen; *Dirigierrolle*; Admont; and
Künzelsau (which however, has no Ascension). Bozen has an unusual
Ascension play with long preliminaries involving prophets, all the
apostles and the Virgin (117). Included are the healing of the blind man
(John 9: 1–7); the Charge to Peter (John 21: 15–17); the request by the
mother of the Zebedees that her sons may sit on each side of Jesus in
the Kingdom (Matthew 20: 20-4); and a request that Jesus will teach
the disciples to pray, answered by the *Pater Noster* (Luke 11: 1–13).
Matthew and John ask for help in writing their gospels and the Virgin
is granted power to intercede for sinners. After a communion meal,
instrumental music covers the move to the place of Ascension.

In the Latin liturgical texts, Italian *laude* and many plays (Alsfeld 840;
St Gallen, I 263; Admont, I 103; Chester 313 and Lucerne, III 111);
Jesus, as he ascends, sings the antiphon for the feast of the Ascension,
'*Ascendo*' (I ascend [to my Father]; St Gallen and Lucerne are in
vernacular). Angels appear and address the apostles, often in Latin,
with the biblical words, '*Viri Galilei*' (Ye men of Galilee: Acts 1: 6). The
actual ascent may be managed very simply with steps (*Dirigierrolle* 371)
but a number of plays suggest some kind of raising machinery or lift
(N. town 383; Gréban 438). Mons 449 makes use of the lift inside the

mountain used for the Transfiguration. An elaborate arrangement of cords and pulleys is described for Florence by Abramio in 1439 and the Toledo *Ascension* waggon in 1500 had a lift and a cloud that descended at the same time, covered with coloured paper and adorned with stars.[86]

Some cyclic plays end the episode with the apostles returning to Jerusalem to await the coming of the Holy Spirit, but several texts have a scene in Heaven with Jesus seated on the right hand of God, surrounded by angels and the redeemed while hymns and anthems are sung. In Alsfeld 828, where Jesus' triumphal entry with the redeemed souls into Heaven follows the Harrowing of Hell, the angels sing *Gloria in excelsis*. In *Ordinalia*, II 189 and Chester 374 different orders of angels welcome the triumphant Jesus with the Ascension Day anthem: 'Why then is thy apparel red, and thy garments like theirs that tread in the winepress?' (Isaiah 63: 2). In Rouergue *Ascension* Jesus preaches a long sermon in which he talks of five 'articles of faith': belief in his Conception, Birth, Crucifixion, Descent into Hell and Resurrection. To these he now adds a sixth: Ascension (88). He then ascends and is greeted by Seraphim and Raphael with this anthem. In Arras, Jesus is shown seated at God's right hand accompanied by the blessed, who are now wearing albs (277). In Gréban, God the Father tells the angels to arouse *Dame Musique* and *Dame Rethoricque* by their sweet and harmonious sounds (440). In Angers 823, Jesus ascends by lift with paper figures representing the rescued souls attached to his robe, while the actors pass into Heaven by a secret way. Then the 'fifty-one' patriarchs and prophets sing a response before being enthroned by Jesus among the nine orders of angels; as he seats each one, Jesus crowns and kisses him (cf. 1 Peter 5: 4); Isaiah and Jeremiah have each a double crown.[87] In those plays which continue with the scene of Pentecost, the apostles, while awaiting the promised Holy Spirit, elect Matthias to be the twelfth apostle in place of the traitor, Judas. It is at this point that many passion plays end, in the same way that, during the Ascension Day liturgy, the Paschal candle is extinguished in churches to signify the end of the redemptive life of Jesus.

CHAPTER 10

Pentecost to Judgement

THE COMING OF THE HOLY SPIRIT

But when he, the Spirit of truth, is come, he will teach you all
truth.   (John 16: 13)

The liturgy of Pentecost was often enlivened by symbolic representations of the descent of the Holy Spirit on Whitsunday (Acts 2: 1–4). The
ceremonial with dove, rays of light and flames used in Ferrara
cathedral for centuries was banned by the bishop in 1590 (D'Ancona,
Origini, II 183). In Florence there was an annual play of the Descent of
the Holy Spirit in the church of Spirito Santo: in 1471 the flames
destroyed the whole building (ibid., I 273). The descent of the Holy
Spirit was included in the (probably Latin) *Ludus Christi* from Cividale
in 1298/1303 and there are also seasonal *laude* from Perugia, Siena,
Aquila and Abruzzi.[1]

Several plays include here or earlier the scene of the apostles
composing the Creed. A probably unique liturgical Creed play is
recorded in a fifteenth-century ceremonial from Perpignan. After the
descent of the Spirit – in the form of a dove bringing fire from which
the apostles and the Virgin light candles – the former then sing in turn
their sentence of the Creed from prepared '*rotols*'.[2] In the Angers
Resurrection 866 the apostles wait impatiently for the promised gift, each
expecting it on a different day of the week for a different reason. For
example, James the Less expected it to come on Sunday because on
that day God created light; Jude on Friday, the day of the Passion.
Finally a burning flame (created with the help of *aqua vita*) descends on
the twenty-one persons present (including the Virgin and other women)
with a thunderous noise from the organs, 'using large, well-matched
organ-pipes'. The hymn '*Veni creator spiritus*' is sung (881). After
composing the Creed and arranging for John to make several copies of

it, the apostles bid farewell to the Virgin and set out on mission.[3] In Rouergue *Ascension* 108, after the Descent of the Spirit, Peter preaches his customary sermon (Acts 2: 14–36).[4]

Although Pentecost was a favourite season for performing vernacular passion plays, few of them include this event, most having ended, like the gospels, with the Resurrection appearances or, at latest, the Ascension. In French, only the Arras/Gréban group includes the election of Matthias and the coming of the Holy Spirit – followed in Gréban 450 by a '*moralité finable*' which reintroduces the Four Daughters of God. Having welcomed the triumphant Jesus back to Heaven, Mercy and Truth embrace, Peace and Justice kiss one another (Psalm 84: 11).[5] Alsfeld is the only German *Passion* to include the election of Matthias and the descent of the Spirit (852). The play ends with Jesus sending Michael down to dispatch the apostles on their missionary journeys.

Whereas Pentecost is the end of the passion plays it is followed in the English cycles and the *Actes des Apostres* as performed in Bourges in 1536, by a number of episodes which may include legends of the apostles, the Death and Assumption of the Virgin, Antichrist and the Last Judgement.

ACTS OF THE APOSTLES

Many wonders also and signs were done by the apostles in Jerusalem.

(Acts 2: 43)

Since a large part of the material in most of the post-Pentecost plays is legendary, the plays on the apostles will be noted only briefly. The Bourges *Actes*, like other French plays, is inclusive rather than selective: some 62,000 lines long and performed over forty days, it treats at length the post-gospel lives of all the apostles (including Paul) together with the Assumption of the Virgin.[6] Elsewhere the playwrights are more exclusive. Some of the Dutch dramatisations of the early chapters of Acts are strongly anti-papist.[7]

The Conversion of St Paul (Acts 8: 9–24) is the single most popular subject; Paul also appears with St Peter in plays based on the early chapters of Acts, especially the story of Simon Magus, which forms a whole *livre* of the Bourges *Actes*, culminating in the martyrdom of both saints.[8]

The story of Mary Magdalene (*Legenda*, 25 July), though omitted by the Bourges *Actes*, proved attractive to other dramatists. The Digby *Mary Magdalene* and the Florence *Miracolo di Santa Maria Maddalena* both begin with scenes of the worldliness and conversion of Magdalene. The rest of the legend of the penitent who became the saint of Marseilles goes beyond the biblical limits of the present study. Several performances of a Mary Magdalene play are recorded in France in the sixteenth century but we have no idea of the precise content: the *Vie de Marie Magdaleine* which begins, after Pentecost, with Lazarus selling his goods (cf. Acts 4: 34) was first printed in 1605.[9]

THE ASSUMPTION OF THE VIRGIN

Although the doctrine of the bodily assumption of the Virgin Mary was not formally declared dogma until 1950, it had been widely accepted in both Eastern and Western churches since the eighth century and plays on the feast-day (15 August) were, and still are, particularly common in Spain, which has the only extant liturgical play of the *Assumption*. The text, from Vich, includes the *Quem queritis?* trope, with the '*sepulcro*' referring here to the grave of the Virgin (Donovan 96). Catalan *Assumption* plays survive from Prades and Valencia. The latter, a fifteenth-century actor's role for Mary with detailed stage directions, was performed in church over the two days of the feast: the death (Dormition) of Mary on the 14 August and the Assumption on the 15 August. The frequent musical interludes and use of the *aracoeli* (mechanical lift) indicate a performance very similar to that of modern-day Elche. Innsbruck and N. town also make much use of music. In *Legenda* and many plays the '*Exitu de Egypto*' is sung during the funeral procession.[10] Most plays follow fairly closely the story as given in *Legenda*: the apostles leave Jerusalem to preach the gospel. Mary goes each day to visit the sites associated with Christ's Baptism, Fasting, Passion, Burial and Ascension.[11] Realising she is near death, Mary prays that she may see the apostles again before she dies. God sends Gabriel with a palm from Heaven as a sign that her plea has been heard. The apostles (including Paul but often not Thomas) are transported by angels to her house from all parts of the world. Mary takes leave of them and dies and Jesus comes and takes her soul to Heaven. In Valenciennes 20-day and late editions of the *Actes* he sends Gabriel (see Lebègue, *Actes* 164). The disciples prepare to bury her. Jews try to disrupt the funeral procession but they are struck blind and when their leader tries to throw down the coffin, his hands remain fixed to it. They are only healed by conversion and prayers to the Virgin.[12] Mary is buried in the valley of Jehosaphat. The following day, Jesus returns, bringing her soul which is placed in the coffin in the presence of the apostles. Then the Virgin rises from her coffin and is taken bodily up into Heaven where she is crowned and seated next to her Son.[13] The York *Appearance of Our Lady to Thomas* is unusual in form. During Thomas's journey from India he recalls the Passion; then he finds himself alone in the Valley of Jehosaphat where, to the accompaniment of music, he sees Mary borne aloft by angels. She tells him to take the news to his brethren and gives him her girdle as token. He bids her farewell and meets the apostles, who refuse to believe him and upbraid him for not having come to the funeral. Even the girdle does not convince them till they see the empty grave; then, reunited in brotherly love, they return to their mission fields.[14]

THE DESTRUCTION OF JERUSALEM

Jerusalem, Jerusalem, thou that killest the prophets ... Behold your house shall be left to you, desolate.

(Matthew 23: 37–8)

In popular Christian writings, Josephus' historical account of the siege and destruction of Jerusalem in 66 AD (believed to be foretold by Jesus in the gospels, cf. Matthew 24: 2) soon acquired legendary accretions, culminating in the eighth-century Latin text, *Vindicta Salvatoris (Vengeance for the Saviour)* in which the Roman destruction of Jerusalem is portrayed as a deliberate act of vengeance on the Jews for the death of the Saviour. Vernacular prose and verse narrative accounts based on the *Vindicta* are extant from the twelfth century onwards in many languages.

Legenda also includes the first part of the incident: the story of the healing of the leprous emperor, Vespasian, by Veronica's holy-image cloth, and the account of the death of Pilate, based on apocryphal texts of the *Mors Pilati* (Death of Pilate). A play of these two episodes is intercalated into the Resurrection play of the *Ordinalia* (II 121). The emperor (Tiberias in this version), hearing of the miracles wrought by Jesus, sends messengers to Pilate to send Jesus to Rome to cure him of his diseases. They arrive to find Jesus has been crucified by Pilate but learn of Veronica's miracle-working relic and persuade her to come to Rome with them. She denounces Pilate, who is taken to Rome as a prisoner. Tiberias is healed by Veronica and converted, but Pilate has managed to obtain Jesus' robe (see p. 254), and when he is wearing it no one can harm him, as Tiberias discovers. Eventually Pilate is forced to remove it, is imprisoned and commits suicide. His body will not rest in the earth and is finally put into an iron box and thrown into the sea. The devils take him to Hell.[15]

The stories of Veronica and Pilate form the first part of the three-day French *Destruction of Jerusalem (Vengance Jhesuchrist)* composed in about 1435 by Eustace Mercadé of Arras.[16] The emperor having been healed by Veronica, the Romans determine to avenge the death of Christ and, after a long debate on the ethics of their actions, set off for Jerusalem on a crusade. The last part of the *Vengance* describes the horrors of the siege in great detail followed by the slaughter of the Jews after famine has forced them to surrender. The Innsbruck destruction scene, which forms the second part of the *Assumption*, omits Veronica and Pilate. Here the destruction of Jerusalem is seen rather as the result of the Jews' rejection of the apostolic mission.

A number of performances of Mercadé's *Vengance* (often in conjunction with a *Passion*) are recorded, especially in northern France and the Burgundian Netherlands.[17] It is not surprising that these plays, with their emphasis on arms and the deeds of knights, should have appealed particularly to the Dukes of Burgundy or to the nobles who gathered to see the play in Metz in 1437.[18]

The destruction of Jerusalem was a subject less open to criticism on grounds of 'popery' than the story of the Passion, which is probably why the burghers of Coventry presented a *Destruction* cycle play in the late sixteenth century after the Corpus Christi plays had been banned. The details of this cycle have not survived and it is uncertain if the English plays included the legends of Pilate and Veronica which link the earlier versions with the biblical drama.[19]

ESCHATOLOGICAL PLAYS

> For these are the days of vengeance, that all things may be fulfilled, that are written.
>
> (Luke 21: 22)

Closely connected with the biblical cycles is the group of plays linked with the Second Coming of Christ on the Day of Judgement, as foretold in Matthew 24–5, and including the parable of the Ten Virgins, first dramatised in the twelfth-century bilingual *Sponsus* play.[20]

Since the parable is essentially about the Last Judgement, the plays are not moralities, where repentance and penance may achieve belated but effective salvation. The wise virgins are unable to share their oil ('merits') because it is made clear in the gospel that, at the Last Judgement, it will be too late to ask for help from anyone. In the plays even the Virgin Mary is powerless. According to the chronicles, when a play of the *Ten Virgins* was performed at Eisenach in 1321, the Landgrave Frederick was so appalled at Mary's inability to protect the foolish ones that he suffered an apoplexy from which he never completely recovered.[21]

In Künzelsau 179 the story is explained by the Rector, who emphasises the judgemental element strongly; the wise virgins are briefly summoned and received into Heaven by God, and the rest of the play is devoted to the foolish ones who appeal in vain to Peter and then to the Virgin before being taken off by Lucifer and his fellows. The Thuringian plays follow a similar pattern (though here the wise virgins are given a larger role before being received and crowned by the Virgin). One version includes much of the biblical text in sung Latin elements, the other emphasises the character of the foolish virgins especially their slothfulness.[22] The most elaborate play is the Dutch one in which the wise virgins are named Fear of God, Hope, Faith, Charity and Humility. At the end, instead of a judgement scene in the presence of the Virgin Mary, a voice announces the arrival of the Bridegroom for the wedding feast. Heaven opens to show the waiting Bride; with music and incense, the wise virgins are individually welcomed, crowned and seated; after more music including the *Te Deum*, Heaven is closed and Hell opens. The foolish virgins (who are also named)[23] knock at the door of Heaven but are turned away by the Bridegroom because, he says, 'You have prayed too late.' A lengthy devil-scene and lamentation follows as they are taken to Hell.

The parable of the Ten Virgins was not the only story to come out of the prophecies and warnings about the Second Coming, which, for the writers of the New Testament, was not a distant prospect but imminent (cf. II Thessalonians 1: 7–10). The most apocalyptic book in the New Testament, the Apocalypse or Revelation of John the Divine, also gave rise to plays: the *Apocalypse* by Louis Choquet (1541) dramatises the visions of St John on Patmos as described in Revelation, alternating them with scenes from the persecution of the Christians. In Antwerp, plays on each of the first seven chapters of Revelation were performed on waggons in successive years.[24]

It was also from Revelation that writers took the events that fleshed out the story of the false prophet foretold in the gospels and in the epistles of John: Antichrist.[25] A major development in the legend of the false messiah, the antithesis of Christ, came in the *Libellus de Antichristo* (*Little book of Antichrist*) composed by a monk, Adso, in the tenth century. This formed the basis of the first extant Antichrist play, the celebrated twelfth-century Latin text from Tegernsee. This elaborate drama which includes kings, emperors, soldiers, prophets, Jews, Christians, *Synagogua* and *Ecclesia*, shows Antichrist's rise to power and domination of the world by means of fake miracles and the help of the hypocrites. The prophets Elijah and Enoch are sent back to earth to fight against him. They are put to death and Antichrist declares himself God; thunder peals out and he falls. The horrified spectators are brought back to the Christian faith by *Ecclesia*.[26]

The vernacular Antichrist plays include a brief scene in Künzelsau, which omits all the kings and warriors but brings in apostles and devils. The fourteenth-century Besançon *Judgement* includes an Antichrist preface linked with the Great Schism. The followers of Antichrist include false bishops and cardinals while his principal opponent is the (true) Pope (237). The only English version, from Chester, is preceded by the *Prophets of Antichrist*, in which Old Testament prophecies by Ezekiel, Zechariah and Daniel are followed by John's forecast of the coming of Enoch and Elijah and an exposition of the Fifteen Signs of Judgement.[27] Chester *Antichrist* play includes scenes of wonders worked by Antichrist culminating in apparently raising the dead; kings bow down to him as the new Messiah. Enoch and Elijah appear and challenge Antichrist, explaining that his 'miracles' were but '*mervelles thinges*' (424) done with the help of the devil, and proving it by the power of consecrated bread. Antichrist slays them and the kings who have turned against him, but then Michael appears, tells him his allotted time is over, and kills him. Devils come and remove the body and Michael raises up Enoch and Elijah and takes them to Heaven.

The stress in these plays is on the marvels of Antichrist rather than the violence. The balance is redressed, however, in the three-day *Antichrist* (culminating in the Last Judgement) performed in Modane (Savoy) in 1580 and 1606. Only part of the text has survived but sufficient to show that here Antichrist is specifically identified with Protestantism. A 'prelate' disputes with Antichrist's followers who reject the doctrine of Purgatory, and concludes: '*Voilà une raison certaine/ contre la secte lutheriste*' (117), while among the elaborate list of *feintes* (many of which involve blood from the corpses and tortures) the organiser had to arrange to put out the eyes of '*le catholique*' (another opponent of Antichrist).[28]

And many of those that sleep in the dust of the earth, shall awake: some unto life everlasting, and others unto reproach.

(Daniel 12: 2)

The third group of eschatological plays is also the largest. Plays, tableaux and mimes with verses depicting the Last Judgement featured in many Corpus Christi processions and cycles. There are no Latin liturgical texts but there are dramatic *laude* for the season of Advent (during which the congregation was asked to meditate on the four last things: Death, Judgement, Heaven and Hell) including a substantial play from Perugia which begins with a short Antichrist scene (I 40). There are also independent plays of the Judgement from Rouergue, Modane, Florence, Mondovi, Majorca and several towns in Germany.[29]

As with the parable of the Ten Virgins, the core of the Judgement plays is found in the gospels, especially Matthew 24–5. Jesus tells his hearers of the signs and warnings that will precede the Son of Man's 'coming in the clouds of Heaven with much power and majesty' (Matthew 24: 30). The angel will sound the Last Trump, then the quick and the dead will be summoned and divided: the 'sheep' (the saved) on Christ's right hand and the 'goats' (the damned) on the left hand. The distinction will be based entirely on good works: feeding the hungry, tending the sick and dying, and clothing the naked, for (to use the familiar words from the Authorised Version of the Bible) 'Inasmuch as ye have done it unto one of the least of these my brethren, ye have done it unto me' (Matthew 25: 40; hereafter referred to as the 'Inasmuch' clause).[30]

In most plays, from the Perugia *lauda* of 1330 to the extensive plays of the fifteenth and sixteenth centuries, the souls are summoned and divided on the 'Inasmuch' clause. In three of the English cycle plays the souls are anonymous and the emphasis is on the spectacle of Christ in Majesty and the appearance of the Hell's mouth to which the devils take the damned (see fig. 8). Chester goes further by introducing pairs of souls – popes, kings, queens, emperors – one saved and one damned. The judge and the merchant are both damned (448). Exceptionally this text stresses that the saved died repentant and have been through Purgatory. Künzelsau adds to an otherwise very simple play a debate between the Body and Soul as to who is to blame: Lucifer firmly takes possession of both (208) but in a similar dialogue in Welsh, the Soul is saved by the intercession of the Virgin.[31]

In the (generally longer) non-cyclic plays, the main interest is the selection of the damned. A few examples of these variations must suffice. Majorca, Perugia and Rouergue all introduce personifications of the Seven Deadly Sins: the costumes in Majorca are graphically described (see *Staging* 144). Perugia includes a strong attack on sodomites (I 49) and hypocritical members of confraternities (I 52) – criticisms echoed in Florence, where a hypocrite who has joined the 'sheep' is winkled out by Michael and moved over to the 'goats' despite his protests of regular churchgoing, fasting and alms-giving (III 502). Michael points out to this premature Tartuffe that his actions were only for show and that God sees the heart: 'all you did was for praise' (cf. Jesus' denunciation of the pharisees: Matthew 23: 13). More surprisingly, Solomon too is damned in the Florence play, despite his claims to have built the Temple, written the Books of Wisdom and been a prophet (III 503).[32] The Besançon *Judgement* 249 damns a usurer with his wife and child, as well as a lawyer who asks leave to appeal: this is disallowed (385). Other paving stones on the road to Hell are gaming, lying and sins of the flesh. Rheinau adds oath-breaking, failing to honour father and mother, and failing to keep the sabbath (I 292).

The German plays, Florence, and Rouergue include the intercessions of the Virgin Mary as in some of the Ten Virgins' plays. In all cases she is unsuccessful though she tries hard and in Rouergue even intercedes for the devils. In Rheinau, Christ tells her firmly to sit down and stop talking: 'in my heart there is no mercy' (299). Elsewhere he is equally firm but more tactful. In Perugia for example he asks her 'to please be silent' (*per tacere ormaie te piaccia*: I 44). In Florence *Judgement*, individual groups appeal in vain to their patron saints: merchants to St Nicholas; prostitutes to Mary Magdalene; clerics to St Peter. Even the poor are rejected by St Francis because they have not borne their poverty willingly but been malicious, resentful and proud (III 507).

It is rare for the Judgement plays to end with the blessed being led into Heaven. Much more usual and perhaps more effective as a warning to the audience is a final emphasis on the tortures of the damned. In Rouergue, this takes the form of a series of dummies, representing the Deadly Sins, being tortured on stage, one by one, by the devil who represents their particular Vice: Mammon tortures Avarice, Satan: Envy (164). Then Satan speaks an epilogue, reminding the audience of their fate if they do not repent and reform: 'May God protect this audience from evil.'

5. Painted animals: Chester Noah play (Leeds, 1984).

6.   Mercy: the Parliament of Heaven (York, 1994).

7.   Crucifixion with painted wooden Christ (Poland, 1970s).

8. Vertical mansions with Hell's mouth: the Last Judgement (Chester, 1992).

Conclusion: survival and revival

THE AGE OF TRANSITION

In the sixteenth century, as in the twelfth, religious drama underwent a series of fundamental changes. The civic and liturgical plays which had existed side by side since the twelfth century continued to flourish but were now challenged by a new religious drama. A detailed analysis of these developments is beyond the scope of the present study and only a few examples can be given here of the polemical, historical, humanist and school drama which, combined with the development of the professional theatre, with its need to cater to the taste of the paying audience, eventually overwhelmed and replaced the essentially amateur and theocentric civic cycle and passion plays of medieval Europe.

Factors which militated against the continuation of the medieval tradition included religious reform, political change and the influence of classical humanism on literature and the arts; but neither Reformation theology nor renaissance humanism was directly the cause of the disappearance of the mysteries. The situation was more complex than that and varied considerably from one country to another.

Least influenced by the new developments was Spain. Apart from Catalonia, religious drama had only developed after the *Reconquista*, and the Peninsula had never had the strong independent civic drama of, for example, England or Germany. Virtually untouched by Protestantism, the Spanish church in the sixteenth century was dominated by the Jesuits, whose teaching on church and lay order and discipline was to be spread throughout Catholic Europe by the Counter-Reformation and the edicts of the Council of Trent. Some changes there were: plays in church were expressly forbidden by Trent, thus putting an end to many of the Catalan Christmas traditions and presumably the Majorcan *Consuetas* performed in Palma cathedral. One exception to the ban was the town of Elche which, by a papal bull of Urban VIII in 1632, was authorised to continue its ancient traditional *Festa d'Agost* which includes a play in church of the Dormition and Assumption of the Virgin Mary, first recorded in 1370 and still performed annually.[1] More widespread in Spain, and not affected by the Tridentine ban, were the Holy Week ceremonies and tableaux and especially the Corpus Christi procession which also continues today with unabated enthusiasm and popularity.[2] The Castilian plays of the Madrid codex, mentioned frequently in the course of this study, witness to the subject-matter of these plays in the middle of the sixteenth century: religious allegory and episodes from the Bible or lives of the saints. The crucifixion is never staged though plays include symbols or allegories of the Passion. Christmas plays were composed for Corpus Christi as well as court performance.[3]

In Italy which, like Spain, remained more or less unitedly Catholic, the fate of the extra-liturgical drama was rather different. As d'Ancona puts it, the plays were not suppressed, they just fell from favour.[4] The successors of the noble or patrician rulers of Florence and Ferrara who had supported and inspired the *sacre rappresentazioni* turned their attention to the new comedy and then, when that palled, to the even newer delights of the melodrama and the opera. For a time *Commedie spirituali* were popular, for example the plays of Cecchi, many of which were written for and performed by religious houses. Gradually the Church's attitude hardened, influenced by St Charles Borromeo who was totally opposed to church drama of any kind. In the south at least however, there is evidence that Holy Week and Christmas plays continued to be written and performed.[5]

The situation in France, Germany and the Netherlands was more complex, because there Reformation and Counter-Reformation confronted one another with military as well as philosophical forces. There were a small number of Catholic anti-Protestant polemical plays as well as more indirect attacks such as the Modane *Antichrist*.[6] In France, the development of the drama after the middle of the sixteenth century has to be considered in two parts: Paris, and the rest of the country. As already mentioned, the ban on the religious plays of the *Confrérie de la Passion* in 1548 was as peculiar to that company and city as the original monopoly had been: the *Confrérie* was barred from putting on any religious plays in Paris, but elsewhere passion and other biblical plays continued to flourish at least till the outbreak of the wars of religion. In the more remote provinces, including Brittany, Dauphiné and Savoy, passion and saints plays (structurally revised to suit the changing tastes of the time) are recorded up to the Revolution.[7]

PROTESTANTS, PURITANS AND THE PLAYS

In the early days of the Reformation, both Calvinists and Lutherans allowed, and sometimes even encouraged, the writing and performing of plays on biblical subjects.[8] Luther, though opposed to dramatisations of the Passion, was willing to see Christ portrayed on stage in school plays but not as a man to be wept over and pitied. Even the strict moralist and predestinarian Calvin prohibited only the clergy from acting and, albeit reluctantly, allowed performances of biblical plays in Geneva, where the *Acts of the Apostles* were performed in 1546.[9]

Since the Protestants saw themselves as the successors to the Old Covenant which linked Man directly with God without the intermediary of the Church, the majority of Protestant plays are from the Old Testament. Particularly popular were stories which could be used to draw parallels with the contemporary situation: in 1550 Calvin's successor in Geneva, Theodore of Beza, published his successful *Abraham sacrifiant*, which contains an attack on idolatry and a clear political allusion to the pressures that had led Beza and many other Huguenots to abandon the 'land of false gods' (France) and seek refuge elsewhere.[10]

For those Huguenots who remained in France, the bitter political struggle between powerful Huguenot nobles and the weak Catholic King led to open warfare after the St Bartholomew's day massacre in 1572. A dramatic footnote to the struggle is the performance in the Huguenot stronghold of La Rochelle (while it was under siege from the Catholic forces of the Crown in 1572–3) of a tragedy of *Holofernes* whose author, Mme de Soubise, however, '*n'a pas imité l'exemple de Judith*' (did not follow Judith's example).[11]

Some Protestant plays, especially Bale's *God's Promises*, and Rueff's *Adam* and *Passion*, are in the medieval tradition and have been included in the analysis of biblical texts. On the other hand, Bartholomew Krüger's five-act cycle play produced in 1580, though it follows medieval tradition in the range and choice of material (from the Fall of Lucifer to the Last Judgement), is highly original (and strongly Lutheran) in its treatment. In Act One Lucifer complains that the place on God's right hand occupied by Jesus Christ belongs by right to him.

He enters Heaven, with his followers, carrying his chair, and tries forcibly to interpose it between the Father and the Son: God the Father expels him from Heaven. Christ is also (exceptionally for Germany) included in the Trial in Heaven scene where the Son offers to help man (who has just fallen) even before Justice obliges God to expel man from Paradise for his fault. The middle three acts present scenes from the Nativity, Baptism, and Burial of Christ (the Crucifixion is reported by Satan) followed by the Harrowing of Hell, Resurrection and Ascension. The fifth act presents the Last Judgement, but though the division of the saved and the damned is made on the customary 'Inasmuch' principle (see p. 151), those saved are all Lutherans who have faith in Jesus Christ, while the damned include Catholic clergy and monks who claim they have helped the poor and the hungry by saying Masses for them or by faithful repetition of the Office.[12]

Though biblical plays might be permitted in Lutheran towns, liturgically linked plays were not. In 1561 Hans Sachs composed a play of the whole Passion, designed for a Christian audience: *vor einer Christlichen Versammlung zu spielen*. It starts with the Last Supper and is a conflation of the four gospels with virtually no additional material. Yet already, in Sachs's Nuremberg, the traditional Easter celebrations had been gradually abolished: in 1498 it was decided to move the *Osterspil* (Easter play) presented on *Osternacht* (Easter night) to Good Friday. In 1526, the Protestant religious leaders of the town wrote to Strasburg to say that in future the Litany, Processions and Way of the Cross, the Entry into Jerusalem on Palm Sunday, with the *Palmesel* (figure of Christ on a donkey) and the passion play on Good Friday were all to be given up 'on good Christian grounds'. Also abolished was the Resurrection play at the sepulchre in the church and the procession of the sacrament on Corpus Christi through which 'Christ is made an actor' (*spilman*), together with all the '*histori*' (plays?) presented on that occasion.[13] This theme is echoed in a 1569 Dutch Calvinist satire on the Catholics who process about in the street and '*there play and counterfeite the whole passion, so trimlie with all the seven sorrowes of our lady*'.[14] A number of Protestant texts from the middle of the century used farce and allegory to dramatise their virulent and explicit mockery and criticism of Catholic beliefs and practices.[15]

In England, too, in the reign of Elizabeth, papist feasts like Corpus Christi were quickly abolished (1567) and the independence of the towns which had staged the plays was also curtailed by the prudent and increasingly absolutist monarch. Despite changes to the texts and a reduction in the role of the Virgin Mary (even, in Coventry, a change of subject-matter from the Passion to the Destruction of Jerusalem; see p. 148), the cycle plays had been finally and definitely banned by the end of the century, though this was as much, it seems, on political as on dogmatic grounds.

Plays on biblical subjects continued to be written and performed for some years, but, either for political reasons or at the insistence of the Puritan element (especially in the Calvinist branch of the Reformed Church) God was eventually banned from the professional stage in Protestant Europe.[16] The disappearance of God and the Virgin (accompanied by angels) led also to the disappearance of the devil in his powerful if comic medieval form. Marlowe's Mephistopheles is the last stage devil to possess still a certain stature. Thereafter, devils dwindle away and are trivialised, not because men did not believe in Hell – there were devils at Loudun and witch-hunts at Salem – but because, it seems, they had lost faith in mercy.[17]

HUMANIST AND SCHOOL DRAMA

The humanism which is reflected in many of the later French *mystères* also encouraged the development of Latin school and university drama by both Catholics and Protestants. The Latin *Theothanatos* (*God's Death*) by the Italian Stoa (written probably while he was teaching in France and published there in 1515) presents some of the events of Holy Week with long laments and speeches, and a use of messengers and narrators reminiscent of (though much inferior to) the *Paschon Christos* which was published in 1542.[18] The *Theothanatos* was probably never staged but it influenced a more successful work by a Frenchman, Barthélemy. His *Christus Xylonicus* (*Dying Christ*) was favourably viewed by the contemporary humanists, twice published, and was imitated by, among others, Nicholas Grimald in his *Christus redivivus* (*Risen Christ*) composed in Oxford in 1543. Both Barthélemy and Grimald introduce some comedy into their plays, imitated from Plautus.[19]

One of the most successful humanist writers was George Buchanan, who was born in Scotland and educated in France. He claimed to be a Catholic but was accused of Lutheran tendencies and was even tried by the Inquisition in Lisbon. During a stay in the Collège de Guienne in Bordeaux (1539–42) he composed plays on Jephthah and John the Baptist. In *Baptistes*, the story of John the Baptist and Herod is explicitly treated as an attack on Henry VIII's execution of Thomas More for refusing to support Henry's divorce from Katharine of Aragon. Although the play is therefore favourable to the Catholic martyr against the English king, the play was performed in Cambridge in the reign of Elizabeth (1562–3).[20]

The most influential and long-lasting creators of school drama were the Jesuits, whose schools, throughout Europe, regularly presented Latin and Greek dramas performed by the pupils.[21] Nor did the Jesuits limit their pedagogic drama to Europe: their missionaries carried the tradition to the Far East, Japan and South America. The first Jesuit plays were recorded in Manila in the Philippines in 1610 and the tradition evidently survived, for a picture of the Holy Week celebrations in the Philippine island of Marinduque in 1978 (published in the *Observer* magazine for 28 April) shows a masked and costumed Longinus, whose repentance and martyrdom are apparently the culmination of the festivities there.

COMEDY OF FEAR AND THE THEATRE OF CRUELTY

Though the Edict of Nantes, which finally ended the wars of religion in 1598, guaranteed political and religious freedom for Huguenots, France remained essentially a Catholic country.[22] In the provinces, community drama and feast-day processions continued as in the rest of Catholic Europe; but in the capital, which ultimately dominated the cultural thinking of France, the medieval play was dead: in 1597, the *Confrérie de la Passion* had persuaded the new king, Henri IV, to authorise them to play '*mystères sacrés*'; eighteen months later the Parlement banned them again and the king conceded the point.[23]

The professional companies who now rented the Hôtel de Bourgogne from the *Confrérie* did not present the *Acts of the Apostles*, with its scenes of torture and execution so beloved of earlier audiences, nor did they aim at the neo-classical imitations of Seneca played there after the original ban in the middle of the century: they staged historical plays full of scenes of torture and violence – a theatre of cruelty, with multiple staging, sensationalism and atrocities equal to the most blood-boltered on the English Jacobean stage.

A fundamental difference exists, however, between the theocentric medieval biblical *Actes* and these anthropocentric historical plays in their attitude to evil. In the former, the scenes of violence are interspersed with comedy embodied in the devils or their avatars such as the ubiquitous, globe-trotting executioner who tortures all the

apostles in turn. Daru takes a fiendish delight in his skills: he is not just
an executioner, but *the* executioner:

> Good at hanging, good at flaying,
> Good at roasting, good at slaying.
> Cutting off men's heads for burning;
> To draw or flog I'm most discerning;
> In all I am the best by far.
>
> (My translation).[24]

This kind of black humour not only distances the audience from the
horrors, it distances the horrors from men. The medieval audience
could console itself for the violence inflicted by seeing the perpetrators
as diabolically inspired. Behind Herod, Judas, Pilate or the tormentors
of Christ were all the infernal legions, tempting them. Moreover, since
the protagonists were God and his saints, their suffering, though
agonising, was not dehumanising. It inspired pity and admiration
rather than horror. The audience could be entertained by the devils
who inspired the torture of the martyrs or actually performed the
torments of the sinners in Hell, for Heaven awaited the faithful, and
God's mercy (especially when mediated by the Virgin) was more
powerful that man's sinfulness.

But the professional theatre of cruelty was dealing with men, not
devils; history, not pious legend. The difference can be illustrated from
two late sixteenth-century plays from the Books of Maccabees. The
Haarlem *Der Machabeen* and the French *La Machabée* both treat the story
of a mother forced to watch her seven sons tortured to death before her
eyes, before she herself is killed (II Maccabees 7). In the Haarlem play
(which also includes the story of Eleasar, II Maccabees 6) the emphasis
is on the pressures brought by King Antiochus to force the Jews to
conform to local heathen custom and eat pork: a valid dramatic subject
in a period of religious oppression. Most of this play follows the biblical
discussion between King Antiochus, his advisors and Eleasar, or the
steadfast defiance of the sons and the mother while the deaths –
detailed and violent as any in the *Acta sanctorum* – take place off stage. A
very different approach is used by Virey de Gravier in *La Machabée*,
where the stage is occupied by gloatingly described tortures being
inflicted on the sons and eventually the mother. Unlike the medieval
saints' plays, there is no comic devil or consoling angel to relieve the
suffering. Instead, lest the audience should miss one detail of the

horror, King Antiochus directs operations from his throne like a surgeon in Rembrandt's *Anatomy Lesson*:

> Ouvrez lui l'estomac, car je veux qu'on lui voie
> le poumon, intestins, et les lobes du foie.
> (Open up his body, for I want to see his lungs,
> intestines and the lobes of the liver.)

The smooth formalism of the alexandrines only emphasises the plain nastiness of the subject-matter. Any audience watching this play could indeed feel that like Macbeth it had 'supped full with horrors'.[25]

CLASSICISM, THE ENLIGHTENMENT AND THE BIBLICAL PLAY

This melodramatic theatre was a comparatively short-lived phenomenon.[26] In the age of Classicism and the Enlightenment, although plays based on the Old Testament and Jewish history were performed in the professional theatre,[27] the New Testament, especially the Passion, virtually disappeared from the public stage even in Catholic countries. These changing fashions will be briefly examined through three texts, one on each of the three facets of the *Ludus Christi*: Nativity, Passion and Judgement.[28]

The tradition of composing wide-ranging plays for the Christmas season survived in Spain and the Spanish colonies in Mexico and South America right through to the nineteenth century[29] and probably inspired the large number of Christmas plays, both learned and popular, composed and performed in the Spanish-governed Kingdom of the two Sicilies (southern Italy and Sicily).[30]

The *Nascitá di Gesu' Bambino* (1759) by the Sicilian author Catalano, for example, survives in two forms, one popular and one learned. The latter is in three acts of some 1,200 lines each: the first two include short scenes of Mary and Joseph travelling to Bethlehem, hampered by the devil and assisted by angels; in Act Three the Child is born and the shepherds come to the manger. Around this core (which forms the bulk of the short, popular, prose text) is woven a long romantic melodrama involving King Herod and his wife, Amoralba, who is in love with Herod's faithful attendant, Stillandro, who is really a woman in disguise. Between whiles, Nymphs and Neptune mingle with Lucifer and Bezebuc while Arcadian shepherds celebrate their pastoral life. The love intrigue involving Herod's queen may have been inspired by the historical account of Herod killing his wife, Mariamne, for alleged infidelity. The episode had formed the basis of Pordage's English *Herod and Mariamne* (1673) which has a different but equally complex plot, and the theme subsequently achieved tragic status in Hebbel's *Herodes und Mariamne* (1850).[31]

Even more wide-ranging is the curious evolution of another Sicilian play, the third part of a Latin trilogy composed in 1569, by the Jesuit, Stefano Tuccio of Messina. Designed for school performance, his play consists of a nativity (*Christus nascens*), a passion (*Christus patiens*) and a judgement play (*Christus judex*). The *Christus judex* (which included the story of Antichrist) was performed in Latin in Rome in 1573–4 with considerable success. A contemporary description suggests a complex structure with a large cast and some form of multiple staging.[32] It was translated into Italian in 1584, and a revised translation was printed in Verona in 1596. A hundred years later another revision, duly updated, was published in Rome, this time with musical additions including an introduction and a duet between Lucifer and Michael. Not content with this, the same reviser, Antonio Cutrona, rewrote the whole work as a music drama (published in Florence in 1721) in three acts with interludes and choruses: Antichrist was a (presumably *castrato*) mezzo-soprano; Enoch, a bass; Jesus, a tenor; and God, a baritone. Meanwhile the original Latin text had been performed and published in Germany (1603); a Polish version was printed in Warsaw in 1725 and a Serbo-Croat edition also came out during the eighteenth century.[33]

The Last Judgement does not feature again in drama or music theatre until the revival of the English cycles in the twentieth, but Passion plays have a more continuous tradition though information about them is rare with one notable exception: Oberammergau. But even the best-known passion play in the world has had a varied textual and performance development.[34] The text used for the first perfor-mance in 1634 was based on a fifteenth-century version from Augsburg; it was '*widerumben renovirt*' (again renewed) for the 1664 performance, when the Augsburg play was conflated with a humanist text by Sebastian Wild, who himself also borrowed elements from Grimald's *Christus redivivus*, published in Cologne in 1543.[35] Performances continued at ten-year intervals (moving to the beginning of the decade in 1680) with various text revisions: in 1740 it was rewritten in alexandrines, on the lines of an Italian opera, with allegorical figures representing Sin, Death, Avarice and so on. In 1770 a general official censure of passion plays meant that for the only time in its history the play was not performed at all, but in 1780, thanks to the intervention of friends in high places, the play was once again officially sanctioned. Later performances were disorganised or postponed temporarily by war but never again was the play banned.[36]

In the nineteenth century, the text was revised and simplified first by Father Weiss from the monastery at Ettal and then by Weiss's pupil, the parish priest, Alois Daisenberger, whose script has been standard since 1860. The music was also rewritten: 'The music of the Passion Play has preserved that originality which Rochus Dedler, schoolmaster at Oberammergau gave to it in 1820. The Haydn–Mozart style is evident.'[37]

Although the Oberammergau *Passion* was never, therefore, really a medieval play it shows marked affinities with the German passion texts of the fifteenth and sixteenth centuries, especially from Lucerne and the Tyrol. Daisenberger's text is strongly biblical but he retains (or restores) some of the traditional additions, such as the scene of Christ's farewell to the Virgin and the disciples in Bethany, which is found in Augsburg and many other medieval texts (see p. 127.) The absence of devils and comedy is typical of the south German passion tradition and it is really only the classical-type choruses, which have replaced the *Proclamator*'s exegesis in Augsburg or the Latin antiphons and responsories of the Eger or Tyrol plays, that distinguish the modern Oberammergau text from its remote German medieval ancestors.

After visiting the play in 1890, Dean Farrar wrote of his impressions and defended the play against accusations of blasphemy and commercialism but expressed his doubts about the desirability of its survival: 'It may well be questioned whether the suppression of the play has not at last become desirable. When it degenerates into a European spectacle criticised in all the newspapers by hundreds of reporters as though it were an opera in Dresden or Vienna, it becomes alas! a fatal anachronism. It is endangered by an alien atmosphere.'[38] Blasphemy? Anachronism? Commercialisation? The same questions have been asked many times since; nevertheless Oberammergau has not merely survived, it has become part of the great revival of the Play of God in modern Europe.

Oberammergau has also inspired other passion plays: in 1900, a priest from Nancy visited the play and was moved to copy the example of the Bavarian village in his much larger town in Lorraine. In 1904, the Nancy clone of the German play was performed in the courtyard of the presbytery of St Joseph's parish in order to raise funds to build a new church. It was repeated annually for some years, then at approximately four year intervals (except 1939–69) in a purpose-built theatre and on a much larger scale. One of the original participants who, at four years old, was blessed by Christ during the Entry into Jerusalem, commented in 1981: '*C'était du théâtre, bien sûr mais j'y croyais presque*' (it was a play, of course, but I almost believed it).[39] Although the text and structure of the play and stage are very similar in the two instances, the effect is quite different because they are staged by different types of people.

Oberammergau's passion is a community play: it involves all the members of the village, many of whom are woodworkers or potters. Nancy is a large industrial town where, like the *Confréries de la Passion* of medieval France, a small proportion of the population drawn from all walks of life join together under the President of the *Théâtre de la Passion* to stage the play on behalf of the rest of the townsfolk. The emphasis at Nancy, as at Mons or Bourges or Châteaudun, is on the visual, with rich costumes and decors (though the modern ones are carefully planned to be as biblically authentic as possible), and the publicity leaflets describe the *Jeux de la Passion* as '*la plus grande fresque biblique jouée en France*' (the biggest biblical fresco performed in France). The difference betwen the French and German *Passions* (as relevant for the fifteenth as for the twentieth centuries) is well summed up in a letter to Anton Lang by a Canadian clergyman who in 1922 saw both of them (as well as one at Erl in Tyrol): 'he called Erl a "religious spectacle for the people", Nancy a "display of theatrical effects", and Oberammergau "divine service"'.[40]

MEDIEVAL TRADITION AND THE MEDIEVAL TEXT

If Dean Farrar had been able to see ahead some thirty years he would have been even more afraid that Oberammergau might be contaminated by publicity and commercialism, for in 1922 'an American motion picture company made an outstanding offer of several millions' to make a film of the passion play.[41] The American offer was ignored, despite the depression of the German mark which meant that the receipts of the 1922 performance barely covered the costs of the play. But a new element had entered the history of the biblical play – the cinema, whose popular appeal and possibility of unlimited performances may be considered the most important new development in the field since the beginning of professional drama four hundred years earlier.[42]

In 1912 the first of many films was made on the life of Christ, the greatest probably being the 1927 *King of Kings* with H. B. Warner as Christ, a simply told, beautifully photographed and acted presentation of the gospel story. Though the many subsequent treatments of the subject have had the benefit of colour and modern special effects, these, like the machinery in Florence or the *feintes* at Bourges, have served only to make bigger, rather than better, productions.[43] Television has not had a good record in biblical drama but radio generated one of the most successful modern passion cycles: Dorothy L. Sayers's *The man born to be king*.[44]

Concurrently with the early biblical films, revivals of the medieval plays also began to be staged. In England, Nugent Monk and his successors had to struggle against the Lord Chamberlain's ban on putting any member of the Trinity on stage (only finally removed in 1968), but Gustave Cohen in France had no such problems to compete with and the '*Théophiliens*' (named after their first production, the *Miracle de Théophile*) performed adaptations of the Anglo-Norman *Adam* and Michel's *Passion* in Paris in the 1930s.[45] Cohen's programme notes for one of these performances contains an interesting comparison: '*[Le] fameux dialogue de Notre Dame et de Jésus qui n'est pas inférieur en grandeur aux stichomythies de la tragédie antique*' (the celebrated dialogue between Our Lady and Jesus which equals the great stychomythic dialogues of classical tragedy).[46]

Cohen's aim was not so much to explore the peculiarly medieval nature of the plays as to show that (with careful pruning and despite a lack of the unities) they were capable of equalling the classics in power and dignity.

Nevertheless the move to reinstate medieval plays was gaining force and when in 1951 through the efforts of E. Martin Browne, parts of the York cycle were performed in the city for the first time in nearly four hundred years, the dam was breached and a flood of performances followed.

In the English-speaking world, this 'medieval' drama can be divided into two kinds: the first includes those productions which follow the medieval tradition of community, usually (but not essentially) amateur, drama, often with a church or other religious background. The text of these plays is usually modernised and selected from different parts of the English cycles – Chester *Noah* and Wakefield *Second Shepherds* being particular favourites.[47] Less medieval in inspiration though more accurately medieval in text are the 'reproductions' by academics which seek to recreate the productions and costumes as well as the language of the originals. Not all plays produced by scholars belong to this category, however, though some attempt at historicity is often found.[48]

The growing interest in medieval plays has led to increased awareness of the surviving 'medieval' traditions on the Continent. The Oberammergau and Nancy *Passions* continue to attract thousands of spectators; the Elche *Assumption* play has been filmed and televised and draws large audiences each year, as do the other traditional Holy Week and Corpus Christi plays and ceremonies in Spain and Italy, or the dramatic processions in the Netherlands, such as the Bruges *Ommegang* or the penitential processions in Veurne. Popular and academic traditions do not necessarily conflict: the SITM triennial colloquia have encouraged the public production of plays from many languages and traditions, thus recreating a form of play contest in the old tradition of the Netherlands but with prizes limited to the plaudits of the local public or the reviews of academic colleagues. On such occasions medieval tradition and medieval text can be seen to blend.

The biblical drama of medieval Europe began in the churches with the *Visitatio sepulchri*. It is fitting therefore to end this brief survey of the resurrection of the medieval plays with a mention of a new *Visitatio sepulchri* drama, by James Macmillan, premiered at the Edinburgh Festival in 1993, a thousand years after the original first performance. A reviewer spoke of 'such a charged spectacle of resurrection drama ... that it didn't occur to me until afterwards to wonder why Jesus (a key-player, you might think) made no appearance'.[49] A medieval audience would not have expected to see Jesus at the sepulchre for the Play of God does not depend on his presence but on his activity: nowhere was he more active than in the Resurrection.

Appendix: the liturgical context of the plays

This account of the structure and music of the Catholic liturgy aims only to provide enough information to explain the references in the body of the main text and in the plays.[1] There were many local variations in the rite and in this Appendix, the Latin texts are drawn from the first printed edition of the *Missale romanum* of 1474; most of the English translations of the Latin texts are from the 1662 Book of Common Prayer (BCP) which is virtually identical with the earliest official English version of the liturgy in the Prayer Books of Edward VI (1539 and 1542).

THE LITURGICAL CALENDAR AND THE CHURCH YEAR

The Church year contains two parallel series of feasts.[2] The *Temporale* (based on the life of Christ) begins with Advent and runs through from Christmas to Pentecost. The date of Easter, the principal festival of the Church, is not fixed, so many feast days can occur on a range of dates. The limits for the major feasts are included in the calendar below. The *Sanctorale* lists feasts of Our Lady and the saints throughout the year.

The week begins on *Dominica* (Sunday, or *feria i*, though the latter term is rarely used) followed by *feria ii–vi* and *Sabbato* (Saturday; *feria vii* is also rare). A ferial day may be a saint's day which then takes precedence, liturgically, with certain exceptions.[3] Major feasts of both the *Temporale* and *Sanctorale* are celebrated for a whole week or octave: for example, the Sunday after Christmas is *Dominica in octavam Nativitatis*. Sundays are sometimes also known by the opening words of the Introit. Thus the Fourth Sunday in Lent where the Introit begins *Laetare Jerusalem* (Rejoice Jerusalem) may be called *Laetare* Sunday.

The following list shows the principal festivals and holy days relevant to the drama. Since the Church calendar was the normal form of dating for all kinds of documents in the Middle Ages, not only English, but also other vernacular translations are included, mainly French and German since Spanish and Italian are usually very similar to Latin. Where more than one is given, French precedes German; the language of any other variant is given in brackets. (*D.*= *Dominica*. *In f.* = *In festo*: on the feast. *BVM* = *Beatae Virginis Mariae*: (of the) Blessed Virgin Mary. JB = John the Baptist. Feasts marked * are only found in later editions of the *Missale).*

The Church year 1: Temporale

Nov. 27–Dec. 3 *D. Prima de Adventu:* Advent Sunday (Fourth Sunday before Christmas, followed by three more Sundays *in Adventu*)

Dec. 24 *In vigilia Nativitatis Domini:* Christmas Eve

Dec. 25 *In Nativitate Domini:* Christmas Day, *Noël, Weihnacht, Nadal* (Catalan)

Dec. 28 *In f. SS Innocentium*: Holy Innocents, Childermas

Jan. 1 *In die Circumcisionis Domini*: Circumcision of Christ

Jan. 5 *In vigilia Epiphaniae Domini*: Twelfth Night

Jan. 6 *In Epiphania Domini*: Epiphany, Twelfth Day, *Jour des Rois, Dreikönigsfest*, followed by up to five Sundays *post Epiphaniam*[4]

Feb. 2 Presentation of Christ in the Temple. (See *Sanctorale*: Purification of the BVM) (The sequence of preparation for Passiontide and Easter may overlap the Purification)

Jan. 18–Feb. 22 *D. in Septuagesima*: Ninth Sunday before Easter followed by *Sexagesima* and *Quinquagesima* Sundays

Feb. 3–Mar 9 *In vigilia Cinerum*: Shrove Tuesday, *Mardi gras, Fastnacht* (end of Carnival Season)

Feb. 4–Mar. 10 *Feria quarta Cinerum*: Ash Wednesday.[5] This marks the beginning of the forty days of *Quadragesima:* Lent, *Carême, Fasten*[6]

Lent 4: *Laetare* Sunday: mid-Lent, *mi-carême*, Mothering Sunday[7]

Mar. 8–Apr. 11 *D. de Passione*: Passion Sunday (Lent 5)

Mar. 15–Apr. 18 *D. in Palmis*: Palm Sunday, *les Rameaux*, begins the *Hebdomada Major*: Holy Week, *Karwoche, Semaine sainte*[8]

   Feria v In Cena Domini: Maundy Thursday, *Jeudi saint, Gründonnerstag*[9]

   Feria vi in Parasceve: Good Friday, *Vendredi Saint, Karfreitag*

   Sabbato Sancto: Holy Saturday, *Karsamstag*

Mar. 22–Apr. 25 *Dominica Resurrectionis*: Easter Day, *Pâques, Ostertag*
   D. in octavis Pasche: D. in Albis, Quasimodo, Low Sunday. Four more Sundays after Easter: *post Pascha*

Apr. 30–Jun. 3   *In f. Ascensionis Domini*: Ascension Day (Thursday)
   (*D. infra Octavam Ascensionis*: Sunday after Ascension)

May. 10–Jun. 13   *In die Pentecostes*: Whit Sunday, Pentecost, *Pentecôte, Pfingsten*

May. 17–Jun. 20   *In f. Trinitatis*: Trinity Sunday

May. 21–Jun. 24   *In f. gloriosissimi Corporis Christi*: Corpus Christi, *Fête-Dieu, Fronleichnam, Antlass* (Thursday after the octave of Pentecost)

The rest of the Sundays in the *Temporale* are simply numbered after Pentecost.[10] See under *Sanctorale* for the feast of the Transfiguration.

The Church year 2: Sanctorale (saints' days)[11]

Nov. 30   *In die S Andree Apostoli*: Andrew

Dec. 6   *In S Nicholai*: Nicholas[12]

Dec. 8*   *In Conceptione BVM*: Conception of Mary

Feb. 2   *In Purificatione S Marie (In lucem domini)*: Purification of BVM, Candlemas, *Ste-Marie Chandeleor, Lichtmess*

Mar. 25   *In Annuntiatione S. Marie*: Annunciation, Ladyday

May. 3   *In Inventione S. Crucis*: Finding of the Holy Cross, Holy Cross day

Jun. 24   *In die S Johannis Baptiste*: Birth of John the Baptist, *St-Jean, Johannistag*, Midsummer

Jun. 29   *In die Apostolorum Petri et Pauli*: Peter and Paul

Jul. 2*   *In Visitatione BVM*: Visitation, *Maria Heimsuchung*

Jul. 22   *Die S. Marie Magdalene*: Mary Magdalene

Jul. 25   *Die S. Jacobi*: James (the Great, son of Zebedee), *Santiago* (Spanish)

Jul. 26*   *In f. S. Anne matris BVM*: Anne, mother of BVM

Aug. 6   *In f. Transfigurationis Domini*: Transfiguration

Aug. 15   *In Assumptione BVM*: Assumption

Aug. 29   *In decollacione JB*: Decollation of John the Baptist

Sep. 8   *In Nativitate BVM*: Birth of BVM

Sep. 29   *In festivitate S. Michaelis archangeli*: Michaelmas

Nov. 1   *In die Omnium Sanctorum*: All Saints, *Toussaint, Alleheiligen*

Nov. 2   *Commemoratio omnium fidelium Defunctorum*: All Souls, *Jour des Morts, Alleseelen*

Nov. 21*   *In f. Presentationis BVM*: Presentation of Mary in the Temple

PROCESSIONS

Processions with banners and relics form part of the liturgy of most major feasts, either inside or outside the church. In central and eastern Europe, the Palm Sunday procession often included a wooden representation of Christ on a donkey (*Palmesel*); in England the Host, representing Christ, was carried with the relics. However, only Corpus Christi is essentially a procession of the Sacrament. In addition a church or town might celebrate the feast of its patron saint with a patronal festival including a procession with tableaux or plays, for example St John's day in Florence.[13]

THE MASS AND THE BIBLE

Although the central Canon of the Mass (which includes the Prayer of Consecration or Eucharistic prayer) was laid down in the fourth century and remained virtually unchanged, elsewhere there was considerable variety of verbal and musical usage during the Middle Ages.[14] The Epistles, Gospels and other items 'proper' to the Mass of the day throughout the year are prescribed according to the calendar; the Propers vary in both text and music depending on the particular Sunday or feast day. Other elements of the service are 'common' all the year round; the Common (or Ordinary) of the Mass always has the same text but may vary musically.[15]

The following outline of a Solemn or High Mass according to the Roman rite gives only the principal elements of the service, identifying the participants and marking them C. (Common) or P. (Proper). Numerous local variants are found.[16]

Introitus (Introit)	Choir P.
Kyrie eleison (Lord have mercy)	Choir C.
Gloria	Choir C.
Collect	Celebrant P.
Epistola (Epistle)	Sub-deacon P.
Graduale (Gradual)	Choir P.
Alleluia (or Tract)	Choir P.
Evangelium (Gospel)	Deacon P.
Nicene Creed	Choir C.
Offertorium (Offertory)	Choir P.
Praefatio (Preface)	Celebrant P.
Sanctus (Holy, holy, holy)	Choir C.

The Canon of the Mass   Celebrant C.
Pater Noster (Lord's prayer)   Celebrant C.
Agnus dei (Lamb of God)   Choir C.
Communio (Communion)   Choir P.
Ite missa est (Dismissal)   Deacon C.

THE CANONICAL OFFICE (DAILY HOURS)

The Office, established by St Benedict in his *Rule* according to the liturgical customs of the earliest Church, consisted of eight short services or Hours said at intervals through the day: Mattins, Lauds, Prime, Terce, Sext, Nones, Vespers and Compline.[17]

Mattins (morning): the 'night Office'

Lauds (praise): immediately after Mattins or at dawn

Prime: first hour

Terce: third hour

Sext: sixth hour (noon)

Nones: ninth hour

Vespers: the evening Office

Compline (*Completorium*): 'completed' the Hours.[18]

Whereas the Mass, with the Words of Institution at the Last Supper and readings from the gospels and epistles, is centred on the New Testament, the biblical backbone of the Office is the Psalter. A number of psalms are appointed to be sung in each of the Hours, together with prayers and a brief reading (*Capitulum* or Little Chapter). The Little Hours (Prime, Terce and Sext) only have one variable – the antiphon which is 'of the day'. The principal Hours, however, especially Mattins and Vespers, also include a number of other elements, some based on biblical texts.[19]

Mattins, the longest of the Hours, contained from three to nine lections 'of the day', arranged in nocturns, each of which consisted of three psalms, each sung under its own antiphon, followed by three readings with their responsories. The readings of the first nocturn were drawn from the Bible or the Legendary (lives of the saints). On major feasts the readings of the other two nocturns included sermons on the relevant topic by the Fathers and doctors of the Church. Many details of the material used in the plays are drawn from these lectionary sermons.

In addition to the lections, three canticles from the gospel of Luke are included in the Office: the *Benedictus* (Blessed be the Lord God of

Israel) sung by Zacharias at the Birth of John the Baptist (1: 68–79), at
Lauds; the *Magnificat* (My soul doth magnify the Lord), the song of the
Virgin Mary at the Visitation (1: 46–55), at Vespers; the *Nunc dimittis*
(Lord, now lettest thou thy servant depart in peace) sung by Simeon at
the Presentation in the Temple (2: 29–32), at Compline. The *Hymnum
trium puerorum* (Song of the Three Holy Children: Daniel 3: 57–88)
beginning '*Benedicite, omnia opera*' (Bless ye, all the works) is recited by
the priest at the end of Mass on his way to the sacristy.[20]

The *Te Deum laudamus* (We praise thee O Lord), described as a
canticle but actually a third-century hymn, is sung after the ninth
responsory at Mattins, at the end of High Mass on feast-days, and at
other celebrations, including the end of many plays.[21]

In the later Middle Ages the Office was supplemented by a number
of popular devotions of Our Lady. The Angelus is based on the angelic
salutation (*englische Grüss*) to Mary at the Annunciation: '*Ave Maria gratia
plena*' (Hail Mary full of grace); the *Ave Maria* is also the principal
prayer in the devotion of the Rosary.

HOLY WEEK

A number of special rites and ceremonies may be added to the liturgy
during Holy Week.[22]

Tenebrae (darkness) refers to a custom practised during the night
Offices of Mattins and Lauds of the *Triduum*: while the lections from the
Lamentations of Jeremiah are sung the candles are gradually extinguished leaving the church in darkness. The *Improperia* (reproaches),
also from Jeremiah, are sung on Good Friday during the Adoration of
the Cross.[23]

The ceremonies of Easter Eve include the kindling of the new fire
and the blessing of the paschal candle. Then follow Old Testament
lections of the Creation, Noah, Abraham and Exodus, followed by
prophecies from Isaiah, Jeremiah, Ezekiel, and the story of the fiery
furnace from Daniel.

MUSICAL LITURGICAL TEXTS

The basic elements of liturgical devotion are prayers, readings from the
Bible and recitation of psalms. 'Additions consist principally of
conventional formulas for introducing and ending each of these
elements ... In these latter places music ... plays an important role.'

The 'additions' most often used in the plays are the *responsorium,* (respond, responsory), antiphon and trope.[24]

A *responsorium* was a chant which followed and commented on a lection, and its theme was therefore 'of the day'. It had two parts: a verse (versicle) sung by a cantor and a response sung by the choir.[25]

Antiphonal chants originally meant simply a piece sung by two alternating choirs, one singing the psalm and the other repeating the refrain (antiphon) between each verse. This principle was later simplified in various ways, so that, for instance, the Offertory or Communion of the Mass, originally antiphonal chants, now consisted of a single verse sung by the whole choir.

The term 'antiphon' may also be used for any separate uncategorised piece sung for a special purpose, e.g. the 'Great O Antiphons' sung instead of the usual antiphon to the *Magnificat* at Vespers in Advent 3 and 4. The name comes from the opening words of the text, e.g. '*O Clavis David*' (O key of David).[26]

The term 'trope' was variously used to describe a musical or verbal (or both) addition to an already existent text.[27]

The differences of liturgical practice between different countries and communities is echoed in the varied use made of the liturgical material in the plays. An index of *Incipits* (opening words) of medieval musical items is given by Hughes.[28]

LITURGICAL BOOKS

The three books needed for the Mass, i.e. Sacramentary (containing the prayers), Lectionary and *Cantatorium* (containing the sung items) were combined into one Missal in the eleventh to twelfth centuries. In the early centuries, when both priests and religious said the Office in church, the Office books were also divided into sections, but with the founding of the mendicant orders in the early thirteenth century, an abridged, combined Office book was needed that could be carried round by an individual friar. This was the Breviary. The chants for the choir continued to be copied in special manuscripts with musical notation, for example a *Processionale,* antiphoner, troper, or *Liber gradualis*.[29]

THE *SYMBOLUM* (CREED)

One of the earliest parts of the liturgy to be established was the Apostles' Creed (*Credo, Symbole des Apôtres, Glaubensbekenntnis*) which contains the basic tenets of the Christian faith. Its formation is dramatised in a number of plays and its stress on the triple activity of God as Creator, Redeemer and Judge provided the tripartite structure of many Corpus Christi cycles.

The *Symbolum* was glossed and commentated on in devotional and iconographic works, and the following list, showing which part was attributed to which apostle is based on Joinville's *Credo* which also includes related prophecies.[30]

(1) *Credo in Deum Patrem omnipotentem creatorem celi*   Peter (Jeremiah)
et terre
(I believe in God the Father almighty
maker of heaven and earth)

(2) *Credo in Jhesum Christum filium eius unicum*   Andrew
Dominum nostrum   (Nebuchadnezzar)
(and in Jesus Christ his only Son our Lord)

(3) *qui conceptus est de Spiritu Sancto natus ex Maria*   James (Isaiah)
Vergine
(who was conceived by the Holy Ghost
born of the Virgin Mary)

(4) *passus sub Pontio Pilato crucifixus et mortuus et*   John (Esdras)
sepultus
(suffered under Pontius Pilate was crucified
dead and buried)

(5) *descendit ad inferos tertia die resurrexit a mortuis*   Thomas (Hosea)
(he descended into Hell the third day he
rose again from the dead)

(6) *ascendit ad celos, sedet ad dexteram Dei Patris*   James the Less
omnipotentis   (David)
(he ascended into Heaven and sitteth on
the right hand of God the Father almighty)

(7) *inde venturus est judicare vivos et mortuos*   Philip (Joel)
(from thence he shall come to judge the
quick and the dead)

(8) *Credo in Spiritum Sanctum*   Bartholomew
(I believe in the Holy Ghost)   (Zechariah)

(9) *sanctam Ecclesiam catholicam*   Matthew (Solomon)
(the holy Catholic Church)

(10) *sanctorum communionem remissionem peccatorum*   Simon (Micah)
(the communion of saints the forgiveness of
sins)

(11) *carnis resurrectionem*. Jude (Thaddeus)
    (the resurrection of the body) (Ezekiel)
(12) *vitam eternam*. Amen Matthias (Daniel)
    (and the life everlasting) Amen

The Apostles' Creed is recited in several of the canonical Hours (including Mattins) but not during Mass, where it is replaced by the Nicene Creed which omits the words 'he descended into Hell' (see article 5) but is otherwise merely a fuller version of the *Symbolum*.

The *Quicunque vult* (Whoever wishes) or Athanasian Creed, replaces the Apostles' Creed on certain feast days; it is primarily concerned with the nature of the Trinity. When dealing with plays where the central character, Creator, Redeemer and Judge, may simply be called *Deus* throughout it is well to be reminded that: 'the Father is God, the Son is God and the Holy Ghost is God. And yet there are not three Gods but one God.'

Notes

In addition to the general Abbreviations listed on p. xix, the following are used in the Notes:

OT   Old Testament
NT   New Testament
VT   *Viel Testament*
MS (S)   Manuscript(s)

To avoid overloading the already substantial Notes section, only authors and short titles of works cited are given here, with full references in the bibliographies. Short (mainly English) reference titles are used for plays throughout. The bibliographical index, arranged alphabetically by these reference titles, normally includes an original language title. Arabic numbers after a title or description refer to the pages of the editions cited.

INTRODUCTION: CHRISTIAN EUROPE AND THE PLAY OF GOD

1 For the text of the Creed and its traditional medieval attribution to different apostles see Appendix.

2 Egeria (also known as Etheria or Silvia) went on a pilgrimage to Jerusalem in the fourth century soon after Constantine had made Christianity the official religion of the Roman Empire, see L. Duchesne, *Christian worship* 547–77. Egeria also highlights the language problems of the Church: in Jerusalem the rites were always in Greek (with simultaneous translation into Syriac) and the Latin pilgrims had to be content with the assistance of bilingual religious among the congregation (ibid. 576).

3 For Palm Sunday ceremonies in Poland from the Middle Ages to the present day see T. Bela, *Palm Sunday ceremonies in Poland*, and H-J. Diller, *A Palmesel from the Cracow region*.

4 The True Cross was believed to have been rediscovered by St Helena, the mother of Constantine. See *Legenda Aurea* Invention of the Holy Cross (3 May).

5 The distinction between Orthodox and Catholic did not come into use for the two Churches until after the schism of 1035.

6 *St John Damascene on Holy Images* 15. The Second Council of Nicaea (787 AD) restored the cult of images, see G. Dumiège, *Histoire des Conciles*, IV 187–9.

7 The main source of information on these sermons is the study by G. La Piana: *Le sacre rappresentazioni nella letteratura bizantina*. I am most grateful to my former colleague, Leslie Barnard, who translated some of these Greek texts for me when I was working on the Byzantine drama for the SITM Dublin Conference of 1980.

8 For details of these passion plays see chapter 2.

9 Two indispensable reference books are the *Cambridge History of the Bible*, vol. II. *From the Fathers to the Reformation*, and Beryl Smalley, *The study of the Bible in the Middle Ages*, henceforth referred to as *Cambridge Bible* and Smalley, *Bible* respectively. The *Vetus Latina* was used by a number of the early patristic writers, including Augustine, so that some of their OT quotations are from the Septuagint (*Cambridge Bible* 98–100). Jerome also included from this Greek translation of the Hebrew Bible (made in Alexandria probably in the second century) a number of works treated as apocryphal in the Hebrew text and modern translations from it. Among these so-called 'deutero-canonical' texts are the Books of Tobit and Judith, and the stories of Susannah and Bel and the dragon from the Book of Daniel which have been used as subjects for vernacular plays.

10 Jerome's Vulgate became, and has remained, the standard Bible of the Catholic Church, providing the lections of the liturgy and the Latin texts of the biblical plays. However, from the tenth century onwards, vernacular translations of the scriptures in both prose and verse began to appear for private reading and devotional study, culminating in the appearance *c.* 1260 of a complete translation of the Bible into French prose, authorised by the University of Paris. (See S. Berger, *La Bible française au moyen âge*; J. Bonnard, *Les Traductions de la Bible en vers français au moyen âge*, and *Cambridge Bible* 338–491.)

11 See *The Rule of Saint Benedict*, chs. 8–18. (For the *Rule* in England and the early plays see p. 14.) For details of the *Opus Dei* and the seven daily Hours see Appendix.

12 For a full list of the biblical lections for the Church year see *Cambridge Bible* 234. Herman of Valenciennes, who translated parts of the Bible into French verse in the twelfth century, followed the lectionary in his choice of material from the gospels (see Herman of Valenciennes, *Li Romanz de Dieu et de sa mere*, ed. I. Spiele, 40–5).

13 In *The seven ages of the theatre* Richard Southern points out that for theatre there must be a minimum of two 'pieces ... the Player and the Audience. Take these apart and you can have no theatre' (1).

14 Cf. C. Morris, *The discovery of the individual, 1050–1200*.

15 'The keynotes of the age were two – restless activity and uncontrolled sentiment' (K. E. Kirk, *The vision of God* 362). Kirk sets out very clearly the importance of these changes for the spiritual life of both clergy and laity.

16 See Marjorie Reeves, *The development of apocalyptic thought: medieval attitudes* 51.

17 These two works were widely known throughout Europe both in Latin and in vernacular translations. In the analysis of the plays any detail

borrowed from them is simply ascribed to *Legenda* or *Meditationes* with no attempt to identify the particular version used in a particular play. The page references for *Meditationes* are to Ragusa's English translation.

18 A useful guide to the influence of Nicholas of Lyra on the French plays is in Roy *Mystère* 207–39. Woolf's invaluable study *The English mystery plays* has a rich variety of source details, including some for the continental texts.

19 Among the most influential were the *Passion des jongleurs*, the English Northern *Passion* and the German epic, *Die Erlösung* (*The Redemption*). These narratives bequeathed to the vernacular plays the use of contemporary realism in their interpretation of life in Jerusalem in the time of Jesus: eating and drinking, buying and selling are basic both to the Bible and the medieval bourgeois, while violence and torture add spice to the spiritual significance of gospel scenes and saints' lives.

20 For the different kinds of groups and their plays see chapter 2.

21 Only in the Netherlands with their urbanised aristocracy did the burghers actually take part in the tourneys and hastiludes, but in many countries the jousts were held in specially constructed wooden halls or in market places surrounded with spectator stands: see R. Barber and J. Barker, *Tournaments: jousts, chivalry and pageants in the middle ages* 43–5.

22 Kirk, *Vision of God* 96.

23 The chronicler's account: *De repraesentatione ludi Christi* and details of the later credal cycle are printed in Young, II 540 and De Bartholomaeis, *Origini* 486.

24 These words come from the opening prologue composed specially for the Mons performance by Jehan Fossetier, a priest from Ath (G. Cohen, *Livre des prologues* and *Matinee IIIe* 7). Cohen's edition of the *Livre de Conduite ... de la Passion joué a Mons en 1501*, is the only source for this special version of the *Passion* (referred to hereafter as Mons *Passion*). Only the directors' copies, with stage directions and the first and last line of each speech, have survived together with the separate book of prologues and the full text of one day.

25 For the lack of liturgical and early vernacular drama in Spain and Portugal see Donovan ch. 2. The political changes are discussed in D. Hay, *Europe in the fourteenth and fifteenth centuries* 150–7.

26 It is regrettable that the Proceedings of the SITM conference in Dublin in 1980, which dealt with the drama of Eastern Europe, have not been published. Some of the material cited here is from the draft texts made available during the conference. The Croatian drama has presented particular difficulties because of the political situation in former Yugo-slavia and I am grateful to Ivona Ilić for translating the quotations in the typescript of Slobodan Novak's paper on the subject. I have not been able to see a copy of F. S. Perillo, *Le sacre rappresentazioni croate* (Bari, 1975). There are no extant medieval play-texts from (Catholic) Slovenia but the text of an early eighteenth-century processional passion play from Skofja

Loka, intended for performance on Good Friday, contains a long scene for Death which echoes the medieval Dance of Death; those under Death's power include: 'popes, bishops, canons and cardinals'. I am grateful to Alasdair McKinnon for sending me this reference and translating the speech for me.

27 See J. Veltrusky, *Medieval drama in Bohemia*. Texts of some of the plays are given with English translation in the same author's *A sacred farce from medieval Bohemia*. 'John Huss was widely regarded as a Wycliffite' (Hay, *Europe* 346) and in 1557 John Bale lists among the biblical and classical plays performed at Hitchen school in Hertfordshire a tragedy *De Io. Hussi damnatione*. (Bale's letter is cited by T. H. Vail Motter in *The school drama of England* 226.)

28 See György E. Szönyi, European influences and national tradition in medieval Hungarian theater, 159–72. See also Hay, *Europe* 241–4.

29 Among the first plays performed at the newly established theatre at the court of Czar Alexis (1645–76) were translations from German biblical plays including 'comedies' of Adam and Eve, Joseph, Esther and Judith. (Unpublished SITM Dublin paper by J. Roberti.)

30 See Bela, *Palm Sunday ceremonies*. I am grateful to Irena Janicka-Śviderska for information on *The history of the glorious Resurrection*. The draft of the Dublin paper by Eleonora Udalska (who also sent me photographs of modern Polish performances) mentions a scene of the Marys buying spices from 'Ruben', the importance of the role of the devils and the influence of the *Glorious Resurrection* on later Polish religious drama.

31 For Dublin and Cornwall, see Lancashire's *Dramatic texts and records* which are arranged alphabetically. The Kilkenny Corpus Christi tradition is studied in Fletcher's The civic drama of old Kilkenny. Brittany has close links with French plays; see G. Le Menn, *Histoire du théâtre populaire breton XVe–XIXe*.

32 See Mill, *Medieval plays in Scotland* 113–293. The civic records are arranged alphabetically.

33 See A. E. Davidson, *The Quasi–dramatic St John Passions from Scandinavia and their medieval background*, and *Holy Week and Easter ceremonies and dramas from medieval Sweden*. For a Swedish vernacular miracle of the Virgin see S. K. Wright, Iconographic contexts of the Swedish *De uno peccatore qui promeruit gratiam*, in *Medieval drama on the Continent of Europe*. Unfortunately this book appeared too late for me to make full use of the material in it.

34 St Anselm, *Basic writings*, trans. S. N. Deane 35.

35 The essential changes in both Protestant and Catholic traditions are analysed in Kirk, *Vision of God* 429–38.

1 LITURGICAL AND FEAST-DAY DRAMA

1 For the different early liturgies see L. Duchesne, *Christian worship, its origin and evolution* ch. 3.

2 These new forms include tropes, sequences and responsories (see Appendix).

3 The St Gallen troper containing this text dates from the tenth century (Young, I 201).

4 The translation used here is from the edition of the *Regularis concordia* by T. Symons.

5 Fleury's 'observance would have been substantially that of Cluny' (Symons xlvii).

6 For the distinctions between the private Mass and the public Mass as said, for example, by the pope, see Duchesne, *Christian worship* ch. 6. The later history of the liturgy can be found in L. Eisenhofer and J. Leichner, *The liturgy of the Roman rite*.

7 For this and other texts of the Christmas tropes see Young, II, ch. 17.

8 Midwives first appeared in the nativity story in the apocryphal gospels. For references see chapter 7 below.

9 There is a *Tractatus stellae* from Zagreb and a number of plays called after the increasingly important character of Herod: *Ad Herodem faciendum* (For presenting Herod). See Young, II, ch. 19.

10 The distinctive features of the Freising text are the variety of incidents included in the play and the strong characterisation of Herod, who first appears here in the form which will become common in later drama, as *Herodes iratus* (raging Herod).

11 According to some commentators it also covered two years: Herod's instruction to kill all the children under the age of two led to a belief that the wise men took that time to reach Bethlehem.

12 For examples of liturgical plays at Ascension or Pentecost see p. 18.

13 The simplest dramatised version of the *Sermon*, from Salerno, survives only from the sixteenth century (Young, II 133. Cf. Donovan 111). For the *Ordo prophetarum* see p. 83.

14 The north–east of Spain, having been the first area to be freed from the Moors, had been put under the diocesan rule of the French bishop of Narbonne and seems to have shared the French enthusiasm for liturgical plays. The eleventh-century troper from the abbey of Ripoll and the customaries of the cathedrals of Gerona and Palma include many references to dramatic ceremonies and plays from an early date. Cf. Donovan, chs. 7–11.

15 The *Sponsus* (Bridegroom), a bilingual text with musical notation for both languages, is preserved in a MS from the monastery at St Martial de Limoges but with no indications of where, when, or by whom it was performed.

16 MSS of every country attest to the continuing role of the basic *Visitatio* play (in its simpler as well as its more complex forms) right through to the late sixteenth century. The numerous texts printed in Young or in Lipphardt do not unfortunately include the important music of the plays. The most useful collection with music is still that of E. de Coussemaker, *Drames liturgiques du moyen âge*.

17 The translation used here is from *Staging* 226–7.

18 The use of a vernacular hymn and the reference to the *populus* (people) are found in several German texts of the Easter play; other language groups end the play with a Latin hymn, usually the *Te Deum laudamus*, even when the 'people' are present. (The *Te Deum* was sung at Mattins, see Appendix). It seems probable that this difference is merely the result of the greater similarity between the Romance languages and the Latin texts compared to the Germanic forms.

19 Since both feast and play were closely connected with the presence of the papal court at Avignon during the so-called Babylonian captivity, it is not surprising that the play does not seem to have survived the Great Schism which followed the death of Gregory XI in 1378 and the return of the papacy to Rome. A translation of the whole *Ordo* is given in *Staging* 207–25.

20 For details of these ceremonies see part two.

21 For the Assumption trope see Donovan 97. An indication of the extreme popularity of the feast comes from Montauban in France (1442) where the Canons and the Carmelites who produced the Assumption play in alternate years quarrelled over who should be allowed to perform when a year had had to be omitted because of plague. The matter was referred to the bishop for judgement. The verdict is not recorded (Petit de Julleville 15–16).

22 It may have been sung during the ceremony of the Adoration of the Cross or, more probably, afterwards, since the elaborate gestures of the characters would have been inappropriate while other liturgical activity was going on. The presence of the crucifix, however, seems certain.

23 The Jasenitz *planctus* is sometimes linked with Bordesholm, a related monastery (Neumann 817). For Laval see Petit de Julleville 203; there is a translation of the Italian incident in *Staging* 248–9. A collection of sermon-plays are described in Szönyi, *Hungarian theatre*, including a performance script of a sixteen-scene passion intercalated into an Easter sermon. The sermon MSS are in Latin but Hungarian translations and records of performances are found from the early sixteenth century. These plays are very different from the Greek sermon-plays, which do not appeal to the emotions.

24 In its surviving printed form the Breton *Passion*, which owes much to that of Jean Michel, dates only from 1530. There is some evidence that it goes back to the fifteenth century.

25 The Cervera play, which has only recently been edited, was revived early this century. The Tyrol texts were collected up and preserved early in the sixteenth century by the painter Vigil Raber of Sterzing, near Bozen; he also revised and directed the performance of many plays in the region. Records from the different towns reveal details of performance and the actors included the local clergy and religious, town officials and members of local guilds and businesses. Cf. J. E. Wackernell, *Altdeutsche Passionsspiele aus Tyrol*, especially XCIV–CIII and CCXXIX–CCXXXV.

26 For the origin and growth of the *disciplinati* and their *laude* see C. Barr, *The Monophonic Lauda*.

27 For texts and history of these plays see De Bartholomaeis, *Origini*, ch. 5.

28 Extracts from these lists are translated in *Staging* 139–40.

29 Some plays, like the Florence *Ascension*, came under the patronage of the Medici and will be considered with the civic plays in the next chapter.

30 According to Arnold von Harff the play included the flogging, crucifixion and Judas' hanging himself, see Neumann 923.

31 'As the Bull shows, the creators of the Corpus Christi intended the celebration to stress the dogma of redemption' (J. Sentaurens *Séville et le théâtre* 36). '*Tunc psallat fides, spes tripudiet, exultet charitas*' (then faith sings aloud, hope dances, charity exults; ibid. 37).

32 See Miri Rubin, *Corpus Christi: the Eucharist in late medieval culture*.

33 This is a variant on the well-known story of St Gregory's Mass (described in *Legenda*, St Gregory, March 12), but in Bolseno the celebrant is not the great pope trying to convert a doubting woman, but a priest who is himself the doubter. The emphasis on the German nationality of the doubting *priest*, suggests a deliberate attempt by the Italian author to belittle the official origin of the feast in German-speaking Liège. The great Dominican theologian, Thomas Aquinas, is said to have composed the Office of the feast shortly before his death in 1274.

34 *Commentaries of Pius II*, trans. F. A. Gragg and L. C. Gabel, XXX 378.

35 The scene of the Last Supper in Michel's *Passion* includes a sequence of speeches by the apostles reminiscent of the Innsbruck play. The lost Creed play from York was also associated with the feast and belonged to the Corpus Christi guild (see *REED*: York).

36 Yarmouth had a Corpus Christi guild and possibly a separate play on Corpus Christi day; in 1350, the Cambridge Corpus Christi guild presented a play '*de filiorum Israelis*' (of the children of Israel). The subject might have been the giving of the Manna to the Israelites in the wilderness, which was a well-known figure of the Eucharist (Lancashire 94). Aberdeen staged a '*haliblude*' (holy blood) play at least twice as well as paying for a Corpus Christi play on an unknown subject (Mill 115–17). It is probable the '*haliblude*' was a Corpus Christi play: in the Tyrol, *Heiligblutstag* (Holy Blood day) was a popular name for Corpus Christi (Dörrer, *Die Bozner Bürgerspiele* 114–15).

37 For the Theseus play see D'Ancona, *Origini*, I 279.

38 For patronal and Rogationtide processions see Appendix.

39 The celebrations in 1462 in Viterbo near Rome, where the pope had a summer palace, are described in the memoirs of Pius II. The Cardinals and other local dignitaries had spent enormous sums on lavish draperies and set-pieces along the route of the procession and several semi-dramatic items are also mentioned including the Resurrection and the Assumption. (*Commentaries of Pius II*, XXXV, 551–6.)

40 For Bohemia, see Veltrusky, Drama 51. Neil Brooks, Processional drama

and dramatic processions in Germany in the Late Middle Ages, treats the German Corpus Christi processions in detail. For the Tyrol see also Dörrer, *Bozner Bürgerspiele*, especially chs. 4–5. Catalan processions are discussed by Shergold.

41 In Castile, the Corpus Christi processions developed a little later but by the middle of the fifteenth century they were established in Seville (Sentaurens, *Séville* 47–50). The accounts of the Cathedral chapter in Toledo for the end of the fifteenth century are rich in details of the procession and the plays performed as part of it (see C.Torroja Menéndez and M. Rivas Palá, *Teatro en Toledo*, Appendix, for the accounts of 1493). The records of the feast in Oviedo are mainly from the sixteenth century onwards (C. C. G. Valdes, *El teatro en Oviedo (1498–1700)*, ch. 1). They include information on the traditional '*gigantes*', the giant figures which are still a feature of Spanish festivities whether for Corpus Christi or the Opening of the Barcelona Olympic Games.

42 For these processions and the feasts of Our Lady from Lille, Leuven and Brussels, see chapter 2. A useful introduction (with map) on the development of the Burgundian Netherlands especially in the fifteenth century is given by Peter Spufford in *The splendours of Flanders. Late medieval art in Cambridge collections*, ed. A. Arnould and J. M. Massing. For the chronicler's account of the Bozen *Umgang* in the seventeenth century, see Dörrer, *Bozner Bürgerspiele* 166–74. For references in the city accounts see Neumann 131–43.

43 Bologna is the only Italian Corpus Christi play for which a dramatic text survives but there are also records from Modena, where the confraternity of St Peter Martyr performed the play of Nebuchadnezzar and the fiery furnace, in both the cathedral and the town on a moving waggon stage. Similar subjects are found in other processions in Italy (D'Ancona, *Origini*, I 279, 288); for Turin see A. Cornagliotti, *Passione di Revello* xvii–xix.

44 Valencia seems at one time to have had plays in the cathedral before the procession set out, for an edict of 1444 ordered the procession to leave the cathedral immediately after Mass without such performances 'for in this much time is lost' (Shergold 67). For city records of the sixteenth-century Corpus Christi plays see Valencia 150.

45 Processional Corpus Christi plays or tableaux from France are recorded from Draguignan and Béthune (Petit de Julleville 208–10, 211–14). In Oudenaarde in the Dutch Netherlands there was a continuous tradition of Corpus Christi and passion plays, the former organised by the Friars Minor (*Kronyk* VI 380). There were also inter–city play-contests (*Landjuweel*) with substantial prizes. Sometimes the subjects were religous and biblical (see p. 39) but in the later sixteenth century Rhetoric became the 'God' of the procession and the meeting. See John Cartwright's description of the procession of Rhetoric in The Politics of Rhetoric: the 1561 Antwerp *Landjuweel*. A 1498 Corpus Christi list from Dublin includes the Nine Worthies and King Arthur with his knights as well as the more usual

biblical episodes (Lancashire 328). Modest–scale guild plays are recorded from Edinburgh and Aberdeen after 1530 and many English towns had processions with dramatic episodes including biblical and saints' plays. (See Mill and Lancashire; the recently published *REED Hereford and Worcester* includes additional references to such mixed processions.)

46 Valencia had Creation and Judgement in a mixed Corpus Christi cycle (150) and Löbau for Holy Cross day (Neumann 433). For examples in passion cycles, see p. 190.

47 In Seville, for example, the craft guilds were responsible (under the direction of the cathedral) for the Corpus Christi processional plays until 1554. In 1532, the Chapter of the cathedral arranged for special places to be prepared for the 'representations' to be staged, and wanted the guilds to include Adam and Eve, the Magi, the Descent from the Cross, Conversion of Constantine and the Judgement, with, if possible, the Ascension and Pentecost. This is virtually a credal cycle of plays. Seville at this date was the principal port of Spain and a flourishing industrial centre, so that the power of the different guilds might be sufficient to take all the financial responsibility for the performances (Sentaurens, *Séville* ch. 1). It is surely significant that the only guild cycle recorded from Spain should also be the only Corpus Christi procession to include the Judgement. Another curiosity is the account of the Corpus Christi processions from Béthune on the border between France and the Netherlands. A series of dramatic processions are recorded for the sixteenth century, but only one, that of 1549, was specifically presented by the craft guilds and, although there is no Creation, a cycle from Annunciation to Doomsday was presented in twenty-eight separate scenes (Petit de Julleville 211–14). There are possibly other similar records still undiscovered in the archives of the towns of France or Italy or Spain.

48 Sometimes in Germany the cycle is only a series of tableaux with no dialogue but at Zerbst, for example, certain episodes were given full dramatic treatment and performed during the procession. Freiburg im Breisgau had a passion play presented by the town's leading guild, the Butchers, every seven years in its proper place in the procession. Biberach guilds performed a full cycle play every ten years on a stage in the market place after the procession in which the guilds also took part; see Brooks, Dramatic Processions 146–56, and Wilhelm Breuer, Aufführungspraxis vorreformatorischer Fronleichnamsspiele. Unusually for France, Bordeaux had both a Corpus Christi procession and also a passion play done by a parish group; the accounts for 1487, for example, show payments at Corpus Christi for those who carried the tabernacle and those who *jogueren la Passion* (acted the *Passion*; see C. Mazouer, *Histoire du théâtre en Bordeaux* 27).

49 For the growth of 'free towns' in the Empire see Hay, *Europe* 199–205.

50 See the facsimile of the N. town manuscript edited by P. Meredith and S. J. Kahrl.

2 CIVIC AND COMMUNITY DRAMA

1 For these texts see Young, II, ch. 25.
2 The absence of play records from Fleury is at first sight surprising, since it is cited as one of the sources for the texts in the *Regularis Concordia* (see p. 14). However, Fleury in the tenth century was subjected to the Cluniac reforms which were opposed to embellishments in the liturgy. It was Cluniac monks who, after the *Reconquista*, restored Christian worship in Spain; the first province to be reconstituted was Toledo in 1086 (Bernard Reilly, *The Medieval Spains* 147). Liturgical Latin plays are virtually unknown in Spain except in Catalonia which had been reconquered earlier (Donovan 70).
3 For the St Nicholas plays from Hildesheim and Einsiedeln see Young, II, ch. 26.
4 The other twelfth-century Latin *Daniel*, performed by the clerks of Beauvais and preserved in a MS with the Office for the feast of the Circumcision (1 Jan), only prescribes the *Te Deum* at the end. It may be significant that at Beauvais the Feast of Fools (the day sacred to the *clercs*) was celebrated on 1 Jan.
5 In later vernacular plays this parable was often closely associated with the Last Judgement: see p. 148.
6 See the introduction to Aebischer's edition of *Adam*, 14–18. Moreover, the MS also includes other works: at the beginning are some Latin hymns and fragments; immediately after the abrupt (perhaps incomplete) end of the prophet play which forms the third episode of *Adam*, there is a French text of the Sibylline prophecy of the Fifteeen Signs of Judgement. If *Adam* was originally written for an Anglo-Norman aristocrat, it could easily have found its way, with him or his family, to the large areas of south-western France which had come under the Norman crown by the marriage of Henry II of England to Louis VII's former queen, Eleanor of Aquitaine. Perhaps having already lost its ending, it was then copied by a rather inept Provençal scribe into a collection of pieces for another noble patron in the south.
7 For the veiling of the cross at Passiontide, see A. Fortescue, *The ceremonial of the Roman rite observed*, ch. 24.
8 For details of the Holy Week forms and ceremonies, see J. W. Tyrer, *Historical survey of Holy Week. Its services and ceremonial.*
9 See Young for the details of the Latin Resurrection plays.
10 The date is much disputed and the play is possibly little older than the manuscript, though Tuilier, the recent French editor, accepts the sixth century as a reasonable date. 'The author belongs to the same period as Gregory of Nazianzus, since the *Paschon Christos* is certainly an ancient work.' (*Paschon Christos* 71. My translation.)
11 The introductory speech is translated in *Staging* 61.
12 For discussion of this text and its relation to Sulmona, see S. Sticca, *The Latin passion play: its origins and development.*

13 The texts are printed by Young but more recent scholarship can be found in the articles by C. Flanigan in *Medieval European Drama*, ed. E. Simon.

14 See Young, II 542 for the chroniclers' accounts of these performances.

15 Young, II 540. The presence of Last Judgement plays links these cycles with the Corpus Christi plays discussed in the previous chapter, and especially with the sixteenth-century three-day play from Freiberg in Saxony which staged the Creation on the first day, the Passion on the second and the Last Judgement on the third (Neumann 327–37). This seems to be the ultimate development of the credal cycle in a non–liturgical context.

16 For example the rubrics in the manuscript from Origny (Young, I 413–19).

17 For details see Notes to the Introduction and the analysis of texts in part two.

18 See the Introductions to the Palatinus and Autun play editions and Grace Frank, *Medieval French Drama*, ch. 13.

19 Where no other source is quoted, references for France will be found in Petit de Julleville, *Les Mystères*, II, under the date and place.

20 All references to Mons are to the introduction to Cohen's edition of the Mons *Passion* of 1501.

21 Plays performed during a guild's annual meeting were not of course contrary to the charter and are known to have been staged, but apart from the *Nativity* included in the Miracles of Our Lady performed for the goldsmiths' guild in the fourteenth century, there is no evidence of biblical plays among these guild performances, which were normally either saints' lives or miracles (see G. A. Runnalls, Medieval trade guilds and the *Miracles de Nostre Dame par personnages*).

22 Contrary to popular belief this ban only applied to Paris. Passion and other religious plays continued to be performed in the provinces throughout the sixteenth century and, in some areas, up to the Revolution. (See Chocheyras, *Savoie* and *Dauphiné*).

23 Gréban's text has been edited twice; all quotations are from the more recent edition by Jodogne. It is one of the bases for the (unpublished) Valenciennes plays of 1547 and 1549 referred to as Valenciennes 25-day and Valenciennes 20-day respectively. The former (extant in two MSS in the Bibliothèque nationale) was definitely performed in the town. The latter, though preserved in the library of Valenciennes, was almost certainly not played there.

24 For the details of the German plays see Bergmann's *Katalog* which lists more than two hundred different religious play-texts including fragments, directors' copies and actors' roles.

25 Because of changing political boundaries the distinction between Low German and Dutch plays is not always clear: the Maastricht play has been described as both. Arnold Immessen's Low German *Sündenfall* (tradition-ally referred to by title not author) has close textual and linguistic associations with the Dutch *Eerste Bliscap*.

26 In addition to the text of the play (edited by Wyss), the Lucerne records are printed in Bergmann and discussed in detail in M. Blakemore-Evans, *The passion play of Lucerne*.

27 Rueff's texts are not included by Bergmann. There is a reference in the Lucerne records (Bergmann 445) to a certain tailor, named Rappenstein, who, inspired by the '*Zwinglisch gifft*' (Zwingli's 'poison' was his Protestant teaching), left Lucerne for the Protestant city of Zurich. This tailor, who had played the part of Christ in 1528, might perhaps have acted instead in one of Rueff's Protestant plays.

28 The Tyrol group of plays were analysed and partially edited in J. E. Wackernell, *Altdeutsche Passionsspiele aus Tyrol*, which is still the main source of comparative information on performance details. The complete records are printed by Neumann and the plays are being re-edited in the series of *Sterzinge Spiele*.

29 Details of the different plays are given in the analysis in part two. Some of the towns have changed their names since the Middle Ages: for example, Bozen is now Bolzano. The old forms are used in the text and maps, with the modern forms cross-referenced in the Index.

30 It is listed with other Italian play–manuscripts in N. Newbigin's *Sacre rappresentazioni fiorentine del quattrocento* liv–lv.

31 Details of the production and of other performances in Piedmont are given in Cornagliotti, *Revello* xiv.

32 It has survived in more than one manuscript (though the others are only fragments) and shows links with the Catalan texts.

33 See the edition of the text and the records in *Toledo* 159–80. The cathedral's involvement with the feast did not usually include writing the plays, which from the end of the fifteenth century were commissioned by the performing guilds from professional playwrights.

34 Bergmann 117–19. See also Brooks, Processional Drama.

35 See P. Meredith, N. town *Passion* 2. There are references to passion plays from Reading though no texts or details survive. I am grateful to Alexandra Johnson for this information from her forthcoming Berkshire *REED* volume.

36 A sixteenth-century dramatisation of the story was printed as *Le Mystère du saint sacrement* and performances are recorded from Metz and Laval (see Muir, The Mass on the medieval stage 317).

37 The epilogue to the seventh Joy, the Assumption, lists the Seven Joys of Mary as Annunciation, Nativity, Epiphany, Finding Jesus in the Temple, Resurrection, Pentecost, Assumption. For an account of the 1556 Brussels *Ommegang* cf. P. Leenderts jr., *Mittelnederlandsche Dramatische Poëzie* 488–95. The French town of Le Puy had a famous statue of Our Lady which was processed annually and for which a special play was composed in 1518; in 1468 scenes, or mimed tableaux, from the Old and New Testament were presented at the *carrefours de la ville* (crossroads of the town) as part of the festival (Petit de Julleville 197). The Leuven procession is described by Meg

Twycross from the sixteenth–century drawings in a Leuven Museum in
The *"liber boonen"* of the Leuven *ommegang*. The history of the Bruges
procession has been studied by W. M. Hüsken in a paper to be published
in the *Proceedings* of the seventh SITM conference at Gerona, 1992. I am
grateful to him for an advance copy of his paper.

38 The Lille plays are being edited by Alan Knight and I am most grateful to
him for making available to me an advance copy of these unusual plays so
that I could include them in this analysis. St Peter's church, which
sponsored the plays from the beginning, possessed the relics of the Virgin
(the precious milk and lock of hair) which were the *raison d'être* of the
Procession de Lille. The plays are not cyclic and there is no indication of
how many plays on what subjects were performed in any one year.

39 Elsewhere in Scotland, as in England and France, the Abbot of Bon
Accort or a similar character presides over secular farces, *sotties*, May
games and Robin Hood plays. For details see Lancashire, Mill, and Petit
de Julleville, *Les Comédiens en France au moyen âge*.

40 See Newbigin xxxix. D'Ancona, *Origini* describes several of these processions (I 233, 245n, 256–7, 273). An eye-witness account of the plays in 1439
is translated in *Staging* 240–2.

41 The Bordeaux Procession is described in Mazouer, *Bordeaux* 30. It was
abolished in 1578 and the deed of abolition states that it was performed by
the *tonneliers* (coopers) of the parish of St Michael and included a play of
the Baptism of Christ. The actors wore long wigs, ecclesiastical vestments
and haloes of wood with their names on them. The same parish also
staged the *Passion* for Corpus Christi. (Wooden haloes were also used in
Valencia 92.)

42 For the accounts of the *Dresdener Spiel*, see Neumann 279–95. An interesting
item for 1502 is *1 groschen* for *stecknadel den juncfrauenn in spil* (pins for the
young ladies in the play). It is not clear if these were actresses or female
roles but the use of the term *juncfrau* makes the former more likely. For
English references see Lancashire.

43 The play from Oberammergau began as the result of a vow in 1634 and
originally used a medieval text from Augsburg. Sometimes these plays
were based on the life of one of the saints noted for intercession against
plague, such as St Adrien, St George or St Sebastian. Four performances
are recorded in Savoy in the mid-sixteenth century; the first from Beaune
in 1546 was also the result of a vow. In Abbeville, parts of the Old and
New Testaments were staged to 'avert the threat of pestilence'. (Petit de
Julleville 54). In 1476, the St John's day ceremonies and '*edifici*' (mansions
on floats) were cancelled in Florence because of the risk of infection being
brought into the city by '*gente di terre ammorbate*' (people from infected areas)
coming to view the spectacle (Newbigin xlvi).

44 School and university drama also existed from the fourteenth century
onwards, probably in Latin, see Lancashire and my article in the *Cambridge
guide to world theatre*.

45 The thirteenth–century *Confrérie des jongleurs et bourgeois d'Arras* may well have been responsible for the only thirteenth–century biblical play in French, *Courtois d'Arras*, a free adaptation of the parable of the Prodigal Son.

46 L. Lefèbvre, *Les Origines du théâtre à Lille aux XVe et XVIe siecles* 15. It is these same neighbourhood groups who performed the *Procession de Lille* see n. 38.

47 In 1444 on their return from Brussels they received 25s as a token of appreciation (*en courtoisie*); but when they won first prize in Aire in 1462 the town gave them £25 towards their expenses. (£sd was the standard money of account in medieval France). They acted on a single waggon which moved from place to place and the city council paid them 4d for each play towards the cost of the '*cars*' (ibid. 357)

48 De-Pas, *Saint-Omer* 347–8. In Mons the rhetoricians are organised both in neighbourhood groups and larger chambers. In 1469, the inhabitants of one district organised a contest for plays (500–600 lines long) on 'an earthly or heavenly subject in honour of God the Creator and Redeemer'. Some of the rhetoricians who took part in a contest in Ghent in 1498 (when the prize went to the Mons Crossbowmen) acted in the Mons *Passion* of 1501 (Mons xiv–xv).

49 See John Coldewey, That enterprising property player. A role somewhat similar to that of the property player was undertaken by Pierre Gringoire, author and actor, who was paid a substantial sum (£100 *parisis*) to organise the *mystères* for the entries into Paris of Louis XII (1498), the Papal legate (1502) and the Archduke (Maximilian of Austria) in the same year. The actual performers were apparently trade guilds and Gringoire's task was to oversee the construction of the scaffolds and the distribution of the costumes (Petit de Julleville 201). In 1542 a certain Lope de Rueda in Seville contracted with one of the guilds to produce an Assumption play on two carts for Corpus Christi: for the sum of twenty-six gold ducats he undertook to provide actors, singers, costumes, scenery and properties (Shergold 100). For more general details on the financing of the plays see below p. 52.

50 S. W. Deierkauf-Holsboer, Les Représentations à Athis-sur-Orge en 1542.

51 See Das Schwäbisches Weihnachtsspiel, ed. E. Simon. A group from the district of Porta Borgne in Perugia performed the story of Jonah on the piazza in the afternoon of the feast of St John; other groups played on other feast-days (D'Ancona, *Origini*, I 279).

52 See Hummelen's *Repertorium* and the plays cited in part two. There is a supplement to the *Repertorium* by H. van Dijk and others in *Dutch Crossing*, 22. 1984.

53 The German account is cited in E. K. Chambers, *The Mediaeval Stage*, II 101. The London clerks had been performing major cycle plays before the king and nobility of England at Skinners Well since 1384; cf. Lancashire 113.

54 See G. Kipling, 'The idea of the civic triumph: drama, liturgy and the royal entry in the Low Countries'. Details of the French Entries are given in Petit de Julleville 186–208.

55 See Lancashire 182 and G. Kipling, The London pageants for Margaret of Anjou.

56 See Petit de Julleville 198.

57 See Mill, *Scotland* 189–91.

58 Petit de Julleville 200–2.

59 See *REED* Coventry 40.

60 Mons xiii.

61 Shergold 116–18.

62 See Neumann 258–60.

63 See C. Port, Documents sur l'histoire du théâtre à Angers 75–7 and A. Lecoy de la Marche *Extraits des comptes du roi René* 323–30. One of the water-pots from Cana was kept as a relic in the principal church in Angers. I am grateful to Roger Middleton for sending me copies of these records.

64 The extent of his involvement is clearly set out in the recent edition of the accounts from Châteaudun by Runnalls and Couturier.

65 There is a detailed analysis and bibliography for the *Cena Cypriani* in De Bartholomaeis, *Origini* 151–61.

66 The Tegernsee text is printed in Young, II 371–87.

67 See Shergold 40–2 and Patt 91.

68 G. A. Runnalls, *Le Mystère de la Passion à Amboise au moyen âge* 10–12.

69 D'Ancona, *Origini*, I 290–5.

70 See Cioni, *Bibliografia delle sacre rappresentazioni*. For Cecchi's plays see D'Ancona, *Origini*, I 408, and the bibliography by Bruno Ferraro.

71 See Patt and Surtz for these and other Spanish examples.

3 PERFORMANCE AND THE COMMUNITY

1 Many of these records have been published; the commonest sources are cited by the abbreviations listed on pp. xix–xx. Performance details from a range of countries are collected in W. Tydeman's *The Theatre in the Middle Ages* and translations of many texts are given in *Staging*.

2 Court drama will not be considered here, since little is known of its staging; nor will the indoor plays of Italian confraternities, French guilds and *puys*, or the Dutch chambers of rhetoric. Like court and university plays, these were mostly on a relatively modest scale with an audience consisting of the members of the community or court concerned. Generally speaking, the size of the location dictated the form of play: a single set with minimum movement and a small cast. The principal members of the audience were probably seated. Characteristic of these plays is their emphasis on words rather than actions, and reliance on the interest of the treatment and perhaps a certain magnificence in costuming

to hold the attention of potentially well-behaved spectators – at least in court plays where the audience was under authority.

3 Particular details of decor and costume will be noted in the analysis of subject-matter in part two.

4 See pp. 19–20 and Muir, *Liturgy and drama in the Anglo-Norman Adam*. Congregational singing in the vernacular is first noted in the eleventh century; see Young, I 176.

5 For processions and general movement and behaviour in church see Fortescue, *The ceremonies of the Roman rite*, especially ch. 5. This form of presentation was used successfully in Canterbury Cathedral in 1992 for a performance of a sequence of medieval plays drawn from the extant cycles and staged in different parts of the building.

6 For flagellants and the Mézières play see pp. 19, 21. The *lauda* of the Decollation of John the Baptist staged by the *Gonfalonieri* in Rome (probably in the church of St John Lateran) includes a direction to carry the body to the sacristy. Herod and his queen wear the vestments of sub-deacons (De Bartholomaeis, *Origini* 262–3).

7 See *Staging* 76–7 for the prologue to the *Seinte Resurreccion*.

8 The introduction to the Esther play in the Majorcan codex requires four stages in the church, set up in pairs on opposite sides of the nave (Majorca *Esther* 277).

9 The modern Elche play of the Assumption is still close to its medieval roots, though the present church with its specially built *aracoeli* dates only from the seventeenth century.

10 The plans for multiple sets inside churches which have survived from Bozen and Villingen, are reproduced in E. Konigson, *L'Espace théâtral médiéval* 46, 127. The Tyrol passion plays were also staged in church and a single scaffold is mentioned in Bozen in 1516 (Neumann 213)

11 The Abramio text is translated in *Staging* 243–7. I am grateful to Cyrilla Barr for sending me an advance copy of her article on the Florence confraternities and their records.

12 Lorenzo and other members of the Medici family were members of the *Compagnia* and supported the productions.

13 The machinery for the play was first designed by Brunelleschi, the architect of the Duomo. According to Abramio, during the Annunciation the angel Gabriel came flying down from a gallery over the north door towards the stage on virtually invisible ropes.

14 For *Herodes iratus* see p. 184 and Donovan 95.

15 The traditional celebrations of the younger members of the community on Innocents' Day or the Feast of St Nicholas frequently led to complaints and attempted restrictions. See Young, II 106–110.

16 See below, Women in the theatrical community.

17 Digby *Conversion of St Paul*, epilogue to Act I.

18 The early floats were carried by men but when superstructures ('*rocas*') were used for the decors the carts were moved along the streets on wheels

(Shergold 86). Some of the decors are clearly two-tiered (ibid. 91–5; for the Madrid stational performances see 418–20). For Innsbruck see W. Breuer, Aufführungspraxis 56.

19 From Florence comes the story of the German who clambered aboard a waggon and attacked Octavian (*Staging* 241).

20 The inclusion of names on the haloes or the carrying of traditional attributes (e.g. Peter's keys) helped to identify the apostles in each scene since they would be played by different actors. In Michel's fixed-location *Passion* the apostles first appear in their '*habits mechaniques*' (tradesman's costume: 51, 56); later (it is not specified exactly when, but before the Arrest) they have an '*habit d'apostle*' (Mons 161) of crimson (*vermeil*, Mons 292). This would serve to distinguish the apostles at a distance amidst a large crowd of 'extras'. See Muir, Aspects of form and meaning in the biblical plays 116.

21 The devils' role is much reduced in the cycle plays compared to the simultaneous texts.

22 The plays were mimed at stations along the route of the procession in the morning, then performed in the main square the same afternoon, after which the prizes for the best plays were awarded. See A. Knight, The sponsorship of drama in Lille 278–9.

23 See Neumann's Index under *Spielorte* and references in Petit de Julleville and Lancashire. H. Reyflaud, *Le Cercle magique* mentions a whole series of staging sites, plans and contracts. In Florence there is indirect evidence for outdoor performances in the *frottola* or framework of real-life scenes which bracket several of the plays. In the play of Isaac, for example, a father takes his son to see the play and afterwards the father congratulates the players and gives them one or two useful pieces of advice on speaking clearly and so on.

24 There are no statistics available for the Cornish play but the stage plan shows the disposition of the mansions round the edge of the central *platea*. Unusually, Heaven and Hell are near each other (only the torturers' 'mansion' comes between) rather than at opposite poles.

25 Châteaudun 14–16.

26 The Strasburg records include both £sd and florins among their monetary references: see Neumann 674–6. Stolberg actually charged admission at the town gates for visitors or those living 'outside the market' (which suggests the residents of the *Marktplatz* were entitled to a free show). This is very unusual in German tradition (see below, Paying for the plays). Eger does not seem to have used a raised stage, merely a central area which each group entered from the '*deserto*'. Occasional references to a *locus* (place) for a particular character may suggest a simple form of mansion (133). For the different stages used in German Corpus Christi processions see Breuer, Aufführungspraxis.

27 The plans showing the locations of all the different mansions and the stands for the audience are reproduced in *Staging*. Of all the known

directors, Cysat best exemplifies the motto: *presentia ordina, futura provide, preterite recordare* (Organise the present, prepare for the future, record the past). His minutely detailed memoranda for the performances include an attempt to keep women out of the playing area altogether, which suggests that here, at least, the audience was carefully controlled.

28 Gréban *Passion*, ed., G. Paris xix. For Cysat's lunch schedules see Evans 221–3.

29 Where devils are not used there is sometimes a comic parody of the Commentator in the form of a peasant (*rusticus, villein*) or a fool (*sot, fou*) who recurs constantly with topical and local comments on the action, e.g. the *fou* in the Troyes *Passion*, or *Rusticus* in Semur. From the eleventh-century *Sponsus* onwards, the bad or the foolish were taken off stage by devils. In the Old Testament, of course, everyone goes the same path: in the Anglo-Norman *Adam*, the devils take Cain off to Hell to the accompaniment of a positive cacophony of noise, but Abel they lead 'more gently'. See Muir, *Liturgy and drama* 139 n. 29 on the use of Hell not Limbo here and R. Rastall, The sounds of Hell.

30 For the 1501 *Passion*, Mons borrowed a church organ (xcviii). Lucerne frequently uses horns and other instruments. The Châteaudun accounts show an exceptional amount of music for the 1510 *Passion*. The first trumpeters (*basteleurs trompetes*) auditioned wanted too much money (instrumental musicians had been professionals for several centuries), so three others were employed who received altogether 69 and a suit of livery each. There were also a tambour player and his boy. Altogether the music cost £117 (Châteaudun 62–4).

31 Having obtained their charter from the king (see previous chapter) they needed a place to perform. The first one they found was the hall of the Hospice de la Trinité which they rented, from the community which ran the Hospice, for more than a century. When they had to return it, they then moved briefly into the Hôtel de Flandres and finally, in 1547, they prepared to move into their newly refurbished and converted auditorium in the Hôtel de Bourgogne. In 1548, the *Parlement de Paris* banned the *Confrérie* from performing religious plays but the Hôtel de Bourgogne became a major Paris theatre of the golden age of classical drama. The records of the last few performances by the *Confrérie* (the only ones we have) clearly indicate a mixed audience, some standing and some seated. S. W. Deierkauf-Holsboer's *Le Théâtre de l'Hôtel de Bourgogne* includes measurements of the theatre as rebuilt soon after 1548 and though her figures have been questioned it seems reasonable to postulate an average audience for the *Confrérie*'s productions of 2,000 people. A purpose-built theatre in Lyons in 1538–41 was the first such venture outside Paris. It was subsequently sold. In Meaux there was a theatre from 1547–8 but it was then demolished; see Muir, Audiences 12.

32 Numerous appeals for quiet are recorded, see Muir, Audiences 18; Tydeman 233; *Staging* 68.

33 See Michel 107; Port, Angers 77. One author at Lille had a more erudite approach: at the beginning of the play of the birth of John the Baptist, the Prologue reminds the audience that bees, the collectors of honey, did not like places where there was Dame Echo or loud noises. Since the play they are about to present is scriptural honey for the benefit of the spectators they should not frighten away these 'honey–bringing bees' with loud noises.

34 This is one of the rare mentions of university students in relationship to a civic play. (See also below under Paying for the plays). Angers had a long tradition of theatrical productions, and perhaps also of trouble at them. For the production in 1486 (the first of Michel's *Passion*) see Port, Angers 76.

35 Petit de Julleville 105. The play, incidentally, was free – which may explain the size of the audience, though not the behaviour of the spectators.

36 It seems likely that this was only for the standing area. Certainly at Romans, children must have been allowed to share the superior and expensive boxes (complete with lock and key and a child-proof rail) erected at the back of the open tiers of seats, with the further comfort of privies at each end of the row.

37 Chocheyras, *Dauphiné* 44.

38 For stage disasters see the performances at Metz and Seurre in Petit de Julleville 12–13; 68–70; the latter is translated in *Staging* 259–62. In Naples in 1506, a preaching friar arranged a grand presentation of the '*Vita di Cristo*' but the staging was so poorly constructed that it collapsed and several people were killed (De Bartholomaeis, *Origini*, 450). In Bautzen in 1413 so many people climbed on the roof of a building to see a play of the martyrdom of St Dorothy that the walls gave way under their weight: thirty-three were killed and many others injured (*Staging* 67).

39 See L. de Gouvenain, *Le Théâtre à Dijon 1422–1790* 275. Other brawls are recorded from Caen, Auxerre and Mende; see Muir, Audiences 18.

40 When the actors were members of the clergy, they were not of course paid, though occasionally in civic plays a priest might be compensated for his time. However, in 1376, the accounts of the cathedral of Cambrai at Easter include payments for the preparation of the sepulchre, thunder for the Resurrection, gloves and shoes for Christ and 30s for the *compagnons* who acted the Mystère de la Resurrection. Other similar payments are recorded (Petit de Julleville 5). Were these *compagnons* laymen or religious? If the former, the play was most likely in French and is one of the first recorded performances in France of a vernacular play in a cathedral. In the French civic plays, where actors had to provide their own costumes, wealthy bourgeois who were not involved in the play might help a poor man with his costume; in Mons 509, 551–2; and Châteaudun 157, the authorities paid for special clothes for Christ. In Valenciennes, men (and women) bound themselves by contract for the duration of the preparations

and performance. They received a meal allowance on the performance days and those who contributed to the costs shared also in the eventual profits. The Contract is translated in *Staging* 43–5. In Eger (Neumann 296–302); Künzelsau (ibid. 428–30); and Zerbst (ibid. 789–99); the civic records are full of entries of small payments for items for the Corpus Christi plays, usually including beer or wine for the actors. Genuine professional groups begin to appear in the religious drama in Spain at the end of the fifteenth century and elsewhere during the sixteenth.

41 In Florence the city fathers had seats outside the Signoria for the St John's day processional plays. In the later years of the York Corpus Christi play audience stands were erected by the citizens at fixed stations, which were allocated by the town on request (and probably for a consideration). In Mons, the Canonesses of St Waudru regularly paid for a stand or window for the town plays, while for the *Passion* of 1501 a special arrangement was made for the wife of the *Baillie* (the Archduke's representative in the Netherlands) to watch in comfort from the window of the Town Hall (Mons xvi–xviii, lxv).

42 Several French plays were instigated by or under the direct patronage of princes. René d'Anjou rewarded generously groups or towns which staged plays for him and also contributed costumes; see Lecoy de la Marche, Roi René 323–30. In 1510, when the town of Châteaudun undertook a passion play on the orders of their local overlord, Dunois, the Duc de Longueville, the Duke contributed £185 *tournois*, as well as paying for copying the Amboise text (Châteaudun 70). In 1459 the Duke of Burgundy contributed half a measure of wood worth £8 to the organisers of a passion play at Aire in Artois (Arras *Passion* xxii). For other examples of royal patronage see the previous chapter.

43 In Germany, however, although the craft guilds were responsible for the plays, the local authorities often contributed to the cost. Mill, *Scotland*, also refers to arguments over guild precedence in the processions in Aberdeen (126) and Edinburgh (179).

44 In Spain although the church usually organised and oversaw the Corpus Christi and other plays, they were paid for by the guilds who performed them. In Seville, in 1554, the guilds complained about the expense involved and subsequently it was decreed that the cost should be borne by the city (Shergold 101).

45 If players brought credit to a town they were often rewarded with a gift of money or wine, see de Pas, *Saint-Omer* 357–9. An interesting case is that of the players in Compiègne who in 1474 acted the life of St Barbe: the town gave them 60s to cover the costs of staging, costumes and so on. The following year they did the same play and the town paid everything, to a total of more than £4,000 (Petit de Julleville 38–9). Was the first attempt a test of their ability? We shall unfortunately never know. In Lucerne, on the other hand, the burghers paid to take part for the glory of it (Evans 112–14).

46 For the text, see *Staging* 36–7.

47 For details of the charges see Muir, *Audiences* 14–15 and Petit de Julleville, *Les Mystères*, I, ch. 12.

48 See Muir, *Audiences* 15; Chocheyras, *Dauphiné* 42 and *Savoie* 45. The moving spirit in these undertakings might be the town council or a group of citizens; it was not usually a guild or confraternity. Generally the town council then appointed a group of senior officials (*echevins*) to oversee and organise the production and they might contract with a carpenter for the stage and call in a professional '*machiniste*' (maker of cunning devices) to undertake the special effects. A number of contracts have survived. The carpenters' contracts from Alençon and Bordeaux are in *Staging* 74–6. Specialist workers – carpenters building stages, or tailors making costumes – were paid at their usual daily rate (see details from Mons and Romans accounts in Muir, *Audiences* 15). There are also numerous records of payments to craftsmen in the German records. A rare reference from Vienna tells of a workman who in 1517 refused to take any money for renewing the wood of one of the thieves' crosses (Neumann 739). Overall these play accounts provide a rich and hitherto almost untapped source of information for economic historians.

49 The players had begun by taking up a collection which proved to be insufficient (Port, *Angers* 78 n.1.) The University reference is cited by Petit de Julleville 51. Collections were also a common method of financing in England, see the Essex records in Coldewey, *The property player*, and the examples from *REED* Reading cited on p. 39.

50 Several days of rain threatened the production at Seurre in 1496 (*Staging* 260); in Bourges, a worsening political situation, coupled with an unprecedented expenditure on costumes and effects for the Acts of the Apostles in 1536, apparently ruined many of the townsfolk (R. Lebègue, *Le Mystère des Actes des Apôtres* 103). The rivalry involved was considerable: Bourges put on the Acts in 1536 because nearby Issoudun had done such a successful *Passion* two years before. Châteaudun envied Amboise and borrowed their text, see *Châteaudun* 35. Jehan Larrivé, the messenger sent to Amboise by the local lord, the duc de Longueville, was part of the ducal household (69). He played God in the *Passion* (140).

51 In Rabelais' *Tiers livre* (1546), ch. 3, Panurge recalls playing God in the *Passion* at Saumur surrounded by angels and cherubim; this is possibly the 1534 production, for the painter who prepared the *Paradis* at Saumur that year proudly claimed it was the 'most beautiful Paradise you have ever seen – or ever will!' (Petit de Julleville 126). Occasionally, as well as dazzling their audience with special effects, the players or the entrepreneur of the play might bribe them with free wine and food (Muir, *Audiences* 17–18).

52 Hrotsvitha's plays are not biblical and are therefore outside the subject of this book. They have been acted this century in Latin quite successfully.

She was not a nun, but a *Stiftsdame* (noble lady living in a convent). For Hildegard of Bingen see *The 'Ordo Virtutum' of Hildegard of Bingen*, Ed. A. E. Davidson.

53 See Young, I for other records of liturgical plays performed by women, mainly *Visitatio* texts.

54 Donovan 124

55 R. Amstutz, *The Thuringian 'Ludem de decem Virginibus'*.

56 The text is in Young and a translation in *Staging*.

57 See the introduction to the Liège plays by G. Cohen. For the Holy Kinship see p. 221.

58 For a discussion of these two plays and the question of who played the male roles see Muir, Women on the medieval stage in France.

59 Notable women patronesses include Isabella d'Este (D'Ancona, *Origini*, I 337–9) and the Canonesses of St Waudru in Mons (Mons xi–xix). For other examples see Lancashire, Petit de Julleville and Neumann.

60 For Marguerite de Navarre see p. 225.

61 The St Barbe at Nancy may have been a *jongleresse*, a professional female entertainer, though this does not quite fit the term *'femme'* used in the records. The first record of a professional actress in France is in 1600.

62 See *REED Chester* 23, 37, 517.

63 Many of the Deventer references are to the feast of the Circumcision, a well-known occasion for scholastic merrymaking and boy-bishops, but this hardly seems relevant to girls. In 1380, the last year to mention these plays, there are payments (all on the same day: 2 Jan.) to the *joncfrouwen*: £2 8s, the *cleriken*: £2, the *schutten* (archers): £2, and the *basselierres* (bachelors/ students?): £3 (Neumann 272–4). All the entries are 'for their play'. Further details of the Deventer records generally, are in the paper by Gerald Nijsten, Feasts and public spectacles: late medieval drama and performance in the Low Countries. I am grateful to Professor Nijsten for giving me a copy of his paper. For the Basle reference, see Neumann 125.

64 For details of this and other Metz plays see Muir, Women on the medieval stage 113–6. A husband and wife played Mary and Joseph in Saragossa in 1476 (*Staging* 55).

65 For a full list of these roles and the ages of the participants, see Muir, Women on the medieval stage 107–112. Cf. also R. Rastall, Female roles in an all-male cast.

66 For the Romans play of the *Trois doms* and the Grenoble *Passion* see Chocheyras, *Dauphiné*, chs. 2 & 4. For Châteaudun see the edition of the accounts by Runnalls and Couturier. See also Muir, Women on the medieval stage 111–13.

67 See Wackernel, *Tyrol* CCXLIV–V. Neumann 190–202, gives the full cast lists.

68 See Muir, Women 113.

69 The incident is recorded in Wackernel, *Tyrol* CCXLV.

4 CREATION AND FALL

1 Throughout this part of the book, page references to the editions quoted in the bibliographical index of plays are given for the exact page of a quotation or for the beginning of a scene or incident. Page numbers separated from the title are put in ( ). References for unpublished texts will be to the folios of the manuscript. Page references are not yet available for the Lille plays.

2 The late French *Viel Testament* (*VT*), which ranges from Genesis to Job, only survives in printed editions of the fifteenth and sixteenth centuries, one of which was the text used for the OT cycle known to have been performed in Paris in 1542 (Petit de Julleville 141). The Fall sequence has been edited separately by Craig and page references are to Craig's edition up till the Expulsion.

3 This procedure is used in the modern Oberammergau and Nancy passion plays.

4 See Muir, *Liturgy and drama* 53. Possible links between the Seven Ages and the English cycles are examined in V. A. Kolve, *The play called Corpus Christi* 88–9. Kolve also mentions a representation of the scene in a Canterbury cathedral window which links the six water–pots of the marriage in Cana with the Ages of the World (89–90). Unique in its structure is the *Breve historia de Deus* by Gil Vicente, whose OT sequence includes the death of Adam and Eve, the death of Abel, Job and the prophets David and Isaiah. The only NT scenes are the death of John the Baptist and the Temptation of Jesus. *Morte* (Death) appears as a frequent character in this play and in a semi-dramatic dialogue, the *Mors de la pomme* (Bite of the apple), which, playing on the words *Mors* (bite) and *Mort* (death) shows Death sent by God after the Fall of Man. The death of Abel is followed by a series of death scenes – a son with his mother, two lovers and so on – culminating in Jesus' death on the cross after which Lucifer declares he has lost his power over man (568). Death is also personified elsewhere (sometimes as one of the devils, cf. Habakkuk 3: 5, 'Death shall go before his face and the devil shall go forth before his feet'). Death appears in person in Semur at the death of Adam (25); in N. town at the death of Herod (195); and in Rouergue *Judgement* 243. Such personifications and allegorical figures are a natural way of expressing abstract ideas (good or evil) on the stage; other examples are the Four Daughters of God in the Trial in Heaven scenes or Pride, Despair and the other Sins who tempt Lucifer, Judas, or Mary Magdalene.

5 God may have the role–name *Deus*, *Deus Pater* or simply *Creator*; in Künzelsau he is *Salvator in creacione* (3). In other parts of the play he is also referred to as the *dominica persona in temptacione; – in deserto*; or *– in resurrectione* (259). In Anglo-Norman *Adam*; *Eger*; and Künzelsau, God is called *Salvator* from the beginning. Creation by the Son/Saviour is based on the Nicene creed: 'Jesus Christ ... by whom all things were made.' (See Appendix for Creeds.)

6 *Alpha et Omega* (cf. Revelation 1: 8) is used in the English cycles, Maastricht, Eger and the Cornish *Creation*. There are two Cornish versions of the Creation: the first Day of the three-part *Ordinalia* and a separate, later redaction referred to here as the Cornish *Creation*.

7 R. H. Charles, *The Apocrypha and Pseudepigrapha of the OT in English*. For an alternative view of the fall of the angels, associated with Genesis 6: 1, see E. Pagels, *Adam, Eve and the serpent* 42–3.

8 Satan appears in the OT (Job 1: 6) as one of 'the sons of God' who is allowed by God to tempt Job. The word in Hebrew means simply adversary (I Chronicles 21: 1; Zechariah 3: 1), but it early became synonymous with the devil. In the gospels it is used several times both in this general sense and more specifically as tempter (e.g. Matthew 4: 10; 16: 23). In Revelation 22: 3 Jesus himself has become the Morning Star, replacing the one who in his pride sought to make himself equal to God. (Similarly, Adam, by eating the fruit, is tempted to make himself equal to God, whereas Jesus, being 'equal with God ... humbled himself, becoming obedient unto death' (Philippians 2: 6–8). The fall of Satan was treated at length by Augustine in the *City of God*, Books X & XI.

9 No text survives from Regensburg but it seems certain that the plays were in Latin. Extant plays of the Fall of Lucifer include English, French, Dutch, Celtic, Italian and German. In addition there is a narrative account at the beginning of the Lucerne *Osterspiel* (Easter play; although the text is so-called it is in fact a full cyclic *Passion*). The Dutch *Eerste Bliscap* (First Joy) includes a dialogue between Lucifer and *Nijt* (Envy: 57) in which the fall of the angels is used to justify Lucifer's hatred for man, who is to replace him in Heaven. 'For God created man incorruptible ... but by the envy of the devil death came into the world' (Wisdom of Solomon 2: 23–4). The devil's envy of man is a common theme in exegesis of the Fall. *Ordinalia* 5 has a stage direction for Lucifer but no reference in the text, suggesting the scene was cut.

10 N. town 22 and Valenciennes 20-day, f. 3r combine them with the stars or the sun, moon and stars. (Valenciennes 20-day is unedited except in unpublished theses of the University of Louvain (now Leuven) in Belgium.) *VT* (followed by Troyes) includes a description of the creation of the four elements based on Peter Comestor (46). In Cornish *Creation;* Towneley 3; and Eger; the whole creation is first of all completed except for Man (cf. Genesis 1: 1–26).

11 The hierarchies were originally set out by Pseudo-Dionysius and then adopted by the medieval schoolmen including Aquinas. All the names are biblical, the middle five being derived from two references by St Paul (Ephesians 1: 21; Colossians 1: 16). The nine orders are usually arranged in three hierarchies of three choirs each: Seraphim, Cherubim and Thrones; Dominations, Virtues and Powers; Principalities, Archangels and Angels. Only the last two choirs have direct contact with Man.

12 For the importance of the *Te Deum* in the early liturgical plays see p. 185

13 In Orvieto, I 340; one MS of the Florence *Creation* 13n; and Revello I 230: v.5603n; he is called not Lucifer but Lucibello (beautiful light). The late Breton *Creation* play also includes the form Lucibel (IX 175) but after his Fall God changes it to Lucifer (IX 183: all references are to the pages of the parallel French translation).

14 In *Sündenfall* 103 and Cornish *Creation* 15 there is a rebel from each of the different orders; elsewhere they appear to be of a separate order altogether.

15 N. town 23; Chester 6; Towneley 4. In the Italian plays; Semur 6; Gréban 14; and Valenciennes 20-day, f. 4r he proposes to set his throne in the north (*aquilonis* cf. Isaiah 14: 15; Ezekiel 8: 5).

16 *Oysseuse* is a character from the *Roman de la Rose*. The idea of a Court of Hell is stressed later in Semur by the inclusion among the devils of the *Coquus Inferni* (11) and *Clamator Inferni* (33), the cook and herald of Hell. 'Princes' and 'Kings' with their courts were common in medieval confraternities, especially those like the French *basoche* or the English Inns of Court made up of lawyers or law students. It is perhaps significant, therefore, that Jehan Floichot, the author/copyist of the Semur *Passion*, was a notary. See Petit de Julleville, *Les Comédiens en France*, ch.5, and A. Wigfall Green, *The Inns of Court and early English Drama*.

17 God acts personally in the English plays; Breton *Creation* (IX 185); Maastricht 303; and Vienna, I 306. *VT* 57; Semur 8; and Gréban 14; all refer to Lucifer as 'dragon'. In Eger, Michael is helped by the seraphim with a fiery sword (7) and the Cornish *Creation* includes a full stage-battle using puppets for the falling devils (27).

18 The Protestant Rueff's *Adam und Eva* (1520) begins with the angels narrating the fall of the angels, after which Lucifer is driven out and laments (120). In the Vienna *Passion* a very Miltonic and dignified Lucifer takes his place on a throne in Hell and proceeds to send Satan to tempt Adam and Eve (I 308). The Bozen *Ascension* is followed by a scene in which the angels remind the spectators of what happened to Lucifer; then Michael pushes a falling devil with a sword, rebuking him. '*Ibi incenditur diabolus*' (then the devil is set alight: 49).

19 The texts *Dic tu Adam* (with its refrain 'Do not trust a woman') and *Adam, Adam, primus homo* (first man) preserved from Padua are parodies of the Pseudo-Augustinian prophet sermon (De Bartholomaeis, *Origini* 496). In addition to the plays mentioned in the analysis, other vernacular texts recorded include a Corpus Christi play from 'Audenaarde' (= Oudenaarde: *Belgisch Museum* 7 239–44) and the lost Adam and Eve play performed fourteen times in Toledo between 1493 and 1510 (46). I have not been able to see the Foligno *Expulsion* (De Bartholomaeis, *Origini* 279), the Berlin Fall play (Bergmann 21) and five *autos* from the Creation to Noah preserved in a sixteenth-century printed book from Barcelona illustrated in G. Wickham, *A history of the theatre* 135. Numerous tableaux of the Temptation are recorded in Corpus Christi processions.

20 Valencia, Lucerne, Orvieto and Florence *Creation* include no theological material.

21 The classic doctrine appears in Eger; *Ordinalia;* Norwich; Chester; Vienna. York has a variant of it called the abuse of power – by killing Jesus, the good man, the devil loses his power over all mankind.

22 The Anselmian doctrine is the basis of, among others, Gréban; Arras; Bologna; *Bliscap; Sündenfall* and two Castilian *autos* of the Fall: the *Peccado* and the *Prevaricatione di Adam.*

23 This may be a ditch (Semur 13) or a '*tonbel*' (tomb: Rouergue 2). In the St Genevieve plays of the *Nativity* and *Resurrection* which both begin with scenes of the Fall, Adam and Eve are hidden by a covering (*Nativity* 99; Resurrection 317); while Lucerne specifies a pit (later the Saviour's grave) with a lid or covering of green branches over it (I 83). A few texts mention a 'rib' among the properties but usually the creation of Eve from Adam's side is mimed only. In Valenciennes 20-day the angels bring the clay to God to form the body of Adam (f. 5v), elsewhere God picks it up himself. Rouergue 4 has a unique scene in which, after Adam's creation, God sends the four archangels to the four cardinal points to find a suitable name for him. Each brings back one letter, the initial of a bright star, making the name Adam. The idea comes originally from Augustine's tract 8–9 on the gospel of John – the episode of the Marriage in Cana (cf. *Cambridge Bible* 182). Anglo-Norman *Adam* (which does not stage the act of creation), *Sündenfall* and Eger are built up on a series of responsories (sung in Latin and drawn from the liturgy for Septuagesima) based on the Genesis text beginning with the words 'and God made man' (Genesis 2: 7).

24 The Florence *Creation* (16), which formed part of the procession on St John the Baptist's day, has three stanzas in which Adam names in turn the fish, birds and beasts; Cornish *Creation* includes the serpent 'with various birds and snakes' (34) while Breton *Creation* IX 195 catalogues plants, fish and birds and Rueff's *Adam und Eva* 23 devotes more than two hundred lines to the naming, with each animal being described in a separate quatrain. In N. town (24), God instructs Adam to give names to fish and fowl and tree and fruit and beasts and to his wife also, but the incident is not shown on stage.

25 Leather suits are used in Cornish *Creation* 29; and Toledo 54 where the suits were touched up with red. Body-stockings were used in Lucerne (Evans 181). In Perugia in 1426 God had a flesh-coloured garment with stockings and in Coventry in 1452 he wore tawed leather (*Staging* 140, 142). For the alternative use of vestments see Muir, *Liturgy and drama* 37. A fifteenth-century Latin morality play, the *Liber apologeticus* of Thomas Chaundler, includes a scene of the Creation of Man (83) who is then clothed with a garment of immortality. After the Fall (treated here as the victory of Sensuality over Reason), Adam finds he has lost this garment and knows he is naked. In the illustrations, Man is shown wearing a royal mantle decribed as the *pallio immortalitas* (41; the *pallium* was the symbol of

authority bestowed on bishops by the Pope). After the Fall, Valenciennes 20-day refers to Adam and Eve's having lost '*la robe de immortalité*' (f. 8r) which may indicate a similar type of costume.

26 There are also explicit references to marriage in Künzelsau 9; and Troyes 35 which, as usual in this part of the play, follows *VT*.

27 The warning against eating the fruit often takes place after the creation of Eve not, as in Genesis 2: 17, before.

28 The Bologna play uses none of the feudal vocabulary that distinguishes Anglo-Norman *Adam*, but contains a short dialogue between Adam and the devil, when the latter explains why he hates Adam and his intention of continuing to harm him (III 206). This scene probably derives ultimately from the apocryphal *Vita Adae* in which Adam and Eve, while doing penance for their sins, are tempted to give up by the devil disguised as an angel of light. Adam resists and Eve succumbs. In Bologna, after the Expulsion, there is a similar scene of the penance of Adam and Eve, with the return of the tempter: Eve succumbs again. In Breton *Creation*, Satan explicitly rejects the idea of tempting Adam as being too difficult (IX 337). The play also includes the scene of the second temptation based on the *Vita Adae* (XI 435). In the Castilian *Auto del peccado*, II 138, Lucifer says that Eve will be easier to tempt. (Plays described in the analysis as Castilian are from a sixteenth-century codex containing ninety-six *autos, farsas* and *coloquios*, edited in four volumes. The play numbers are given in the bibliography.)

29 There is considerable diversity in the plays on the identity of the tempter. Genesis only mentions the serpent but Lucifer is named as tempter in Mons though he is replaced in performance by a youth in a serpent 'skin' of woven osier because Paradise is 'too far away' from Hell (10); in *Sündenfall* he climbs the tree and speaks through the serpent (119); in the *Peccado* he is accompanied by Greed and Avarice; in Cornish *Creation*, Lucifer forces the female serpent to allow him to enter her (43). In Künzelsau (11) Lucifer sends Satan to tempt Eve; Anglo-Norman *Adam* calls him *Diabolus* but both Adam and Eve address him by name as Satan; the St Genevieve plays both have a devil called Belgibus, and other plays do not name the devil. A few plays include only a serpent (Lucerne, I 87; Florence *Creation* 18; Valencia 102). In *Bliscap* the serpent is briefed by Envy (61).

30 Ultimately derived from the *Historia scholastica*, the female serpent is found in *Ordinalia*; Lucerne; *Sündenfall*; *VT*; Gréban and Chester. In Semur, the serpent says it will transmute itself into a woman: the stage-direction specifies a figure with the bust of a woman, feet and tail of a serpent and wearing a skin of red feathers; it is sent out by Lucifer and when it reaches Eden it greets Eve as sister, woman to woman (15). The idea is very common in art, see J. K. Bonnell, The serpent with a female face; Pagels, *Adam* 67; and Woolf 115.

31 The tempter flatters Eve notably in Anglo-Norman *Adam* (35) and briefly

in N. town (26). In Valencia, it addresses Eve in a '*ueu amorosa*' (amorous voice). In a seventeenth-century Dutch play, *Lucifer treuerspel*, the beauty of Eve is stressed by the devil Appollion, who expresses his envy of the newly created bride and bridegroom and the misery of being only 'one' and not a pair. I am grateful to Agnes Zwanenfeld for this reference.

32 Some French plays show Eve already tempted by the apple's appearance even before the serpent/devil appears (Gréban 18; St Genevieve *Nativity* 101; *Resurrection* 320).

33 In Anglo-Norman *Adam* a serpent *artifiose compositus* (cunningly contrived) appears at this point and seems to speak to Eve (39). In Gréban, Adam eats in full knowledge that '*mal en vendra*' (ill will come of it: 19), whereas in Troyes he is sure that only good can come of it (56).

34 Their later garments of fur (Genesis 3: 21) may be given to them before the expulsion (Mons 12; *Sündenfall* 124; Rouergue 11; Lucerne, I 91) or found on earth afterwards (*VT* 101 and Semur 20). In St Genevieve God tells Adam he must now dress in the '*robe de honte*' (garment of shame: *Nativity* 104; *Resurrection* 325).

35 In Mons, the boy in the osier serpent crawls on his belly as far as Hell (12); in the Breton *Creation* the serpent, having no hands or feet, is carried out by devils (IX 353). In Cornish *Creation* 77, Lucifer comes out of the serpent which remains in the tree while he himself slinks along the ground. In Troyes (which is independent of other texts for the last part of this episode) Satan comes down from the tree after the expulsion and cheerfully prepares to return to Hell and relate his victory (71).

36 In N. town, at the Expulsion, Adam tells Eve she must now spin '*Oure nakyd bodyes in cloth to wynde*' (34) while in St Genevieve *Nativity* Eve declares her intention of spinning sheets, towels and kerchiefs (105).

37 Some texts include a role for the Blood of Abel (cf. Genesis 4: 11; *Ordinalia* 45; Mons 16; Semur 23).

38 There had been a few such realistic touches already, like Eve's spinning (cf. note 36) or Adam lamenting because the corn he had planted was filled with weeds (Anglo-Norman *Adam* 56; Breton *Creation*, X 453). After the Expulsion two plays include a scene of Adam and Eve building (or finding ready) a house into which they retire, to emerge first with infants and then with grown sons (Mons 13; Breton *Creation*, X 210); in the latter Adam laments the lack of the necessary tools needed for life on earth (X 443). A few texts include Adam instructing his sons in the need to sacrifice to God and in the meaning of tithing (Cornish *Creation* 91; Troyes 94; Gréban 22). In *Ordinalia* 33 it is God himself who instructs Adam.

39 The symbolic smoke occurs in Gréban 23; Castilian *Auto de Cain e Abel*; Lucerne, I 97; Valenciennes 20-day, f. 10v; Troyes 101. The Florence *Abele e Caino* is unpublished. The theme is also common in iconography and forms one of the intercalated figures in the Oberammergau play.

40 The jawbone is used in Valenciennes 20-day, f. 10v; Cornish *Creation* 93;

and all four English cycles. In *Ordinalia* the weapon is not specified but Cain hits Abel 'on the jawbone' (41). In Ville Toustain's *Tragédie de la naissance ou création du monde*, published in Rouen *c.* 1614, Cain strikes Abel with a '*lourde et massive machoire*' (large and heavy jawbone. See H. C. Lancaster, *A history of French dramatic literature in the 17th century*, I 81.) Anglo-Norman *Adam* has a stage direction for Abel to have a pot (*ollam*) hidden under his clothes which Cain is to strike as if he was killing Abel (62). Cf. also O. F. Emerson, Legends of Cain.

41 In Lucerne, Abel is carried off by four stretcher-bearers 'dressed in black' and 'looking as alike as possible'. They later remove the bodies of John the Baptist, the son of the widow of Nain, Lazarus, and the Penitent Thief (Evans 203). In Künzelsau both Cain and Abel address the audience *after* the murder (18). In *Ordinalia* 43 and Anglo-Norman *Adam*, Abel is taken to Hell; in Florence *Creation* an angel takes Abel's soul away from the devils (24); in a sixteenth-century Castilian *auto* (cf. Rouanet Appendix B) and Breton *Creation*, XI 305, the spirit of Abel is taken to Limbo, as the first of the righteous.

42 Some plays extend the scene considerably: Cain is told that the earth will not give him food (cf. Genesis 4: 11–12) in Eger 23; Castilian *Cain*, II 161; Lucerne, I 99; *Ordinalia* 45.

43 Troyes 119; Cornish *Creation* 119 (cf. Genesis 4: 19, 23). The Hebrew tradition that Lamech killed the boy who helped him aim at what he thought was a wild animal is dramatised in Florence *Creation* 27; Eger 25; N. town 47 (intercalated into the Noah play) and *VT*, I 183 which identifies the youth as Lamech's son, Tubalcain (cf. Genesis 4: 22). In Florence the devils take Cain and Lamech but the angel insists the boy was guilty only of an accident and takes him to join the righteous in Limbo (28).

44 The birth of Seth is described in Troyes 121, and *VT*, I 126. *Bliscap* includes several other 'children' of Adam (80) and in Cornish *Creation* Adam says he has thirty-two sons and thirty-two daughters in addition to Cain and Abel (161; this is nearly the same as *Legenda*, where he has thirty sons and thirty daughters as well as Cain, Abel and Seth). The title page of Breton *Creation* lists the stories of Seth, Noah and Abraham but they are not available in print or in translation.

45 *Legenda* includes the story of the Rood under the feast of the Invention of the Holy Cross, with a brief reference under the Resurrection. There are several variants of the story for there were many versions of the legend of the Holy Rood which traces the wood of the cross from the death of Adam to the reign of Solomon and then describes its rediscovery by St Helena, mother of the Emperor Constantine (R. Morris, *Legends of the Holy Rood*). The full legend is dramatised only in *Ordinalia* which uses it to link together its OT selections.

46 Ordinalia 53; Troyes 127; Cornish *Creation* 141. In the Bible, Eve dies before Adam but in the plays this may be reversed to allow Eve to lament and bury her husband (Semur 25). In *Bliscap*, Adam begs not to die but Envy and

Lucifer, representing Hell, appeal to God, who gives judgement for them (80).

47 The grass is burnt in Semur 25; *Ordinalia* 55; Cornish *Creation* 143. In Troyes 127 and Valenciennes 20-day, f. 13r it has withered. (In *VT*, I 100, Adam commented on the grass withering under their feet as they left Paradise). *Legenda* (Invention of the Holy Cross: 3 May) gives three versions of Seth's meeting with the angel: in one, Michael says simply that the Oil will not be available for 5,500 years; in the second he gives Seth a branch of the 'miraculous tree', ordering him to plant it on Mount Libanus; in the third version, Jacobus adds that this was the tree which caused Adam to sin and that when Seth was given the branch he was told that the day it bore fruit his father would be made whole.

48 The seeds are from the fruit of the Fall (*Ordinalia* 63); or the tree of life (Cornish *Creation* 151). Seth is told to plant them in Adam's grave, either between his tongue and his teeth (*Ordinalia*); or one in his mouth and one in each nostril (Cornish *Creation*). Valenciennes 20-day omits the visions of Paradise but includes the grains to be buried in Adam's mouth (f. 14v). In Semur, Seth is merely told by Cherubim that after five thousand years a maiden will bear a prince who will be the Oil – there is no mention of seeds. The angel tells Seth to bury the branch under his father's head (*Bliscap* 84); he plants the branch on the tomb of his father, who is dead when he returns (Gréban 29) and repeats the Lord's prayer over the grave (St Genevieve *Nativity* 111). See E. Quinn, *The penitence of Adam* for a special French version of the legend of Seth.

49 In Semur, *Mors naturalis* comes to kill Adam and his soul is taken to Hell (25). In *VT*, God creates Limbo as the abode for fallen man where they will await '*la grace du mire*' (the grace of the healer: I 151). In Cornish *Creation* Death strikes Adam with a dart and his soul is taken to Limbo by an angel while his body is buried 'in a fine tomb with church songs' (169). None of the English cycles contains a play of Seth though one is listed among the Corpus Christi pageants for Beverley.

50 Cornish *Creation* 170; and *VT*, I 142; introduce here the story of the taking up into Heaven of Enoch who 'walked with God and was seen no more because God took him' (Genesis 5: 24). *VT* sets him in Earthly Paradise surrounded by fire and foretells his role in the fight against Antichrist (I 210; cf. Hebrews 11: 5 and p. 150).

51 In the Cornish *Creation*, Enoch warns the people of the consequence of their sins – a theme taken up by his father Seth, who foretells the Flood and prepares two pillars, one of marble to withstand water and one of terracotta to withstand fire. In these he puts books containing the knowledge of mankind to preserve it for posterity (177). In *VT* the pillars are built by Tubal and Jubal, the grandsons of Lamech, killer of Cain. In Cornish *Creation* 187 these two mock Noah for building the ark and swear no flood could destroy the world but in *VT* Jubal claims they are acting reasonably in taking cognisance of Adam's warning of the coming of two

floods, one of water and one of fire (I 221). They specify that the books they are hiding contain all manner of knowledge including the husbandry of Jabel and the knowledge of music, coming from Jubal himself (Genesis 4: 20–1). In addition they save several memoirs made by Enoch and the art of weaving wool discovered by Noema. The last named seems a particularly medieval science to include. The episode derives ultimately from Josephus, cf. Picot's introduction to *VT* which gives sources and parallels for all the episodes at the beginning of each volume.

52 For the marriage of the Sons of God and the Daughters of Men as an explanation of the origin of demons, see Justin Martyr, cit. Pagels, *Adam* 42.

53 Cf. the footnotes to these verses in the modern Douay edition. *VT* telescopes the sequence of generations given in Genesis 5, and has Caynam, grandson of Seth, woo Noema, daughter of Cain, while she is weaving cloth of mingled silk and wool (from which, she tells her mother, they can make fine clothes without having to wear skins). Other daughters of Cain, including the two wives of Lamech, also accept the sons of Seth as lovers (I 192). In Valenciennes 20-day the dying Adam tells the children of Seth to have nothing to do with the children of Cain, the murderer and outcast; after Adam's death his grandsons decide to marry the daughters of Cain (f. 17r).

54 For a possible origin of this scene in Mons see the Judgement of Jesus Christ plays, p. 243

55 The Flood is mentioned in all the lists of floats in the Corpus Christi procession from Zerbst. Noah with his three sons (no ark is specified but it was surely there) were presented by the Sadlers at Ingolstadt (Bergmann 374, 154). Valencia in 1400 regilded the ark and in 1424 the ark had its own float at Barcelona (Shergold 54). Noah's ship is mentioned among the floats at Dublin (Lancashire 327). An unusual parallel is that drawn by the rector of the Künzelsau Corpus Christi processional play who describes the ark as being the Virgin Mary (20).

56 There are no extant Flood plays from Spain or Italy, nor does Noah feature in the list of plays performed in Toledo between 1493 and 1515.

57 Künzelsau; Valenciennes 20-day and Eger omit Noah's wife altogether. In *Sündenfall* 146 she is called Semiramis and in *VT*, I 217, Phuarfara; both are very obedient as are the unnamed wives in *Ordinalia* 77; Semur 29; and Mons 24. The Mons Flood play was thought to be unique until part of it was identified in Valenciennes 20-day, f. 22r. See M. Foley, Two versions of the Flood (under Mons in the bibliographical index of plays).

58 This legend, which seems to combine Delilah's betrayal of Sampson (Judges 16) with the story of the drunkenness of Noah (Genesis 9: 20–1), is discussed in A. J. Mill, Noah's Wife again; see also Woolf 136–8. The devil uses Mrs Noah to enter the ark himself but is expelled by the return to the ark of the Holy Spirit in the form of the dove.

59 She appears as quarrelsome and shrewish (York 84 and Towneley 32);

refuses to enter the ark without her 'gossips' (Chester 50); and insists on taking certain possessions because they cost a lot of money (Cornish *Creation* 197).

60 Chester 48; Semur 28; and *VT*, I 233 – though the last-named apparently has real animals for the entry into the ark (I 220). Mons has quite an extended scene for the children of Noah collecting up the different unclean beasts and pushing them into the ark '*par petites esquiellettes toutes propices*' (through suitable small openings: 25). Mons is also the only text which describes how a real flood is to be managed: the stage is covered with turf and in one section where the wicked are feasting it is carpeted with violets. At the signal of the director, the water pours down through lead pipes, concealed by clouds, from the barrels located in Heaven. The wicked disappear through trapdoors in the stage as if drowned (27). It seems likely that a similar method was used in the staging of *VT* which specifies the addition of some non-speaking extras to be drowned (I 228).

61 In Eger he appears sitting on the rainbow (28, cf. Revelation 4: 3). In Cornish *Creation* the sacrifice is accompanied (like the funeral of Adam) with good church songs (201). *Ordinalia* allows each member of the family to make a sacrifice and Noah insists on a full tithe, apparently forgetting that he has only limited stock in hand with which to repeople the whole earth. God accepts the offering and institutes the law of not eating meat that has blood in it (93, cf. Leviticus 7: 26).

62 The mocking of Noah was a figure of the Mocking of Christ. *VT*, I 254, then introduces Ham's grandson, Nembroth (Nimrod: Genesis 10: 8–9) who, determined to prevent Noah's curse from coming true, declares he will lead the family in battle against his brothers; Nimrod is subsequently associated with Ninive, the legendary founder of Nineveh in a unique staging of the building of the Tower of Babel (I 259 cf. Genesis 11: 1–8) with a rare comic scene for the masons.

63 Noah comments that the drink is stronger than he had anticipated (31) before he goes away to sleep it off. Chanaam (Ham) had already revealed himself as the 'bad son' by his refusal to join in the sacrifice after the Flood: when all the others are thanking God he declares he is hungry and prays for 'plenty of beans to eat' (30).

5 THE COVENANT AND THE KINGDOM

1 *VT* starts with a legendary account of the death of Abraham's brother, Aram (I 280, cf. Genesis 11: 28), and the marriage of Abraham and Sarah followed by the calling of Abraham and his travels to Canaan including the visit to Egypt (Genesis 12). The quarrel between the herdsmen of Abraham and those of his nephew Lot (I 315) leading to the settling of the latter in the area of Sodom and Gomorrhah (Genesis 12–13) are dramatised also in the Castilian *auto* of *Abraham in Canaan* and the Dutch *Abraham's journey* (Hummelen 246: many of the sixteenth-century Dutch

plays are not yet edited and are cited from summaries in Hummelen's descriptive *Repertorium*).

2 Melchisedech is also referred to in Psalms: 'Thou art a priest for ever after the order of Melchisedech' (Psalm 109: 4; cf. Calderon's *El órden de Melchisedech*). *VT*, I 332, and Castilian *Abraham and the Kings* include the episode without any symbolic additions; in Künzelsau there is a short speech for Melchisedech in which he explains that a priest is coming who will be eternal, to whom man will offer bread and wine (24; cf. Hebrews 7: 16–17). In Chester the stage directions of certain MSS specify a chalice and paten for the offering (60n). In *Sündenfall* a monologue by Melchisedech follows the Moses scene (157). Melchisedech is also mentioned among the figures listed for the Corpus Christi processions at Ingolstadt and Zerbst. The Lille *Abraham and the angels* refers to the meeting but does not actually stage it, see also Muir, The Mass on the medieval stage 320. Only *VT*, I 369 and Lille include the story of Lot leaving Sodom and Gomorrhah, Lot's wife's being turned into a pillar of salt and Abraham's continued travels (Genesis 19–20).

3 God's covenant with Abraham and the promise of an heir (Genesis 15; *VT* only) is followed by the story of the birth of Ishmael whose mother, Hagar, is Sarah's bondswoman (Genesis 16. cf. Galatians 4: 22–31). In *VT*, I 342 it is Hagar's mocking of Sarah's barrenness which leads to their rejection, but in the Florence *Abraham and Hagar* (where the story is treated as a parable of two brothers, with Ishmael as the bad son and Isaac the good one), Hagar and her son are banished by Abraham because Ishmael mocks Isaac for his obedience and piety. (Some editions of the text have a *frottola* or framing play, in which two similarly contrasted brothers are taken to watch the play by their father: I 3.) The Castilian *Exile of Hagar* shows Abraham reluctantly exiling Hagar and Ishmael on God's orders; they are consoled by an angel with the promise of a land and nation of their own (cf. Genesis 21: 17–18). There is a Dutch *Flight of Hagar*, and Hagar and Ishmael also appear in Leuven, where Hagar is described as 'an Egyptian woman' and wears a turban (Twycross, Leuven *Ommegang*). In the Haarlem *Abraham's Sacrifice*, Sarah forces Abraham to exile them because she is jealous of Ishmael (f. 54v). A large collection of plays belonging to the rhetoricians of the Haarlem *Trou Moet Blijcken* company in the sixteenth and seventeenth centuries are currently being edited in facsimile with transcript. The four volumes which have so far appeared contain several biblical plays entered in the bibliographical index under 'Haarlem'; references are to the folio numbers of the transcript.

4 The versicle of the same responsory mentions the belief that the three angels represent the Trinity: 'Abraham saw the Lord God as in a figure of the holy Trinity.' In the Zutphen fragment of the role of Sarah in this episode, Hagar helps Sarah serve the meal to the three visitors. For the visit of the three angels in art, see G. Schiller, *Iconography of Christian Art*, I 41.

5 The sacrifice of Isaac features in many processions including Toledo, Löbau, Freiburg im Breisgau and Zerbst. Dundee in 1450 has a props list which includes Abraham's hat (Mill 173). Texts of the three sixteenth-century French versions of the *Sacrifice* are printed in B. Craig, *The Evolution of a mystery play*. Belcari's *Abraham and Isaac* play is the most popular recorded from Florence: Cioni lists twenty-two editions between *c.* 1485 and 1600.

6 Isaac carries the wood in *Sündenfall* 152; Lucerne, I 103; Haarlem *Abraham's Sacrifice*; and Eger, in which Abraham orders him: 'So, take the wood on your neck' (28). This is the type of Christ carrying the cross in the Heidelberg *Passion* 221.

7 *VT* begins with a scene in Heaven with God foretelling the crucifixion and condemning his own Son to death irrevocably (II 15). God tells Mercy that the son will consent as well as the father (II 24) and Isaac's acceptance is immediate (II 48; cf. also N. town 54). In Aversa the devil appears to Isaac on the way to the sacrifice and tells him of Abraham's intention; Isaac sends him away and, once he realises it is the will of God that he be sacrificed, he accepts it (251: cf. also Chester 71; Belcari 51; Brome 48. York 93 follows Peter Comestor in making Isaac a grown man). In *Ordinalia* 103, Isaac tells his father to bind him firmly lest he try to move away when the flames burn him. The role of Sarah is emphasised in the Greek *Abraham*, from Crete, which may date from the sixteenth century and shows definite Italian influence. *VT* somewhat ineptly includes Ishmael in the sacrifice episode, showing him accompanying them on the journey and earlier enjoying a pastoral feast with Isaac and other youths (II 9).

8 Rebecca at the well (Genesis 24: 13–20) was used in the Heidelberg *Passion* 63 as a figure for the frequently dramatised scene of the Samaritan woman whom Jesus meets at the well (John 4). Rebecca also figures in Ingolstadt Corpus Christi cycle.

9 For the debate of *Ecclesia* and *Synagogua* see p. 138. The Towneley play of Jacob which has a scene of Jacob's dream (Genesis 28: 11–16) is incomplete (52 cf. L. R. Muir, *Contexts for medieval English drama*). There is also a play from Lille, and the *Bendicion (Benediction) de Isaac* performed by the Embroiderers in Seville in the 1552 Corpus Christi procession was probably on the same subject (Sentaurens, *Séville* 55).

10 *VT*, II 170, stages Jacob's flight from the wrath of Esau, his sojourn in Aran in the service of Laban, his marriages to Leah and Rachel and his eventual reconciliation with Esau. For Castilian plays on Jacob's marriage and his wrestling with the angel see Rouanet IV, XI, XII. The wrestling is also in Ingolstadt. Four texts stage the rape of Jacob's daughter, Dinah, by Prince Sichem (Genesis 34): Castilian *La roba Digna*, *VT*, II 265; Lille and Stonyhurst. The Stonyhurst pageants were written in the early seventeenth century by a Roman Catholic from Lancashire. The collection begins part-way through a pageant of Jacob with this story. Other pageants in the series

will be noted in their place. Although they are late, the texts show strong links with the earlier drama as do the sixteenth–century *Commedie Spirituali* by Cecchi, which include two plays about Jacob.

11 Joseph as a type of Christ is explained by God himself in the divine commentary that precedes the episode in *VT*, II 328 and in Jerome's introduction to the Lucerne Figure (I 121: cf. also Genesis 41: 45: 'And he [Pharaoh] turned his name and called him in the Egyptian tongue, The saviour of the world'). In both texts the parallel is developed by making Judas/Juda the brother who plans the betrayal and demands payment for Joseph of thirty pieces of silver.

12 The two Joseph plays from Florence emphasise the family relationship between the brothers. There is a Dutch Joseph play listed (but not summarised) by Hummelen and two from Lille, on the selling of Joseph, and Joseph in Egypt.

13 The action of this unique play is based on a Greek apocryphal legend which had passed into the *Speculum historiale* of Vincent of Beauvais. (See Rouanet, IV 179–80; and S. Baring–Gould, *Legends of Old Testament Characters*, II 46–8.) Joseph's wife, Assenes (Aseneth), appears in the Leuven *Ommegang* dressed as a woman of rank in the Egyptian manner (Twycross, Leuven *Ommegang* 95).

14 While Joseph is having his feet washed Senec (Aseneth) sees him from a window and is struck by his beauty: he is the sun come from Heaven, the very Son of God (*hijo de Dios*). This last phrase is not in the legend where Aseneth asks: 'What father has begotten so much beauty?' When Joseph rejects her as a heathen she laments her folly in speaking against Joseph, and her heathen practices.

15 In the legend there is no sacramental element in the story of Joseph and Aseneth and the angel gives her honey from the roses of paradise. The divine activity of Joseph is implicit rather than explicit in *VT*, which includes scenes from the seven good years and the seven bad years (Genesis 41: 53–7), between which is a very short interlude with Potiphar, the captain of the guard, upbraiding his wife for her false accusation of Joseph (of which he has apparently just learned) and declaring that he will never more be a husband to her but will geld himself and become the prince of the eunuchs and one of the priests (III 112). This odd scene seems to be an attempt to overcome the problem raised by the Vulgate description of Potiphar as an eunuch (Genesis 37: 36); it also links Potiphar with the probably quite independent high priest, father of Aseneth. The Vulgate makes all Pharaoh's officers eunuchs including the baker and butler (Genesis 40: 1) whose dreams Joseph interprets in prison. In some medieval versions of the story Pharaoh's queen replaces Potiphar's wife, probably for the same reason. See Joinville's typological figures for the different articles of the Creed (Appendix).

16 The Castilian *Finamiento de Jacob* and *VT*, III 186 dramatise the death and burial of Joseph's father, Jacob.

17 *VT* introduces only the last part of the scene and omits the child's refusal
    of the earlier nurses (III 243). For these Jewish legends (included in the
    Speculum historiale), see Baring-Gould, *Legends*, II 75–9.

18 People of Madian were descended from a son born to Abraham late in life
    (Genesis 25: 1). The marriage of Moses was one of the pageants for the
    Entry of Charles the Rash into Arras in 1469 (Petit de Julleville 198).

19 Moses and the Burning Bush occurs in *Sündenfall* 154; *Ordinalia* 107;
    Towneley 67; York 102 and *VT*, III 269, where the angel appears in the
    bush in the form '*du filz de Dieu*' (of the Son of God). All except *Sündenfall*
    include the miracle of the rod that becomes a serpent; the last three also
    have the miracle of the leprous hand (Exodus 4: 1–8). The plagues of
    Egypt (Exodus 5–12) narrated in detail by the messengers in York 106 and
    Towneley 73 are limited in *VT*, III 289, to the slaying of the first-born,
    with the emphasis instead on the eating of the paschal lamb and the
    establishment of the priesthood of Aaron. The same plays then stage the
    Exodus. Eger narrates the Exodus just before the scene of the giving of the
    Law (31). N. town omits the Exodus altogether but God in the burning
    bush gives Moses the Tables of the Law which Moses then expounds to
    the audience (60).

20 For other scenes in the *Ordinalia* from the Rood legend see p. 56.

21 The miracle of the water from the rock (linked typologically with the Last
    Supper) is in *Ordinalia* 141; Semur 38; Lille; Lucerne, I 149; and *VT*, III
    321. The giving of the manna is in Lille; Lucerne, I 143; Castilian *Auto del
    Magna*, I 169; and *VT*, III 314 which also has the quails (Exodus 15 & 16).

22 The giving of the Law is found in Chester 81; Lille; N. town 60; *VT*, III
    342; Eger 36; Lucerne, I 163; and Semur 40. In Künzelsau 29, the
    Decalogue is preached to the audience.

23 Aaron is recorded as an independent figure in plays from Erfurt and
    Ingoldstadt so these are probably linked with the flowering rod (Bergmann
    89, 154); in Bologna, Aaron appears with the Ark of the Covenant
    containing the rod and the manna and prays for the people of Israel (III
    221). *VT*, III 324 and Lille stage the defeat of the Amalekites (Exodus 17:
    8–16); *VT*, III 376 and Cecchi, the punishment of Choron and Dathan
    (Numbers 16: 31). *VT* concludes this sequence with the death of Moses (III
    425).

24 *VT*, III 380; Künzelsau 30; also in Ingolstadt; Freiburg; and Stonyhurst.
    Lille has two plays of Joshua's victories from the Book of Joshua.

25 References are given here from the Vulgate which has four books of
    Kings: I & II Samuel and I & II Kings. Many of these stories were very
    popular in the post-Reformation Protestant drama which was always
    reluctant to introduce God on the stage. Lille, exceptionally for a
    fifteenth-century collection, includes twenty plays from the books of Kings
    – almost one third of the total number of biblical plays in the manuscript.

26 This is particularly clear when considering the plays of the Destruction of
    Jerusalem and the Apocalypse. (See p. 147)

27 Sampson also appears in Künzelsau 30 carrying the gates: cf. *VT*, IV 1; Florence; a Castilian *auto*; and Stonyhurst. Gideon is the subject of a Lille play and a Stonyhurst pageant and appears in processions from Ingolstadt, Ghent and Arras. OT heroes are often treated as 'saints' in medieval writings though only the Maccabees were officially canonised by the Church (feast day 1 August).

28 Draguignan Corpus Christi play includes a scene of Jael and Sisera. Jephthah's rash vow is in Castilian and Stonyhurst. The only play of Ruth is from Lille, though she appears with the gleaners in a tableau (sponsored appropriately by the Thatchers) in the Leuven *Ommegang*. The book of Ruth was included in the OT canon because she was an ancestress of Christ (Matthew 1: 5) but the story had no liturgical or typological associations.

29 *VT*, IV 49, starts its sequence of scenes from these books with the dedication of the child Samuel in the Temple and his calling by God (I Kings 1); Lille has a play of the sons of Eli and the ark (I Kings 4) and the death of Eli.

30 *VT* and Lille include a number of scenes from the story of Saul; David's love for Jonathan and his laments for the death of Saul and Jonathan appear in *VT*, IV 160, Lille and Dutch. Saul appears with David and Solomon in Stonyhurst. Abigail appeasing David is in Lille and Castilian. There are Castilian plays of the anointing of David and the death of Adonias, also found in *VT*, IV 297. David and Goliath was included as a tableau in a Paris procession of 1484 and David appears as one of the Nine Worthies in a number of English processions (see Lancashire). There is a late-sixteenth-century Swedish play of *Absalom*. I am grateful to Terry Gunnell for this information.

31 *VT*, IV 263 and Lille also stage the crowning of Solomon. His Judgement appeared in Eger 39; Florence *Salamone*; Béthune; Lille; *VT*, IV 317 and Ghent. The Queen of Sheba features in Béthune and the 1514 Paris procession. A number of other kings of Israel and Judah appear in plays: Rehoboam (III Kings 12) is in the entry of Charles the Rash into Arras in 1469 (Petit de Julleville 198). There are Dutch, Lille and Cecchi plays of Ahab and Obadiah, Naboth's Vineyard, Ahab and Benadad (III Kings 20–1).

32 There are plays of Esther in Lille, Dutch, Florence and Majorca. Separate plays of Ahasuerus and his queens, Vashti and Esther, appear in *VT*, VI 192, and Castilian. Judith and Holofernes appear in *VT* (where Nebuchadnezzar is, unbiblically, still the monarch: V 231); Lille; Majorca; Dutch; Florence; Draguignan and Ingolstadt.

33 Tobias and the angel appear in *VT*, V 52; Lille; Florence; Haarlem and Castilian.

34 L. Besserman, *The legend of Job in the Middle Ages*, 57–64. There is a play of Job in *VT*, V 1, another French play, *La Patience de Job* and texts in Italian and Castilian.

35 The figure of Jonah also appears in Corpus Christi plays from Ingolstadt and Zerbst.
36 The Latin Daniel plays are in Young, who describes this scene as an apocryphal addition although in the Vulgate this whole story of Bel and the Dragon, like the story of Susannah, was included in the OT canon, see p. 181.
37 There was a tableau of Susannah in Ingolstadt and plays from England; Florence(2); Aquila; Vienna; *VT*, V 130; Lille and Dutch.

6 PROPHETS AND PRECURSORS OF REDEMPTION

1 For texts and discussion see Young, II, ch. 21. The *Sermon* might be read on a number of different days during the Christmas season.
2 Young, II 132 n.1.
3 Ibid. 130–2.
4 For texts and details of the Sibylline prophecies in the liturgy in Spain see Donovan 37.
5 Young, II 133 and Donovan 147–54.
6 For a table of the prophecies in the Latin and Anglo-Norman plays see Muir, *Liturgy and drama* 175.
7 For prophets of the Passion and Judgement see pp. 244, 262. Other plays include from four to a dozen or more prophets (Eger 40; Lucerne, I 189). They may be summoned by God (Künzelsau 46); an angel (Belcari's *Annunciation*, I 169); or *Ecclesia* (Maastricht; and Semur, where Moses' prophecy comes at the end of a long narration of the plagues, Exodus and crossing the Red Sea: 41). The Maastricht play is the only one to include Virgil (310). Balaam appears, with his ass, in Revello and Bologna and without it in the St Gallen Christmas play I 143. (The editor, Mone, calls it the *Kindheit Jesus* (Childhood of Jesus) but I have followed Bergmann's *Katalog* in referring to these texts as Christmas plays.) There are mentions of prophets in tableaux from Spain and they are quoted by shepherds or hermits in several of the Spanish Christmas plays. In Yanguas's *Egloga en loor de la Natividad*, one of the shepherds tells the prophets they need suffer no more as they will surely go to the Elysian Fields (B. Patt, *The development of the Christmas play in Spain* 156).
8 D'Ancona, *Origini*, I 332 and his introduction to Belcari's *Annunziazione*.
9 An almost identical prophet play, including Augustine, is found at the beginning of the Frankfurt *Dirigierrolle* and *Passion* texts.
10 This is a common theme in art: see A. Watson, *The early iconography of the Tree of Jesse*.
11 See Appendix and p. 147 for Creed plays.
12 D'Ancona, *Origini*, I 358–60. A translation of the description of the Modena Corpus Christi procession is in *Staging* 268. For Bertrand de la Broquière's story and other records from Constantinople, see S. Baud-Bovey, 'Sur un sacrifice d'Abraham de Romanos'.

13 In Revello twelve sibyls alternate with twelve prophets (21), including the only appearance of 'Baruch' outside of the *Sermon*. Palermo has eight and eight and includes details of the sibyls' costumes. After the Octavian play (see p. 98) in Valenciennes 20-day, twelve sibyls are introduced and their appearance described by the Tiburtine Sibyl (f. 85r). Belcari alternates two prophets and one sibyl. The Florence *Purification* (which like the Coventry *Purification* has a prophet prologue) begins with the prophetess Anna, continues with a series of patriarchs (including Noah and Sampson) and a dozen prophets and finishes with three sibyls. For a table of the Italian *Prophetae*, see Revello xlii. A liturgical MS from Cordoba in Latin and Castilian records an *Ordo sibillarum* with each of eleven sibyls presenting a brief prophecy of the Nativity (see Bibliography: Records: Spanish: Cordoba).

14 For other sibyl plays see R. E. Surtz, *Historia del teatro en España: Edad Media* 74–5. A list of sibyls and their emblems is to be found at the back of *The Book of Saints* edited by the Benedictines of St Augustine's, Ramsgate.

15 For similar scenes at the beginning of the Harrowing of Hell plays, see p. 138.

16 The comments on Advent are omitted from the English translation of the *Golden Legend* by Ryan and Ripperger. Bale uses these antiphons at the end of each scene of his Old Testament play, *God's Promises*. The Sicilian play adds to the usual six antiphons a seventh, *O Virgo virginum* (appropriately spoken by Isaiah).

17 For the Table of parallels between these plays and a discussion of the scene see P. Meredith & L. R. Muir, The trial in Heaven in the *Eerste bliscap* and other European plays.

18 Mons differs from Gréban, however, in prefacing the Trial only with the prayers of Human Lineage (not the prophets) and making the sequel to the Trial the birth of Mary not of Christ. In Troyes, God narrates the clash of the Virtues and explains that Justice has weakened and Pity gained strength. 'We will give our own Son to save the people of Israel' (145). Semur has a special variant where Charity and Hope ask God how man can be saved (instead of telling him) and God then ponders, aloud, on how he can reconcile his Truth and his Mercy and decides it can only be done by creating a new Paradise with a new Tree (Mary) whose Fruit of Life (Jesus) man can eat: the Eucharist (46).

19 See also Valenciennes 20-day; Rouen; Castilian *Justicia divina contra el peccado de Adam*; Revello; Vicente *Trial in Heaven* and Belcari's *Annunciation*. The Trial forms the opening scene of the Valenciennes twenty-five-day *Passion* which survives in two MSS. (Hereafter referred to as Valenciennes 25-day.) The text is unpublished and cited here from the Bibl. Nat. MS 12536. Konigson's study of the play uses this MS but also includes the rubrics from the Rothschild MS. In *Sündenfall* the Trial follows God's decision to harken to the prayers of the prophets (210). Judging by the cast–list, the Dutch *Bruijt Christi* (Bride of Christ, listed but not summarised

by Hummelen), like the Castilian *Farsa de la esposa de los cantares*, is a Trial in Heaven play based on the Song of Songs.

20 L. R. Muir, The Trinity in medieval drama, analyses the N. town and *Bliscap* texts. A simpler version of the debate, featuring only Justice and Mercy, is intercalated at intervals in *VT* from the Fall to the end of the Flood sequence. For the disappearance of the Four Daughters in the sixteenth century from the scene of the Assumption in the *Actes des Apostres*, see Lebègue, *Actes* 172. Debates are also found in Maastricht 306, Bologna, III 219 and Künzelsau 39. In Vicente's Portuguese *Auto de Deos Padre e Justiça e Misericordia*, a prophet and sibyl play, introduced by the prayers of Joseph and Mary, follows the debate in Heaven.

21 For a tabulated schema of this group of plays, see Meredith and Muir, Trial in Heaven.

22 The three source texts are all printed together in *Apocryphal Gospels, Acts and Revelations*, trans. A. Walker. A few play-texts contain only the Marian material, but in others it is part of a larger whole from a Christmas play to a full Corpus Christi cycle. The *laudario* from Orvieto, compiled at the beginning of the fifteenth century from older material, has two different plays of the Conception (Orvieto A and B) both prescribed for 8 December (I 348, 355). The only English text is in N. town *Mary*, a play from the Conception to the Visitation grafted on to the Corpus Christi cycle between the Prophets and the birth of Christ. The Rouen *Nativité* of 1474, which makes great use of *Meditationes*, is the longest extant Christmas play – 30,000 lines which do not include the visit of the magi. The play ends with Octavian entertaining the Sibyl and the shepherds rejoicing. (The editor of this text mentions also a play of the Immaculate Conception performed in Rouen in 1499.) The late fifteenth-century *Mystère de la Conception ... de Marie ... avec la Nativité de Jésus-Christ* extant only in early printed editions, also combines the Marian material with the Christmas story. *Mystère* formed the first day of the huge cyclic passion in Paris in 1507 and influenced Valenciennes 25-day (see note 19). It is unpublished and folio references are given here from the undated, Paris edition by Lotrian and Janot in the British Library. The cast list survives from Toulon of a nativity play performed there in 1333. Petit de Julleville (3) mentions only a few of the characters but the full list printed in the *Revue des sociétés savantes* (259) makes it clear that the play included Mary in the Temple and the Marriage of Joseph and Mary as well as the Christmas story.

23 For details of the Marian feasts see R. W. Pfaff, *New liturgical feasts in medieval England*. Spain has a very large number of Christmas plays especially from the sixteenth century. Patt, *Christmas play*, lists sixty-eight extant texts linked (sometimes tenuously) with the Christmas season and a further thirty-four titles of unpublished or lost plays up to about 1650. (This includes plays from the whole Peninsula, in Catalan, Castilian and Portuguese.)

24 The priest is named Reuben in *Pseudo-Matthew; Orvieto* B; *Sündenfall* 204; Valenciennes 25-day, f. 6r; but Ysachar in *Nativity of Mary*; N. town *Mary* 33; Eger 46; Mons 53. In *Mystère*, f. 14v he says he is 'Ysachar, surnamed Reuben'. By Jewish law a barren wife could and should be divorced after ten years (Pagels, *Adam* 11).

25 N. town *Mary* (later in the play) and Valenciennes 20-day include acrostics on her name. This was a common theme in religious lyrics. See P. Meredith, N. town *Mary* 98.

26 The doctrine was opposed by many leading schoolmen, including SS. Bernard, Bonaventure and Thomas Aquinas, but it achieved such widespread popular and theological support that Pope Sixtus II in 1477 approved the Feast of the Immaculate Conception with its own Mass and Office. The choice of date – 8 December – was dictated by the already existing Feast of the Nativity of Mary on 8 September. The doctrine was not formally declared dogma till 1854.

27 Mézières also composed the Propers of the Mass for the feast. The play was performed twice in Avignon during the schism but then disappears: cf. *Philippe de Mézières' Campaign for the Feast of Mary's Presentation*, ed. William E. Coleman.

28 A rare representation of Mary weaving the purple is included among the mosaics in the twelfth-century church at Kore, in Istanbul. In a Greek homily on the Annunciation attributed to St Germanus the angel tells Mary 'the purple you hold signifies royal dignity' (*Patrologia graeca*, XCVIII, 324; see also note 48).

29 For this play see De Bartholomaeis, *Origini* 270.

30 Cf. N. town *Mary* 99.

31 In St Gallen *Christmas* Cleophas addresses Joseph as 'brother' (I 154). See *Legenda*: James the Less and note 37 for the Holy Kinship.

32 One of the lections for the Third Sunday in Advent is from a sermon by St Bernard explaining that it was necessary for Mary to be married to conceal from the devil the divine nature of the child she would bear. In Valenciennes 20-day Gabriel tells Joseph this at the time of Joseph's Doubt (f. 74r).

33 The phrase 'your mother and your brethren' (Matthew 12: 47) was originally explained as a reference to sons of Joseph by a previous marriage but after the second century they were described as Joseph's nephews or cousins. From very early days the idea of the Virgin bearing other children was rejected completely.

34 At the end of the Limburg *Echtverbintenis van Maria* there is a statement that 'Joseph was thirty-three years and three months old at the time: by the Jewish ten-month calendar he is therefore forty' (134). The source for this account is included in the same MS and claims to be a Dutch translation of a fifteenth-century Latin text based on the 'Nazarene books'. Most of the source is similar to the *Nativity of Mary* (though the Dutch version mentions three bishops, two of them named Abiachar and Ysachar). It

also includes a scene in the Temple when the priest tries to change the prophecy 'a virgin shall conceive' into a 'young woman shall conceive', but it is changed back each time by an angel. The priest is rebuked by the elderly Simeon (138). This incident, with Simeon as the one trying to alter the text, occurs in the Chester *Presentation* based on the *Stanzaic life of Christ* whose source for it is unknown (205).

35 The story of Agabus, excluding the pact with the devil, is cited (unfortunately without source) in A. S. Rappoport, *Medieval legends of Christ* 32. The Carmelites and the cult of St Anne are discussed in *Interpreting cultural symbols: St Anne in late medieval society*, ed. Ashley and Sheingorn.

36 In *Protevangelium*, Joseph left Mary alone while he went away to build houses, being a carpenter. In Rouen it is stated that Mary went back to her parents' home in Nazareth. For other references to the family in Nazareth see, chapter 7, The Flight into Egypt.

37 *Mystère*, f. 28r (following *Legenda*) dramatises the two other marriages of Anne: after the death of Joachim she is married first to Cleophas, by whom she has a daughter Mary who later marries Alpheus and becomes the mother of James the Less, Justus, Simon and Jude. (This James is also called the brother of the Lord (Galatians 1: 19) but this was explained in *Legenda* as being because he looked very like his cousin, Jesus. For this theme in relation to the kiss of Judas see p. 131.) After the death of Cleophas, Anne marries Salome by whom she has another daughter called Mary who marries Zebedee and is the mother of James and John. This Holy Kinship is frequently represented in art in the Middle Ages. See Ashley and Sheingorn, *St Anne* 169–227.

38 In addition to the plays discussed here, there are also a few relevant 'figures' recorded in civic entries or processions. Ingolstadt Corpus Christi play of 1507 has figures of the Annunciation to Joachim and Anne and the Marriage of Mary and Joseph. There is also a reference to a Golden Gate but linked with the Visitation to Elizabeth, not with Joachim's meeting with Anne (Bergmann 154). Bozen Corpus Christi procession includes Mary in the Temple (which needed repainting in 1504 and again in 1509: ibid. 254). One of the pageants which greeted Margaret Tudor when she came to Edinburgh in 1503 to marry James IV, combined the Annunciation with the Marriage of Joseph and Mary (Mill 178).

39 John is the only saint other than the Virgin Mary whose nativity is celebrated: normally saints were commemorated on their death. Augustine and others taught that John's birth was miraculous not just because of the age of his mother, but also because he was purified in the womb from Original Sin at the Visitation.

40 A dialogued antiphon of the Annunciation prescribed for the last Friday in Advent is cited by De Bartholomaeis (*Laude*, I viii) from the Roman Antiphonar. The Advent commemoration reflects the practice of the churches, especially in Spain, of celebrating the feast in December rather than in March when it often fell in Lent (Young, II 245).

41 The Dutch *Birth of John the Baptist* makes the story of Zacharias and Elizabeth the excuse to emphasise the need for more Christian charity and brotherly love between the *Gues* (the Dutch reformist opponents of Spain) and the Catholics.

42 Ceremonies connected with the feast of the Annunciation and the *Missa aurea* (Golden Mass) are described in Young, II 245–50. Annunciation tableaux appeared in many of the non-dramatic Corpus Christi processions including Béthune, Draguignan, Barcelona, Valencia, Ingolstadt, Zerbst. The importance of the Annunciation as symbol of the Incarnation is shown by a mid-fifteenth–century illustration to Dante's *Paradiso* by Giovanni di Paolo: in Canto VII Beatrice's explanation of the mystery of the Redemption is pictorially represented by a triple scene of the Fall, the Annunciation and the Crucifixion, see Dante, *Paradiso* 94–5.

43 For the *Bliscap* see p. 36.

44 See D'Ancona, *Origini* for Abramio (I 246) and Ferrara (I 334).

45 This follows Nicholas of Lyra's comment that, as the annunciation to Zacharias was made while he was serving in the Temple, that to the Virgin would surely find her praying. This is cited explicitly by Rouen and obviously known to others. For Lyra's influence on the French plays especially Gréban, see Roy *Mystère* 207. A variant of this scene is included in Gil Vicente's *Auto de la Sibila Cassandra*. The Trojan prophetess has three sibylline aunts – Erythraean, Persian and Cimmerian – who are trying to persuade her to marry Solomon. After much discussion on the relative merits of marriage and singleness, Cassandra finally admits she wishes to remain virgin, because God will be born of a virgin and she thinks she will be the one. She is rebuked by her prophetic uncles – Moses, Abraham and Isaiah – for her pride: the one chosen by God is the humble Mary. The play, which includes many prophecies of the Incarnation, Passion and Judgement, ends at the manger where Cassandra confesses her fault and all join in a final *Te Deum* (Patt, *Christmas play* 134).

46 For the various titles of Mary including the fleece of Gideon, see York prophet-prologue to the Annunciation (110) and the chapter on the Annunciation in J. Vriend, *The blessed Virgin Mary in the medieval drama of England*. The metaphor of the sun through glass is quoted also by John the Baptist in his introduction to the Towneley *Baptism* 195. In Troyes 156, Mary addresses Gabriel as '*ange de Dieu secretaire*', a somewhat free translation of *angelos* (messenger).

47 This seems an unusual and not very felicitous variant on the theme of Joseph's flowering rod or the legend of Judas and the capon, see p. 246. In the Florence play seen by Abramio, he describes Gabriel bringing a rod from Heaven and giving it to Mary; the prophecy of the rod of Jesse is among those quoted by the York Annunciation prologue.

48 The homilies are discussed in La Piana, *Le sacre rapprezentazioni* 110–18. Mary's words to the angel and Joseph's to Mary are from a homily

attributed to the eighth-century patriarch, St Germanus (*Patrologia graeca*, XCVIII 322–8).

49 Doves featured in both Latin and vernacular plays; in Besançon an elderly man representing God was located in the gallery from which the dove descended. In Padua, Mary received the dove and put it under her cloak symbolising the conception (Young, II 245–50). Troyes 156 says the dove descends from Paradise, Valenciennes 25-day has a dove 'in a sphere which opens' (rubric to the third day in the Rothschild MS) and Valenciennes 20-day, f. 72v has it surrounded with light. In Barcelona in 1453 a mechanical dove was required which would issue from the mouth of God the Father, descend to Mary with light and fire and return the same way (Shergold 58). The beam of light appears in representations of the Annunciation in art, often with a dove in the beam, and sometimes leading to Mary's ear as a symbol that she conceived the Logos, the Word of God. In a sermon attributed to St Gregory Thaumaturge, when God gives Gabriel his instructions for the Annunciation, Gabriel reflects 'as was consistent with reason' on the amazing condescension of God who, to a daughter of Eve, 'announces the advent of his very person; indeed he promises an entrance through hearing' (*Patrologia graeca*, X 1175).

50 The Visitation is included in processions from Freiburg, Ingolstadt and Zerbst (Bergmann 121, 154, 374). The N. town MS has genealogies of Mary and Elizabeth including a reference to the latter's mother, Emeria. The name occurs in the gospel of *Pseudo-Matthew* (N. town *Mary* 87). In Valenciennes 20-day, f. 72v, Mary says Elizabeth is the daughter of '*ma tante Esmeria*' (cf. Ashley and Scheingorn, *St Anne* 14–16, and note 37).

51 In Künzelsau 52 the *Magnificat* is sung antiphonally in Latin by Mary and a chorus; N. town *Mary* 80 has it sung antiphonally by Mary, in Latin, and Elizabeth, in English. Chester 100 and Towneley 98 (where the Salutation of Elizabeth is a separate play) have vernacular paraphrases. Gréban cuts the *Magnificat* by half, whereas Arras, followed more or less verbatim by Lille (Knight 45) and Valenciennes 25-day, expands it to eleven stanzas at the end of which Elizabeth exclaims: '*O ma cousine quel cantique!/Quelz langaige de rhetorique!*' (O my cousin what a canticle! What rhetorical language! (15)), In Semur 58, Mary recites the *Magnificat* in Latin on the way home from Elizabeth.

52 Joseph's concern over Mary's possible punishment is described in *Protevangelium*; he fears that she might be innocent despite the evidence.

53 This play was composed *c.* 1470, for his sister who was abbess at Calabaçanos (Patt 69).

54 La Piana quotes these homilies from a thirteenth-century codex in the Naples library in which the dialogues (exceptionally) are not set in a commentary but arranged in dramatic form. It is tempting to see this as an influence of Western traditions on Eastern sermon-plays.

7 THE BIRTH AND CHILDHOOD OF JESUS

1 The tax is set at one silver *denarius* (*denier, pfennig*, penny: *Legenda;* Valenciennes 20-day, f. 75v; Künzelsau 54; Eger 55). Rouen 8 has ten *deniers*. In Chester 112, Joseph asks if the poor have to pay as well as the rich since this is unfair. On a more legalistic note, Arras 20 and Valenciennes 25-day, f. 44r have the whole decree read out in Jerusalem by the high priest, Reuben. Written in prose, it is very long and uses much formal legal terminology. The effect is of a translation of a genuine Latin document.

2 Although the Bible talks of Caesar Augustus, the plays follow *Legenda* (25 December) where he is called the Emperor Octavian ('who was also called Caesar, after his uncle Julius Caesar, and Augustus because he augmented the Roman Republic'). The church of the *Aracoeli* stands on the site of the meeting of the Emperor and the Sibyl on the Capitoline hill in Rome.

3 In Semur 82 (where the tax is four *deniers*) Octavian tells the Sibyl that the money raised by the new tax he has just imposed will go to make good, straight roads leading to Rome in order to receive the new king worthily. This seems to be an echo of Isaiah 40: 3, quoted about John the Baptist in the synoptic gospels: 'Prepare ye the way of the Lord, make straight in the wilderness the paths of our God' (Luke 3: 4). Valenciennes 20-day, f. 80v includes other miracles from the night of the Nativity: the death of the Sodomites; the fountain of oil and the vision of three suns as a symbol of the Trinity (*Legenda*). The *Dialogo del Nascimiento* by Torres Naharro, a comprehensive if undramatic presentation of the Nativity story from prophets to Magi, includes all the Roman miracles except the death of the Sodomites (cf. Patt, *Christmas play* 145–54). No other Spanish play includes any of the miracles in Rome. Woolf 178 gives a detailed comparison of the English versions.

4 Fragments of more traditional Catalan plays on this subject are also extant (cf. Surtz, *Teatro* 74–5). There is a fragmentary scene of the Emperor and the Sibyl in one nativity play from the Majorcan Codex (which contains several *Consuetas de Nadal*). A very special variant of the scene from Hungary is described by an Italian diplomat: 'in Buda on Corpus Christi day in 1501, a Turkish mosque was constructed in front of the cathedral containing Mohammed's coffin, and surrounded by Turkish worshippers. Suddenly fire from Heaven destroyed the coffin and a student dressed as the Sibyl, appeared on the roof of the church and prophesied the fall of the Ottoman empire.' (See Szönyi, *Hungarian drama* 169.)

5 Gréban 62; Eger 56; Mons 62; Semur 63; Chester 113. For Nicholas of Lyra see Roy, *Mystère* 208–9. The ox and ass were seen as the fulfilment of Habakkuk's prophecy, 'He shall be seen between two beasts', which is included in the *Pseudo-Augustinian Sermon* from the Septuagint. It is not in the Vulgate. Cf. also 'The beast of the field shall glorify me' (Isaiah 43: 20).

6 Cf. Daniel's prophecy in the *Sermon*, 'When the most Holy One shall come your anointing will cease', based on Daniel 9: 25.

7 Marguerite de Navarre (also sometimes referred to as Marguerite d'Angoulême), sister of Francis I of France and consort of Henry II of Navarre, wrote a group of sacred comedies.

8 This miracle is found in the French poem of the *Enfances de Christ* which is freely adapted from the Latin Infancy gospels. In a prose version of the *Meditationes* prepared for Jean, duc de Berry, in the late fifteenth century this miracle is recorded in almost identical terms but attributed to the child Jesus (see the Introduction to Whittredge's edition of the St Genevieve *Kings*, 48).

9 In the Cangé *Nativity*, Zebel, who is not a midwife, shows Joseph and Mary where to stay and remains with Mary for the birth; later Joseph returns with Salome, the official midwife, and the usual scene follows (I 210). Semur intercalates a scene in the synagogue where the Jews and *Synagogua* foretell in comic terms the end of their rule (64). (The principal Jew, Damp Godibert, becomes a regular character throughout the play, mainly comic but sometimes serious.) *Ecclesia* and *Synagogua* then debate and the latter acknowledges defeat. *Ecclesia* sings verses of the '*Veni redemptor*' expanded with comments on the Incarnation in French; Innocence and Humility sing the refrains.

10 The tradition of three Masses on Christmas Day dates from the sixth century (Eisenhofer and Lechner, *Liturgy* 222).

11 Midwives were first introduced into the Nativity story in *Protevangelium* where their purpose was to bear witness to the Virgin Birth. There are two of them: the believer (called Zemoli in *Pseudo-Matthew* and *Meditationes;* Zebel in *Legenda* and most plays) who accepts Joseph's words at once; and Salome (*Protevangelium* and all plays) who refuses to believe Joseph's story that Mary is a virgin and the mother of God. For details of the various legends of the midwives see Chester, II 91 Notes.

12 Honestasse is subsequently called Anastaise. The association of St Anastasia (feast 25 December and commemorated during the second Mass of Christmas Day) with the Nativity is peculiar to the French tradition. The source of the legend of the hands is probably the martyrdom of two different Anastasias (feast days 28 October and 15 April) who both had their hands cut off (Roy, *Mystère* 18*). There is also a link with the so-called *Arabic Infancy Gospel*, where Joseph brings to Mary an old Hebrew woman who is healed of palsy when she touches the child (Walker, *Apocrypha* 100–1). The St Genevieve version is taken from the *Roman de Fanuel*, which includes the birth of St Anne and other stories of the Virgin and Christ, see Whittredge, *Nativité* and Vriend, *Virgin Mary* 112, note C. Anastaise is in the cast list of the 1333 Toulon *Nativity* (as well as the midwives Salome and Zael) and she also features in the fourteenth-century Provençal *Esposalizi (Marriage of Mary)*. Anastaise is described as the servant of Joseph and Mary in a magi play from Manosque in

Provence. Meyer refers to a late-fourteenth-century prose translation in Provençal of the Nativity sequence of the *Roman de Fanuel*, which may be the source of these three occurrences. For Anastasia in a Purification play see p. 109.

13 The angels sing, among other pieces, '*Noe, Noe*' (Valenciennes 20-day, f. 79r); '*Hodie christus natus est*' (Benediktbeuern, II 180); '*Veni creator spiritus*' (St Genevieve 147); '*Gloria in excelsis*' (Eger 59; Hesse, III 909); '*Puer natus est*' (Lucerne, I 201, which prefaces the moment of birth with a blast of trumpets; Troyes also mentions the use of instruments in heaven to accompany the vernacular angels' song: 215).

14 The Liège plays were composed *c.* 1480 by a Sister Katharine Bourlet of the community of the White Ladies of Huy for performance in her convent. (See Cohen, *Nativités* and *Le Théâtre français en Belgique au Moyen Age* 28) The plays include unique scenes of the adoration of the infant Jesus by St Anne and the Virgin's sisters.

15 There is also a lullaby sung in the Tyrol Christmas play. In Encina's *Egloga interlocutoria* the shepherds discover Joseph singing and dancing to entertain the Child (Patt, *Christmas play* 104. For dancing shepherds, see p. 104).

16 See Szönyi, Hungarian drama 167.

17 In addition to the plays cited here there are others still unpublished including the NT Catalan *Consuetas* listed by Llabres in his *Repertorio* of the Palma MS. The OT and saints' plays have recently been edited.

18 See Young, II, ch. 17. The bilingual Shrewsbury fragment gives the English words of the role of the Third Shepherd interspersed with sung Latin texts (including music), one of which is part of the shepherds' reply to the midwives.

19 The strongly liturgical *Natività* from Siena requires the angels and shepherds to be in position before the Mass. At the time of the *Gloria*, an angel appears holding a light and begins the '*Gloria in excelsis deo*'. The choir responds. After the end of Mass, an angel announces the *festa*, then speaks the annunciation to the shepherds. 'Then there shall be a sudden flash of light and crackling' near the shepherds (II 212). This suggests a use of fireworks.

20 Patt, *Christmas play* 101.

21 From the earliest days the people presented, before Mass or at least before the singing of the Gospel, gifts of food, clothing, wax, oil and so forth, for the support of the clergy and the poor. They also offered *oblata* of bread and wine for use in the Eucharist itself. Although in the later Middle Ages the ceremony of offering was reduced in length, the general practice has remained, though nowadays the gifts are usually money (G. Dix, *The shape of the liturgy* 104, 142).

22 Other gifts include toys for the baby (rattles, bells, and a wooden calendar from which he can learn his letters); cups and a shepherd's crook. The discussion of the gifts may be symbolic in tone or humorous, or even both. Vicente's *Auto dos quatro tempos* exceptionally includes only one offering,

made here by King David, who has come to encourage the shepherds to go to the manger, the gift being a humble spirit and contrite heart: cf. 'A sacrifice to God is an afflicted spirit: a contrite and humbled heart, O God, thou wilt not despise' (Psalm 50: 19). Cf. Patt, *Christmas play* 142.

23 The English shepherds seem to have little genuine concern for their sheep (Woolf 187); in contrast, one shepherd in Lucerne tells his fellows he will stay behind and guard the sheep while they go to the manger (I 204), and in Florence *Christmas*, I 193 Nencio is told to stay by his fellows but insists he wants to go as well. A few plays also include a 'boy' to whom the task may have been entrusted while in Valenciennes 20-day they say the dogs will protect the sheep from the '*loupz rabis*' (ravening wolves: f. 82v).

24 They sometimes eat before the angelic announcement (St Genevieve 151; Chester 131) or before setting out for Bethlehem. In Semur the shepherds are joined by their wives and they cook a meal of milk and eggs; after his return, *Primus pastor* quarrels with his wife in very outspoken terms over the meal she has prepared, alternating his criticisms with words of veneration for the sight he has seen. In Florence *Christmas* they eat before setting out (I 194) and another meal is taken with Joseph in the stable after the adoration of the Child: having walked for three hours the shepherds are very hungry (198).

25 These texts may include four evangelists as shepherds, all quoting their own gospels, or a wise shepherd instructing the younger ones; the plays end with a formalised obligatory scene of the Stable and the Adoration. See plays by Encina and Vicente among others in Patt, *Christmas play*.

26 In Valenciennes 20-day, a similar glorification of the pastoral life, which might stem from purely literary pastoral convention, nevertheless contains elements that relate to contemporary experience, as when the shepherds talk of the importance of being free from the rule of king or regent (f. 82r). The country was at that time (1549) under the rule of Philip II of Spain and his regent in the Netherlands.

27 This dance play is discussed by Patt (*Christmas play* 247) and translated in *Staging* (174) which also mentions other examples of dance in the plays. For the association of dancing with the feast of Corpus Christi in Spain see Valdes, *Oviedo* 54–75.

28 Roy, *Mystère* 209, claims that this follows the *Summa theologiae* very closely.

29 In Valenciennes 20-day, f. 90v there is a speech of twenty-eight lines in praise of the Holy Name, each line beginning: 'Jesus'. Mary laments over the pain her infant son must suffer.

30 Plays of the kings are particularly numerous, occurring not only in all the Corpus Christi and passion cycles but in many separate texts: there are three different plays of the kings from Neuchâtel, for example. The exception to this general popularity is Spain. Catalonia has a tradition of kings' plays and a notable text from the Valencia Corpus Christi cycle but elsewhere there is very little – even in Toledo it was only performed once, in 1502, though it should be noted also that the Nativity and Shepherds

were never performed at all (46). The twelfth-century *Auto de los reyes magos* is the only Spanish magi play before the sixteenth century and then there are very few although the Christmas plays with shepherds are extremely numerous.

31 They are sometimes shown as astronomers even when they are kings (St Gallen, I 164, Valenciennes 20-day, f. 87r).

32 Because their relics were preserved in the cathedral of Cologne, they are sometimes referred to as the Kings of Cologne, as in the Welsh *Y tri brenin o Gwlen* (*The three kings of Cologne*), the only Celtic play on the childhood of Christ. A few plays also mention the age variation and it is common in art. In Florence *Christmas* they are unnamed and described simply as the old, the middle and the young *magus*: I 198; Valenciennes 20-day, f. 87r has Jaspar as the eldest; in St Genevieve, Melchior, introducing them to Herod, refers to Balthasaar as '*anciens*' and Caspar as a '*jouvenceaulx*' (youth: 168). There is also considerable variation in their countries of origin, though Caspar is usually from Arabia. In the fifteenth century, in art, he was often shown as a Moor, but in Lucerne, Balthasaar is dressed '*Mörisch*' and Caspar is '*arabisch*' (Evans 186). In Grandi's *Resurrection* 36, where the story is narrated by the kings during the prophet play, one is from the Levant. In St Genevieve *Kings*, Melchior is from Serile (?Syria: 161).

33 Processional versions sometimes include only the journey to the stable and adoration with gifts (Bologna, Florence *Magi*, and many liturgical ceremonies). Marguerite de Navarre begins her *Comédie de l'adoration des trois Roys* with a lengthy scene in which the kings are disciplined by Tribulation, Inspiration or Philosophy so that they can receive Divine Understanding.

34 The source of these visions is an old legend attributed (erroneously) by Rappoport, *Medieval legends* 58, to John of Hildesheim. The source is otherwise unidentified.

35 For liturgical Epiphany processions see Young, II, ch. 18. In the Leuven *Ommegang* as portrayed in the *Liber Boonen* illustrated MS (1594), the kings' mounts (including a camel) are made of wickerwork and borne by two men whose feet show underneath (Meg Twycross, Leuven *Ommegang* 96). In the Bologna Corpus Christi procession they accompany the Nativity waggon with a retinue, trumpets and much pomp (III 226).

36 This play (one of a group from the town of Erlau in Hungary) uses a number of liturgical Latin responsories and the kings speak in both languages.

37 In the Herod play from Sicily (II 61), Arras 41 and Valenciennes 25-day, f. 54v, the advisors erroneously attribute to Isaiah (who never mentions the town) Micah's prophecy of Bethlehem as the Messiah's birthplace.

38 Abondance's *Joyeulx mistère* (*c.* 1540) is one of three extant kings' plays from Neuchâtel. The *Offertorium Magorum* (1500) is a strongly liturgical piece. The *Discours pour le jour des roys* (1640) shows a continuous dramatic Epiphany tradition in the area for more than 150 years.

39 In *Mystère*, f. 66v; Valenciennes 20-day, f. 86v; and Chester 158 the kings talk of Balaam as their ancestor – a tradition inspired by Balaam's prophecy of the star of Jacob (Numbers 4: 17). Cf. Schiller, *Iconography*, I 96.

40 For the liturgical scenes of *Herodes iratus* see p. 184.

41 The absence of this motif in the continental plays may be due to their having already treated the theme in the story of Octavian. Thus although in English the character has passed into proverb, 'to out-Herod Herod' would have little meaning in, for example, French. There is an interesting early example of this expression in a Catalan text of about 1200, the Vich Antiphoner, where one of the reasons given for not reciting the *Invitatorium* on the Feast of Epiphany is lest they should 'seem to out-Herod Herod' in cunning and deceit ('*Ne Herodidemus Herodes*': Donovan 95).

42 The ease with which this is achieved may reflect a deliberate contrast with the problems met by Joseph and Mary. Presumably the people gathered for the census have now left. York 146 introduces an *ancilla* (maidservant) who, in an echo of the scene with the midwives in many Latin shepherd plays, asks the kings whom they seek, and tells them to draw near as they have reached their goal.

43 Valenciennes 20-day, f. 94v; *Mystère*, f. 67v; Gréban 92 and Perugia, I 82. This may have been associated with the tradition of the sovereign's Epiphany offering: in 1378, for the visit of the Emperor Charles V, the King of France (also Charles V) had two sets of offerings prepared, one for each ruler, each consisting of gold, incense and myrrh. The royal gift was actually given to the archbishop by three knights, each presenting one in turn, but it is explicitly described as 'l'offrande du roy' (Young, II 432–3). The tradition of the royal offering has survived in England: each year, two Gentlemen Ushers to the Queen present gold, frankincense and myrrh on behalf of Her Majesty to the Dean of the Chapel Royal in London.

44 Elsewhere they just lie down on the stage. In Semur they sleep very near the stable and take their leave of Mary and Joseph the next morning before setting off home (88).

45 Most of these responsories are found in the *Officium stellae* and Latin Herod plays; cf. Young, II, ch. 19.

46 On his return from Rome, Herod sees the ships, believes they are those used by the kings and burns them. Nicholas of Lyra tells of the kings' return home by sea and adds that Herod in anger burnt the ships of Tharsis (cf. Roy, *Mystère* 211, and Psalm 47: 8 – 'Thou shalt break in pieces the ships of Tharsis'). In Gréban 94 the kings take a boat to Tharsis; in Valenciennes 20-day the dream is not staged but narrated by the kings, who then set off towards the coast. *Mystère* is similar. Ships and sea-battles on stage are rare in the biblical drama but not unknown in saints' plays, such as the English and French Mary Magdalene plays or the French lives of St Louis.

47 Coventry and Chester follow this practice and moreover combine the

episode of the Purification with Christ and the doctors in the Temple. Digby follows straight on from the Flight and Slaughter of the Innocents to the Purification regardless of logic. (For a detailed analysis of the solutions used by the English cycle plays see Woolf 195–6.) The German processional plays either omitted the Purification (Künzelsau) or staged it in the logical sequence (Freiburg im Breisgau). The Latin, Italian and Spanish texts usually treat the stories in separate plays.

48 St Gallen, I 175; Arras 53; Semur 91. For details of the French handling of this scene see Muir, Aspects of form and meaning in the biblical drama. Revello's solution is to intercalate a scene of Herod, after instructing his men to search for the Child, journeying to Rome and back because summoned by the Emperor (55). Gréban 103 follows the tradition (based on Herod's orders to kill all the children under the age of two) that the star appeared two years before the Nativity. Having discovered this, Herod gives orders for the slaughter *before* he sets off for Rome.

49 Gréban 94; York 151; Towneley 181. In Bozen *Candlemas* – where he is described as *modicum incurvatus ad modum senum* (somewhat bent like an old man) – Simeon has a servant who mocks him as an old fool for praying to a child and talking about a virgin mother (178). Simeon is promised the sight of the Messiah by an angel (N. town 182) or the Holy Spirit (Perugia *lauda*, I 94). Anna is sometimes omitted (Eger; Perugia). Joseph and Mary may be accompanied by members of the family (Mons 91), and may offer both doves and pigeons (Mons 92; Arras 50), whereas in the Bible a choice is given: 'a pair of turtle doves or two young pigeons' (Luke 2: 24). In Chester, Simeon tries to change the wording in the book of the prophecy of Isaiah (see p. 220). In Lucerne, I 224, the priest who offers the child is Zacharias, father of John the Baptist. In Coventry *Presentation* 47, Joseph complains about his age and infirmity because he has to trap the birds for the offering himself. In Eger 79 he buys them from a vendor in the Temple.

50 The feast is often called Candlemas (see Appendix for French and German forms) and candles were used in the liturgy of the day because of the reference in the *Nunc dimittis* to Christ as the 'light to lighten the gentiles.' In Eger 79, Mary gives a candle as part of the offering for the Child but in Chester 209 and Cangé *Nativity*, I 225, the candle is a symbol of Mary's own purity. For Candlemas processional plays see p. 37.

51 In this play the five gold pence for the redemption of Jesus, and the candle come from the gifts of the magi (cf. *Legenda*). I am most grateful to Graham Runnalls for letting me have a copy of this unusual play before it was published.

52 In one version of Lucerne, Herod is specifically tempted to the deed by the devil (I 229n).

53 For example, Hiczenplicz, Windeck and Schlachinhaüffen (Eger) add a vigour to the written text not supplied by *Primus*, *Secundus* and *Tercius Miles* (Semur).

54 The Latin plays of the slaughter are sometimes called *Ordo Rachelis*: for texts see Young and Donovan). In Semur 94 the two women are Rachel and Zebel (the midwife); in Künzelsau 87 all three are Rachel. In Marguerite's *Comédie des Innocents*, Rachel has an extended lament or *planctus* at the end of the slaughter (II 166) while in St Gallen, I 179, the lament is by Rachel speaking as Christendom.

55 Arras 57; *Comédie*, II 162. In Gréban 107 the nurse is called Medusa. In Mons 103 the '*enffant futif*' (wooden doll) is being taught to walk in a babywalker; usually the dolls are being held by their mothers. In a few plays the women attack the soldiers (Coventry 30; Digby 107). In Florence *Christmas* 207, the women are invited to bring the children to the palace where they are seized and killed. Some texts have stage directions or dialogue suggesting that the soldiers proudly display their lances and swords laden with spitted corpses. In *Mystère*, f. 75v the soldiers guess the age of the babies by their weight. Several plays claim a total death toll of 144,000 (Lucerne, I 236; Liège 32; in Arras 59 Satan tells Lucifer this). The figure was taken from Revelation 7: 4 where the number of the saved is shown as 144,000. The Innocents were venerated as the first Christian martyrs because 'their martyrdom conferred baptismal innocence upon them; in other words it purified them from Original Sin' (*Legenda*; many martyrs of the early Church were held to have been 'baptised in blood' if they died without the sacrament of Church Baptism).

56 Sometimes he is tempted to kill himself by devils (*Mystère*, f. 78r; St Genevieve 195) and in Valenciennes 20-day, f. 108r he himself summons them. Arras 63 and Gréban 110 follow the *Legenda* account of Herod's using the knife with which he is peeling an apple to kill himself in a frenzy of pain (cf. also Mons 107). In Troyes 370 and *Mystère*, f. 78r the knife is given him by his sister Salome (in *Legenda* she is his daughter). In other plays, Herod is eaten by worms (Benediktbeuern, III 896; *Mystère*, f. 78r; in Chester 201 he describes his rotting flesh). In N. town 197 Death refers to himself as worm-eaten. In Benediktbeuern, Chester and many French plays Herod is taken off to Hell by devils.

57 Usually this is a brief, simple scene. In Hesse 936, Joseph is afraid to go to town to buy bread for the journey lest he be attacked by one of the mourning mothers. The scene ends with them going off '*zu dem guden bier!*' (to the good beer!). In Erlau, III 949, Mary agrees with Joseph that they should set off, then there is a stage direction: *Et sic recedant, supra vehiculum sint Maria et Joseph* (And so they withdraw; on the vehicle are Mary and Joseph). There is no other indication in the texts or records that the Erlau plays were on waggons or other 'vehicles'. Marguerite de Navarre's *Comédie du désert* is a lyrical, semi-dramatic text (very different from her other plays) in which allegorical figures mingle with the Family. The desert is seen to blossom like a rose and the lion lies down with the lamb (cf. Isaiah 35: 1, 2; 66: 25).

58 Somewhat confused versions of the story of the sower occur in St

Genevieve 182 and Valencia 126 (where there are three sowers). In Semur 93, the soldiers meet the *Rusticus* and his wife, instead of the sower, and get no information from him, only obscenities.

59 Perugia, I 85, includes both fountain and bowing tree; Arras 56 includes the bowing tree. Both are mentioned in *Legenda*. In Revello 57 the tree offers Mary dates, which she picks. In German, the episode is included only in the Kreuzenstein (Bergmann 182) and Himmelgartner fragments. Only the last-named (a semi-dramatic thirteenth-century adaptation of the gospels) follows *Pseudo-Matthew* in having the child order the tree to bow and give its fruit (393). In the plays a doll is probably used for the child. A version of the legend is used in N. town 153 during the journey to Bethlehem, though here the tree is a cherry not a date palm (cf. the English *Cherry tree carol*).

60 *Meditationes* rejects the other miracles 'since few authentic things are known', but does include the idols because they are scripturally based: 'as was prophesied by Isaiah' (68). The same distinction is followed by several French plays (Arras 57; *Mystère*, f. 78r; Gréban 102) who include a dialogue between the priests of the Temple in which the idols fall. In Troyes the *Sot* (fool) tells the priest their idols are useless and offers them his '*marotte*' (fool's doll) as a suitable substitute (347). Benediktbeuern has a most unusual and confused Flight play including kings of Egypt and Babylon and even Antichrist (see H-J. Linke, Der Schluss des Weihnachtsspiels aus Benediktbeuern).

61 A very few plays record the return of the Family from Egypt to Nazareth. There is a brief instruction from Gabriel to Joseph in Lucerne, I 237, and the French plays introduce a family reunion in Nazareth, leading into the preparations for going up to Jerusalem with the twelve-year-old Jesus (Arras 66 and Valenciennes 20-day, f. 114v, include St Anne and Elizabeth in the group; Gréban 111 has Joseph's kin). In Valenciennes 25-day Gabriel 'flies' to Egypt to tell them to return (Rothschild MS, rubric to seventh Day).

62 The meeting with John in the desert is briefly described in *Meditationes* 82. In the Burgos *Flight* a pilgrim meets John and tells him of the birth of Christ. John asks the pilgrim to take a message to his mother. The pilgrim does so and on his return tells John to persevere in his desert solitude.

63 The discussion on the fulfilment of prophecy is based on Nicholas of Lyra (cf. Roy, *Mystère* 214) and does not appear in *Meditationes*. Losing her son on this occasion is one of the 'Sorrows of Mary'. Hummelen lists a play of the twelve-year-old Jesus and the scene also occurs in the Haarlem *Doctors*, f. 165r. The subject is treated briefly in Lucerne, I 239 and elaborated in Gréban 113 and *Mystère*, f. 81v. Valenciennes 20-day and 25-day have a shortened version of Gréban and also introduce two *chevaliers du Temple* (an echo of the *Templiers* or Knights Templar?). These violent defenders of Judaism, rejoicing in the names of Osanna and Sabaoth, are borrowed from Arras 69, where, however, the discussion is on the Commandments,

with Christ attacking the doctors for failing to live up to the Commandments they preach (73, cf. Matthew 23: 3–4). Four English plays use the
discussion on the Commandments, with reference to the gospel debate on
which is the greatest (Matthew 22; York 177; Towneley 189; Chester 213
and Coventry). In N. town, original as ever, the topic for discussion is the
Trinity (199).

64 The prophecy, associated in the gospel with the question from John the
Baptist's disciples: 'Are you the one we expect?' refers to the healing
miracles that the Messiah will work. Jesus tells the disciples to describe to
John (in prison) the miracles they have seen.

8 THE PUBLIC LIFE OF JESUS

1 Although modern commentators prefer to call it the Fourth Gospel rather
than John's gospel, the traditional (and medieval) title is used throughout
this study.

2 The selection of incidents from the public life of Jesus varies enormously
from one play to another. Generally the processional plays limit
themselves to the Baptism, Transfiguration and Raising of Lazarus with
one or two healing miracles and some teaching. The passion plays,
however, are more extensive.

3 As well as the cyclic plays already mentioned, a number of substantial new
plays including the Alsfeld, St Gallen and Heidelberg *Passions* begin with
the Baptism of Christ; Michel's *Passion* (based on Gréban but much
developed and enlarged) becomes an influential part of the French group
of *Passions*. The Auvergne *Baptism* survives and has been edited separately
from the rest of the *Passion*. In addition to the texts discussed here there is
an unpublished Dutch play of the *Decollation* which includes the Baptism
(Hummelen 30), and a 'comedy' of the *Preaching of John the Baptist* by John
Bale. Four cycle plays omit the Baptism: Mons, Eger, Künzelsau and
Chester. There is a missing '*journee*' in Troyes at this point.

4 The farewell to the Virgin occurs in Auvergne *Baptism* 74 and the two
versions of the Abruzzi *Deserto* (Temptation) play (114, 121). In Revello 62
he takes leave of both Mary and Joseph. In Michel 22, Jesus tells Mary
(who is accompanied by Gabriel) about his work and the witness of John
the Baptist, in a long speech based on John 1: 1–14.

5 He is summoned by God (Auvergne *Baptism* 54), Raphael (Mons 133) and
an angel (Lille; Towneley 197). In York 181 he introduces himself at some
length. The Towneley play stresses throughout the sacramental nature
and importance of baptism. John says to the angel '*By this I may welle
understand / That chylder shuld be broght to kyrk*' (197).

6 Alsfeld and St Gallen include Latin responsories side by side with the
spoken German text throughout. Gréban, Michel and their dependants
open with long sermons addressed to the spectators, either by a Prologue
or by the Baptist himself (both in Michel). They then continue with the

various groups of dramatic characters, including Jews who question John about himself: are you the Messiah, or Elijah? (also in Abruzzi *Decollation* 42; Florence *Decollation* 116; Heidelberg 6). Lille and Lucerne, I 247, follow Matthew's gospel in characterising the interlocutors by occupation: workman, soldier and so forth. In Lille the 'soldiers' include Joseph of Arimathea and other knights. In Semur 96, Christ preaches on the Ten Commandments before he is baptised.

7 The organisation of the water was in the hands of the *Brunnenmeister* (stream-master; cf. Evans 145, n.25). Some plays mention the removal of clothing, implying baptism by immersion (Michel 26; Auvergne *Baptism* 78). In Revello 67 the angels who are present help Jesus resume his garments). The Frankfurt *Dirigierrolle* uses the common liturgical word '*aspergat*' (sprinkles: 342) and Semur also implies affusion with '*infundendo*' (pouring: 100). The cast list for the Toledo *Baptism* play includes a 'water-carrier' (68). Towneley – which, like the other English plays, Revello and Auvergne *Baptism* suggests affusion with John pouring water over Jesus' head – is the only play to mention the other concomitant of the sacrament: the mixture of oil and balsam known as Chrism (200).

8 John points at Christ in N. town 208 and Revello 72. The finger of John the Baptist was a venerated relic in the Middle Ages because of this action, see *Legenda*, Decollation of John the Baptist. In Towneley 201, Jesus gives John a lamb as his symbol.

9 The dove is omitted by Lille and, although foretold by the angel, does not appear in York (183). In Toledo it came down from a cloud, surrounded by rays made of tin (68).

10 In Florence God's words are to be spoken by '*una voce nascosa che dica per quella colomba*' (a hidden voice which speaks through this dove). In Auvergne *Baptism* 78, *Deus pater* addresses his remark to the angels who, in Revello, Florence and Towneley, escort Jesus throughout this scene. Towneley 199 specifies two angels because Jesus is both God and Man.

11 The Decollation of John the Baptist is celebrated on the 29th August. He was the patron of Florence and a performance of the Florence *Decollation* on the feast-day in 1451 was attended by fifty thousand people (Newbigin 109). Decollation plays are found in a few Corpus Christi cycles (Künzelsau, Zerbst and Toledo). There are also independent Castilian and Italian plays, and scenes in the French, German and Italian cyclic *Passions*.

12 Valenciennes 25-day shows Herod's first wife who, learning of his infatuation, decides to leave him and return to her father (f. 83r; the event is reported to John the Baptist by a Jew in Michel 42). In most plays the new queen is called Herodias but Gréban and the Abruzzi play use the form Herodiades. Both forms are found in the Vulgate, depending on the case-ending. (Künzelsau has Heroida.)

13 The disciples of John visit Jesus asking 'Art thou he that art to come?' (Matthew 11: 3) in both Rome *lauda* 139, and in Revello 78, where Jesus

preaches on baptism as the replacement for circumcision (Matthew 22). In Auvergne 116, Christ reads this prophecy in the Temple in Nazareth. The priest '*cantet sicut in secunda dominica*' (sings as for the Second Sunday [in Advent]). Then Jesus preaches on the fulfilment of the prophecy.

14 Although the name Salome is already found in Josephus (third century AD) it is never used in the plays. Often she is an unnamed *filia* (daughter). Occasionally she is given a name apparently at random: Florence (Michel 99 and Mons 188, where the role was played by a girl); Eglantine (Semur 111); Drusiana (Abruzzi 47); Rea (Lucerne, I 339). Her dance is variously described as a *morisco* (Mons 189); a *morisque* (Semur 111); a *stampita* then a *bassedance* and *saltarella* with one of the courtiers (Revello 83); and a *zitella* (Rome 146). In Auvergne 91 she changes into *habitus moriscarum* (the dress of a morisque dancer) and then with two courtiers makes an *intragium moriscem* (morris entry; Michel 99 has an *entree de morisque*). In Künzelsau 96 she dances *cum aliis puellis* (with other girls). A variety of musicians and instruments accompany the scene.

15 In Florence *Decollation* 128, Herod tries to refuse, and the *filia* pretends to cry. The courtiers insist he must keep his word. Abruzzi, Michel, Mons and Valenciennes 25-day follow *Historia scholastica* (cited by *Legenda*) in showing that Herod and Herodias plan the whole thing in advance.

16 The Casteldurante *Decollation* is described in a letter. The writer gives an eye-witness account of a play of John the Baptist, performed on a specially erected stage with many locations (see *Il Teatro italiano*. Ed. E. Faccioli, I 696–7). One year, Toledo paid three separate actors to represent John: one preaching, one in prison watching Salome dance and one being executed. The waggon was obviously arranged in a triple tableau (59).

17 Herodias's revenge is described in Lucerne, I 344; Michel 103; Arras 85. In Valenciennes 25-day the dagger in the head and the spouting blood is noted as one of the 'marvels' of the twelfth day in the Rothschild MS. I have not been able to identify the source. In Mons and Auvergne the disgusted guests rapidly depart at this point; mother and daughter are taken off to Hell by devils (Künzelsau 101). At Casteldurante, the devil carried the (unnamed) queen off to Hell '*per una corda*' (by a rope). This might suggest a downward 'flight' similar to that of the angels from Heaven '*sopra una corda*' (on a rope) earlier in the play (Casteldurante *Decollation*, I 697). In Florence 133 the earth opens and swallows Herodias. *Legenda* cites this as the fate of her daughter.

18 Revello 87, Castilian *Decollation* II 59 (where the disciples include Santiago = St James). The scene is clearly modelled on the gospel account of Joseph of Arimathea asking Pilate for the body of Christ. In Heidelberg 41, Herodias declares her intention of sinking the head in deep water so it can never be reunited with the body. Disciples bury the body. In Auvergne 109, Herod orders the head to be taken away and the gaoler, repenting of what he had had to do, buries the head with the body.

19 In addition to the Temptation plays discussed here, there are two Majorcan *consuetas* and a Dutch play (Hummelen 84). The episode was staged four times in Toledo. In Künzelsau it occurs much later in the sequence after the anointing by Mary Magdalene (107). It is omitted in Mons, although the construction of the pinnacle of the Temple is mentioned in the accounts (485). Some of the German plays are very brief and biblical (Lucerne; Heidelberg; Künzelsau). St Gallen and the *Dirigierrolle* from Frankfurt include sung antiphons. There is a brief scene of the Temptation at the beginning of the second Day of the *Ordinalia* before the Entry into Jerusalem.

20 The infernal council features in N. town 213; York 186 (the devil has a long speech); Gréban 141; Michel 27; Semur 116; and Abruzzi 116, 124. It forms the opening scene of the Alsfeld and Tyrolean *Passions*. In Revello 68 the devils sit in their prescribed places in the middle of the scaffold, with Lucifer in a higher seat. In Auvergne *Baptism* 108, they are given letters of authorisation by Lucifer. This may be an echo of the formal permission which God gave Satan to tempt Job (Job 1: 12).

21 He is sometimes accompanied by a second devil with whom he can discuss his plans (Gréban 142; Michel 27; Auvergne *Baptism* 108). In Revello 71 he has demons who are eventually put to flight by Michael, who chains Satan and takes him back to Hell.

22 *Meditationes* 122 comments on Jesus' humility. In Revello 70 Satan takes Jesus' hand and leads him up the mountain but in Michel 37 and Valenciennes 25-day (rubric to the eighth day) Jesus sits on Satan's shoulders and they are raised by machinery. Subsequently the devil descends the same way but Jesus returns 'secretly'. In Semur 118 after Satan has gone Jesus asks the angels to bring him down from the mountain.

23 When Satan shows Jesus 'all the kingdoms of the world' he sometimes names specific countries: Perugia *lauda*, I 109; N. town 218; Abruzzi 118; Gréban 144; Michel 39.

24 The scene occurs in St Gallen; Lucerne; the Sterzing *Gospel* plays and all the Gréban group (except Troyes which has a *journee* missing) but not in the other French *Passions* or Revello. Maastricht has only the end of the scene. The Greek word used by John for 'miracle' is *semios*: a sign, which he distinguishes from the usual miracles. The turning of water into wine was read during Epiphany because it was held to be a further 'manifestation' of Christ's divinity (C. H. Dodd, *Fourth Gospel* 297–383). In Michel, after the miracle, a servant comments that if he had this power he'd 'turn the whole Sea of Galilee into wine and there would never be another drop of rain-water' (71). In Valenciennes 25-day, (according to the introduction to the episode in the Rothschild MS), over a hundred members of the audience drank the wine that had been miraculously converted. The episode was recalled nearly a century later in an account of the play in the *Histoire de Valenciennes* of 1629 (see E. Konigson, *La*

Représentation d'un mystère de la Passion à *Valenciennes* 23, 92). Audience involvement in the multiplication of loaves and fishes (another 'type' of the Eucharist) is also mentioned but here by 1629, the number who shared the meal has swollen from the hundred mentioned in the play MS to more than a thousand (Konigson 23, 103). This latter episode is found otherwise only in the Tyrol gospel plays and a Perugia Lent *lauda*, I 156.

25 The 'ruler of the feast' is called *architriclinus* ('steward' or 'butler') in the Vulgate. Then Architriclin (Archideclin: Gréban) became a proper name. In Maastricht 327 he is the bride's father. See D. A. Trotter, Influence of Bible commentaries on Old French Bible translations.

26 This was a well-known theme in the lives of saints, for example, St Alexis.

27 In John's gospel (and a few plays) the Marriage at Cana is immediately followed by the Cleansing of the Temple. Most plays and the synoptics put the Cleansing after the Entry into Jerusalem and it will be considered then.

28 Although the feast of the Transfiguration, celebrated on 6 August, was popular in the East, it was only confirmed in the Western Church in 1457. There is no record of a Transfiguration scene from Germany or Holland. The Auvergne *Passion* (which omits the Transfiguration and has Jesus withdraw merely to pray alone) includes a vivid scene of the disciples trying in vain to heal the boy, while the devil makes him fling himself in the water. He is pulled out by the disciples but they cannot heal him. The incident is conflated with the healing of the dumb boy (Matthew 12: 22), for the possessed child is also deaf and dumb and can only make noises '*On, on, on, on*'. Eventually Jesus returns and heals the demoniac (157). In the gospels the disciples' failure is only referred to by the father who tells Jesus, 'I brought him to thy disciples and they could not cure him' (Matthew 17: 14–20).

29 See *The Oxford dictionary of the Christian church* and Ashley and Scheingorn, *St Anne* 27.

30 Bergmann lists twelve other healing miracles in the German plays as well as the raising of Jairus's daughter, the son of the widow of Nain and Lazarus. Most of these miracles also occur in French and many healing miracles are dramatised in the Italian *laude*; cf. Perugia, I 140, 147, 161.

31 Sometimes miracles become conflated: in Auvergne 127 and Semur 140 the son of the ruler in Capernaum becomes the son, not the servant, of the Centurion (whose rank, like the status of Architriclin, is often treated as a proper name; Matthew 8: 5–13). Both stories are also staged elsewhere. The healing of the ruler's son was John's second sign: 'This is again the second miracle that Jesus did ... in Galilee' (John 4: 54). Like the wedding in Cana, this episode is omitted by the Corpus Christi cycles though healing miracles may be intercalated into other episodes such as the Entry into Jerusalem (York 213; N. town 264).

32 See p. 51 for Michel's use of the raving of the daughter of the Canaanite woman to encourage silence in the audience. In Mons at the exorcism,

fireworks explode and a devil appears (through a trapdoor) and rushes off to Hell (184). For fireworks in the plays, see P. Butterworth, 'Gunnepowdyr, Fyre and Thondyr' and the records in Vitale-Brovarone's edition of the Provençal *Director's notebook*.

33 See the Dutch *Gebooren Blinde*, Revello, Perugia and Provençal. The German and French texts are analysed in Wildenberg-de Kroon, Die Blindenheilung 162–3. Jesus' attacks on the moral blindness of the Jews inspired another Dutch play: the Predestined Blind (*Ghepredestineerde Blinde*). In the Cyprus *Passion* the blind man and the cripple bear witness to their healing during the trial of Jesus. Longinus who thrust a spear into Christ's side at the Crucifixion, is described as blind in *Legenda* and in Semur he appears with his attendant 'boy'.

34 The fifteenth-century French *Passion d'Isabeau* begins not with the Entry into Jerusalem but with the Raising of Lazarus because, as it says, this was the final cause of the Jews' decision to kill Jesus.

35 The theme of repentance and conversion informs a number of other episodes such as the Woman taken in Adultery (also from John's gospel – 8: 1–11) which is included in most German and French *Passions* (in Gréban and Michel she is called Jhezabel); Künzelsau and all the English cycles (except Towneley). The Chester Expositor (following the exegetes) says Jesus wrote on the ground the sins of the accusers (229); and the Dutch play of this episode is called *Christ schrift in der Erden* (Christ writes on the ground; Hummelen 150).

36 For a detailed study of the Magdalene story in the plays, see J. Accarie, *Le Théâtre sacré de la fin du moyen âge* 136–230). The worldliness of Magdalene is not found in any Corpus Christi cycle and only Künzelsau and Zerbst include her Conversion. Perhaps Christocentric episodes were considered more appropriate in Corpus Christi plays. An incomplete French *'Moral à six personnages'* which includes Magdalene, Martha and Lazarus stages only the worldliness. (See Petit de Julleville, *Le Répertoire du théâtre comique en France* 77.)

37 It has been suggested that the vernacular song and dialogue used in the mainly Latin Benediktbeuern *Passion* (I 520) indicate that the scene comes from an older folk play which may also lie behind the Bohemian *Play of Gay Magdalene* (Veltrusky, Drama in Bohemia 55) but there is no concrete evidence of this folk element.

38 This story is clearly a form of *psychomachia*, as found in saints' lives or morality plays. Mary's lovers include one of Herod's knights (Michel 126; Alsfeld 632); Pilate's nephew, with whom she plays chess (Donaueschingen 60); Centurion (Rouergue *Lazarus* 77); and young men (Florence *Conversion* 263; Vienna 306). They may be the devil Belial (Eger 102) or the Seven Deadly Sins (Digby 38). In Alsfeld her servant is a devil called *Natyr* (Nature?) and she dances with Lucifer and the Sins (632). In Erlau *Magdalen* 95, the play opens with devils conspiring to tempt her. These texts are obviously influenced by the Lucan reference to Jesus casting out

seven devils. In N. town Jesus casts them out during the scene in Simon's house before the Last Supper (270). Michel picks up the theme of the Seven Deadly Sins at the very end of the conversion sequence when the penitent Mary confesses her sins, enumerating each in turn in much scholastic detail with sub-divisions (162).

39 In Florence *Conversion*, Martha is equated with the woman healed of an issue of blood (Matthew 9: 20; cf. *Meditationes* 167); in other plays that woman appears as a separate character, who in Cyprus *Passion* 181 witnesses to her healing during the trial before Pilate). Mary agrees reluctantly to hear the preacher and insists on going first for two days to Bethany with her own servants.

40 In other plays Jesus preaches on the parable of the sower (Auvergne 137); and expounds the beatitudes (Frankfurt *Passion* 413; Alsfeld 637). In Michel, where the text is 'No one knows the hour', Mary's friends invite her to go and hear this exciting new preacher and at her request describe his appearance and clothes in detail and glowing terms: 'Is he very good to look at?' – 'He is tall and straight, wise, controlled, constant and cold.' 'Well made? – Fairest in the world' (143). In the Cyprus *Passion* 145 the harlot (she is not named in this text) tells the vendor of ointment that Jesus 'is well-shapen' and quotes Psalm 44: 3. 'Thou art fairer than the children of men.' Mary is already penitent in Abruzzi *Magdalene* 144.

41 He is variously referred to as Simon Leper or Simon the Pharisee: Michel uses both. In the Florence *Miracolo di S Maria Maddalena* (which, like Digby, includes the conversion of Mary before treating of her later missionary work) he says he is 'the Pharisee, Simon the leper whom you healed' (I 393). Usually Simon criticises Jesus for allowing Mary to touch him but in St Genevieve *Passion* 101, she asks Simon's permission to enter and he himself takes her to Jesus.

42 Mary washes and anoints Jesus' feet in Benediktbeuern, I 523; Donaueschingen 65; Semur 138; Arras 118; the 1526 Sterzing *Gospel* play 188; and a Perugia *lauda* for the Monday of Holy Week (I 198).

43 She anoints Jesus' head and feet in Eger 106; Frankfurt *Passion* 422; Heidelberg 123; *Ordinalia*; Provençal *Passion* 18; Revello 99.

44 In Donaueschingen 64 she tells the apothecary that she wants the finest salve as an offering to honour the physician who heals all the sick. In Abruzzi *Magdalene* she takes with her some ointment she once used on herself. A stage direction in this play has Mary creep in under the table (*socto la mensa*, 145; cf. Michel 164; Autun 73 and Arras 118). This image is also found in art: see Schiller, *Iconography*, II, fig. 27. In Auvergne 139 there is much rustic humour as the servants prepare the meal and quarrel in patois over the catching of the fish and game they need. These two comics recur at intervals throughout the play.

45 This parable appears in Benediktbeuern *Passion*, I 523; Fleury *Raising of Lazarus* II 200; Heidelberg 125; Donaueschingen 66; Semur 138; Auvergne

153; Arras 119; Provençal *Passion* 20; and *Ordinalia* 261. There is a separate dramatisation of this parable in Lille.

46 In Palatinus *Passion*, where the scene precedes the Last Supper, Judas swears to get his own back by selling Jesus to the Jews (99). In Troyes 549, Judas comments that it is just like a woman – wasting everything! In Abruzzi *Magdalene* 146 the chorus warns the audience not to risk damning themselves by rejecting the need for repentance.

47 This whole scene, nearly a hundred lines long, seems to have been intended to show the status of the family at Bethany and their knowledge of proper etiquette (Revello 100). According to *Legenda*, Mary, Martha and Lazarus were of royal birth and held the towns of Magdala, Bethany and part of Jerusalem from their mother. The Revello play was supported by and played before the local overlord, the Marchese di Saluzzo, who could be expected to appreciate such a scene. Lazarus's lineage is indirectly mentioned in Michel 78 where he is shown as a wealthy young nobleman given to hunting and hawking before he is converted to a less worldly life.

48 The subject is discussed at length in *Meditationes* chs. 45–58. In several plays Martha has a serving maid called Marcella (various spellings. Castilian *Hospitality of Martha*, II 440; Florence *Conversion*, I 263; Frankfurt 414; Heidelberg 103). In Frankfurt 414 Narcilla cries out to Jesus 'Blessed is the womb that bore thee' (Luke 11: 27). Alsfeld 638 says Martha's servant calls out and in Auvergne 165 a 'woman of the people' called Marcella speaks these words. The link between the name, the incident and Martha comes from *Legenda* (see entry for Mary Magdalene). The cast list for a proposed Pentecost play at New Romney (Kent) in 1555 included Mary, Martha, Lazarus and Martha's servant (Lancashire 233). A probably unconnected Marcella is the porteress at Peter's Denial in Gréban 258.

49 Based on a narrative poem, the description of Hell is found in most of the French plays and Breton *Passion*, where it is one of the first incidents staged (9). In Revello 106, Lazarus describes his vision only to Mary and Martha. In Towneley 390 and Rouergue *Lazarus* 86 the scene immediately follows the Raising so that Lazarus is still wearing his shroud. In St Genevieve 126 the narrative is part of the Last Supper at which Lazarus is present. The stage directions of the Angers *Resurrection* 191 call for separate locations for Hell, Limbo, Purgatory 'under Limbo and containing souls tormented by fire' and a separate Limbo for uncircumcised infants. These are the four regions described by Lazarus in Michel's version (203).

50 An Umbrian *lauda* of the Raising was performed on the feast of St Lazarus (29 July). Aversa *Lazarus* begins with Lazarus trying to convert an incredulous Jew, and several plays show Lazarus and his sister Martha trying to reform Mary Magdalene. Sometimes the meal at Bethany is confused with the meal with Simon the Leper, probably because the name Lazarus means 'leper' and the two characters were confounded. There is also sometimes confusion with the beggar called Lazarus in the parable of

the Rich Man and the beggar (Luke 16: 19–31; see p. 122) and in French Lazarus is often referred to as *Le Ladre* (the leper).

51 Even more than religious prejudice, anti-Jewish political persecution in the later Middle Ages was a matter of economics. Because the Church did not allow Christians to lend money at interest, the Jews were the principal money-lenders, including royalty among their clients. When debts became too big, it was more convenient to persecute the Jews than pay them. The Jews were expelled from England in 1290 and from France in 1306. Though they continued to be tolerated in the Empire attacks and criticisms were frequent (Hay, *Europe* 356). For the growth of the Inquisition in Spain see Reilly, *Medieval Spains* 198–203.

52 Fleury specifies that the house of Simon (from which he has now departed) can be used for the death-scene in Bethany. In the church plays, Lazarus's tomb was sometimes the Easter sepulchre (Young, II 210; see also Scheingorn, *The Easter Sepulchre in England*). In Arras 106 he is buried in a ditch with earth put over him; in Valenciennes 25-day, f. 170v, there is a stone over the grave which can be lifted up for the Raising.

53 In St Genevieve *Passion* 109, Jesus' weeping over Lazarus follows the Raising and he explains that he weeps because Lazarus will have to suffer death again.

54 In Arras, where the Raising precedes the Conversion of the Magdalene, Lazarus '*tous couzus dedans son suaire*' (all sewn up in his shroud) narrates his vision of Hell, thanks Jesus for raising him and kneels to him. In Florence *Conversion*, I 301 he and his sisters join in a paean of praise of Jesus and the play ends with the conversion of all present. The Perugia *lauda* of the gospel for the Friday before Passion Sunday ends with the news of the Raising of Lazarus being taken to the pharisees (I 174).

55 There are also several non-cycle versions associated with the liturgical commemoration of the Four Last Things (Death, Judgement, Heaven and Hell) during Advent. For all these texts see under Eschatological plays.

56 There are three plays of the Prodigal Son extant in French; two from Majorca (Llabres); two in Dutch (Hummelen); one in Castilian and one in German (Bergmann). The Italian version is called the *Vitello sagginato* (Fatted calf; see Newbigin 29). Partly, perhaps, because it invokes no dogmatic or doctrinally controversial ideas, the story retained its popularity in the post-medieval period with many versions extant in Latin and the vernaculars.

57 Composed in Arras in the first quarter of the thirteenth century, *Courtois d'Arras* has survived in four MSS. The other two French plays on the theme are much later, see Petit de Julleville, *Répertoire* 57.

58 There are obvious parallels here also with the story of the Fall and Redemption of Adam, see especially the *Liber apologeticus*.

59 In the gospel, the play is a straight denunciation of riches (Kirk, *The Vision of God* 70) but the medieval versions usually add an element of deliberate lack of charity (as in the case of the Prodigal Son's elder brother) to point

the moral and justify the damnation of the rich man. There are two plays in German (Bergmann); one in French (Petit de Julleville, *Répertoire*); three in Dutch (Hummelen). In Italian both characters are called Lazarus: *Lazaro ricco e Lazaro povero*. This parable is also popular in art.

60 The MS is dated 1539 but Vigil Raber says he has copied it from a text of 1520. The play is intended for performance and is arranged in a series of scenes separated by the closing and opening of a curtain. After the prologue a stage direction says the curtain should be taken away or pulled back (*so thue man das thuech weg oder ab*, 240).

61 Hummelen's *Repertorium* lists more than twenty parable plays including (in addition to those already mentioned) two versions each of the Unjust Steward (Luke 16: 1–13); the Guest without a Wedding Garment (Matthew 22: 11) and the Labourers in the Vineyard (Matthew 20: 1–16) which, like the Two Debtors (Matthew 18: 23–35), is also found in Lille. I am indebted to my colleague, Wim Hüsken, who is currently editing some of these plays, for help in sorting out the different parables. There are also two versions of the parable of the Wheat and Tares (Matthew 13: 24–30; the Vulgate translation has 'cockle' for 'tares') which appears also in a dumb-show in the scene on earth of the Anglo-Norman *Adam* 50, symbolising God's words to Adam, 'Thorns and thistles shall it bring forth to thee' (Genesis 3: 18).

62 In Vicente, the Law and the Sacrifices cannot help Adam, who is counselled in the Inn of Holy Church by the four doctors: Gregory, Jerome, Ambrose and Augustine. The allegorical interpretation of the parable, based on Bede (Lille refers to *Benda, venerable docteur*), is also found in Langland's *Piers Plowman*.

63 See the formalities in the Trial before Pilate and the episode of the Trial in Heaven with which this group of plays shows some affinities. A staging description from the beginning of the Provençal *Director's notebook* includes mansions (*mais[os]*) for 'the angels of *Umana natura* with his councillors and the seat of Law who will summon Our Lord'; 'when Jesus Christ has been condemned to death by them the Virgin Mary will appeal' (4). Clearly this play included a Judgement of Christ scene or scenes. Linguistically it is linked with Rouergue but there are no precise subject similarities.

64 Aquinas, *Summa theologiae* (trans. McDermott 524). Despite its title, Bale's *Comedy concerning three Lawes of Nature, Moses and Christ … corrupted by the sodomytes, pharyses and papystes (1538)*, is not a discussion on the necessity for the Passion (like the Judgement plays) but a polemic against the corruption of the Church.

65 For a detailed study of the sources and dramatic evolution of the theme (excluding the Tyrol play) together with the text of the *Sermon*, see Roy, *Mystère* 433.

66 In the *Sermon*, the plaintiff is referred to as *genus humanum* 469; in Rouergue 22, *Natura humana* (an old man, decently dressed) enters from Hell. In Abondance, *Nature humaine* is a leprous woman (Roy 503). In Tyrol 194, the

plaintiff is the *Redner der menschen* (Spokesman for mankind). Rouergue presents the whole trial according to strict procedural rules. Each move is formalised, there has to be a spokesman for each group of Judges, and the summonses are all in writing and delivered by the 'sergeant' Roma (26). Tyrol omits much of the formality but retains the sergeant (here called Malcho) and before the Judges enter to give their verdict in each scene, the plaintiff, defendant and counsel have to leave the court (199), perhaps because a small stage was being used. Abondance and the *Licentia* simplify even more, omitting all the juridical details.

67 The defendant is variously Jesus (Rouergue); the Innocent (Abondance); and Christus (Tyrol; *Licentia*). Rouergue, alone, follows the *Sermon* with counsel for and against Christ in each scene.

68 In Tyrol, Noah has a different figure: the ark by which he was saved was of wood, so man must be saved by wood (201). In the Castilian *Donas que embio Adan a Nuestra Senora* which has some similarity to the Judgement plays, the Virgin is described as the ark who brought salvation (II 393; for another instance of Mary as the Ark see p. 210). In this play, *La Humanidad* obtains from the Virgin an agreement (in writing) that Christ shall suffer on the cross.

69 The *Sermon* (Roy, *Mystère* 472) and Tyrol 203 also introduce the figure of Joseph who was betrayed by his brothers, so Christ must be betrayed. The *Licentia* begins with a dispute between Charity, who wants Christ to die for man, and Innocence, who claims he is guiltless. They appeal to *Natura* who takes council of the patriarchs (excluding Joseph) and then gives the judgement (Roy, *Mystère* 465).

70 The Judge here is *Scrittura (Licentia)*; David is spokesman for the prophets (Rouergue). The counsel for the plaintiff is Truth (*Sermon;* Rouergue; *Licentia;* Tyrol).

71 The *Sermon* and Tyrol add Zechariah. In the first *paso* (scene) of the Burgos *Passion*, the same four prophets are asked by the Virgin to spare her son but they all reluctantly declare he must die: 'because our salvation depends on his suffering' (957). This scene is evidently based on a Judgement play.

72 The *Sermon* and Rouergue mention also the eleven apostles as advisors. Revello omits the Law of Grace sequence. In the Castilian *Christ's farewell to his mother*, Adam enters carrying a cross and appeals to the Virgin for help in obtaining redemption (II 418).

73 The *Sermon* here follows closely the text of the late fourteenth-century *Passion d'Isabeau*. The crucifixion in Abondance is allegorised and performed by *Envie* (the Jews) and *le Gentil* (the Gentiles. Roy, *Mystère* 506). Rouergue continues with the play of the Raising of Lazarus. The Tyrol play ends with a *planctus* by the Virgin.

74 It seems possible that a version of this Sermon was the source for the *Moralité* which, Cohen suggested, was the basis for the role of *Humain lignaige* in the Mons *Passion* (xxxii). He first appears after the death of

Adam (18) and has many short scenes. He is tempted by the devil in the orgy before the Flood, in which he is drowned but reappears just before the scene of Abraham's sacrifice of Isaac with a prayer to God (33), and then has a scene with the prophets in which David and then Isaiah intercede for him to God and comfort him (34). As the speeches in this last section are fairly short it is easier to follow the sense of the sequence. David's last words are: 'Let these things be written down'(*Ces choses cy soient escriptes*: 35). Isaiah tells him the time will soon come (35). In the New Testament scenes *Humain lignaige* constantly reappears praying to God for deliverance or (after the Resurrection) referring back to Christ's suffering (441). In the absence of the full text of the speeches any source can only be tentatively suggested.

9 THE PASSION AND RESURRECTION

1 For Palm Sunday processions in the Middle Ages see Young, I 90–8. The scene figures in the Corpus Christi processions and plays from Freiburg, Bozen, Ingolstadt and Zerbst, but is omitted by Künzelsau and Bologna. There are also two surviving fragments of Palm Sunday plays from Bohemia (Veltrusky, Medieval drama 55). Figures of Jesus on a donkey were (and still are) used in many Palm Sunday processions throughout Europe and medieval ones are still preserved in churches and museums, see Teresa Bela, Palm Sunday Ceremonies in Poland: the Past and the Present. In Heidelberg 111 the *turba* (crowd) watching David's fight with Goliath prefigures the crowd at the Entry into Jerusalem.

2 The frequent references to finding the ass at a castle or *castellum* are based on the use of *castellum* in the Vulgate (Matthew 21: 2). None of the gospels names the apostles Jesus sends but in most of the French and German texts, Towneley and Revello they are Simon Peter and John, perhaps because they are the ones who will later be sent to arrange the Passover meal. However York 207; Chester 256; Rouergue 97; Alsfeld 657; and Heidelberg 119 send Peter and Philip. N. town *Passion* 231 has James the Less and Philip. In *Ordinalia* they are Matthew and James the Great (237). York 207 and Lucerne, II 36 describe the ass as being 'common property' that can be borrowed by anyone.

3 Latin or vernacular versions of the *Hosanna* and *Benedictus* (found also in the synoptics) are sung in Chester 259; Abruzzi *Entry* 144; Rouergue 99; Michel 221; and the Castilian *Entry* 270; Semur says the crowd sing *Hosanna* 'as on Palm Sunday' (*Dominica Ramos Palmarum*: 157). In Lucerne, II 37 the Synagogue sings the *Sanctus, Benedictus* and *Agnus Dei* from the Common of the Mass (see Appendix). In Eger 121 there are six different choruses who sing responsories in Latin and German. Troyes (which here is independent of Gréban) has an extensive scene where groups of boys greet Jesus with anthems (568). In *Ordinalia* 239 (whose passion play begins here, after a brief Temptation) the children

talk of picking the branches and throwing down their clothes, then greet Jesus with 'Joy to thee'.

4 Among other parallels, he is hailed as Salvation, Redemption, Light of the World and Glory of Heaven. The similarities between York and the liturgy are conceptual, not verbal.

5 A number of plays include Jesus' lament over Jerusalem (Luke 19: 41–4). In Michel 222 it is in the form of a *ballade*.

6 The liturgy of Holy Week provided no certain guide for the order of events since from Palm Sunday till Maundy Thursday the gospel for the day was the Passion according to each of the synoptics in turn: Matthew on Palm Sunday, Mark on Tuesday and Luke on Wednesday. The Passion according to John was sung on Good Friday. A number of semi-dramatic Passions survive from sixteenth-century Scandinavia; see Davidson, *The quasi-dramatic St John Passions*.

7 In Abruzzi 143 the disciples fetch the donkey from the Temple gate, and in several plays the children greet Jesus there again with *Hosannas* (Matthew 21: 15).

8 Sometimes the Jews complain to the authorities immediately (Sterzing *Passions* 13 and 213; Revello 113). In Arras, after the Cleansing, Jesus tells the sellers he is the 'Son of God, the second person of the Trinity'; they cry out 'Blasphemy' and want to stone him but he disappears (126). Versions of this scene, based on John 10: 29–39, occur in many plays, at different points in the story.

9 There are farewell scenes in Lucerne, II 55; Michel 230; and a very long one in Breton *Passion* 20. *Laude* on this theme were sung on both Sunday and Wednesday of Holy Week in Perugia, I 197, 205, and a possibly fourteenth-century dialogue on the theme is preserved in a Bolognese MS (D'Ancona, *Origini*, I 209). In the Abruzzi *Passion*, Jesus asks 'leave' (*licentia*) of his mother to depart after she has tried in vain to persuade him not to risk the anger of the Jews by returning to Jerusalem (155). In Michel 255 and Eger 140, when the Virgin fails to achieve her wish, she ironically turns to Judas, who is present, and begs him to look after her Son for her (cf. also Brixen (Tyrol 364) and Hall (ibid. 287) where Judas addresses the Virgin as '*fraw mueter*' (lady mother)).

10 For the first, see above, The Judgement of Jesus Christ. For the others, Jesus explains that since he must suffer for all men it must be a bitter suffering. He must die before his mother does as he must enter first into glory in fulfilment of Scripture. Lastly, he cannot take away the feeling and understanding which make her the *digne creature* (worthy creation) that she is (230). In Breton *Passion*, Jesus tells her that it would be contrary to reason for her to be able to view his sufferings without emotion (38; this is the only text I have found which includes (44) the common iconographical image of Jesus in the Winepress: cf. Schiller, *Iconography*, II 129). However, he does promise that at least her own death shall be without fear or pain. The dialogue is found in a number of French narrative *Passions*, especially

the 1380 *Passion Isabeau*. At the end of Michel's version is a particularly effective stichomythic dialogue (also found in Valenciennes 25-day) in which the Virgin begs that her son's death should not be cruel or public (234).

11 These scenes have been discussed above. Only Luke sets the scene well ahead of the Passion; Matthew, Mark and John all set it just before or during the early days of Passiontide.

12 The tithe is explicitly mentioned in Michel 245; Provençal *Passion* 29; Frankfurt 443; Abruzzi *Passion* 148; and Coliseum *Passion* 20. In the Tyrol *Passions* the devil tells him to ask for thirty pieces of silver because it is a tithe of the money (Tyrol 34). In Donaueschingen 133, Judas is promised thirty pieces of gold, not silver. In Revello 118, Judas actually refuses more money in order to get the proportion he wants. In York 223 and Towneley 212, which do not include the episode of the anointing, Judas nevertheless tells the story to the Jews to explain his decision to betray Jesus. Some texts include the motif of the counting of the money on stage. Often the devil appears and tempts Judas to betray Jesus (Künzelsau 123; Tyrol 36n; Eger 129; Frankfurt 443; Breton 61; and N. town *Passion* 77).

13 In Heidelberg 127 the betrayal is preceded by the figure of the selling of Joseph by his brothers. It was traditionally held that the betrayal took place on the Wednesday of Holy Week (which is why Wednesdays were fast days – Maastricht mentions the day specifically). The legend of the birth of Judas is dramatised in Michel 45 and references to it occur in Towneley 393; Revello 80; Abruzzi *Passion* 172; Freiburg im Breisgau; Gréban 149; Provençal *Passion* 22; Semur 173. In a Catalan *Ministry* fragment, Judas explains that his mother exposed him outside Bethlehem to save him from death during the Slaughter of the Innocents. Semur 173 and Abruzzi *Passion* 172 include a different legend of Judas and his mother: when she learns of his treachery she says Jesus is God and will rise again; Judas retorts that the capon on the table will stand up and crow first: it does. (The same story forms the basis of the carol of King Herod and the Cock.)

14 In the Cyprus *Passion* the Harlot's repentance and the Betrayal are immediately followed by the scene of the Washing of Feet at the Last Supper but it is not certain whether the scenes are intended to be linked (149). The term *Weyhenpfinztag* ('Weeping fifth-day') for Maundy Thursday appears in medieval Austrian records from, for example, Bozen (cf. Neumann 140), where the term *Antlass* (used in modern times for Maundy Thursday, see Appendix) referred rather to the commemoration of Maundy Thursday on Corpus Christi (*Gottsleichnam*) referred to popularly as '*hl Blutstag, Antlass oder ... Kranzl- und Prangtag*' (Dörrer, *Bozner Bürgerspiele* 114–15).

15 The OT types for the Eucharist are usually the meeting of Abraham with Melchisedech, and the manna in the wilderness; Heidelberg 142 uniquely prefigures the Last Supper with Ahasuerus summoning his followers to a

feast (Esther 1:3–8), perhaps on analogy with the parable of the man who gave a great supper (Luke 14: 16). In Admont, I 20, Jesus opens the scene with a Latin responsory based on this parable, and during the eating of the Paschal Lamb angels sing the Easter Anthems.

16 Semur; Revello; Frankfurt; Eger; N. town; *Ordinalia*. Most French texts use the word sacrament and some also include references to Jesus as the priest. For details see Muir, Mass on the medieval stage.

17 In the church in Saint-Omer this ceremony and the Mass were followed by a second semi-dramatic ritual meal in a room near the church involving the collegiate clergy and leading local citizens and included the washing of the feet of the townsmen; cf. Muir, Liturgy and drama at Saint-Omer.

18 In Mons 280 the host sends for water (apparently at Jesus' request: the text is incomplete) and a water-carrier brings it in but does not help with the washing. In St Genevieve 129 Jesus asks the servant, Malquin for a basin, water and a towel 'without delay!'. In *Ordinalia* Jesus asks for *warm* water and John brings it. Felix Fabri, when visiting Jerusalem in the fifteenth century, saw the place where the water was heated for the washing of feet (Felix Fabri, *The Wanderings*, I 309). In Semur 170, where Simon provides water and a white cloth, Jesus' upper garment is described as a chasuble (*casulam*: a priestly vestment). In Michel 264 the under-garment is described as being like a long *jaquete* (coat). In Eger 147, during the washing, the apostles compose the Creed.

19 Peter is the only apostle in the gospels to have a sword, so it is natural that he (and/or his brother Andrew) should be the most usual person to speak these lines (Frankfurt 452; Donaueschingen 144; York 233; *Ordinalia* 295; Michel 274); in St Gallen 129 the speaker is Bartholomew. For the Arras scene, see Muir, Aspects of form and meaning. In Valenciennes 25-day, f. 201v, the apostles answer in chorus.

20 *Meditationes* has a long section on the Agony and Bloody Sweat (323). The seven Blood-sheddings of Christ: the Circumcision, Bloody Sweat, Scourging, Crown of Thorns, Tearing-off of the blood-caked robe, Crucifixion and Longinus's spear-thrust, are mentioned in the English religious lyrics (see Woolf, *The English Religious Lyric* 222–7). They were also a recognised iconographic series, found, for example, on a panel in the church at Hamstall Ridware in Staffordshire (I am grateful to Peter Meredith for this reference). Seven plays of *Die Bloedstortinghe* (Blood-sheddings) of Jesus were performed in Oudenaarde during Eastertide in 1524, and a play on the same subject, by a Brussels group, won the twenty-eighth prize at the play contest in Antwerp in 1496 (*Kronyk von Audenaarde*, VI 29, 405). Some plays make Jesus apply the words 'The spirit is willing but the flesh is weak' to himself rather than to the disciples (York 237; Towneley 220; N. town *Passion* 82; Gréban 249; St Genevieve 136). This interpretation, which goes back to Bede, also occurs in the *Passion Isabeau*.

21 Lang, who played the *Christus* in 1900, 1910 and 1922, visited the Holy

Land in the late 1920s. His *Reminiscences* (published in 1930) span more than fifty years of his involvement in the play, from a child in 1880 to his performance as the Prologue in 1930, and provide fascinating insights into the experience of staging a community passion play.

22 The Provençal *Director's notebook* includes detailed notes (and a few drawings) on how to create various special effects as well as costumes and movements for a Passion play. Michel 284 includes a stage direction: *Icy sue sang par le visage* (Here he sweats blood from his face) but the effect is apparently achieved only verbally: Christ refers to the blood he is sweating. Valenciennes 25-day notes the Bloody Sweat as one of the effects on the nineteenth day (f. 203v).

23 Gabriel (Maastricht); Michael (Lucerne, Künzelsau). In Revello 129, Uriel shows Jesus a cloth displaying the Passion. Michel (followed by Mons and Valenciennes 25-day) includes all three archangels and a scene of their dispatch by God the Father. However, the illustration to this scene in the Valenciennes 25-day MSS simply shows an angel with a cross (f. 203v). In Towneley 221 the speaker is the *Trinitas*. In Breton 65, Jesus has a dialogue with *Raison* before the angel appears. An angel appears in the Umbrian *Lauda* 43 and Frankfurt 456; with a chalice (Eger 157; Coliseum 25); and a chalice and host (N. town *Passion* 83). He brings a chalice and cross (Abruzzi *Passion* 166, Admont I 33); or the instruments of the Passion (Toledo *Passion* 162; Donaueschingen 149). Gréban introduces a brief dialogue between God the Father, Mercy and Justice, with the last-named insisting, despite Mercy's pleas, that even the Bloody Sweat is not sufficient suffering and Christ must be crucified to satisfy her (249). This scene has echoes of the Judgement of Jesus Christ plays.

24 The first part of the *Gospel of Nicodemus*, the *Gesta Pilati* (Acts of Pilate), begins with the Arrest and Trial of Jesus. In the first Greek form (Walker 126), the Jews involved include Dathaes, Gamaliel, Alexander, Nephthalim and Levi who all appear in various plays: Auvergne; Semur; Rueff; Breton; Arras; Valenciennes 20-day. In Lucerne, II 93 the guards turn aside to arrest Barabbas. In Revello 149 Barabbas is arrested during the trials. '*Judas his lanterne*' is listed among the relics at St Denis in 1612 in *The travel diary of an English catholic* by Sir Charles Somerset (77).

25 See above for the Holy Kinship. N. town *Passion* 71; and Hall 307 mention the likeness; Frankfurt 458 says both James and John are like Jesus. Lucerne specifies that his hair and beard are like the Saviour's (Evans 202). In Michel, James at his calling is dressed more or less like Our Lord: *vestu et habillé pres ou environ comme Nostre Seigneur* (58).

26 In John's gospel this follows the words 'I am he', but the plays are very varied, some having as many as three falls and rarely coinciding with the exact gospel timing. In St Gallen 131 the soldiers say they fell as if drunk; in Breton 72 the apostles comment on the soldiers' falling. In Michel 287, Judas falls with the soldiers and Jesus himself comforts them. In Abruzzi *Passion* 168, Judas touches the soldiers to make them get up; in Alsfeld 691

he strikes them; in Künzelsau 132 he tells them they are not hurt; and in Frankfurt 460 he tells them they are drunk.

27 In the Coliseum *Passion*, Jesus rebukes Peter but apparently does not heal Malchus (27). The omission may merely indicate a faulty text. Most plays treat the ear incident straightforwardly. The Provençal director prescribes a whole false head with built-in blood supply and easily detachable/ replaceable ear (30).

28 The identification with John derives from the *Passion des Jongleurs*. *Ordinalia* 315 correctly specifies a linen cloth, but most plays call it a cloak. In Frankfurt the cloak is seized and John is threatened at the Crucifixion for being a follower of Jesus. A Jew, however, makes the soldier return the cloak, saying that John had had a right to be at the house of Annas where he is well known (510). In Mons 292, John loses his crimson apostle's cloak. In Michel his subsequent flight takes him to Bethany, where he gives the news of Jesus' arrest to the Virgin and other women; Martha gives him a fine white silk robe to cover his 'near nudity' (296). A similar scene (without white robe) is in Revello 135. In N. town *Passion* 87 the messenger is Magdalene.

29 Pilgrims to Jerusalem could visit the location where the Virgin stood near the door of Caiaphas's house (Fabri, *Wanderings*, I 320). She is also present at the trials in Frankfurt; Abruzzi; Umbria; Burgos 958 (briefly); and Auvergne. In Umbria she declares that Judas' avarice has cost her dear (315). In Michel 339, Judas first of all curses the money which has tempted him, and returns it; then he explicitly rejects the idea of asking the Virgin for mercy – no mother could pardon one who had caused her son's death. In a great '*Cry*' of a hundred lines he summons all the forces of Hell, Misery and Evil, including representatives of the Seven Deadly Sins. Hearing him, Lucifer sends *Desesperance* (Despair) to bring him to his death. Judas' love of money, which led him to betray Christ, is mentioned in several plays. In Breton the Virgin asks Judas: 'If you wanted to sell him why not offer him to me? With my family's help, I could have given you a bigger price' (129). In Revello, after the Harrowing of Hell, Mamona, who has previously lost a fight with Beelzebub over Judas' soul, is imprisoned in the lowest depths of Hell because it was through her machinations that Judas betrayed Jesus, thus leading to the overthrow of Lucifer's empire (182). The theme echoes the story of Pilate's wife's dream.

30 In Alsfeld the devils bring him the rope and sing a chorus with the refrain '*Du armer Judas!*' (O poor Judas!). After his death they carry him off noisily to Hell (702). In Benediktbeuern 296 the devil takes Judas and hangs him, and in Revello, after taking the soul, the devils come back with a cart to remove the body (159).

31 Many German plays formalise the scenes with liturgical Latin texts intercalated into the vernacular dialogue, including versions sung by Jesus himself of the *Improperia* or Reproaches sung on Good Friday (see Appendix). Jesus sings them during the *Via crucis* in Alsfeld 464; and the

Sterzing *Passions* 90 and 294. (As the actors were laymen, the music included in the Sterzing MS is a simplified version of the liturgical chant.) Translations of *Nicodemus* and several plays include vernacular versions of the Reproaches: during the Scourging (Castellani 316); the Crowning with Thorns (Coliseum 37); the *Via Crucis* (Arras 184; Michel 393; Valenciennes 20-day, f. 327r); before the Crucifixion (Eger 229; Frankfurt 505; and Rueff's Protestant *Passion* (1549) 182); and on the cross (Towneley 265; York 327).

32 The former usually takes place in the house of Caiaphas and includes the 'blind man's buff' sequence of the blindfolded Jesus being challenged to say who hit him. Heidelberg prefigures the flagellation with a scene from Job in which *Salvator*, sitting bound on stage, plays the role of God and gives Satan permission to torment Job (182). The mocking, here associated with the Crowning with Thorns, is prefigured by Elisha being mocked by children who are immediately eaten by bears (210).

33 In Montecassino 70 the cock crows and Jesus looks at Peter (cf. Luke 23: 61). Breton and *Ordinalia* omit the cockcrow but Breton 82 includes a speech by Jesus to Peter, and in *Ordinalia* (where Thomas introduces Peter into Caiaphas's house) Jesus 'looks back' at Peter (337). Bodley *Resurrection*; Castilian *Resurrection*; and Gréban include Peter's lament on Easter Day. In Toledo *Passion* the lament is punctuated with the refrain: '*Ay dolor!*' Later John narrates the Trials to the Virgin in the form of a lament with the same refrain (168). In the Perugia Easter Day *lauda* 260, Peter is pardoned by the Virgin, and it is she who obtains Peter's pardon from the crucified Christ in *Paschon Christos* 193. After the Resurrection, Pilate refuses to believe the disciples have stolen the body because they were so frightened that the mocking of a girl made them deny their master (*Paschon* 321).

34 Both scenes derive from *Nicodemus*. Revello 138 and Alsfeld 706 have both episodes; Cyprus 173 and Frankfurt 483 only the cloak; York 262 and Arras 157 only the standards. For 'pomping' (boasting) speeches, see Welsh 155; Towneley 243; and Alsfeld, which uniquely intercalates in the Pilate scenes one of heavenly praise of the Passion (705).

35 As the incident comes in the *Gospel of Nicodemus*, the defender is usually Nicodemus. In *Nicodemus*, Cyprus 179, Frankfurt 493 and one version of Michel where the defender is Lazarus, the sick themselves describe their cures (Addition IV 457). In Revello 154 they are narrated by the defender, a Jew called Samuel. In St Genevieve 181 the defender is Pilate's wife. In Toledo *Passion* 174, Pilate uses the same list of miracles to justify sentencing Jesus for sorcery.

36 In Cyprus 187, Herod goes to Pilate and exchanges signs of friendship with him. In Heidelberg 207; *Dirigierrolle* 359; and Frankfurt *Passion* 481 they embrace on stage. One version of Michel includes a scene of the original quarrel between the two (Addition II, 443).

37 She is sometimes anonymous but her traditional name, Procula (various spellings) occurs in *Nicodemus* and many plays. In Lucerne, II 167, she is

Livia; and in Eger 206 Pilatissa. The devil (cf. Nicholas of Lyra in Roy, *Mystère* 229) appears in York 259; *Ordinalia*, II 375; Semur 197; Arras 165; Frankfurt 488; Lucerne, II 167; and Eger 206, where he tells her he is an angel. In Hell, Satan informs Lucifer that he has caused Jesus to be condemned. Lucifer, however, foresees the consequences and sends Satan to Pilate's wife to try to stop it (Gréban 313; N. town *Passion* 109; Frankfurt 488).

38 It also appears in processions (Zerbst; Bruges; Paris (1313); Béthune; Bozen). Some plays stress his Roman legalism and sense of justice. In Auvergne he interrogates Barabbas and has him admit his guilt but has to free him. The two thieves, Dismas and Gestas, are made to swear on the saints that they are guilty before he condemns them (171). In Hall 323, Pilate pronounces sentence on Jesus in legalistic terms. In Abruzzi *Passion* the lengthy sentence is announced by one of the soldiers, who emphasises he is not a Jew (173).

39 In Auvergne 175 he tells the soldiers to take off the purple robe and put on Jesus' own clothes 'gently' (*doucement*: this contrasts with the fifth Bloodshedding). Either here or in the earlier scenes in Caiaphas's house, many plays show Jesus bound to a stone pillar, being beaten. This pillar (*statua*) was a prized relic in Rome and the scene is one of those put forward for the contemplation of the faithful in *Meditationes* 328. In Künzelsau 146 the Crucifixion is replaced by a procession with expositors in which one *Salvator* carries the pillar, another the crown of thorns and a third the cross. At the end is a priest holding the Cross and singing the Good Friday antiphon 'Behold the Wood of the Cross' (also sung in Eger 235). The Bologna procession consists of angels carrying the instruments of the *Passion* (including the pillar) followed by Christ showing his wounds, the Penitent Thief and the Virgin (226).

40 For OT episodes in the Legend of the Rood see pp. 54, 56 and Morris, *Legends of the Holy Rood*. In Gréban 318 the beam in the Temple is mentioned briefly in a scene between the tormentor and the carpenter, who is only interested in being paid. Michel 383 says it is eighteen feet long; Valenciennes 20-day, f. 322v, says ten to fifteen feet. Both agree it is very heavy and rough. The production notes at Mons call for a hollow cross to be used for the carrying and a solid one for the actual Crucifixion (501). In Toledo *Passion* 176 and N. town *Passion* 117 Pilate gives orders for the Crucifixion, with much sadistic detail about the cross and nails. The Aversa *Factura crucis* (*Making of the Cross*) presents two smiths (*fabri*) who discuss whether Jesus is God while making the cross (151). Nicodemus and a Hebrew join the discussion and the play ends with complaints against the cross by John and the Virgin.

41 The story is included in the narrative *Passion des Jongleurs* and in some English Rood legends. Arras 181 has no names but the wife is called Grumaton in Semur 203; Maragonde in St Genevieve 187 (husband Galant). She is Ysaude in Valenciennes 20-day, f. 321v; Valenciennes 25-

day, f. 240r; and the 1548 Béthune procession (Petit de Julleville 213). Auvergne 177 omits the miracle of the hands, and when the smith, Grimance, refuses to make the nails, he is made to work the bellows while his wife, Malembouchee, forges and sings. In Palatinus 149 the order for forging the nails is given by Herod. Alsfeld includes a smith (*Faber*) at the Crucifixion who provides a hammer and the nails (768). Revello 165 has a smith (Farfala) and wife (Furiana) at the Crucifixion: the latter produces the nails but there is no forging. In Cyprus 193 the nails are hammered in by a Gipsy Smith.

42 The fourteen Stations of the Cross are portrayed in churches in painted or carved representations. In Heidelberg the carrying of the Cross is prefigured by the sacrifice of Isaac (221).

43 *Meditationes* 330 comments at length on the events, with a special emphasis on the physical and mental sufferings of Christ.

44 In a number of plays the Virgin is brought to the place by John, who tells her Jesus has been condemned. In Revello she is told by Joseph of Arimathea and Nicodemus, who take her a brown dress and cloak to put on instead of her fine clothes (157).

45 In France she is sometimes equated with the shroud-seller from whom Joseph buys the shroud for Jesus (Michel 389; for details of the French shroud-sellers see p. 137). In Revello 163; Arras 185; Semur 206; Jesus asks Veronica for the cloth; elsewhere she uses the cloth herself (Breton 124; Eger 221; Heidelberg 231; Gréban 324). In Alsfeld 763; Admont 66; Donaueschingen 204; Lucerne, II 184; she asks Jesus for a memento of him, he takes the cloth, wipes his face and gives it back with the image on it. In Cervera *Passion* 115 Veronica asks Jesus to comfort his mother, he tells her to do that herself and asks her to wipe his face. She does so and the image remains.

46 In St Genevieve 192 they are called '*magdelaines*', implying a more pejorative interpretation of the Latin *filia*. In Michel 389, Pasiphae and Perusine are former attendants on Mary Magdalene.

47 Mons, using Michel's text, adds a stage direction: Mary shall pretend to put on the cloth but Jesus will already be wearing one (365). In Frankfurt *Dirigierrolle* 360 the Virgin puts the cloth round Jesus. In Coliseum 53, after the nailing, the Virgin asks permission to cover Jesus and after some discussion Pilate grants it. In Revello, Mary Salome asks, and one of the soldiers takes her veil and does it for her (167).

48 Jesus prays in Coliseum 44; Castellani 320; Revello 166; Rueff 182; York 316; in Abruzzi *Minor Passion* he addresses the cross and embraces it as a sign of his willingness to die for mankind (201). The Welsh *Passion* 189 gives the Testament of Jesus whose bequests include his soul to his Father, his mother to John, his body to the Jews, Heaven to the righteous and his Passion to the penitent. There is a Testament of Judas in Breton *Passion* 97. Moses setting-up of the brazen serpent prefigures the Crucifixion in Heidelberg *Passion* 232.

49 In Poland it was normal to use a painted and jointed figure of Christ for the Crucifixion and the Resurrection (see fig. 7). The speeches of the Towneley soldiers use the ironic image of a knight being put on his horse (261). In Alsfeld 775; and N. town *Passion* 121 the Jews dance round the cross and in Semur they say that Jesus with his 'wreath' is dressed for a dance (212). Jesus is also described as a parchment stretched out of shape and his wounds are the many bloody letters written on this book (Bodley *Burial* 149).

50 In Lucerne, II 199, one tormentor asks another to steady the ladder while he climbs up and fixes it.

51 In Auvergne, contrary to the gospel (Matthew 27: 34), Jesus accepts the wine he is offered. The thieves also accept the wine gladly and declare it is good strong wine. Several plays transfer Jesus' refusal to drink to the moment when he cries out '*Eli Eli lama sabachthani*' (IV) or 'I thirst' (V) and is offered vinegar from a sponge on a reed (cf. John 19: 29). In Freiburg im Breisgau, Malchus gives Jesus wine to drink when he says 'I thirst' because he healed his ear. More usually Malchus is a bitter enemy of Jesus.

52 The most elaborate lament by Mary (the *planctus*) may either come here or follow the Deposition when Mary takes the body of Jesus on her lap. Referred to iconographically as the *pietà*, this is the fifth of the Sorrows of Mary (cf. Schiller, *Iconography*, II 176). It was included five times in the Toledo procession (46). Mary's lament occurs in several Croat texts including the *Muke* (*Passion*). The texts were cited in an unpublished paper by Slobodan Novak for the Third SITM conference in 1980 and I am grateful to Ivona Ilić for translating them for me. In German there are a large number of separate dramatic *planctus* texts in addition to those in the passion plays: Bergmann lists 147 MSS and seventeen printed texts. There are also a number among the Italian *laude* for Good Friday (Perugia *Death and Deposition*, I 239; Umbrian *Planctus* 169; Siena *Tractato* 288). Within a passion play the *planctus* may be very long and use a variety of verse forms; cf. Semur 225; Revello 167; and Alsfeld 779. Gréban 338 is over a hundred lines long; in Abruzzi *Minor Passion* 207 the Virgin takes off the crown of thorns and apostrophises it. There are many *planctus* lyrics in English and the 187-line speech in Bodley *Burial* 160 includes well-known lyric refrains such as: 'Who cannot weep come learn of me'. In Montecassino 77, Mary stands by the cross 'as if showing Jesus the womb that bore him'. In two Bozen *Burial* plays (61; 359) Simeon brings the Virgin a sword, literally recalling his own prophecy (Luke 2: 35). In Künzelsau 148 John holds a sword to the Virgin's breast. In *Paschon Christos* 181 the actual Crucifixion is described by the messenger, then Mary goes to Calvary and has a long dialogue with the crucified Christ, during which the Words are paraphrased and glossed.

53 In an Old English version of the *Regularis concordia* prepared for a community of women, during the singing of the passion on Good Friday, 'when *Partiti sunt vestimenta mea* is read, the two deacons who are standing

on both sides of the altar shall tear the sewn raiment which lies upon the altar ... in the manner in which the saviour's garment was divided'. Several of these details are peculiar to this version of the *Regularis*. (The translation is taken from the forthcoming edition of *The Regularis concordia adapted for nuns*, ed. J. Hill.)

54 *Ordinalia*, II 447; Frankfurt *Passion* 512. In Revello one soldier tries on the robe before he has won it and a quarrel ensues, followed by a detailed dice game (168). In Arras 191; Gréban 342; and Michel 412, Satan teaches one of the Jews to play dice. The different numbers on the dice are given a blasphemous meaning, e.g. five signifies the five wounds of Christ. Draguignan's Corpus Christi props in 1544 included *la raubbo de Nostre Seigneur* (Petit de Julleville 210). No other costumes are mentioned, which suggests it was a prop in a dicing scene or even a scene with Pilate. In Lucerne, II 198 the seamless robe is taken to Pilate by the winner, Cyrus, who offers it to him with the question: were we right or wrong to kill him? Pilate ignores him, but in Towneley a whole play, the *Processus talentorum*, presents Pilate dicing with the soldiers for the Robe and taking it by force from the real winner. This links up with the apocryphal Death of Pilate included in *Legenda* and dramatised in the *Ordinalia*.

55 St Denis, who became patron saint of France, was believed to be the same as Dionysius the Areopagite, converted by Paul on Mars Hill in Athens (Acts 17: 34). He is here also conflated with the author of the *Celestial hierarchy*, an influential medieval study of angels: see *Legenda*: St Dionysius (9 October).

56 In Valenciennes 20-day, f. 335v, all the wonders are described by *Dieu le Pere* in Heaven. In Coliseum 59 and Gréban 348 the angels in Heaven lament the death of Jesus. In Michel, which ends with the Entombment, the heavenly host sing part of *Tenebrae* (see Appendix) and may conclude their laments with a Latin *chant royal*, 'sung most pitifully' (418). Cervera 122 prescribes artillery for the earthquake, which in Coliseum 63 is described by pilgrims. In *Ordinalia* 461 the tormentors are frightened by the Risen Dead who also appear in Michel 417 and speak in Semur 219 and Arras 201. In Châteaudun 154 they (and Jesus) wore bed-sheets for shrouds. The sheets were stolen and the widow who had lent them for the play was paid thirty *sous* in compensation.

57 *Nicodemus* and Cyprus 199 equate Centurion and Longinus. (Centurion is regularly treated as a proper name not a rank.) Centurion discusses the events with Pilate (Frankfurt 530; Coliseum 68; Provençal 70) or with Pilate and Caiaphas (Towneley 309). The Aversa *Tumulatione* (*Entombment*) shows Centurion becoming a Christian hermit (53). In Auvergne 276 after talking to the Centurion Pilate laments his actions and tells his wife she was right all along.

58 A detailed comparative study of the different French plays of the Death and Resurrection of Jesus is given in Wright, *Themes of the resurrection*.

59 Valenciennes 25-day, f. 239v had a special effect for the blood to flow from

Jesus' wounds: his hands, feet and side (rubric to the twenty-second day). In the Frankfurt *Passion* 525 the wounds are painted on already. In Semur, Longinus and his servant Ganymede appear several times and their relationship repeats the theme of the farce of *Le Garcon et l'aveugle* in which the blind man is cheated by his boy: see G. Cohen, La Scène de l'aveugle et de son valet. Cohen mentions parallels in Arras and Angers (663 in the new edition). In St Genevieve 210 it is Pilate who gives Longinus the lance. In Revello 172 the soldiers make fun of Longinus's helmet, saying it came out of the ark (*fu fatto al tempo di Noè*).

60 In St Genevieve 224 the Jews try in vain to make Pilate rescind the permission and are rebuked by Nicodemus. In the Castilian *Descendimento*, IV 23, Joseph laments his late arrival at Calvary and determines to humble himself and go to Pilate to ask for the body. In Frankfurt 530, Joseph asks for Pilate's messenger to help with the deposition. Other plays include John, a servant or boy, and in Cyprus the smith reappears to help (203). In Lucerne, II 223, Longinus and Centurion help with the burial. In Towneley 278 Joseph and Nicodemus act alone.

61 In Auvergne 237 and some texts of the *Gospel of Nicodemus*, the seller is the woman whom Jesus had healed of an issue of blood; in Michel 429 the seller is Julie; in Gréban, while Nicodemus is buying ointments, Joseph buys a shroud for ten silver besants from a woman silk-merchant (357). For details of the shroud-buying scenes and possible links between the French plays and the Turin shroud see Muir, The holy shroud in medieval literature.

62 In Michel 439 the guards insist on checking that the body is actually inside the tomb before it is sealed, which in Heidelberg 265 is done by the guard. Mons 399 directs Caiphas to affix a large seal of red wax, while in Florence *Resurrection*, I 330, Pilate lends his official seal-ring to seal the tomb. This echoes the Old Testament when Daniel is put into the lion's den, a stone is put in front of the door, and the king seals it with his own ring (Daniel 6: 17).

63 The arrest and imprisonment of Joseph of Arimathea are dramatised in Heidelberg; Tyrol plays; Revello; Arras; Gréban; Valenciennes 25-day and Perugia. Rouergue has a whole play on the subject. Joseph appears also in the French *Vengeance* plays. A number of passion plays end with the Death and Burial, including Michel; Frankfurt; Heidelberg; Benediktbeuern; and Auvergne (where God comforts the Virgin with a promise of resurrection). The 20,000-lines-long Angers *Resurrection* (attributed probably erroneously to Jean Michel) begins here. An edition of the early Chantilly MS has just been published.

64 The debate between *Ecclesia* and *Synagogua* goes back to one of Augustine's sermons where it is linked with the prophecies of the Incarnation – in Semur it is introduced just before the Nativity (64). The theme was common in iconography where it is linked with the Cross; see Schiller, *Iconography* II 110.

65 See Young, I, ch. 5. For details of gospel and patristic references see Wright, *Resurrection*. The subject was also popular in the Byzantine sermon-plays. In a fourth-century homily attributed to St Epiphanius, Christ is accompanied by all nine orders of angels who take part in the traditional dialogue based on Psalm 23 (Septuagint Greek version). When Hades (within) asks, 'Who is this King of Glory?' all the Orders reply together: 'The Lord of Power is the King of Glory!' (See La Piana, *Sacre rappresentazioni* 74).

66 In the Anglo-Norman *Adam* both Cain and Abel are taken to Hell, though Abel is led 'more gently'. Only from the thirteenth century onwards was Limbo, the resting place of the righteous, a separate part of the nether regions.

67 Limbo is sometimes portrayed on stage as a tower or prison. The most detailed description is in the three-day Angers *Resurrection* 189 (see *Staging* 92: Paris *Resurrection*, where it is translated from another MS). In a few plays the rejoicing of the souls is linked with the appearance of a bright light, and/or the arrival of John the Baptist telling of the approaching end of their suffering. The Angers *Resurrection*, which develops all the Resurrection material at extreme length, directs that among the forty souls in Limbo there should be a dozen good musicians who sing the hymn *Veni redemptor gencium* (98).

68 For the Oil of Mercy see p. 71. Several plays follow *Legenda*, Aquinas and others and show the *Anima Christi* (Soul of Christ) harrowing Hell while the body of Jesus hangs on the cross or rests in the tomb: Semur 247; Arras 241; Gréban 349; Welsh 213; *Ordinalia*, II 11; N. town *Passion* 143. In the Angers *Resurrection* the white-clad *Anima* kneeling by the cross gives thanks to God that his body, now dead, has conquered death (155).

69 In the *Dirigierrolle* 363 he is 'triumphantly garbed' in a dalmatic and a red chasuble, wearing a crown and carrying a *vexilla* (a staff with the small triangular white pennant with a red cross on it, traditionally associated with the Risen Christ; in Gréban he uses it to break the gates of Hell). Elsewhere angels bring a crown and banner (Sterzing (1486) 139; Admont 84; Donaueschingen 236); in Semur 239 he is crowned and given gold rings as the Bridegroom of Holy Church; in Revello 179 and Valenciennes 25-day, f. 254r, he has a mantle, worn to show his wounds, and a banner.

70 For the use of this verse on other liturgical occasions see Young, I 161–70. Christ's victory may be signalled by the collapse of the gates of Hell (*Ordinalia*, II 13); in Künzelsau 240 Christ kicks them open. Sometimes the devils fight back: Toledo specifies fireworks (56); the Angers *Resurrection* 172 mentions '*couleuvrinas, balistas et cetera*' (culverins, catapults etc.). In Grandi's Sicilian *Resurrection*, the souls greet Jesus with praises including the 'great O antiphons' (see Appendix); in addition to the usual patriarchs and prophets, Jesus frees the innocents, kings and penitent thief; Enoch and Elijah appear and the latter recalls meeting Christ on the Mount of the Transfiguration (38). The innocents also appear (in a post-Harrowing

scene) in Angers together with many other Old Testament figures including Judith, Esther and Noah's wife (634). In the Burgos *Resurrection* Jesus first leads Adam and Eve to the Virgin, whose forgiveness they implore (972).

71 York 338; Alsfeld 822; Semur 244; Angers 180. The argument between Christ and the devil over the redemption of Man is also found as a separate dialogue, especially in Italian. (For texts see *Contrasti*). There is a *Procès de Bélial* in the Bourges Actes as part of a healing miracle. (See Lebègue *Actes* 175 and n., for other examples in French.) The Castilian *Accusacion contra el genero humana* and French *Advocacie Notre Dame* introduce the Virgin defending man against the devil. See also the Last Judgement plays below.

72 A few plays show the devils immediately setting out to restock Hell: Sterzing 180; Semur 246; Chester 338. In Vienna *Passion* 312 a similar scene follows the Fall. In Palatinus, Satan escapes from Hell and goes off to Lombardy 'in spite of Jesus Christ' (197).

73 For scenes following the Ascension, see note 87.

74 The four Bozen *Osterspiele* and the *laude* from Perugia and Assisi are virtually translations of the Latin *Elevatio* and *Visitatio* ceremonies described in Young, I, ch.4.

75 Sterzing (1486) 140; Bozen *Easter* 91; Donaueschingen 237; Admont 83; Eger 282. In Gréban 387 the Virgin sings '*Exurge*' then continues with a vernacular lament addressed to her companion Gabriel. In Lucerne, II 238, as Christ steps from the tomb angels sing '*Christ ist erstanden*', then Christ sings 'I slept', also in vernacular.

76 Several plays refer to the angels removing the stone, or to Jesus stepping out of the tomb; even to the guards sleeping on top of the tomb (*Ordinalia* II 33; Welsh 213). Clearly, therefore, a standing table monument was normally used rather than the cave in a rock described in the gospels. The illustration to the twenty-third day of Valenciennes 25-day shows such a tomb being carried into a cave. However, in the next drawing the cave has gone and only the tomb remains.

77 The visit to Mary is uncanonical but 'it is the common belief that Our Lord appeared first of all to the Virgin Mary' (*Legenda*). The scene occurs in Welsh 227; *Ordinalia*, II 37; Revello 184; Perugia, I 264; Florence *Resurrection* 336; N. town *Passion* 146; *Paschon Christos* 299; Alsfeld 845; Gréban 387; Angers 351 and one Castilian *Resurrecion* (IV 72. The other Castilian *autos* (Rouanet LX & LXI) are pastoral dialogues in which the Harrowing and Resurrection are discussed by the shepherds).

78 For the *Quem queritis?* trope see p. 15. Some plays (e.g. Delft; Eger; Künzelsau; Innsbruck) mix Latin and vernacular dialogue in this scene.

79 In Sterzing (1496) the scene was optional: 'Here you may introduce the *Medicus* with his servant if you like' (155). For the *Mastickár* and the German comic scenes from Innsbruck, Muri and Erfurt see Veltrusky, *Sacred farce* 107.

80 In Semur one guard has a dream of the Resurrection and Visit of the Marys which he narrates to his fellows; they do not believe him but the *Rusticus* enters and tells in his own comic, crude way the story of a fleeing corpse pursued by three beautiful women (254). The *Gospel of Nicodemus* introduces Joseph of Arimathea into the scene between the guards and the authorities: when the guards are accused of corruption for allowing Jesus' body to be stolen, they challenge the Jews, saying if they can produce Joseph, they (the guards) will produce Jesus. When Joseph is not in the prison (see note 81), the guards insist he has been freed by Jesus. In Angers, the guards are paid four thousand francs, taken out of the Ark which is locked with many keys (527).

81 Jesus appears to Peter in Arras 263; Gréban 393; Alsfeld 845; Florence *Resurrection* 343; Castilian *Resurrection*, IV 96; Angers 426; and to James the Less (following the account in *Legenda*) only in Anger 429 and Gréban 395 (followed by Valenciennes 25-day and Troyes). Those plays which staged the imprisonment of Joseph of Arimathea also include his rescue by Jesus; in the *Ordinalia* Joseph and Nicodemus are both imprisoned under nine keys (II 7). They are later freed by Gabriel.

82 For this scene and the possible link with the Turin shroud see Muir, The holy shroud in medieval literature.

83 In the Bozen plays the Gardener and Jesus are two different actors, the former having a long monologue (or dialogue with his servant) about the plants in the garden and their uses (147, 191). In Semur after the 'Touch me not, for I have not yet ascended to my father' Jesus immediately goes away to Paradise (257). In Revello 185, Jesus ask Mary 'Whom do you seek?', not the usual 'Why are you weeping?'. Then she announces the Resurrection to Frater Symone whose sermon concludes the play. St Genevieve ends with Magdalene's announcement to the apostles, while *Paschon* concludes with Jesus' appearance to the assembled apostles (332).

84 For Latin *Peregrinus* plays see Young, Donovan. Only Cleophas is named in the gospel but many vernacular plays, following the commentators, call his companion Luke (Gréban 409; Bozen 108, 289; Chester 356; Towneley 326). St Genevieve omits most of the appearances and ends after the Marys' announcement to the apostles, with an epilogue in which Centurion addresses the spectators.

85 Mons stage included a 'sea' with a boat on it and the Valenciennes 25-day MS illustration also shows a 'sea' and Jesus with the disciples sitting at a round three-legged table while the fish cooks on a very modern-looking grill beside them. The directions in the Angers *Resurrection* 727 include fishing nets: one empty, and one filled with 143 large fish (John 21: 11 specifies 153).

86 The Abramio description is translated in *Staging* 245. For the Toledo *Ascension* see Toledo 61–3.

87 Some patriarchs and prophets are also given doctors' haloes because they represented the law of Nature (Noah, Melchisedech, Job, Abraham) or

the law of Moses (Moses, Aaron, Samuel, David, Daniel). This is reminiscent of the Judgement of Jesus Christ plays.

10 PENTECOST TO JUDGEMENT

1 The coming of the Spirit may have formed part of the *Magnus ludus* celebrated in Padua in 1208 on Pentecost and the following days (De Bartholomaeis, *Origini* 134). The sixth Joy of Mary in the Brussels *Bliscapen* was Pentecost, but the play has not survived (*Bliscap* 213).

2 It is not clear if the Perpignan '*rotols*' contained any verbal or dramatic additions to the basic words of the Creed (Donovan 156–7). In the traditional play the twelve apostles combine to compose the Creed or Symbol of the faith, each contributing one article (see Appendix). Creed plays or scenes are also found in Künzelsau 154; Innsbruck *Corpus Christi* 147; Innsbruck *Assumption* 24; Bologna, III 229; Angers 884; Arras 280. Mons omits the Gréban *moralité finable* and concludes with an original Creed scene. In Abruzzi *Pentecost* 22, the apostles recite the Creed in Latin together. For the York Creed play see p. 186. Felix Fabri describes the site in Jerusalem where the 'Apostles ... gave the Church the twelve articles of her faith ... wherefore this place deserves to be greatly reverenced' (Fabri, *Wanderings*, I 331).

3 With pleasant (if perhaps unintentional) irony, Peter begins '*Je voly predicar dos motz*' (I would like to say two words: 95) and then preaches for 440 lines with angelic music at intervals. Seven listeners representing Cappadocia, Phrygia, Egypt and so on, declare (partly in gibberish) that they hear him in '*lengua nostra*' (our language: 109). A few other plays introduce the Pentecostal *glossalalia* (speaking with tongues). In Perugia Pentecost *lauda*, I 284, the apostles have a few lines of gibberish and in Lucerne in the proposed addition for 1616, the apostles are 'to speak in different languages' but only Chaldeen is written out (III 184).

4 For John as secretary, see the invitation to a meal at Bethany, p. 119. In one of the Pordenone *Assumptions* the Virgin addresses him as '*segretario del divin consiglio*' (secretary of the divine council), a role evidently derived from his authorship of a gospel, three epistles and Revelation (De Bartholomaeis, *Origini* 438). In the *Passion Isabeau*, Peter, James and John are called Jesus' '*especiaulx secretaires*' (special secretaries: 91).

5 Only Valenciennes 20-day continues with Acts and the Assumption. The Valenciennes 25-day illustrations show the descent of the Spirit as flames falling from a sphere containing a dove. The same sphere appears with a dove in the Baptism (fourth day) and a star for the Three Kings (fifth day)

6 The *Actes des Apostres* was written by either Simon Gréban, brother of Arnoul, or Jean du Prier: the matter is still unresolved. Originally composed *c.* 1450–80 it was printed several times in the sixteenth century. There is no modern edition but a detailed analysis and study in Lebègue, *Actes*. The last four days of Valenciennes 20-day follow closely one version

of the *Actes* though they omit much of the comedy. The play was noted for its special effects of which a long list has survived, part of which is translated in *Staging* 101.

7 The *Dwerck der Apostolen* was published in 1539 (Hummelen). For the development of religious controversy over the plays see Conclusion.

8 Peter, Paul, Stephen and Denis are in the St Genevieve *Cycle des Premiers Martyrs*; Peter and Paul appear with other saints in a sixteenth-century *mystère* printed in Paris and in a Provençal *Peter and Paul* (Petit de Julleville 548). They only appear in German in the Gothaer actor's role. All twelve apostles appear in processions in Zerbst, Bologna, Valencia and Barcelona. A number of individual saints' plays were written in Italian, Catalan and Castilian, including plays of Andrew, Bartholomew, James the Greater (Florence); Simon and Jude (Perugia); Matthew (Perugia, Majorca). For lists and bibliography of saints' plays see Davidson, *The saint play in medieval Europe*.

9 For performances of Mary Magdalene plays see Petit de Julleville 533. In 1491, Chartres had a play of the three saints, Martha, Lazarus and Magdalene, which may have used parts of the extensive Michel text (ibid. 60).

10 Donovan 96. He also quotes a tableau from Majorca and describes the *aracoeli* (145). Young, II 256–7, quotes a ceremonial from Halle but no actual plays. For the Elche play, see p. 19. For stage directions in Prades and Valencia, see *Staging* 79, 230. Three Castilian plays of the Assumption are included in the Rouanet collection (XXXII is the most elaborate, with much music; two other later texts are given in the Appendices). The Assumption was performed at Toledo only in 1493. Two unedited, anonymous, printed French *Assomptions* are described by Petit de Julleville (470). A *Moralité* of the Assumption by Jean Parmentier includes an early example of a character making his entrance from the midst of the audience (Petit de Julleville, *Répertoire* 36). For unedited Italian assumption plays and performances see De Bartholomaeis and D'Ancona, *Origini*. There are only two German plays, from Amorbach (incomplete) and Innsbruck.

11 In the *Sevenste Bliscap* (Seventh Joy) performed in Brussels, her actions are described by the Jews (148).

12 This scene, which resembles the story of the unbelieving midwife, appears in most of the texts and is popular in art.

13 The crowning was represented in the Ingolstadt Corpus Christi procession (Neumann 411). In Siena in August 1458, to celebrate the election of Aeneas Piccolomini as Pope Pius II, Mass was celebrated in the piazza followed by a representation of the Assumption which ended with Mary in Heaven being crowned by the new Pope (D'Ancona, *Origini*, I 282.) In *Legenda* and Innsbruck *Assumption* 77, Jesus asks the apostles what he should do to honour her and James the Less says he should raise her up bodily as he himself rose.

14 The story of the girdle (*Legenda*) also occurs in Perugia, I 306; Orvieto, I 396; and the Rodez *Ascension de Notre Dame* (a separately preserved play related to the Rouergue collection, cf. Petit de Julleville 174). There is a lacuna in the *Bliscap* MS after the burial, followed by Thomas telling the apostles what he has seen and showing them the girdle (205). This suggests a similar scene. In Innsbruck the play continues with the Destruction of Jerusalem.

15 According to another legend Pilate was thrown into Lake Lucerne and *Mons Pilatus* is called after him.

16 Mercadé's play (which has been edited only in unpublished theses), survives in two handsome MSS of the late fifteenth century. An extended version was printed several times in the sixteenth century. The French *Ste Venice* treats of the healing of Vespasian by the 'Veronica'; it ends with Titus and Vespasian preparing to summon their allies and march on Jerusalem to destroy the *faulx juifx*. For a detailed study of the extant vengeance plays see S. K. Wright, *The Vengeance of Our Lord*. The Castilian *Destruction* and the fifteenth-century *Gothaerbotenrolle* – an incomplete acting part for a messenger in a two-day play – tell the same basic story.

17 Veronica's scene was presented, with crusading and other episodes, at the Royal Entry of Philip the Good in Mons in 1455. Later that year a passion play was performed in Mons and costumes from the Entry were lent to the actors, who also presented a vengeance play in 1458 (cf. Mons xii–xiv). Wright overlooked this performance, which is the nearest in date to the main MS copy of the *Vengance*.

18 For details of the Metz performance see Wright, *Vengeance* 118 and Petit de Julleville 12.

19 Wright's survey of the later texts in England, Spain and Italy suggests that only the historical material was retained. The surviving fragments of the Breton *Destruction* are too brief to be helpful: see Lebègue, *Etudes*, I 111, n.1.

20 In the *Sponsus* the gospel story is enhanced by the introduction of the scene with the *Unguentarius* (Oilseller) from whom the foolish virgins try in vain to buy oil. The *Sponsus* was written about 1100 so this predates the oldest *Visitatio* with a *Mercator* scene preserved in the early twelfth-century Ripoll Troper (Donovan 78–81). Perhaps because of the development of the episode in the Easter plays none of the other Ten Virgins plays includes the scene with the Merchant.

21 The chronicle is quoted in Neumann 306. In *The Latin substratum of the Thuringian 'Ludus de decem Virginibus'*, Renate Amstutz suggests that the Thuringian A text was written not merely for a convent but for the Celebration of the Profession of a Nun.

22 Three of the extant plays are followed by Antichrist and the Last Judgement (Lucerne, Marburg, Künzelsau); the two versions of the Darmstadt/Thuringian text; Erfürt Morality; *Sponsus*; and sixteenth-century Dutch *Spel* are independent plays.

23 The names of the foolish virgins are not easily translated: *Hoverdie* (Pride),

Ydelglorie (Vainglory) and *Roeckeloose* (Reckless) are accompanied by *Zottecollacie* who may be linked with Gluttony or Sloth, and *Tijtverlies* (Lost time). Names were apparently also given to the virgins in a sixteenth-century *Commedia dei dieci vergine* performed in a Florentine convent. (D'Ancona, *Origini*, I 160).

24 Details of Choquet's *Apocalypse* are given in Petit de Julleville 615 and Lebègue, *Actes* 43. For Dutch plays see Hummelen.

25 Biblical references include Jesus' warning to his disciples 'For many will come in my name saying, I am Christ: and they will seduce many' (Matthew 24: 5). These unnamed seducers were identified in the epistles of John as Antichrist: 'Little children, it is the last hour; and as you have heard that Antichrist cometh, even now there are become many Antichrists whereby we know that it is the last hour' (I John 2: 18, 22; II John 7). There is a detailed account of the Apocalypse and the legend of Antichrist in the Middle Ages in M. Reeves's The development of apocalyptic thought.

26 For text and discussion see Young, II 371–87.

27 Prophets foretelling the Last Judgement and Doctors reciting the Fifteen Signs appear at the beginning of some German Judgement plays, see note 29. For Enoch and Elijah see The Harrowing of Hell. They also appear in the Mondovi *Last Judgement* and in the fragments of a fifteenth-century Dutch *Antichrist* listed (Item OF1) in the supplement to Hummelen's *Repertorium* appended to A survey of Dutch drama before the Renaissance, by H. van Dijk and others.

28 A substantial part of Day One is published in Le Gros, *Etude sur l'Antichrist de Modane*; other fragments in *Savoie* 202–24. The contract for the *feintes* is translated in *Staging* 104.

29 The unedited Lucerne judgement play was staged alternately with the passion play. Bergmann 534 also lists a number of other (mainly unedited) *Weltgericht* (Last Judgement) plays including texts from Marburg, Munich, Chur, Schaffhausen and Schwabia. The Rheinau text, edited by Mone, will be considered here as an example of the group. Klee's 1906 thesis on the German Judgement plays includes a version of the Donaueschingen text which shows some differences from the Rheinau play.

30 There is a Dutch play of the Seven Corporal Acts of Mercy (*Wercken der Barmhartigheid*) based on this clause listed in Hummelen and another from Haarlem. There are also examples of the theme in art.

31 The debate of Body and Soul also appears in the Berlin *Judgement* (Bergmann 61) and in a number of Italian *Contrasti* (D'Ancona, *Origini*, I 551).

32 Belcari is here following Augustine in having Solomon damned as an idolater: 'when he was now old his heart was turned away by women to follow strange gods' (III Kings 11: 4).

CONCLUSION: SURVIVAL AND REVIVAL

1 See the articles on Elche listed in the records section.

2 See especially Shergold ch. 15 for details of the later Corpus Christi plays. Corbató, *Valencia* has records of the plays right through to the nineteenth century.

3 Patt, *Christmas play* lists Corpus Christi plays of the Visitation, and a Latin *tragedia* of *Lucifer furens* for the Feast of the Circumcision. She also (Appendix I) includes a survey of the Christmas play in the seventeenth century. For other late records see Sentaurens, *Séville* and Valdes, *Oviedo*.

4 D'Ancona, *Origini*, II 166.

5 See Cioni, *Bibliografia* for later printings of *sacre rappresentazioni*. Sicilian texts are discussed in *Drammatiche rappresentazioni in Sicilia dal secolo XVI al XVIII* (see Palermo, Records). The evolution of the Christmas plays is discussed by Musumarra, *La sacra rappresentazione*.

6 See p. 150 for Modane. The Catholic polemical plays are mentioned in Lebègue, *Etudes*, I 197.

7 Lebègue lists examples of performances of *mystères* after 1550 from a considerable number of towns and villages in *La Tragédie religieuse en France* 61–5. See also Chocheyras, *Savoie*, and *Dauphiné*. For Brittany, see Lebègue *Etudes*, I 98–119; 131–43.

8 Farrar, *The passion play at Oberammergau* 9, quotes (without source) Luther as saying: 'such spectacles do more good and produce more impressions than sermons'. Generally speaking, most of the Protestant states in the Empire belonged to one of the Lutheran sects, while the Netherlands, the Huguenots in France and some towns in Switzerland (including Geneva) followed the predestinarian teachings of Calvin.

9 See Lebègue, *Tragédie religieuse* 289–93 and M. Roston, *Biblical drama* 52. For a strongly anti-Catholic Dutch version of the Acts see p. 145.

10 The play was performed in a number of Protestant towns including Lausanne (1550) and Leyden (1559). Lebègue, *Tragédie religieuse* has a long section (289–443) on the Protestant writers. Hans Sachs wrote a play of God blessing the sons of Adam. For other German plays see Robertson, *German Literature* 186–194.

11 Lebègue, *Etudes*, I 199. There is a useful bibliography in Stone, *French humanist tragedy* 211–19. For English plays see Blackburn, *Biblical drama under the Tudors* 64–76; 119–54. Popular biblical plays flourished in the German-speaking border regions of Hungary right through to the 1930s. See Ernyey and Karsai, *Deutsche Volksschauspiele in oberungarischen Bergstädten*.

12 In the unpublished eighteenth-century *Tragédie sur les péchés des premiers anges*, it is Christ's announcement of his plan for the Incarnation that drives Lucifer to rebel against God.

13 For the full text of the letter see Neumann 603. A record from Guben (1516) refers to the former custom of presenting the Passion '*nach papistichem Gebrauch*' (according to papist custom). Catholic practices were banned by

the reformed Church in Holland, but many customs connected with the old feast-days were maintained in the seventeenth century: see Zumthor, *Daily life in Rembrandt's Holland* 183–92.

14 The English translation by George Gilpin (1579) is printed in Young, II, Appendix I.

15 Lebègue, *Etudes*, I 196–8.

16 Roston, *Biblical drama* discusses the various popular manifestations of biblical theatre (141–2).

17 The medieval Theophilus was saved from his pact with the devil by repentance and the intercession of the Virgin. For Faust there is no mercy.

18 Lebègue, *Tragédie religieuse* 467–8 mentions two other editions of the *Paschon Christos* and translations into Latin and Italian before 1600.

19 For Stoa's *Last Judgement* and other Latin texts see ibid. 129–289

20 Blackburn, *Biblical drama* 77–118 and Lebègue, *Tragédie religieuse* 195–254.

21 See L.-V. Gofflot, *Le Théâtre au collège*; J. M. Valentin, *Le Théâtre des Jésuites*; Lebègue *Etudes* II 165–208. Blackburn, *Biblical drama* mentions a number of Protestant school plays from the end of the sixteenth century (122–5). The Jesuit practice of staging 'ballets' between the acts may derive from the tradition of the Roman *tragoedia saltata* (danced tragedy) see Kelly, *Ideas and forms of tragedy* 17.

22 A description of the *modus vivendi* of Huguenots and Catholics in Dieppe in 1612 is given in Somerset's *Travel diary* 53.

23 Lebègue, *Tragédie religieuse* 61.

24 There is no modern edition of *Actes*. The French original of the whole speech (twenty lines) is cited in Petit de Julleville, I 276–7 and with English translation in Muir, *Saint play in medieval France* 155–6.

25 The Haarlem play is in the collection of the rhetoricians of the company *Trou Moet Blijcken* which is currently being published. For *La Machabée* see Rousset *La Littérature de l'âge baroque en France* 81–3.

26 Lebègue, *Etudes* suggests that the theatre of 'horror' found in France, England and elsewhere at this period might usefully be studied comparatively as '*un théâtre baroque*' (I 374).

27 Catholics and Protestants alike used certain Old Testament themes to reflect political situations in the seventeenth century: see Orcibal, *La Genèse d'Esther et d'Athalie*. Descriptions of a play of *Noah* in Lisbon and an (entertainingly bad) *Creation* in Bamberg are quoted in Hone's *Ancient mysteries* 180–90.

28 For biblical plays, including Corpus Christi plays, in the French provinces in the seventeenth century, see Lebègue, *Etudes*, II 80–4 and Carrington Lancaster's comprehensive *History of French dramatic literature in the 17th century*.

29 Patt, *Christmas play* 297–322.

30 In the first part of her study, *La sacra rappresentazione della Natività*, Musumarra lists thirty plays of the Nativity published between 1572 and 1763, the majority in Palermo.

31 Musumarra quotes a description of the text as an '*opera sacro-scenica-tragi-comica*' (65). It is not an opera in the accepted modern sense, though music played an important role in the later evolution of the biblical drama.

The singing of the *Passion* on Good Friday developed, in the hands of Bach, into a full-scale musical performance in the context of a Lutheran service. There were oratorios on many biblical subjects, of which Handel's *Messiah* is outstanding for its cyclic structure and use of a mixture of Old and New Testament texts: the opening section is reminiscent of the medieval *Procession of Prophets*. Successful operas on biblical themes include Verdi's *Nabucco* and Saint-Saëns's, *Sampson and Delilah*, while Britten's 'parables' of the *Burning Fiery Furnace* and *The Prodigal Son* owe much to the traditions of medieval church drama.

32 The account is quoted in D'Ancona, *Origini*, II 184.

33 See Levi, *La leggenda dell'Anticristo* 62–3.

34 Nativity and passion plays are known to have been performed in Bavaria and the Tyrol, Savoy and Dauphiné, even in Brittany, but none on the scale and regularity of the Oberammergau votive play. For Italian biblical plays in the seventeenth century, including *Passions*, see D'Ancona, *Origini*, II 188–91. Hone quotes an account of a Latin cycle play, from Creation to Crucifixion, performed at the Jesuit seminary in Strasburg in 1769 (*Ancient mysteries* 191). Tableaux of the *Passion* including the Agony in the Garden and the Crucifixion, presented in a booth at a fair in Bayonne in April 1904, are described in *From my private diary* by Daisy, princess of Pless: despite seeing the Virgin Mary selling tickets beforehand and the miscellaneous, often inappropriate, music on a piano between the scenes, the princess found it an unexpectedly reverent and affecting performance. (I am grateful to my friend, Judy Stock for this unusual reference).

35 See A. Hartmann, *Oberammergau* 221.

36 For the evolution of the *Passion* text and stage, see E. Corathiel, *The Oberammergau story*.

37 Lang, *Reminiscences* 27.

38 Farrar, *Passion play* 20. It seems unlikely that the burghers of Mons, York, Bourges or Bozen would have shared Farrar's objection to such publicity. Nor did it worry the popes and princes, Hapsburgs and Hohenzollerns who flocked to the little village from all over Europe, while for the many English who visited Oberammergau, its play was a work of simple piety and unexceptionable decorum: a far cry from the crudeness and vulgarity of the medieval English plays. 'Of the sense of life as a violent drama which the medieval cycle plays conveyed there was little at Oberammergau' (Elliott, *Playing God* 40).

39 Quoted in an article in *L'Est Republicain*, 23 June 1981. I am grateful to M. Surdel of Nancy for sending me newspaper cuttings about the 1981 performance.

40 Lang, *Reminiscences* 113. My own most vivid memory of the 1981 performance at Nancy was of the local dancing school, wearing red

harem-trousers, dancing before Herod to the music of Bizet's *L'Arlésienne*. It was all very different from Oberammergau but *le bon roi René*, Duke of Lorraine, would have enjoyed it.

41 Lang, in *Reminiscences* 114, mentions that he also received a number of personal offers from the States both to lecture and to appear in films.

42 Four hundred years earlier still, in the twelfth century, the decisive development had been the introduction of vernacular lay drama. The evolution of biblical drama seems to have followed a four-century cycle.

43 While hundreds of Old Testament films have been made, the life of Christ has been treated only a score of times. The medieval habit of retelling biblical stories in contemporary terms can be seen in works like *Godspell* or *Jesus Christ, Superstar*.

44 Sayers's play-cycle was commissioned by the BBC's Director of religious broadcasting from a professional writer who was a Christian, a theologian, and a medievalist. Throughout, the gospel events were made intelligible to the listeners by the use of scenes of everyday life. Despite some criticism, the series was generally most successful.

45 For details of the revivals in England see Elliott, *Playing God*. The situation in France at the turn of the century is discussed in Lebègue, *Etudes*, II 214–21. He quotes a German thesis on *Das französische Jesus-Christus drama 1539–1936*, which lists 171 plays about Christ, only seven prior to 1800.

46 For this dialogue see p. 169. I am grateful to my colleague Gwilym Rees for giving me his programmes of the *Théophilien* productions he saw in Paris as a student. Kirkup's English adaptation of Gréban, *The true mystery of the Passion*, was produced for radio and television in Bristol in 1961, but in France Cohen found no successor till 1990 when Jaques Ribard of Amiens University staged the Palatinus *Passion* in the cathedral there and subsequently at the SITM conference in Perpignan.

47 For details of the English community performances see Elliott, *Playing God*. *MeTh* contains information about many modern religious dramatic events, including those in Spain: for example, Portillo and Lara's listing of Andalusia's Holy week processions, *MeTh*, 1986, 8: 119–39.

48 These 'reproductions', to use Peter Meredith's useful term, have become increasingly common in the last twenty years both in Europe and the United States, and a number of videos have been made ranging from the Fleury *Visitatio* to the Dutch *Wise and Foolish Virgins*. Many of the illustrations in the present study are drawn from such presentations.

49 Michael White, writing in the *Independent on Sunday*, 29 August 1993. The programme of the festival claims that by the combination of dancers on stage and voices singing in Latin and English off stage, Macmillan is 'using the inherent theatricality of religious liturgy and ancient spiritual texts to create a modern day parallel to the resurrection'.

APPENDIX: THE LITURGICAL CONTEXT OF THE PLAYS.

1 More detailed information can be found in Hughes, *Medieval manuscripts* and Harrison's *Music in medieval Britain*. A full account of the texts of the Mass and the Office according to the modern usage is given in Young, I, ch. 1. A useful introduction to the use of liturgical material in the civic plays will be found in Richard Rastall's forthcoming *The Heaven singing: music in the early English religious drama*. For these and other relevant books see the general bibliography.

2 Cf. Hughes, *Medieval manuscripts* 3–13.

3 The rules establishing precedence are laid out in the Missal and the BCP.

4 If Easter is early and not all the five Sundays after Epiphany are used, they may be added to the Sundays after Pentecost; however, the Propers of the last Sunday after Pentecost are always used on the Sunday before Advent Sunday.

5 The ashes are made from the previous year's Palm Sunday palms.

6 Lent's forty days cover seven weeks, for Sundays are never fast days.

7 A record from Bozen (1484) refers to a '*marckt mitvasten*' (mid-Lent fair) where cloth was bought (Neumann 137).

8 The last three days of Holy Week are also known as the *Triduum*.

9 For the use of the names *Antlass or Weyhenpfinztag* see p. 25. In Austria, special ceremonies were connected with *Antlasspfinztag* (Maundy Thursday). *Antlass* comes from 'entlassen' (freeing) and refers to the reconciliation of penitents which took place on that evening. I am grateful to Dr Bennewitz for sending me information about the *Antlass* traditions. The modern German term, *Gründonnerstag*, dates only from the Reformation. The prefix is variously derived from '*greinenden*' (weeping; cf. Eisenhofer and Lechner, *The liturgy of the Roman rite* 192) or the colour green representing renewal and hope.

10 The *Temporale* also includes periods of special fasting and penitence: the *Quatuor tempora* (Quarter Tense, Ember Days, *Quatre-Temps, Quatember*) were the Wednesday, Friday and Saturday in Advent 3, Lent 1, the Octave of Pentecost and the third week in September (which may be Pentecost 13–17).

11 The calendar of saints' days begins with St Andrew at the end of November because it falls close to the season of Advent when the *Temporale* begins.

12 Perhaps because he was patron of scholars, St Nicholas is the only non-biblical saint to have inspired Latin plays. His feast-day was the occasion of merrymaking (and sometimes clerical rowdiness) in the Middle Ages.

13 See T. Bailey, *The processions of Sarum and the western church* 116 for the Palm Sunday traditions. Other occasions for processions were penitential: the *Feria rogationum* (Rogationtide, *les Rogations, Bittage*) were periods of penance marked by litanies of intercession. The *Litania maior* (greater Litany) on 25 April was sung during processions round the fields to invoke a blessing on the new crops. (For the use of a processional cross at Rogationtide see Dix,

Liturgy 411). The *Litaniae minores* were sung on the Monday, Tuesday and Wednesday before Ascension and the preceding Sunday was sometimes called Rogation Sunday (Hughes, *Medieval Manuscripts* 12–13). The Litany (sung also on Easter Eve) invokes the prayers of the saints but emphasises the events of the Incarnation in a series of intercessions, each followed by the prayer *Libera nos, Domine* (Lord deliver us). The penitent recalls in turn the acts of God, Redeemer and Judge: 'by your holy Incarnation (Advent, Nativity, Baptism, Fasting, Cross and Passion, Death and Burial, Resurrection, Ascension)' and concludes: 'by the Coming of the Holy Spirit and on the day of Judgement, Lord deliver us'.

14 In addition to the Roman rite there were the Gallican and Mozarabic rites used in France and Spain respectively, or the Sarum rite in England. Only after the Council of Trent and the Counter-Reformation in the sixteenth century was the Roman usage made compulsory and the (modern) Tridentine rite standardised.

15 For a discussion of these terms see Hughes, *Medieval manuscripts* 81–93. A Bach or Mozart Mass is normally a setting of the Common, and can be used for any occasion except for a Requiem, which has special Propers such as the *Dies irae* (day of wrath). For more detailed comment on the Propers see below after the outline of the Office.

16 Normally only one such High Mass was celebrated on any day, but Christmas, exceptionally, had three with different Propers: the *Missa in gallicantu* (cockcrow, midnight Mass); the *Missa in aurora* (Mass at dawn); and the *Missa maior* or *Missa in die natalis* (Mass of Christmas Day) see Harrison, *Music in medieval Britain* 70 note.

17 Terce, Sext and Nones traditionally commemorated respectively the Condemnation, Crucifixion and Death of Christ (Harrison, *Music in medieval Britain* 55, note 6).

18 Since the medieval day was divided into twelve 'hours' from sunrise to sunset, the times of the Office Hours varied considerably at different times of the year (see the *Rule* ch. 8). For a comparison of the winter and summer timetable see Lekai, *The Cistercians* 364–5. Feast days (following Jewish custom) began at sunset on the Vigil, so there are two Vespers for major feasts, e.g. First Vespers on Christmas Eve and Second Vespers on Christmas Night.

19 See Harrison, *Music in medieval Britain* 56.

20 See Eisenhofer and Lechner, *The Liturgy of the Roman rite* 333–4.

21 Among other hymns and anthems used in the plays are those prescribed for Christmas, Palm Sunday and Easter Day: see the relevant sections of part two.

22 For the Burial of the Cross and other semi-dramatic ceremonies see Young, I, chs. 3–4.

23 See Hughes, *Medieval manuscripts* 248–9. '*Tenebre*', a group including black-clad Marys, John, Centurion and Longinus appeared in the procession at Zerbst in 1507 (Neumann 786). For *Improperia* in the plays see p. 249.

24 See Hughes, *Medieval manuscripts* 21.
25 Responsories are found, among others, in the Anglo-Norman *Adam* and Eger.
26 These antiphons 'usually seven in number but which may be as many as twelve' (Hughes, *Medieval manuscripts* 170) are sung during the prophet scene in Valenciennes 20-day and Grandi's *Resurrection*.
27 The celebrated *Quem queritis?* trope was first used as part of the Introit on Easter Day and was later incorporated in numerous plays.
28 Hughes, *Medieval manuscripts* 418–26. Lists of liturgical items used are given in some play editions, e.g. the Bozen plays (see bibliographical index of plays).
29 The term 'a religious' is used to describe any member of a religious order, male or female. For details of the different MSS and books see Hughes, *Medieval manuscripts* 118–29.
30 Joinville composed this work in the late thirteenth century at the suggestion of St Louis. It is preserved in a magnificently illuminated manuscript of much later date; Friedman's edition of Joinville's *Credo* reproduces all the illustrations. The prophets included suggest parallels with the Processions of Prophets in the plays. Joinville also lists well-known iconographic figures for the different incidents: for example Jonah emerging from the whale is a type of the Resurrection.

Bibliographical index of plays

In this index the plays are arranged alphabetically by the short titles used in the main text, followed by the title in the original language (although long ones may be abridged). Only specific references are indexed, so not all plays listed will have any. For post-1700 plays *see* the general bibliography.

The following abbreviations are used in this index, in addition to those cited on p. xix.

A.   *Auto* (Spanish plays)
JB   John the Baptist
C.   *Consueta* (Catalan plays)
CC   Corpus Christi
Ct   *Conment* (Lille plays)
NME No modern edition
R.   *Rappresentazione* (Italian plays)
Titles in [] are editorial.

The following *short forms* will be used for collections of play-texts in the bibliographical index.

Abruzzi: De Bartholomaeis, V. *Il teatro Abruzzese del medio evo.* Bologna, 1924.
D'Ancona *SR*: D'Ancona, A. *Sacre rappresentazioni dei secoli XIV, XV e XVI.* 3 vols. Florence, 1872.
De Bartholomaeis *Laude*: De Bartholomaeis, V. *Laude drammatiche e rappresentazioni sacre.* 3 vols. Florence, 1943.
Digby plays: Baker, D. C., Murphy, J. L., and Hall, L. B., eds. *The late medieval plays of Bodleian MSS Digby 133 and e Museo 160.* EETS. Oxford & London, 1982.
Froning: Froning, R. *Das Drama des Mittelalters.* 3 vols. Deutsche National-Litteratur, 14. Stuttgart, 1892.
Huerta i Viñas: Huerta i Viñas, F., ed. *Teatre bíblic: Antic Testament.* Barcelona, 1978.
Llabres: Llabres, G. Repertorio de 'Consuetas' representadas en las iglesias de Mallorca. *Revista de archivos, bibliotecas y museos,* 1901, 3rd series, 5. (Contains only list of plays.)

Mone: Mone, F. J., ed. *Schauspiele des Mittelalters*. 2 vols in 1. Aalen, 1970 [repr.].
Non-cycle plays: Davis, N., ed. *Non-cycle plays and fragments*. EETS supplementary series, 1. Oxford & London, 1970.
Sterzing: Lipphardt, W., and Roloff, H-G., eds. *Die geistlichen Spiele der Sterzingearchivs*. Bern, 1981 – (in progress).

PLAYS CITED – UP TO 1700

Jean d'Abondance
Judgement: Moralité . . . nommée Secundum legem debet mori (Partial edition in Roy, E. *Le Mystère de la passion en France du XIVe au XVIe siècle*. 412–33. Paris, 1905) 124, 242–3
Kings: Le Joyeulx Mystère des Trois Roys (In *Trois Jeux des Rois*. Ed. Y. Giraud, N. King & S. de Reyff. Fribourg, 1985) 106–7, 228
Abruzzi plays
Abraham and Isaac: R. di Abramo e Isacco (Abruzzi 26)
Annunciation (3): Lauda dell' Annunciazione (Abruzzi App)
Arrest of Christ: R. dell arresto e del processo di Gesù (Abruzzi 28)
Crucifixion: R. della crocefissione e della deposizione (Abruzzi 25)
Decollation: Decollatione de S Johanny Bactista (Abruzzi 11) 234–5
Emmaus: Apparizione ad Emmaus e agli Apostoli (Abruzzi 20)
Entry into Jerusalem: Entrata di Gesù in Gerusalemme (Abruzzi 21) 244–5
John and Virgin: Annuncio di Giovanni (Abruzzi App)
Magdalene's repentance: Convito in casa di Simone lebbroso (Abruzzi 22) 239–40
Passion (major): R. della Passione (Abruzzi 23) 135, 245–6, 251
Passion (minor): R. de Yesu Christo (Abruzzi 24) 129, 252–3
Passion-sermon: Il Passio volgarizzato (Abruzzi App)
Pentecost: R. della Pentecoste (Abruzzi 6) 259
Resurrection: R. della Resurrezione (Abruzzi 19)
Temptation (2): R. nel deserto (minore/maggiore) (Abruzzi 16/17) 116, 233, 236
Trials of Christ: R. del processo, morte e sepoltura di Gesù (Abruzzi 29) 249
Admont *Passion: Das Admonter Passionsspiel* (Ed. K. K. Polheim. 3 vols. Munich, Paderborn & Vienna, 1972–80) 141–2, 247–8, 252, 256–7
Alsfeld *Passion: Das Alsfelder Passionsspiel* (Ed. E. W. Zimmermann. Gottingen, 1909) 130–1, 133, 135–8, 142–3, 145, 233, 236, 238–40, 244, 248–50, 252–3, 257–8
Angers *Resurrection: Le Mystère de la résurrection. Angers (1456)* (Ed. P. Servet. 2 vols. Geneva, 1993) 142–4, 198, 240, 255–9
Anglo-Norman *Adam: Le Jeu d'Adam. (Ordo representacionis Adè)* (Ed. W. Noomen. Paris, 1971) 29–30, 68–71, 84–5, 197, 202, 205–8, 217, 242, 256, 269
Aquila *laude*
Annunciation: Anunptiatio S Maria (De Bartholomaeis, *Laude*, I) 144
Marriage of Mary: Disponsatione et festa della Nostra Dopna (Abruzzi 13) 90–2
Susanna: Devotione et Festa de S Susanna (Abruzzi 12) 217
Arras *Passion: Le mystère de la Passion. Texte du manuscrit 697 de la bibliothèque*

Chaundler (Ed. with English translation by D. Enright-Clark Shoukri. London and New York, 1974) 205, 241

Liège *Nativity*: *Nativités et moralités liégeoises du moyen âge*. (Ed. G. Cohen. Brussels, 1953) 55

Lille plays (Ed. A. Knight. In preparation. The numbers refer to the order of plays in the edition)

Abigail and Nabal: *Ct Abigaïl rapaisa David* (Knight 22) 216

Abraham and the angels: *Ct Abraham en vit trois et en aoura ung* (Knight 2) 75, 212

Abraham's sacrifice: *Ct Abraham mena Ysaac* (Knight 3) 213

Adam and Eve: *La creation de Adam et Eve* (Knight 1) 204

Annunciation: *[Ct Marie rechut la salutation]* (Knight 45) 223

Ascension: *Ct Jhesuchrist monta aux cieulx* (Knight 61)

Assumption: *[Moralité de l'Assomption]* (Knight 70) 260

Baptism of Jesus: *Ct S JB baptisa Jhesucrist* (Knight 46) 260

Birth of JB: *[La naissance de S JB]* (Knight 44) 222

Conversion of Magdalene: *Ct Marie Magdelaine ploura aux piez de Jhesucrist* (Knight 49)

David and Absalom: *Ct Absalon menoit guerre* (Knight 26) 216

David and Bathsheba: *Ct David fist tuer le chevalier Urie* (Knight 24) 216

David and Joab: *Ct Seba esmut ceulx d'Israel* (Knight 27) 216

David and Jonathan: *Ct David et Jonathas firent alianches ensemble* (Knight 21) 216

David numbers the people: *[Ct David fist nombrer le peuple]* (Knight 28) 216

Death of Abner: *Ct Joab tua Abner* (Knight 23) 216

Death of Ahab: *La mort du roy Achap* (Knight 33) 216

Decollation: *Ct Herod fist decoler S JB* (Knight 50) 234

Eli and the Ark: *Ct l'arche fut prinse des Felistiens* (Knight 17) 216

Elijah and Ahab: *Ct Helye noncha au roy Achab qu'il ne plouveroit point* (Knight 31) 80

Elijah's Ascension: *Ct Helye fut translaté sur ung chariot de feu* (Knight 34) 80

Esther: *Ct Hester impetra grace au roy Assüere* (Knight 40) 216

Gideon: *[L'istoire de Gedeon et la toison]* (Knight 15) 216

Jacob and Esau: *Ct Ysaac donna benedixtion a Jacob* (Knight 5) 213

Jacob's Vision: *L'istoire de l'eschielle que vit Jacob* (Knight 6) 213

Joshua's victories (2): *La prinse ... de la cyté de Haÿ* (Knight 13) 215

    [Ct Josué sauva ceulx de Gabaon du siege des cinq rois] (Knight 14) 215

Judith: *Ct Judich tua Olofernes* (Knight 39) 216

Lazarus: *Ct Jhesucrist resuscita le Ladre* (Knight 58) 241

Machabees (2): *Judas Machabeus contre Nicanor* (Knight, 41) *Ct Heliodorus volt piller le tresor* (Knight 42) 81

Manna: *Ct Dieu envoia la sainte manne du chiel* (Knight 10) 215

Marriage of Isaac: *Le mariaige de Ysaac et de Rebecca* (Knight 4) 76

Marriage of Joseph: *L'istoire de la provision des bledz que fist Joseph en Egipte* (Knight 9) 214

Naaman: *Ct Naman fut gary de sa maladie* (Knight 35) 81

Naboth's vineyard: *La vigne de Naboth* (Knight 32) 216

Performance records and references

(For modern records see the general bibliography)

Aix: Raimbault, M. Une représentation théâtrale à Aix en 1444. *Revue des Langues Romanes*, 1933–6, 67: 263–74.

Alençon: Despierres, G. *Le Théâtre et les comédiens à Alençon aux XVIᵉ et XVIIᵉ siècles*. Paris, 1892.

Amboise: Runnalls, G. *Le Mystère de la Passion à Amboise au Moyen Age*. Le moyen français, 26. Montreal, 1990.

D'Ancona, A. *Origini del teatro italiano*. 2 vols. Rome, 1981 [repr.].

Angers: Port, C. Documents sur l'histoire du théâtre à Angers. *Bibliothèque de l'Ecole des Chartes*, 1861, 22: 69–80.

Antwerp: Willems, J. F. Chronologische lyst van oorkonden Wegens de Antwerpsche Rederykkamers. *Belgisch Museum*, 1837, 1: 147–71.

Athis: Deierkauf-Holsboer, S. W. Les Représentations à Athis-sur-Orge en 1542. In *Mélanges Gustave Cohen*. 199–203. Paris, 1950.

De Bartholomaeis, V. *Origini della poesia drammatica italiana*. 2nd edn. Turin, 1952.

Bergmann, K. *Katalog der deutschsprachigen geistlichen Spiele und Marienklagen des Mittelalters*. Veroffentlichungen der Kommission für deutschen Literatur des Mittelalters der Bayerischen Akademie der Wissenschaften 1. Munich and Zurich, 1986.

Berkshire: Johnston, A. F., ed. *REED: Berkshire*. [In preparation.]

Bordeaux: Mazouer, H. *La Vie théâtrale à Bordeaux des origines à nos jours*. I. Paris, 1985.

Bourges: Lebègue, R. *Le Mystère des Actes des Apôtres*. Paris, 1929.

Bozen: Dörrer, A. *Bozner Bürgerspiele: alpendeutsche Prang- und Kranzfeste*. I. Leipzig, 1941.

Brooks, N. Processional drama and dramatic processions in Germany in the late Middle Ages. *Journal of English and Germanic Philology*, 1933, 32: 141–71.

Bruges: Hüsken, W. H. The Bruges Ommegang. *SITM* 7. [In preparation.]

Cambridge: Nelson, A., ed. *REED: Cambridge*. 2 vols. Toronto, 1989.

Châteaudun: Couturier, M., and Runnalls, G. A., eds. *Châteaudun 1510: Compte du mystère de la Passion*. Société archéologique d'Eure-et-Loir, 1992.

Chester: Clopper, L. M., ed. *REED: Chester*. 2 vols. Toronto, 1979.

Cordoba: Lopez Yepes, J. Una *Representacion de las sibilas* y un *Planctus Passionis en el Ms. 80 de la Catedral de Cordoba. Aportaciones al estudio de los origenes del teatro medieval castellano. *Revista de Archivos, Bibliotecas y Museos*, 1977, *80*: 545–68.

Coventry: Ingram, R. W., ed. *REED: Coventry*. Toronto, 1981.

Cumberland: Douglas, A., and Greenfield, P., eds. *REED: Cumberland/Westmorland/Gloucestershire*. Toronto, 1986.

Dauphiné: Chocheyras, J. *Le Théâtre religieux en Dauphiné du Moyen Age au XVIIIe siècle*. Geneva, 1975.

Devon: Wasson, J., ed. *REED: Devon*. Toronto, 1987.

Dijon: Gouvenain, L. de. *Le Théâtre à Dijon 1422–1790*. Dijon 1888.

Elche: King, P., and Salvador-Rabaza, A. La festa d'Elx (Elche). *MeTh*, 1986, *8*: 21–50.

Castaño, J. Documentary sources for the study of the Festa of Elche. *MeTh*, 1990, *12*: 21–33.

Essex: Coldewey, J. That enterprising property player: semi-professional drama in sixteenth-century England. *Theatre Notebook*, 1977, *31*: 5–12.

Evans: Blakemore-Evans, M. *The passion play of Lucerne: an historical and critical introduction*. New York and London, 1943.

Florence: Barr, M. C. Music and spectacle in confraternity drama of fifteenth-century Florence. The reconstruction of a theatrical event. (In *Christianity and the renaissance: image and religious imagination in the quattrocento*. Ed. T. Verdon and J. Henderson. 376–404. New York, 1990)

Gloucestershire *see* Cumberland.

Herefordshire: Klausner, D. N., ed. *REED: Herefordshire and Worcestershire*. Toronto, 1990.

Hummelen: Hummelen, W. M. M. *Repertorium van het rederijkersdrama, 1500–ca. 1620*. Assen, 1968. [Addenda to the *Repertorium* in *Dutch Crossing*, 1984, *22*: 105–28.]

Ingolstadt: Brooks, N. An Ingolstadt Corpus Christi processsion and the Biblia Pauperum. *Journal of English and Germanic Philology*, 1935, *36*: 1–16.

Kent: Dawson, G., ed. *Records of plays and players in Kent 1450–1642*. Malone 7. London, 1965.

Kilkenny: Fletcher, A. The civic drama of old Kilkenny. *REED newsletter* 1988, *13*: 12–30.

Lancashire: Lancashire, I. *Dramatic texts and records of Britain: a chronological topography*. Toronto, 1984.

Lancashire: George, F., ed. *REED: Lancashire*. Toronto, 1992.

Lecoy de la Marche, A., ed. *Extraits des comptes et mémoriaulx du roi René*. Paris, 1873.

Leuven: Twycross, M. The *Liber Boonen* of the Leuven Ommegang. *Dutch Crossing*, 1984, *22*: 93–96.

Lille: Knight, A. *The sponsorship of drama in Lille. In *Studies in honor of Hans-Erich Keller*. Ed. R. Pickens. 275–85. Kalamazoo, 1993.

Lefèbvre, L. *Les Origines du théâtre à Lille aux XVe et XVIe siècles*. Lille, 1905.

Lincolnshire: Kahrl, S. J., ed. *Records of plays and players in Lincolnshire 1300–1585*. Malone 8. London, 1974.

Lucerne *see* Evans

Majorca: Llabres, G. Repertorio de 'Consuetas' representadas en las iglesias de Mallorca. *Revista archivos, bibliotecas y museos*, 1901, 3rd series, 5.

Mill, A. J. *Medieval plays in Scotland*. Edinburgh and London, 1927 [repr. New York, 1969].

Modane: Gros, L. *Etude sur le mystère de l'Antéchrist et du jugement de Dieu*. Chambéry, 1962.

Neumann, B. *Geistliches Schauspiel im Zeugnis der Zeit. Zur Aufführung mitteralterlicher Dramen im deutschen Sprachgebiet*. 2 vols. Münchener Texte und Untersuchungen zur deutschen Literatur des Mittelalters 84, 85. Munich and Zurich, 1987.

Newcastle–upon–Tyne: Anderson, J. J., ed. *REED: Newcastle–upon–Tyne*. Toronto, 1982.

Norfolk: Galloway, D., and Wasson, J., eds. *Records of plays and players in Norfolk and Suffolk 1330–1642*. Malone 11. London, 1980.

Norwich: Galloway, D., ed. *REED: Norwich 1540–1642*. Toronto, 1984.

Oudenaarde: Vandeer Mersch, D. J. Kronyk der Rederykkammers van Audenaerde. *Belgisch Museum*, 1843, *6*: 378–408; 1844, 7: 15–72; 232–53; 386–438.

Oviedo: Valdes, C. C. G. *El teatro en Oviedo (1498–1700)*. Oviedo, 1983.

Palermo: *Drammatiche rappresentazioni in Sicilia dal secolo XVI al XVIII*. Biblioteca storica e letteraria di Sicilia, 22. Palermo, 1876.

Paris: Thomas, A. *Le théâtre à Paris et aux environs à la fin du quatorzième siècle*. In *Mélanges Gustave Cohen*. 606–11. Paris, 1950.

Provençal *Director's Notebook*: Vitale-Brovarone, A. *Il quaderno di segreti d'un regista provenzale del Medioevo: note per la messa in scena d'una Passione*. Alessandria, 1984.

Saint–Omer: De Pas, J. Mystères et jeux scéniques à Saint-Omer aux XVe et XVIe siècles. *Mémoires de la Société des Antiquaires de la Morinie*, 1912–13, *31*: 343–77.

Savoy: Chocheyras, J. *Le Théâtre religieux en Savoie au XVIe siècle*. Geneva, 1971.

Seville: Sentaurens, J. *Séville et le théâtre de la fin du moyen âge à la fin du XVIIe siècle*. Bordeaux, 1984.

Shergold, N. D. *A history of the Spanish stage from medieval times until the end of the seventeenth century*. Oxford and London, 1967.

Staging: Meredith, P., and Tailby, J., eds. and trans. *The staging of religious drama in Europe in the later Middle Ages: texts and documents in English translation*. EDAM monograph series, 4. Kalamazoo, 1983.

Suffolk *see* Norfolk

Toledo: Torroja Menéndez, C., and Rivas Palá, M. *Teatro en Toledo*. Madrid, 1977.

Turin: Cornagliotti, A., ed. *La Passione di Revello*. Turin, 1976.

Tyrol: Wackernell, J. E. *Altdeutsche Passionsspiele aus Tyrol*. Graz, 1897.

Valencia: Corbatò, H. *Los misterios del Corpus de Valencia: Appendix.* University of
  California Publications in Modern Philology, 16. Berkeley, 1932.
Valenciennes: Konigson, E. *La Représentation d'un mystère de la Passion à
  Valenciennes en 1547.* Paris, 1969.
Westmorland *see* Cumberland
Worcestershire *see* Herefordshire
York: Johnston, A. F., and Rogerson, M., eds. *REED: York.* 2 vols. Toronto,
  1979.

General bibliography

Accarie, M. *Le Théâtre sacré de la fin du moyen âge: étude sur le sens moral de la 'Passion' de Jean Michel*. Geneva, 1979.

Amstutz, R. *The Latin substratum of the Thuringian 'Ludus de decem virginibus'*. Toronto, 1993.

Anselm, Saint. *Basic writings: Proslogium, Monologium ... [etc.]*. Trans. S. N. Deane. 2nd edn. La Salle, 1974.

Apocryphal Gospels, Acts and Revelations. Trans. A. Walker. Ante-Nicene Library, 16. Edinburgh, 1890. [*Evangelia Apocrypha*. Ed. C. Tischendorff. Leipzig, 1853.]

Aquinas, St Thomas. *Summa theologiae: a concise translation*. Trans. and ed. T. McDermott. London, 1989.

Ashley, K., and Sheingorn, P., eds. *Interpreting cultural symbols: St Anne in late medieval society*. Athens and London, 1990.

Augustine, Saint. *City of God*. Trans. J. Healey. Bks 10 and 11. London, 1931.

Axton, R. *European drama of the early middle ages*. London, 1974.

Bakere, J. A. *The Cornish Ordinalia: a critical study*. Cardiff, 1980.

Bailey, T. *The processions of Sarum and the western church*. Toronto, 1971.

Barber, R., and Barker, J. *Tournaments: jousts, chivalry and pageants in the Middle Ages*. Woodbridge, 1989.

Baring-Gould, S. *Legends of Old Testament characters*. (2 vols in 1) vol. II 46–8. London, 1871.

Barr, M. C. *The monophonic lauda and the lay religious confraternities of Tuscany and Umbria in the Late Middle Ages*. EDAM monograph series, 10. Kalamazoo, 1989.

Bartsch, K., ed. *Die Erlösung*. Amsterdam, 1966 [repr.].

Baud-Bovey, S. Sur un sacrifice d'Abraham de Romanos. *Byzantion*, 1938, *13*: 321–34.

Bela, T. Palm Sunday ceremonies in Poland: the past and the present. *EDAM Review*, 1990, 12(2): 25–31.

Benedict, Saint. *The Rule of St Benedict in Latin and English*. Ed. and trans. Justin McCann. 3rd edn. London, 1963.

Berger, S. *La Bible française au moyen âge. Etude sur les plus anciennes versions de la Bible écrites en prose de langue d'oïl*. Paris, 1884.

Besserman, L. L. *The legend of Job in the middle ages*. London and Cambridge, Mass. 1979.

Blackburn, R. H. *Biblical drama under the Tudors*. The Hague, 1971.

Bonnard, J. *Les Traductions de la Bible en vers français au moyen âge*. Paris, 1884.

Bonnell, J. K. The Serpent with a human head in art and in mystery play. *American Journal of Archeology*, 1917, 21: 255–91.

The book of saints: a dictionary of servants of God canonized by the Catholic Church. Compiled by the Benedictine monks of St Augustine's Abbey, Ramsgate. 6th edn. London, 1989.

Bourgeois de Paris: A Parisian journal 1405–1449. Trans. J. Shirley. Oxford, 1968.

Breuer, W. Aufführungspraxis vorreformatorischer Fronleichnamsspiele. *ZDPh*, 1975, 94, Sonderheft: 50–71.

Brockett, C. W. The role of the office antiphon in tenth-century liturgical drama. *Musica disciplina. A yearbook of the history of music*, 1980, 5–27.

Butterworth, P. Gunnepowdyr, fyre and thondyr. *MeTh*, 1985, 7: 68–76.

  Hellfire: flame as special effect. In *The Iconography of Hell*. Edited by C. Davidson and T. H. Seiler. 67–101. EDAM monograph series, 17. Kalamazoo, 1992.

Cambridge History of the Bible. II: The West from the Fathers to the Reformation. Ed. G. W. H. Lampe. Cambridge, 1969.

Cartwright, J. The Politics of rhetoric: the 1561 Antwerp *Landjuweel*. In *Medieval drama on the continent of Europe*. Eds. C. Davidson and J. H. Stroupe. 54–63. Kalamazoo, 1993.

Chambers, E. K. *The mediaeval stage*. 2 vols. Oxford, 1903.

Charles, R. H., and others, eds. *The Apocrypha and Pseudepigrapha of the Old Testament in English*. 2 vols. Oxford, 1913.

Cioni, A. *Bibliografia delle sacre rappresentazioni*. Biblioteca bibliografia Italica, 22. Florence, 1961.

Cohen, G. La Scène de l'Aveugle et de son Valet dans le théâtre français du moyen âge. *Romania*, 1912, 41: 346–72.

Coleman, W. E., ed. *Philippe de Mézières' Campaign for the Feast of Mary's Presentation*. Toronto, 1981.

Corathiel, E. *The Oberammergau story*. London, 1959.

Coussemaker, E. de. *Drames liturgiques du moyen âge*. New York, 1964 [repr.].

Creizenach, W. *Geschichte des neueren Dramas*. I. Halle, 1893.

Crouch, D. J. F. Paying to see the play: the stationholders on the route of the York Corpus Christi play in the fifteenth century. *MeTh*, 1991, *13*: 64–111.

Daisenberger, J. A. *The Passion play at Oberammergau: The whole official text for the year 1934*. Duiessen vor München, 1934.

Daisy, princess of Pless. *From my private diary*. London, 1931.

Dante Alighieri. *Paradiso. The illuminations to Dante's Divine Comedy by Giovanni di Paolo*. Ed. J. Pope-Hennessy. London, 1993.

Davidson, A. E. *The quasi-dramatic St John Passions from Scandinavia and their medieval background*. EDAM monograph series, 3. Kalamazoo, 1981.

ed. *Holy Week and Easter ceremonies and dramas from medieval Sweden*. EDAM monograph series, 13. Kalamazoo, 1990.

ed. *The 'Ordo Virtutum' of Hildegard of Bingen*. EDAM monograph series, 18. Kalamazoo, 1992.

Davidson, C., ed. *The saint play in medieval Europe*. EDAM monograph series, 8. Kalamazoo, 1986.

and Stroupe, J. H., eds. *Medieval drama on the continent of Europe*. Kalamazoo, 1993.

Deierkauf-Holzboer, S. W. *Le Théâtre de l'Hôtel de Bourgogne*. I: 1548–1635. Paris, 1968.

Dijk, H. van., and others. A survey of Dutch drama before the Renaissance. *Dutch Crossing*, 1984, 22: 97–131.

Diller, H.-J. A *palmesel* from the Cracow Region. *EDAM Newsletter*, 1989, 11(2): 27–30.

Dix, G. *The shape of the liturgy*. London, 1943.

Dodd, C. H. *The interpretation of the fourth gospel*. Cambridge, 1963 [repr.].

Dryden, J. R., and Hughes, D. G. *An index of Gregorian chant*. 2 vols. Cambridge, Mass., 1969.

DuBruck, E., ed. *La Passion Isabeau*. New York, 1990.

Duchesne, L. *Christian worship, its origin and evolution*. London, 1904.

Eisenhofer, L., and Lechner, J., eds. *The liturgy of the Roman rite*. Edinburgh and London, 1961.

Elliott, J. R., jr. *Playing God. Medieval mysteries on the modern stage*. Studies in Early English drama, 2. Toronto, 1989.

Emerson, O. F. Legends of Cain, especially in Old and Middle English. *PMLA*, 1906, 21: 831–929.

Emerson, R. *Antichrist in the Middle Ages: a study of medieval apocalypticism, art and literature*. Seattle, 1981.

Ernyey, J., and Karsai, G. *Deutsche Volksschauspiele aus den Oberungarischen Bergstädten*. 2 vols. Budapest, 1938.

Fabri, F. *The wanderings of Felix Fabri* [1482–4]. Trans. A. Stewart. Library of the Palestine Pilgrims' Text Society, 7 and 8. New York, 1971 [repr.].

Falvey, K. Italian vernacular religious drama of the fourteenth to sixteenth centuries: a selected bibliography on the *Lauda drammatica* and the *Sacra rappresentazione*. *RORD*, 1983, 26: 125–44.

Farrar, F. W. *The Passion play at Oberammergau*. London, 1890.

Ferraro, B. G. Catalogo delle opere di G. M. Cecchi. In *Studi e problemi di critica testuale*. Ed. R. R. Spongano. Vol. XXIII, 39–75. 1981.

Flanigan, C. C. The liturgical drama and its tradition: a review of scholarship 1965–75. *RORD*, 1975, 18: 81–102.

Fortescue, A. *The ceremonies of the Roman rite described*. Revised and augmented by J. O'Connell. London, 1951.

Foster, F. A., ed. *The Northern Passion*. EETS. London, 1913.

ed. *A stanzaic life of Christ*. EETS. London, 1926.

Frank, G. *Medieval French drama*. Oxford, 1954.

Friedman, L. J. *Text and iconography for Joinville's Credo*. Cambridge, Mass., 1991.

Gospel of Nicodemus. See *Apocryphal Gospels, Acts and Revelations*. Trans. A. Walker. Ante-Nicene Library, 16. Edinburgh, 1890. [*Evangelia Apocrypha*. Ed. C. Tischendorff. Leipzig, 1853.]

Gofflot, L.-V. *Le Théâtre au collège du moyen âge à nos jours*. Paris, 1907.

Green, A. W. *The Inns of Court and early English drama*. New York, 1931 [repr.].

Gros, G. *Le poète, la Vierge et le prince du puy. Etude sur les puys marials de la France du Nord du 14e siècle à la Renaissance*. Paris, 1992.

Hardison, O. B. *Christian rite and Christian drama in the Middle Ages. Essays in the origin and early history of modern drama*. Baltimore, 1965.

Harrison, F. Ll. *Music in medieval Britain*. London, 1958.

Hartmann, A., ed. *Das Oberammergauer Passionsspiel in seiner ältesten Gestalt*. Leipzig, 1880.

Hay, D. *Europe in the fourteenth and fifteenth centuries*. 2nd edn. London, 1989.

Herman de Valenciennes. *Li romanz de Dieu et de sa mère*. Leyden, 1975.

Hill, J., ed. *The Regularis Concordia* adapted for nuns: CCCC 201, 1–7. In *Reformed Englishwomen? Women and the religious life in late Anglo-Saxon England*. Ed. L. Abrams and D. Dumville. Woodbridge, [in press].

Hofman, R. *Das Leben Jesu nach den Apokryphen*. Leipzig, 1851.

Hone, W. *Ancient mysteries described*. London, 1970 [repr.].

Hughes, A. *Medieval manuscripts for Mass and Office. A guide to their organization and terminology*. Toronto, 1982.

Medieval music: the sixth liberal art. Toronto, 1982.

Hummelen, W. M. H. The biblical plays of the Rhetoricians and the pageants of Oudenaarde and Lille. Trans. S. Mellor. In *Modern Dutch Studies: essays in honour of Peter King*. Ed. M. Wintle and P. Vincent. 88–104 and 288–90. London, 1988.

John of Damascus, Saint. *St John Damascene on Holy Images, followed by three sermons on the Assumption*. Trans. M. H. Allies. London, 1898.

Josephus, Flavius. *Antiquitates*. Ed. with English trans. by H. St. J. Thackeray. London and Cambridge, Mass., 1926.

Kelly, H. A. *Ideas and forms of tragedy from Aristotle to the Middle Ages*. Cambridge, 1993.

Kipling, G. The London pageants for Margaret of Anjou. *MeTh*, 1982, *4*: 5–27.

The idea of the civic triumph: drama, liturgy and the royal entry in the Low Countries. *Dutch Crossing*, 1984, *22*: 60–83.

Kirk, K. E. *The vision of God*. New York, 1966 [repr.].

Kirkup, J. *The true mystery of the Passion*. London, 1962.

Kolve, V. A. *The play called Corpus Christi*. Stanford, 1966.

Konigson, E. *L'Espace théâtral médiéval*. Paris, 1975.

Lancaster, H. C. *A history of French dramatic literature in the 17th century*. Part I: 1610–34. 2 vols. Baltimore and Paris, 1929.

Lang, A. *Reminiscences*. Munich, 1930.

La Piana, G. *Le sacre rappresentazioni nella letteratura Bizantina*. Grottaferrata, 1912.

Lebègue, R. *Le Mystère des Actes des Apôtres. Contribution à l'étude de l'humanisme et du protestantisme français au XVIe siècle.* Paris, 1929.

La Tragédie religieuse en France. Les Débuts (1514–73). Paris, 1929.

Etudes sur le théâtre français. Paris, 1977 [repr.]

Leenderts jr., P. *Middelnederlandsche Dramatische Poëzie. Bijlage 7,* Leiden, 1907.

Lekai, L. J. *The Cistercians: ideals and reality.* Kent State University Press, 1977.

Levi, E. La leggenda dell' 'Antichristo' nel teatro medievale. *Studi medievale,* 1934, n.s.7: 52–63.

Linke, H. Der Schluss des Weihnachtsspiels aus Benediktbeuern. *ZDPh,* 1975, 94, Sonderheft: 1–22.

A survey of medieval drama and theater in Germany. In *Medieval drama on the continent of Europe.* Eds. C. Davidson and J. H. Stroupe. 17–53. Kalamazoo, 1993.

Massip, J.-F. *Teatre religios medieval als paisos catalans.* Barcelona, 1984.

Meditationes vitae Christi. In *S. Bonaventurae ... Opera omnia.* Ed. A. C. Peltier. Vol. XII. Paris, 1868. [*Meditations on the Life of Christ.* Trans. I. Ragusa. Ed. I. Ragusa and R. B. Green. Monographs in art and archaeology, 35. Princeton, N. J., 1961.]

Meredith, P., and Muir, L. R. The Trial in Heaven in the *Eerste Bliscap* and other European plays. *Dutch Crossing,* 1984, *22*: 84–92.

Michael, W. F. *Das deutsche Drama des Mittelalters.* Grundriss der germanischen Philologie, 20. Berlin and New York, 1971.

Migne, J. P., ed. *Patrologiae cursus completus, series graeca.* 161 vols. in 166. Paris, 1857–1904.

Mill, A. J. Noah's Wife Again. *PMLA,* 1941, *56*: 613–26.

Missale Romanum (1472). Ed. R. Lippe, for the Henry Bradshaw Society. 2 vols. London, 1899, 1907.

Morris, C. *The discovery of the individual, 1050–1200.* Church history outlines, 5. London, 1972.

Morris, R. *Legends of the Holy Rood.* EETS. London, 1871.

Muir, L. R. *Liturgy and drama in the Anglo-Norman Adam.* Oxford, 1973.

The Trinity in medieval drama. *Comparative Drama,* 1976, *10*: 116–29.

The Fall of Man in the drama of medieval Europe. In *Studies in medieval culture, 10.* Ed. J. R. Sommerfeldt and T. H. Seiler. 121–31. Kalamazoo, 1977.

Les Prophètes du Christ, cent ans après. In *Mélanges Jeanne Lods.* 447–58. Paris, 1978.

The holy shroud in medieval literature. *Sindon,* 1982, *24*: 23–36.

Women on the medieval stage: the evidence from France. *MeTh,* 1985, *7*: 107–19.

The saint play in medieval France. In *The saint play in medieval Europe.* Ed. C. Davidson. 123–80. EDAM monograph series, 8. Kalamazoo, 1986.

Liturgy and drama at St-Omer in the thirteenth through the sixteenth centuries. *EDAM Newsletter,* 1986, *9*: 7–15.

Audiences in the French medieval theatre. *MeTh,* 1987, *9*: 8–22.

English medieval drama – the French connection. In *Contexts for medieval English drama*. Ed. M. G. Briscoe and J. C. Coldewey. 56–76. Bloomington and Indianapolis, 1988.

Aspects of form and meaning in the Biblical drama. In *Littera et sensus. Essays ... presented to John Fox*. Ed. D. Trotter. 109–24. Exeter, 1989.

The Mass on the medieval stage. *Comparative Drama*, 1989–90, 23: 314–31.

Playing God in medieval Europe. In *The Stage as Mirror; Civic Theatre in Late Medieval Europe*. Papers from the symposium held at the Pennsylvania State University, March 1993. Forthcoming.

Murdoch, B. *Cornish literature*. Cambridge 1994.

Musumarra, C. *La sacra rappresentazione della nativitá nella tradizione italiana*. Biblioteca dell' 'Archivum Romanicum', 52. Florence, 1957.

Nancy: *Le Mystère de la Passion à Nancy: Paroisse de Saint-Joseph*. Nancy, 1920.

Nativity of Mary. See under *Gospel of Nicodemus* in *Apocryphal Gospels, Acts and Revelations*.

Nelson, A. H. *The medieval English stage. Corpus Christi pageants and plays*. Chicago: London, 1974.

Newbigin, N., ed. *Nuovo corpus di sacre rappresentazioni fiorentini del Quattrocento*. Bologna, 1983.

Nijsten, G. Feasts and Public Spectacles: Late medieval Drama and Performance in the Low Countries. In *The Stage as Mirror; Civic Theatre in Late Medieval Europe*. Papers from the symposium held at the Pennsylvania State University, March 1993. Forthcoming.

Orcibal, J. *La Genèse d'Esther et d'Athalie*. Paris, 1950.

Parfaict, F., and Parfaict, C. *Histoire du théâtre françois*. 2 vols. [Paris], 1745–8.

Parry, A., ed. *Passion des jongleurs*. Paris, 1981.

Patt, B. *The development of the Christmas play in Spain*. Ann Arbor microfilms, 1977.

Petit de Julleville, L. *Les Comédiens en France au moyen âge*. Paris, 1885.

Le Répertoire du théâtre comique en France au moyen âge. Paris, 1887.

Histoire du théâtre en France. Les mystères. 2 vols. Geneva, 1969 [repr.].

Pfaff, R. W. *New liturgical feasts in later medieval England*. Oxford, 1970.

Medieval Latin liturgy: a select bibliography. Toronto, 1982.

Pius II. *Commentaries of Pius II*. Trans. F. A. Gragg and L. C. Gabel. 5 vols. Smith College studies in history, 22, 25, 30, 35, 43. 1936–57.

Portillo, R., and Gomez Lara, M. Andalusia's Holy Week processions. *MeTh*, 1986, *8*: 119–39.

Protevangelium. See under *Gospel of Nicodemus* in *Apocryphal Gospels, Acts and Revelations*.

Pseudo-Matthew. See under *Gospel of Nicodemus* in *Apocryphal Gospels, Acts and Revelations*.

Quinn, E., ed. *The penitence of Adam: a study of the Andrius Ms*. Mississippi, 1980.

Rastall, R. Female roles in all-male casts. *MeTh*, 1985, 7: 25–51.

The sounds of Hell. In *The iconography of Hell*. Ed. C. Davidson and T. H. Seiler. 102–31. EDAM monograph series, 17. Kalamazoo, 1992.

The Heaven Singing: music in early English religious drama. 2 vols. Woodbridge, [in press].

Reeves, M. The development of apocalyptic thought: medieval attitudes. In *The Apocalypse in English Renaissance thought and literature.* Ed. C. A. Patrides and J. Wittreich. 40–72. Manchester, 1984.

Reilly, B. F. *The medieval Spains.* Cambridge, 1993.

Rey-Flaud, H. *Le cercle magique: essai sur le théâtre en rond à la fin du moyen âge.* Paris, 1973.

Robertson, J. G. *A history of German literature.* Edinburgh and London, 1949.

Le Romanz de saint Fanuel et de sainte Anne. Ed. C. Chabaneau. Paris, 1888.

Roston, M. *Biblical drama in England. From the middle ages to the present day.* London, 1968.

Rousset, J. *La littérature de l'âge baroque en France.* Paris, 1953.

Roy, E. *Le Mystère de la passion en France du XIVe au XVIe siècle.* Paris, 1905.

Rubin, M. *Corpus Christi: the eucharist in late medieval culture.* Cambridge, 1991.

Runnalls, G. A. Medieval trade guilds and the *Miracles de Nostre Dame par personnages. Medium aevum,* 1970, 39: 257–87.

Medieval French drama: a review of recent scholarship. Part 1: Religious drama. *RORD,* 1978, *21:* 83–90; 1979, *22:* 111–36.

Sainte vie de Nostre Dame, La. In *La vie de Nostre Benoît Sauveur Jhesu Christ.* Ed. M. Meiss and E. H. Beatson. New York, 1977.

Sarum *Missal: Missale ad usum ... Sarum.* Ed. F. Dickinson. Burntisland, 1861–83.

The Sarum Missal. Trans. F. E. Warren. London, 1911.

Sayers, D. L. *The man born to be king.* London, 1942.

Scheingorn, P. *The Easter Sepulchre in England.* EDAM reference series, 5. Kalamazoo, 1987.

Schiller, G. *Iconography of Christian art.* (Trans. J. Seligman.) I, II. London, 1971–2. *Ikonographie der Christlichen Kunst.* III. Gütersloh, 1986 (2nd edn.).

Simon, E., ed. *The theatre of medieval Europe. New research in early drama.* Cambridge, 1991.

SITM: Proceedings of the Triennial Colloquia.
   1. 1974, Leeds: *The drama of medieval Europe. Proceedings of the colloquium held at the University of Leeds 10–13 September 1974.* Ed. P. Meredith. Leeds medieval studies 1. Leeds, 1975.
   2. 1977, Alençon: *Le Théâtre au moyen âge. Actes du deuxième colloque ... Alençon 11–14 juillet 1977.* Ed. G. R. Muller. Montreal, 1981.
   3. 1980, Dublin: Unpublished.
   4. 1983, Viterbo: *Atti del IVo colloquio ... Viterbo 1983.* Ed. F. Doglio. Viterbo, 1984.
   5. 1986, Perpignan: *Le Théâtre et la cité dans l'Europe médiévale. Actes du Veme colloque ... (Perpignan, juillet 1986).* Ed. J.-C. Aubailly and E. E. DuBruck. *Fifteenth-century studies,* 1988, 13: special issue.
   6. 1989, Lancaster: *Evil on the medieval stage. Papers from the sixth triennial colloquium ... 1989.* Ed. M. Twycross. *MeTh,* 1989, 11 [publ. 1992].
   7. 1992, Gerona: In press.

Smalley, B. *The study of the Bible in the Middle Ages*. Oxford, 1941.

Smoldon, W. *The music of the medieval church dramas*. Ed. C. Bourgeault. Oxford and London, 1980.

Somerset, Sir Charles. *The travel diary (1611–1612) of an English catholic*. Ed. M. G. Brennan. (Leeds Philosophical and Literary Society). Leeds, 1993.

Southern, R. *The medieval theatre in the round*. 2nd edn revised and expanded. London, 1975.

The seven ages of the theatre. London, 1986.

Spufford, P. The Burgundian Netherlands. In *Splendours of Flanders: late medieval art in Cambridge collections*. Ed. A. Arnould and J. M. Massing. 1–12. Cambridge, 1993.

Sticca, S. *The Latin passion play: its origins and development*. New York, 1979.

Stone, D., jr. *French humanist tragedy. A reassessment*. Manchester, 1974.

Styan, J. L. *Drama, stage and audience*. Cambridge, 1975.

Surtz, R. E. El teatro en el edad media. In *Historia del teatro en España*. Ed. J. M. Díez Borque. I, 61–154. Madrid 1983.

Symons, T., ed. *Regularis concordia* (with English translation). London, 1953.

Szönyi, G. E. European influences and national tradition in medieval Hungarian theater. *Comparative Drama*, 1981, *15*: 159–171.

Tailby, J. E. The role of Director in the Lucerne Passion play. *MeTh*, 1987, *9*: 80–92.

Die schriftlichen Zeugnisse zur Luzerner Osterspielaufführung des Jahres 1583 und ihr Verhältnis zu den Bühnenplänen Renward Cysats. *Daphnis*, 1989, *18*: 223–49.

Testaverde, A. M., and Evangelista, A. M., eds. *Sacre rappresentazioni manoscritte e a stampa conservate nella biblioteca nazionale centrale di Firenze*. Giunta regionale toscana. Inventari e cataloghi toscani 25. Milan, 1988.

Tragédie sur les péchés des premiers anges et sur la chute d'Adam. (NME; Bibl. Nat. n.a. f.fr. MS 4542).

Trotter, D. A. Influence of Bible commentaries on Old French Bible translations. *Medium aevum*, 1987, *56*: 257–75.

Tydeman, W. *The theatre in the Middle Ages*. Cambridge, 1978.

English medieval theatre 1400–1500. London, 1986.

Tyrer, J. W. *Historical Survey of Holy Week. Its services and ceremonial*. Alcuin Club Collections 29. London, 1932.

Valentin, J.-M. *Le Théâtre des Jésuites dans les pays de langue allemande: Répertoire chronologique des pièces représentés et des documents conservés (1555–1773)*. Stuttgart, 2 vols., 1983–4.

Veltrusky, J. F. *A sacred farce from medieval Bohemia*. Ann Arbor, 1985.

Medieval drama in Bohemia. *EDAM Review*, 1993. *15*: 51–63.

Vriend, J. *The Blessed Virgin Mary in the medieval drama of England*. Purmerend, 1928.

WACE maistre. *L'Etablissement de la fête de la conception Notre Dame, dite Fête aux Normands*. Ed. G. Manuel and G. S. Trébutien. Caen, 1842.

Watson, A. *The early iconography of the Tree of Jesse*. Oxford, London, 1934.

Wickham, G. *A history of the theatre*. Cambridge, 1985.

Wildenberg-de Kroon, C. van den, Die Blindheilung in dem deutschen und französischen geistlichen Drama und in der bildenden Kunst des Mittelalters. *Amsterdamer beiträge zur älteren Germanistik*, 1994, 40: 159–172.

Wisch, B. The passion of Christ in the art, theater and penitential rituals of the Roman confraternity of the Gonfalone. In *Crossing the boundaries. Christian piety and the arts in Italian medieval and renaissance confraternities*. Ed. K. Eisenbichler. 237–62. Kalamazoo, 1991.

Woolf, R. *The English religious lyric in the Middle Ages*. Oxford, 1968.

The English mystery plays. Berkeley and Los Angeles, 1972.

Worp, J. A. *Geschiedenis van het drama en van het toonel in de Nederlanden*. 2 vols. Groningen 1904–8.

Wright, E. A. *The dissemination of the liturgical drama in France*. Bryn Mawr, 1936.

Wright, J. G. *A study of the themes of the Resurrection in the medieval French drama*. Bryn Mawr, 1935.

Wright, S. K. *The vengeance of our Lord. Medieval dramatizations of the destruction of Jerusalem*. Studies and texts, 89. Toronto, 1989.

Iconographic contexts of the Swedish *De uno peccatore qui promeruit gratiam*. In *Medieval drama on the continent of Europe*. Eds. C. Davidson and J. H. Stroupe. 4–16. Kalamazoo, 1993.

Zumthor, P. *Daily life in Rembrandt's Holland*. London, 1962.

Index

This index includes all proper names of places and persons (including personified abstractions who appear in the plays) except post-medieval writers and critics. Biblical names are given according to the usual English form; if the Vulgate or other linguistic variant is noticeably different it is shown in brackets e.g. Elijah (Elie); Ham (Chanaam). Place names are given according to normal English usage or as on the Maps; linguistic variants and modern forms are shown in brackets e.g. Eger (Cheb); Bozen (Bolzano). Non-dramatic medieval texts and dramatic works from the modern period are included here but for early play-texts *see* the bibliographical index of plays.